W9-BQS-711

THE AMERICAN ALPINE JOURNAL

2015

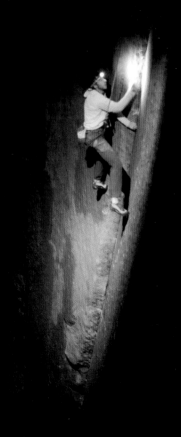

[Front cover] Ales Cesen and Luka Lindic
en route to the summit of Hagshu in India
after climbing the north face (p.319). *Marko
Prezelj* [This page] Tommy Caldwell on the
Loop Pitch of the Dawn Wall (p.12). *Corey
Rich/Big UP Productions/Aurora Photos*

2015 VOLUME 57 ISSUE 89

CONTENTS

12 THE DAWN WALL BY KEVIN JORGESON
The long struggle for the world's hardest big-wall free climb

22 STAIRWAY TO HEAVEN BY KEVIN COOPER & RYAN JENNINGS
Climbing the dreamy ice drips on Mt. Johnson's mythical north face

33 KOREAN DIRECT BY AHN CHI-YOUNG
The first ascent of Gasherbrum V

38 WALL OF ICE BY HÉLIAS MILLERIOUX
A tactical tour de force on the west face of Siula Chico, Peru

46 CHOSS ODYSSEY BY BEN DITTO
Alpine-style and all free on Baffin's big walls

57 BELUGA SPIRE BY JOSHUA LAVIGNE
The all-free first ascent of a legendary wall

62 SENDERO LUMINOSO BY DAVID ALLFREY
Two years of effort to free Mt. Hooker's hardest route

70 VOLCÁN AGUILERA BY NATALIA MARTÍNEZ
The last great volcano of the Andes is climbed

78 ALPINE MENTORS BY STEVE HOUSE
A volunteer program trains the next generation of alpinists

86 SOUL GARDEN BY JIMMY HADEN
A gift from Sean Leary

91 SPEED BY KILIAN JORNET BURGADA
The why and how of a new Denali record

RECON [UNEXPLORED & OVERLOOKED]

96 CLOUD PEAK BY MATT CUPAL, ARNO ILGNER, RAY JACQUOT, MARK JENKINS & DOUGALD MACDONALD
Wyoming's off-the-radar granite paradise

CLIMBS & EXPEDITIONS

108 UNITED STATES—LOWER 48
148 ALASKA
168 CANADA
180 GREENLAND
190 MEXICO
193 COLOMBIA & BRAZIL
195 PERU
206 BOLIVIA
216 ARGENTINA & CHILE
236 ANTARCTICA
242 EUROPE
244 MIDDLE EAST
246 AFRICA
250 RUSSIA
257 KYRGYZSTAN
269 TAJIKISTAN
272 PAKISTAN
282 NEPAL
310 INDIA
338 CHINA & TIBET
358 MYANMAR & BORNEO
361 NEW ZEALAND
364 MARQUESAS

366 BOOK REVIEWS EDITED BY DAVID STEVENSON
373 IN MEMORIAM EDITED BY JAMES BENOIT
385 CLUB ACTIVITIES EDITED BY FREDERICK O. JOHNSON

390 INDEX
400 INTERNATIONAL GRADE CHART

[Photo] The view toward Yerupaja Sur from the second bivy on the west face of Siula Chico, Peru (p.38). *Robin Revest*

CORPORATE PARTNERS

SUMMIT PARTNER [$50,000]

HIGH CAMP [$25,000]

patagonia®

BASECAMP [$15,000]

Black Diamond

PATRON [$10,000]

LOWA   GORE-TEX   SCARPA

BROOKS-RANGE
MOUNTAINEERING   OUTDOOR RESEARCH   STERLING ROPE

PETZL   ASOLO   ARC'TERYX

The American Alpine Journal, 710 Tenth St. Suite 100, Golden, Colorado 80401
Telephone: (303) 384-0110 Fax: (303) 384-0111
E-mail: aaj@americanalpineclub.org
www.americanalpineclub.org

ISSN: 0065-6925
ISBN: 978-1-933056-87-6
ISBN: (e-book): 978-1-933056-88-3

MIX
Paper from
responsible sources
FSC® C004191

[Photo] The endless ice smears of the Odyssey, Pyramid Peak, Alaska (p.121). *Jerome Sullivan*

GREAT RANGES FELLOWSHIP

EIGER

Nicole Alger & Zachary Karabell
Malinda & Yvon Chouinard
Kevin Duncan
Wes Edens
Greg Engelman
Timothy C. Forbes
Clark Gerhardt Jr.
Todd Hoffman
Louis W. Kasischke
James M. Kennedy
Mark Kroese
Craig McKibben
Allen Miner
Mark & Teresa Richey
Jim Simons
Cody J Smith
The Spitzer Family Foundation
Steven Swenson & Ann Dalton
Douglas & Maggie Walker
Lawrence True & Linda Brown
Anonymous (2)

ALPAMAYO

Jim & Karen Keating Ansara
Douglas and Sandy Beall
Edmund & Betsy Cabot Foundation
Chadwick Christine
Maryclaire & Jim Collis
Suzanna Derby
Kit DesLauriers
Philip Duff
Charles & Lisa Fleischman Family Fund
Bruce Franks
Gerald E. Gallwas
Eric D. Green
Rocky & Laura Henderson
Stephen K. Hindy
Bradley Hoffman
Jeffrey Hoffman
David Landman
George H. Lowe III
Jonathon Malkin
Shelly Malkin
Peter Metcalf
James D. Morrissey M.D.
Vanessa A. O'Brien
Wolf Riehle
David Riggs
Carey Roberts
Naoe Sakashita
Bill & Barbara Straka
Ronald Ulrich
Geoff Unger
Finn Wentworth

ROBSON

Warren Adelman
Ralph Burns
Leon P Burris IV
Bruce H. Carroll
John H. Catto
Eric C. Christu
Jeffrey R. Cohen
Madrone Coopwood
Christopher Croft
James M. Crosslin
Matt & Charlotte Culberson
William E. Davis
James & Cheryl Duckworth
Jim Edwards
Gary Evans
Estate of Ruth Ewing
Marilyn Geninatti
Neil C. Gleichman
David V. Goeddel
Peter Sam Addis
Gus Goldman
Wayne & Cynthia Griffin
Syed Haider
Jeffrey S. Hall
Robert B. Hall
Roger Hartl
Sandy Hill
Denny Hogan
Thomas & Kathy Hornbein
Robert A. Horton Jr.
Thomas C. Janson
Mark Kassner
Jamie Logan
Paul Morrow
Karla Pifer
Matthew Pruis
Paul Rose
Charles J. Sassara III
Ulrika & Mark Schumacher
Steve Schwartz
Stephen Scofield
Howard Sebold
A.C. Sherpa
Alan Spielberg
Theodore P. Streibert
Robert P. Strode
Lewis Surdam
Joshua Swidler
Thomas Taplin
David Thoenen
Jack Tracy
Patricia Smith
Richard Tucker
Paul Underwood
James Wilson
Robert A. Wilson
Anonymous

TEEWINOT

Lisa Abbott
Nathan Allen
Jon Anderson
Robert Anderson
Melissa Arnot
Stephen Arsenault
Joseph Ashkar
Deborah Atwood
James Balog
Col. Christopher Bates USA (Ret.)
Robert Behrens
Vaclav E. Benes
Gordon A. Benner M.D.
Brook Bennet
Bob Berger
Stewart Bernstein
Laura Bothwell
James Brady
John Bragg
Tom Bratton
Deanne Buck
Jeff Buhl
Thomas Burch
William A. Burd
David Burton
Ailie Byers
Deirdre Byers
Craig Cammann
Robert J. Campbell
Randall Carmichael
Susan C. Clark
Dan Cohen
Kevin Cooney
Kimberly Coupounas
Nadia Danilenko-Dixon
Karen Daubert
Joseph K. Davidson
Scott E. Davis
Alain De Lotbiniere
Tom Degenhardt
Stanley Dempsey
Ed Diffendal
Newton Dominey
David B. Dornan
Jeff Dozier
Richard Draves
Jesse Dwyer
Bill Egger
Ken Ehrhart
Charles Eilers
Stuart Ellison
Lee Elman
Denise Elmer
Dan A. Emmett
Terrence J. English
Philip Erard
Marc Evankow
John Evans
Chris Flowers
Charlotte Fox
James A. Frank
Jim Frush
Paul Gagner
Ellen Gallant
James & Franziska Garrett
Neil Gehrels
Karl Gerdes
Bill Givens
Charles Goldman
Kenneth Goodwin
Kevin Grant
Richard Griffith
Peter Hackett
Rick Hanheide
Jason Hanold
Robert Hastings
John Hebert
Christopher J. Heintz
Scot T. Hillman
Michael Hodges
Marley & Jennifer Hodgson
Barbara & Floyd Hoffman
Richard E. Hoffman
Scott Holder
Michael Hornsby
Robert Hyman
Thomas Jenkins
Corey Jensen
The Seby B. Jones Family Foundation
William Kennedy
Michael Kidder
Rodney Korich
Phil Lakin
Kyle Lefkoff
Paul Lego
George Lilley
Misha Logvinov
Chris Lynch
Brent V. Manning
Weston Markham
Sheila Matz
John McCall
Jim McCarthy
George McCown
Danny McCracken
Gary Lynn McElvany
Melissa McQueen
Garry Menzel
Doris & Charlie Michaels
Halsted "Hacksaw" Morris
David Morton
Rick Nolting
Alan Pace
John Parsons
Daniel Peck
Alan P. Peterson
Seth Thomas Pietras
David Polan
John Pope
Louis Reichardt
John Reilly
Prof. John D. Reppy
Jim Richards
Michael Riley
Sam Richter
Joel P. Robinson
Darren Rogers
Dan Rose
Howard Runyon
Jeb C. Sanford
Nancy Savickas
Rebecca Schild
Janet Schlindwein
George Shaw
William Sheil
John Sheu
Fred Simmons
Tanya Bradby & Martin Slovacek
George N. Smith
Jordan K. Smith Jr.
De Snook
Vincent E. Starzinger
John L. Stauffer M.D.
Robert & Jennifer Stephenson
Duncan Stuart
Arthur Sulzberger
Jack Tackle
Pete A. Thompson
Martin Torresquintero
John Townsend
Lein Tung
Robert Vaughn
Dieter H. Von Hennig
Roger Walker
Mark D. Wilford
Warren E. Wilhide Jr.
Todd Winzenried
Fred Wolfe
David M. Young
Keegan Young
Rob Ziegler
Anonymous (3)

THE AMERICAN ALPINE JOURNAL

EXECUTIVE EDITOR
Dougald MacDonald

SENIOR EDITOR
Lindsay Griffin

ASSISTANT EDITOR
Erik Rieger

ART DIRECTOR
Erik Rieger

CONTRIBUTING EDITORS
James Benoit, *In Memoriam*
Frederick O. Johnson, *Club Activities*
David Stevenson, *Book Reviews*

ILLUSTRATIONS AND MAPS
Jeremy Collins, Leighan Falley,
Uncharted Project, Clay Wadman

PROOFREADERS
Clark Gerhardt, Dana Gerschel, Damien Gildea,
Allie Levy, Joel Peach, Katie Sauter

INDEXERS
Ralph Ferrara, Eve Tallman

TRANSLATORS
Peter Jensen-Choi, Todd Miller, Pam Ranger
Roberts, Christian Romero, Simone Sturm,
Ekaterina Vorotnikova, Xia Zhongming

REGIONAL CONTACTS
Steve Gruhn, Mark Westman, *Alaska*; Sevi
Bohorquez, Sergio Ramírez Carrascal, *Peru*; Luis
Pardo, *Colombia*, Damien Gildea, *Antarctica*;
Rolando Garibotti, Marcelo Scanu, *Argentina/
Chile*; Rajesh Gadgil, Harish Kapadia, *India*;
Elizabeth Hawley, Rodolphe Popier, Richard
Salisbury, *Nepal*; Tamotsu Nakamura, Hiroshi
Hagiwara, *Japan*; Peter Jensen-Choi, Oh
Young-hoon, *Korea*; Elena Dmitrenko, Anna
Piunova, *Russia, Tajikistan, and Kyrgyzstan*, Xia
Zhongming, *China*

ONLINE EDITORS
Chris Harrington, Joel Peach

ADVISORY BOARD
Andrew Bisharat, Kelly Cordes, Damien Gildea,
Colin Haley, Mark Richey, Freddie Wilkinson,
Emily Stifler Wolfe

WITH HEARTFELT THANKS TO
Erik Lambert, Claude Gardien, Allie Levy, Duane
Raleigh, and all *AAJ* donors and contributors

[Photo] Walker Arm, Baffin Island, in August
2014 (p.57), *Joshua Lavigne*

THE AMERICAN ALPINE CLUB

OFFICIALS FOR THE YEAR 2015

*DIRECTORS EX-OFFICIO

[EXECUTIVE COMMITTEE]

Honorary President
James P. McCarthy

Honorary Treasurer
Theodore (Sam) Streibert

President
Doug Walker*

Vice President
Matt Culberson*

Secretary
Clark Gerhardt*

Treasurer
Paul Gagner*

[DIRECTORS]

Term Ending 2016
Deanne Buck
Philip Duff
Chuck Fleischman
Todd Hoffman

Term Ending 2017
Janet Wilkinson
Phil Lakin
Kit DesLauriers

Term Ending 2018
Brad Brooks
John Heilprin
Ken Ehrhart
Mia Axon
Chas Fisher
Mark Butler
Stacy Bare

[SECTION CHAIRS]

Alaska
Harry Hunt & Cindi Squire
Arizona
Erik Filsinger & Jeff Snyder
Cascade
Erin Schneider & Truc Allen
DC
David Giacomin
Deep South
Michael Kidder
Front Range
Carol Kotchek
Great Lakes
Bill Thompson
Heartland
Jeremy Collins
Idaho
Kammie Cuneo & Jason Luthy

Mid Atlantic
Barry Rusnock & James Kunz
Midwest
Ray Kopcinski
Montana
Kevin Brumbach
New England
Nancy Savickas & Rick Merritt
New Mexico
Pat Gioanninni
NY Metro
Howard Sebold
NY Upstate
Will Roth & Mark Scott
North Central
Mark Jobman

Oregon
Jesse Bernier & Heidi Medema
Sierra Nevada
Karen Zazzi & Kristen Nute
Southern Appalachian
Danny McCracken
Southwest
James Pinter-Lucke &
Tony Yeary
Texas
Adam Mitchell
Utah
Blake Summers
Western Slope
Lee Jenkins
Wyoming
Micah Rush

[STAFF]

Executive Director/CEO Phil Powers
Director of Operations/CFO Nat Matthews
Executive Assistant and Grants Manager Janet Miller
Information & Marketing Director Erik Lambert
Director, Regional Programs & Development Keegan Young
Library Director Dana Gerschel
IT Director Craig Hoffman
Senior Software Engineer Blake Bowling
Accountant Carol Kotchek
Develpment Manager Vickie Hormuth
Development Coordinator Ben Edwards
Marketing Manager Paul Dusatko
Content Manager Whitney Bradberry
Online Store Manager Michelle Hoffman
Graphic Designer David Boersma
Conservation & Volunteer Coordinator Remy Rodriguez
Digital Services Librarian Allison Bailey

Library Manager & Museum Curator Katie Sauter
Facilities Director Philip Swiny
Publications, Executive Editor Dougald MacDonald
Publications, Assistant Editor & Art Director Erik Rieger
Northwest Regional Manager Eddie Espinosa
Western Regional Manager Jeff Deikis
Rocky Mountain & Central Regional Manager Adam Peters
Northeast & Southeast Regional Manager Lisa Hummel
Museum Events Manager Devyn Studer
New River Gorge Campground Manager Paul Nelson
Gunks Campground Manager Paul Curran
Gunks Campground Assistant Manager Ajax Greene
GTCR Campground Co-Managers Gary and Deb Bunten
GTCR Campground Assistant Manager Ryan Butler
Hueco Campground Manager Brian Martin
Hueco Campground Assistant Manager Shaun Gregg

PREFACE

LONG LIVE EXPLORATION

EVERY YEAR MORE BLANK SPOTS on the map are filled and more peaks are crisscrossed with new routes and variations. Inevitably, many climbers decry the disappearance of exploration and adventure in our world. But exploration is only evolving, not vanishing.

To be sure, traditional exploration—stepping into a blank spot on the map—continues even in this age of Google Earth. This edition details many fine examples, from the first teams to explore the South Simvu Glacier in India to the two international expeditions that crossed the Southern Patagonia Icefield in search of distant unclimbed peaks. Exploration also includes evolving methods and ideas. What, for example, might climbers accomplish if they visited the eastern fjords of Baffin Island in the summer months, when almost all teams before had gone in the spring? (Answer: a bonanza of huge, alpine-style free climbs.) And then there are frontiers of difficulty, of which no climb pushed boundaries further in 2014 than the Dawn Wall on El Capitan.

Tommy Caldwell and Kevin Jorgeson's seven-year effort to free the Dawn Wall had some traditionally adventurous elements: long run-outs above marginal protection, two serious injuries, and significant icefall hazard. But no long route in history was better known before it was climbed, down to such minute details as the precisely correct angle of one's foot on a nubbin of granite. In this context, exploration can only be internal: Can it be done? Can *I* do it? This is very different from the adventures of Shipton and Tilman in Asia and Patagonia, or John Clarke in British Columbia. But it is no less valid or exciting.

The Dawn Wall turned off some observers because of the media frenzy that came to surround it. Apart from the bizarre and often amusing attempts to translate what was happening up there for a mass audience, there was genuine concern that something was lost among the Instagram posts and live television feed. During their earlier attempts, Tommy and Kevin had gone dark for days or weeks at a time. On the final push they shared their experience, and the world responded with fascination.

Ultimately, this is a personal choice, not the End Of Climbing As We Know It. Mobile phones and satellite connections have made communication possible anywhere, but many teams do only the bare minimum of communication necessary to satisfy sponsors. Still others whip out their credit cards and pay for trips themselves, with no sense of obligation or desire to post results, in real time or anytime. At the *AAJ* we are well aware that significant ascents each year *never* get reported. As journalists it pains us to leave these climbs undocumented. As climbers we say, "Right on, do what feels right to you." Happily, the world remains big enough to accommodate all forms of exploration, old and new.

— **DOUGALD MACDONALD**, *EXECUTIVE EDITOR*

FIND MORE AT THE *AAJ* WEBSITE

ONLINE VERSIONS of *AAJ* stories frequently contain additional text, photographs, videos, maps, and topos. Look for these symbols indicating additional resources at *publications.americanalpineclub*.

FULL-LENGTH REPORT	ADDITIONAL PHOTOS	MAPS OR TOPOS	VIDEO OR MULTIMEDIA

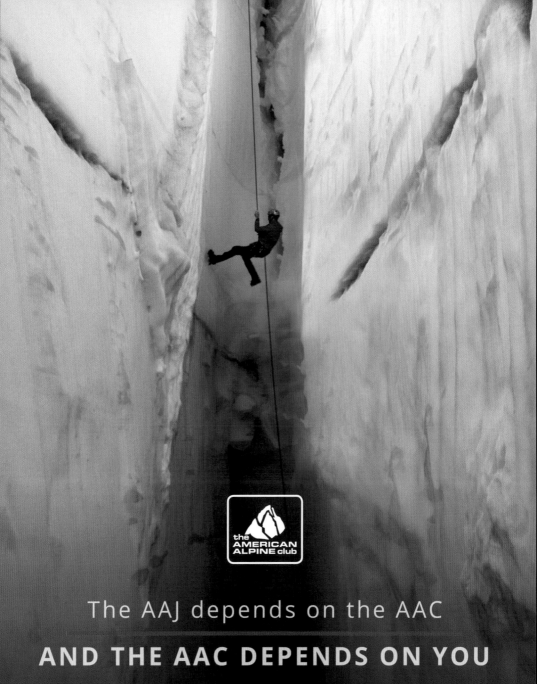

The AAJ depends on the AAC

AND THE AAC DEPENDS ON YOU

The AAJ is only possible because of thousands of hours invested by the AAC and its volunteers. Please consider supporting the publication of this information by volunteering your time or making a donation to the American Alpine Club.

americanalpineclub.org/give

THE DAWN WALL

THE LONG STRUGGLE FOR THE WORLD'S HARDEST BIG-WALL FREE CLIMB

KEVIN JORGESON

Standing at the base of the Dawn Wall on December 27, 2014, I attempt to break the nervous tension. "It's the low-pressure push," I say with a grin. I know it's bullshit. Once we start, we're going to the top. "One pitch at a time," Tommy responds. I nod and start climbing.

Six years earlier, I was sitting on top of a 55-foot boulder at the Buttermilks in Bishop, California. Just a few moments before, I'd been 45 feet off the deck, ropeless, on my most ambitious highball first ascent to date. For the past two years, I'd constantly put myself in positions like this. I was obsessed with pushing the standards of highball bouldering, rolling the dice with each sketchy first ascent. Ambrosia pushed the bar even higher, not just blurring the lines between highball and solo but crossing it. To continue meant becoming a free soloist, and I was unwilling. Not only did I need a new project, I needed a new discipline of the sport.

The climbing film *Progression*, released in late summer of 2009, featured both Ambrosia and Tommy Caldwell's new big-wall free climbing project. When I saw the closing scene of Tommy's segment, I heard an invitation: "I look at this next generation of climbers doing things on the boulders and sport climbs that I can't conceive of. If they could apply that kind of talent to the big walls, that's what it would take to free climb this project. Even if I can't climb this, I want to plant the seed for someone in the future to come and inspire us all."

Was this the opportunity I was looking for? I was completely unqualified. Tommy and I had only climbed together one day. I had never climbed El Cap. I wrote Tommy an email out of the blue, asking him if he needed a partner for the fall season. To my utter shock, he said yes.

A few months later, in October 2009, I met Tommy in El Cap Meadow for the first time. Little did I know this was the first of hundreds of such rendezvous. I was nervous but ready for anything. I had to ask Tommy where the line went—when I looked to the right of the Nose I couldn't see any features to climb. Our plan was to hike heavy haulbags to the top of the wall. For the next five hours, my face was only a few feet from the ground, bent under the load. On top of the labor of the hike, Tommy's dad was crop-dusting me the entire time. When we got to the top, well after dark, I dropped the pig on the ground and felt endorphins rush to my head. "That felt good!" I exclaimed, stretching my arms overhead and looking up at the stars. I would later learn how much these three words influenced Tommy's perception of my grit and durability.

The next morning was my initiation to pioneering a big-wall free climb. My job was to rappel off the top, do 100-foot rope swings from side to side, and figure out how the last four pitches of the climb would reach the summit. I hand-drilled my first bolt. I hollered into the wind with 3,000 feet

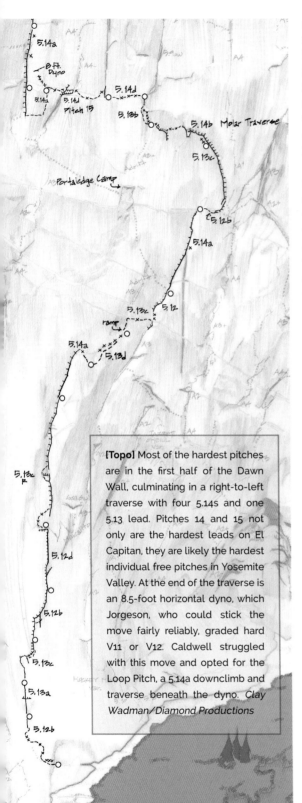

[Topo] Most of the hardest pitches are in the first half of the Dawn Wall, culminating in a right-to-left traverse with four 5.14s and one 5.13 lead. Pitches 14 and 15 not only are the hardest leads on El Capitan, they are likely the hardest individual free pitches in Yosemite Valley. At the end of the traverse is an 8.5-foot horizontal dyno, which Jorgeson, who could stick the move fairly reliably, graded hard V11 or V12. Caldwell struggled with this move and opted for the Loop Pitch, a 5.14a downclimb and traverse beneath the dyno. *Clay Wadman/Diamond Productions*

of air beneath my toes. I showered dirt onto my face as I cleaned mossy finger cracks. As I Mini-Traxioned what would become the last pitch of the climb, I thought about what it would feel like to grab the top of the wall and have it matter. It was only day one, but I was already imagining how amazing the last day would be. I was in heaven. That is, until I tried to lead a pitch.

I was gripped. I quickly found that this style of climbing was different from anything I was used to. I was appalled by the protection. We were in aid climbing territory. No man's land. We had to adapt our style to the canvas, which meant making use of every scrappy piece of aid protection already in the wall and adding no bolts unless absolutely necessary. Tommy tried to assure me that "beaks are like bolts," until I zippered some out of the wall when I fell.

Over the next six years, every one of my 350-plus days on the wall was an education. Tommy had spent the past 18 years climbing on El Cap, and I needed every day I could get in order to catch up to his level of mastery. I was a kindergartener in a Ph.D. class. My education never stopped, right up until the day we started our final push.

Technically, day one of the route is the easiest. Every day after this, we will have to climb at least one pitch of 5.14 until we get through pitch 16. The first four pitches pass smoothly, but pitch five makes me fight. California has just experienced two solid weeks of rain, which means the entire crux of this 5.12d pitch is wet. Pulling onto Anchorage Ledge, pumped and drenched, I'm satisfied with my aggression. I know I want it.

With the positive momentum from day one, we roll through our first week on the wall. Another day, another pitch of 5.14. Our mood is light and energy is high. Day four brings a frigid windstorm and our first rest day. These days are as much about giving our mind a break as healing our bodies. It's a marathon, so it's important to stay as fresh as possible. To pass the time, Tommy and I pile into a portaledge with videographer Brett Lowell, sip bourbon, eat chocolate, and watch *The Wolf of Wall Street*. We laugh awkwardly at the crude humor and nudity. "I feel like I need a shower after watching that," Tommy jokes. In stitches, we forget all about the frigid wind outside and the intensity of the effort we face.

On day six we reach pitch 14, the hardest on the route. Slicing horizontally across the wall from right to left, the pitch is characterized by three vicious boulder problems with rests between each. Six weeks earlier, I fell off the last move of the pitch, so I know I can do it. But I still haven't. Tommy sent this pitch on the same day I fell off the last move, and he's climbing stronger than I've ever seen him. It feels like there's an inevitability to his success. For me, there's the inevitability of the battle, the pressure, the very real fact that now is the moment I have to do what I've never done before.

Honestly, I wasn't that close to climbing the Dawn Wall when we began. Of the six 5.14 pitches, I had only done the two easiest ones. Not only that, but the myriad 5.13+ pitches above the crux were a big question mark for me. Four years earlier, it had been the 5.14b stemming corner and face traverse of pitch 12, the Molar Traverse, that shut me down. But on the last day of 2014 I clipped the anchors within a few attempts, shattering doubts that had defined my reality since 2010. "I never have to do pitch 12 again!" I exclaimed with shock and relief. This breakthrough was critical for my confidence.

Now, January 1, we face pitch 14. Of all the pitches on the Dawn Wall, I have spent the most time working on this one. I know how it should feel. But on my first three attempts, I'm plagued by the finicky first crux, with a microscopic hold on which my left foot stubbornly refuses to stick. It's

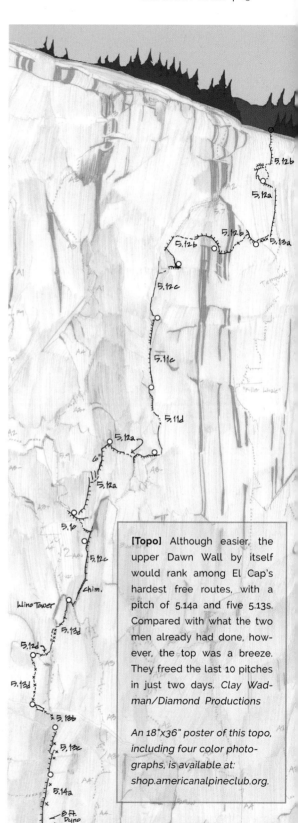

[Topo] Although easier, the upper Dawn Wall by itself would rank among El Cap's hardest free routes, with a pitch of 5.14a and five 5.13s. Compared with what the two men already had done, however, the top was a breeze. They freed the last 10 pitches in just two days. *Clay Wadman/Diamond Productions*

An 18"x36" poster of this topo, including four color photographs, is available at: shop.americanalpineclub.org.

[Photo] Climbing at night provided cool temperatures for better grip and a surprising side benefit: The headlamp cast shadows that made tiny footholds look bigger. *Corey Rich/ Big UP Productions/Aurora Photos*

dark out. We climb after the wall goes into shade and well into the night, in midwinter, because the holds on these crux traverse pitches are too small to use when the temperature is above 45°F. The ironic thing about climbing at night is that the headlamp casts a shadow below even the smallest dimple on the wall, making our footholds appear more positive than they are. In the flat daylight, they look like porcelain. On my fourth attempt the left foot sticks, and after a few breathless moves I'm through the first crux and staring at the final move. Last time I managed the crux I rushed the move to the belay. I won't make the same mistake twice. I force myself to hesitate and focus on the final edge guarding the anchor before committing.

Back at the portaledge 45 minutes later, I send my girlfriend, Jacqueline, a text: "Babe. It's done." It's not even 8 p.m. and the hardest pitch on the Dawn Wall is in the bag for both of us. The mood is light and celebratory as we go about our evening ritual of washing our hands, making tea, taking a nip of bourbon, and cooking dinner.

[Above] The daily ritual of skin care. [Bottom] Jorgeson wills the skin of his fingers to grow faster. *Corey Rich/Big UP Productions/Aurora Photos*

Whereas I had been obsessed with learning the nuances of pitch 14 over the years, I had largely avoided pitch 15, the second hardest on the route. Something about the nature of the climbing always put tension in my chest. I could never find a rhythm on it. When Tommy sent pitch 15, two years earlier, it had dropped down our priority list. I would always justify spending time on some other pitch. Well, there was no avoiding it now. This second traversing pitch is broken into two distinct sections: a 60-foot 5.13c to a big rest, followed by a vicious iron-cross boulder problem on razor blades. Prior to the push, I had never even linked from the start of the pitch to the rest. But I had done the boulder problem on many occasions.

The week that follows is the most intense of my life. Tommy swiftly dispatches pitch 15 after one warm-up burn. With the index and middle fingers on my right hand taped to protect the worn-out skin from splitting open even more, I give four all-out efforts before my power and precision deteriorate. Back at camp, I dismiss the failure. "It's only natural that this route puts up a fight," I shrug. The key takeaway from first round is how much harder the crux feels with taped fingers.

Round two the very next morning confirms this. After one attempt, it's clear

that I have no chance at the pitch as long as two fingers are taped. I force myself to rest the remainder of the day, and the following one as well, while my skin heals. Meanwhile, Tommy has gone on to climb the Loop Pitch, which circumnavigates an 8.5-foot dyno on pitch 16 that has given him a lot of trouble. The Loop partially reverses pitch 15, downclimbs 50 feet, and then climbs 60 feet up an adjacent corner on the left to where the dyno ends. With the Loop Pitch complete, Tommy only has one more pitch of 5.14 left on the entire route.

On day four on pitch 15 I am full of hope and determination. If I can just send tonight, I'll be caught up with Tommy, causing no delay. The skin on my right index finger has healed just enough to climb without tape. I probably have two or three attempts before it splits again. Every go has to count. After four demoralizing close attempts, the tip of my right index finger ruptures. "Fuck!!!" I scream into the night, hanging at the end of the rope. Tommy, Brett, and photographer Corey Rich are all silent.

Back at the belay, my fat, frustrated thumbs tap out a single-word text to my girlfriend. "Devastated." I press send and stuff my phone back into my pocket. Blood seeps through the tape on my fingers as I pull on my gloves. I rappel back to camp, 200 feet below. My eyes, once laser focused on every detail of the granite, take on a thousand-yard stare as we prepare dinner. Pasta. Again. Two more rest days needed. Again.

Inside the sleeping bag, my thoughts churn. *Maybe I should just throw in the towel and support Tommy to the top. I don't want to be the guy that almost climbed the Dawn Wall. What's a few more rest days if it means success? I will rest. I will try again. I will succeed.*

The sound of falling ice hitting my portaledge wakes me around 6:30 a.m. The ice isn't too big; it sounds like hail, but more sporadic. Nearly all the risk on the wall is in our control, but ice falling from the rim is more like roulette. It will be another hour before the sun reaches us, so I try to fall back asleep. The hardest part of this project isn't the climbing, it's the time between the climbing. The waiting game. We've already been up here for more than 10 days: plenty of time for focus, confidence, and determination to crumble.

After breakfast, we check in with our loved ones. Tommy calls his wife, Rebecca, in Colorado and shares the news, both good and bad. He sent the pitches he wanted to the previous night. I didn't. I can feel the nervous energy coming through the phone. Rebecca is wondering if Tommy will push on without me. She's wondering how long he will wait. Have we had "the conversation" yet?

The conversation comes up after breakfast. Tommy keeps it simple: "Hey, man, the weather forecast is amazing. I'm going to keep going until Wino Tower but stop there. I'll go into full support mode at that point for as long as it takes for you to catch up. There's nothing worse I could imagine than finishing this climb without you." Right away, I feel some of the pressure dissolve.

Tommy will climb and I will head up our network of fixed ropes to belay him as he pushes higher. It's hard for me to feel excited for his progress. Likewise, he's probably holding back some excitement after each pitch so as not to discount the battle I'm still waging. It's an unspoken, delicate balance of support, but also distance. We don't talk about it.

Like a machine, Tommy reaches Wino Tower. He will certainly send the Dawn Wall. One hundred and eighty feet below, I'm happy for him, truly. But I'm also hollow. Tommy is only two days from the top—he could probably do it in one. I have a pitch of 5.14d, a 5.14c dyno, a 5.14a corner, and three pitches of 5.13+ before I catch up. Jesus.

Two days later, January 9, I wake feeling calm. Today is my day. The portaledge fly flaps in a cold updraft. A soft, gray light sits in the Valley—it's the one overcast day we've seen in the forecast. One way or another, a conclusion is coming and I'm at peace with it. Today is our 14th day on the wall. Today, I will either send this pitch or sacrifice my dream to make sure Tommy realizes his.

I start my preclimb routine, sanding any abrasions off the soles of my climbing shoes. Then I

[Photo] Tommy Caldwell makes the most of minimal holds on pitch 19 (5.13c), *Brett Lowell/Big UP Productions/Aurora Photos*

[Above] With the crux behind, Jorgeson pushes toward the top. *Corey Rich/Big UP Productions/ Aurora Photos*

do the same for my fingers. Next I coat my split finger in superglue and begin an elaborate, weaving tape job with a special brand of Australian tape donated by Beth Rodden. I tie in with the perfect figure-eight, with the tail passed back down into the knot. I lace my shoes carefully. A jumar goes on the right gear loop of my harness. Gri-gri on the left. I'll need them both to get back to the portaledge if I fall. Last, I strip my top layers down to the same green T-shirt I've been wearing from day one.

This isn't any shirt. It's Brad's shirt. Really, it's the reason I'm even on this wall. Since I was 16, Yosemite has been a place of inspiration and wonder. But this year the Valley held two very real ghosts, neither of which I had wanted to confront.

The first was the ghost of some rough times in my relationship with Jacqui. Last October, for reasons I still don't fully understand, she pressed pause on the relationship. We'd since come back together, stronger, but the Valley held an emotional residue from that experience. It represented the feeling of losing a person and a future that had seemed perfectly, joyously inevitable. Second, the Valley held the ghost of my dear friend Brad Parker, who fell to his death on the Matthes Crest in Tuolumne on August 16, 2014. His passing was the first time I've experienced true grief. True loss. I wasn't alone either. Our whole tribe was crushed—every person he inspired with his bright, daily, "epic" approach to life.

In September, mere weeks before I was to meet Tommy to begin the Dawn Wall season, my heart had been fragile and uncommitted to the impending battle. I trained halfheartedly by bouldering and hangboarding in the gym a few times per week. Before I could feel the uplifting burn of inspiration, I would have to turn my two ghosts into allies.

One night in mid-October, while I was up on the wall attempting to prepare for our push, Brad's girlfriend Jainee texted me that she too needed to confront the emotional trauma of Yosemite. The last time she'd been here, she drove in with the love of her life and drove home alone. I had felt utterly helpless in the wake of Brad's passing. But surely I could help Jainee by taking her climbing. Over the next two days, Jainee and I climbed nothing but easy Valley classics. For years, training and the cloud of pressure around the Dawn Wall had defined my experience with climbing. But for these two days it was pure joy. The experience washed away the memory of emotional trauma and turned grief into celebration. It's exactly what I needed.

Around this time, we started the B-Rad Foundation in Brad's name and designed T-shirts with original art based on a drawing Brad had done on the dirty window of his truck's camper shell. Since beginning the final push on the Dawn Wall, I've been wearing one of those shirts every day. It's the reason I'm even on the wall again. If I'm lucky it will be the reason I stand on top as well.

The moves between the belay ledge and the midpoint rest on pitch 15 are nearly automatic at this point. Despite the highly technical climbing I find a flow. Shaking out on the jug, I alternate holding my hands to the wind, using the icy updraft to harden the calluses on my fingertips. When my heart rate falls to near resting rate, I turn my mind from relaxation to razor focus. A few sharp exhales prep my body for what I'm about to make it do.

The last ten times I've been at this spot the result has been the same. Something has to change. I've decided to revert to a foot sequence from earlier in the season. The difference is subtle, but while holding the crux iron cross, from fingertip to fingertip, I feel the difference I've been seeking. My right foot is secure. Anxiety is replaced by confidence. Trembling is replaced by control. I'm through the crux, with one more bolt of insecure climbing to negotiate. As I grab one of the final crimps, I see the tape on my index finger saturated with blood. Doubt lasts only an instant. Moments later, everything is silent except the strong wind in my ears.

For a few moments there's no celebration, just breathing. Did that just happen? I do a last few moves and clip the anchors at the no-hands stance. My scream reverberates down to the meadow, and cheers echo back up to the wall. Yes, that just happened.

A collective breath is released. Not just by me and by Tommy, but at this point by millions of followers. Momentum is a powerful force, and when nervous anticipation turns into universal celebration, everything shifts. The tide is coming in and I ride it upstream.

SUMMARY: First free ascent of the Dawn Wall (32 pitches, 5.14d), a free link-up of Mescalito and the Wall of Early Morning Light, plus portions of Adrift, Tempest, and previously unclimbed sections of the southeast face of El Capitan. Tommy Caldwell began working on the route in 2007 and was joined by Kevin Jorgeson in 2009, spending 8 to 10 weeks each year on the climb. They redpointed the full route December 27, 2014–January 14, 2015, with each climber leading or following every pitch free (the two led different variations on pitches 16 and 17).

ABOUT THE AUTHOR: Kevin Jorgeson, 30, lives in Santa Rosa, California.

[Right] Success at last. *Bligh Gillies/ Big UP Productions/Aurora Photos*

A STAIRWAY TO HEAVEN THROUGH THE EVIL FACE, MT. JOHNSON   L. FALLEY 2015

STAIRWAY TO HEAVEN

CLIMBING THE DREAMY ICE DRIPS ON
MT. JOHNSON'S MYTHICAL NORTH FACE

RYAN JENNINGS & KEVIN COOPER

RYAN: "A Wild Ride to the Summit of Mount Johnson" reads the *American Alpine Journal*. Beneath the headline, a meaty account of Jack Tackle and Doug Chabot's first ascent of the Elevator Shaft in 1995.

I'm fresh off my first real alpine climb, Hallett Chimney in Rocky Mountain National Park. It's the first time I've sensed the distinct smell of crampons scraping walls of stone. I've found a new love, and I drool over every word in Doug's ghastly accounts of attempts on this mythical Alaskan route—broken hips, rescues, avalanches—weaving tales of grit, determination, and survival. But it is one photo that truly captures my attention: a great pyramid more beautiful than any mountain I have seen.

I linger on this page, studying Johnson's grand north face. The Elevator Shaft cuts vertically up the right side, three-quarters of the way across, but it's the rest of the face—everything left of the Elevator Shaft—that gives me shivers. The dreamy drips I know to be the future fall in near-vertical, undisturbed paths. I must know!

KEVIN: I first meet Ryan in '97 in a bar in Estes Park, Colorado. After a few beers, it seems we both have a similar mindset for climbing, and we quickly make plans to get out in the Park. It's late winter when we gear up for the alpine classic Dark Star on Mt. Meeker. Alpine, big wall, and long trad routes are the topics of choice on our hike in. Ryan enjoys my kind of suffering, and he soon becomes my "go to" guy when I want to go big. Before long we start planning a trip to Alaska. Ryan doesn't know it yet, but I too have my sights on Johnson's nordwand.

RYAN: The headline in the 2003 edition of *Accidents in North American Mountaineering* still makes me cringe. "Rappel Failure – Inadequate Anchor." I remember Cooper shouting, "Oh shit!" Looking up, I fall back into darkness, spinning and sliding, faster now. The block that

[Previous page] Ryan Jennings and Kevin Cooper's 2014 route Stairway to Heaven (4,000', WI4 AI5+ M6 A1) begins in the lower left, skirts the large horizontal roof, then breaks right and climbs the prominent white streak for the length of the face, finishing on the final summit slopes. The Elevator Shaft (*AAJ 1996*) climbs the prominent gash second from right; the Ladder Tube (*AAJ 2008*) ascends the rightmost gash. *Leighan Falley*

once held the anchor slams my shoulder, leaving a scar for life. I think it's Cooper's crampon. Then my ankle snaps, and I'm flying through the air for an eternity. "Should have gone limp!" We fly over the bergschrund, sure to have been our grave, and bounce down the blocks of ice and avalanche debris. Our rescuers are true Alaskan hard men. Eventually we understand that if it weren't for the 1,000-foot fall down our warm-up route on the Moose's Tooth, our main objective, Mt. Johnson, surely would have killed us.

Post-accident, time drifts and we settle into new lives, no longer selfishly ours. We go mixed climbing on small crags and link big, local routes. I trend toward being the cautious one in our partnership. And Kevin hates my badgering. But we've always been opposites attracted. He is the best climber I know, never afraid to take the sharp end, and for this I'll take our differences. One of us brings Johnson up every other year, but the timing is never right.

KEVIN: With Ryan living near Redstone, Colorado, we develop a taste for dirty, soft sandstone, honing our mixed skills on chossy rock with sparse gear, reveling in ice picks pounded into dirt. In RMNP we are treated to years of thin and heady routes. Small victories come, and though we never lose sight of our big objective, we are immersed in families and careers. The Johnson project seems almost a fantasy.

Finally, in 2013 we are ready for something more. But Johnson still feels too meaty an option. We choose Cerro Torre. We train all summer and purchase airfare for late December. Then, in September, all hell breaks loose in Colorado: Estes Park and the entire Front Range are hit with biblical flooding. No way in or out for days. With delivery of materials delayed, my building work shuts down, and the lack of income means I can't afford Patagonia. I'm now faced with an extremely difficult phone call. Ryan will be so pissed.

[Above] Kevin Cooper with the scope locked on Johnson's north face. *Ryan Jennings*

RYAN: I need to know we are going somewhere. After learning the painful way about no refunds on flights, I put a photo of Johnson's pyramid behind my computer's login prompt as inspiration. The image erupts onto the screen and my heart sinks heavy. The brilliantly sharp photo hides too much. *I must know what is in that corner up high. What hides behind the sheets of white down low? Is it ice in that section? How big is that roof?* I draw imaginary lines, realizing work will never get done until I have another adventure.

After the kids go to bed I search the Internet for grant opportunities. Kevin's wife mentions the Mugs Stump Award. I'd glossed over it, not feeling worthy of anything attached to Mugs' name—he is a giant in my mind, and grants like this seem reserved for modern giants. But the form is simple enough, so I take a shot and submit an application. My heart lifts as I take one last look at the screensaver, gently close the laptop, and drift off to peaceful sleep.

KEVIN: It's just another day banging nails in the mountains when I get the call from Ryan. Mugs is shining down on us, granting access to our dreams! Waves of emotion flood over me—fear, excitement, apprehension—knowing we finally may step foot on this monolithic face. When Mugs says go, you go!

On our flight into the Ruth, the first glimpse of Johnson inspires and intimidates. Streaks of white lace the lower half of the face, leading to a huge corner. "Fuck! How could that still not be climbed?" The most beautiful face in the gorge, untouched.

RYAN: A crisp wind sends us gliding down the glacier, eyes focused intently on the pyramid in the distance. Dickey, Bradley, and Wake take their time passing to our right. Apprehensively confident, we yearn to be close to Mt. Johnson. A massive serac blocks access to the wall as we approach. We know its history. Seth Shaw is nearby. The serac calved onto him a decade ago as he stood below to snap a photo. We find a bypass to the left and stay clear of the monster.

We spend the day touring below the base over to the Elevator Shaft. The wall

[Above] Kevin Cooper sets off. The next pitch would traverse left on snow mushrooms to breach the huge roof system. *Ryan Jennings*

seems impossible. At home the photos made it look slabby. On the plane it looked steeper, *but here?* The first half of the wall is overhanging and undoubtedly taller than El Cap. Few lines present themselves; those that do look futuristically daunting. We fan the idea of an Elevator repeat, but wanting more we quickly turn—empty and defeated—back across the base of the wall. Amazingly, the wall tilts at a new angle from this direction and possibilities appear, one on each side of the great roof. Tomorrow we will see which way goes.

KEVIN: All we want is to sink some iron into the gut of the beast. An unusually mild winter has left the north face in prime shape. Quickly dismissing our first option on the right, disappointment hovers as our attention turns to our second and only other option. Dropping from the left side of the roof is a shallow, left-facing corner, barely poking out of the snow—the only semi-distinct weakness visible amongst a sea of smooth slabs. We scurry over and around a few crevasses, surmount the final 'schrund, and arrive at the base.

I quickly grab the rack. Firm snow and rotten rock are the two ingredients on this opening pitch; Spectres and Peckers are the pro of choice. I belay as the corner feature disappears. Ryan follows and we study our next move. Chaotic snow blobs hang precariously below the roof. Just stoked to have started on the wall, we fix a rope and head back to camp. Pitch one, at M5, is an eye-opener. At camp we laugh at Jack Tackle's certainty: "No cracks up there, guys, no cracks." But I know it's too early to be cocky.

Ryan: Multiple snow mushrooms hang into space, blocking our way. I traverse, well protected, under the first blob and place a picket in steep névé before heading vertically between the second and third. I belly-ride the last 'shroom, bound for a blank slab out left, and thoughtful mixed climbing stretches me farther from solid pro. Suddenly, as if destined, a four-inch-deep corner, with ice barely thick enough for picks, hides perfect nut placements. "Hell yeah! We're in there!" I sew it up and delicately dance along micro-edges. We are past the great roof.

Our five-percent-chance-in-hell just jumped drastically. But the thought of the unknown above sinks to my gut and stews as we ski back to camp.

Kevin: Base camp has been kind, but we're down to our last rum. At 3 a.m. I'm amped and bursting out of my bag, trying to motivate a groggy partner. "Calm'er down!" Ryan's famous words erupt. "We've got a long trip ahead of us." Crawling out of the tent, I see two headlamps a few hundred feet up the Escalator on the east side of Johnson. Must be Jewel and Kim. "Yo, Ry! The girls are motoring up Johnson." I yell into the tent, hoping to create some urgency. "Um, Kev? Weren't there two headlamps up high?" Ryan asks. "Yeah, why?" I respond. "Now there's only one and it's at the base of the route."

We both assume the worst and go into rescue mode, first stopping to wake Jack Tackle and Fabrizio Zangrilli. I fear the gruesome sight ahead, but as we near the lone headlamp the sky brightens and we make out two figures moving upward. Just a dropped headlamp. We head back to camp, too mentally worked to head up our route.

Ryan: The morning of the false start, I sense it. Cooper's energy is revved. He's already rushing us. He is not present but lost in the days ahead. Paying attention to your partner's energy is paramount to survival. On the mountain I can feel Kevin's thoughts 200 feet down the rope; here in the tent they're more pressing.

Jack and Fabrizio join us at the headlamp. It feels surreal to have this moment with legends as we ski back to our tents, discussing mortality, family, and a general love of this life. Tension hangs in the air as we tiptoe around our chosen line. I can tell they're concerned about some nobodies attempting it.

Days later, we're back at the top of our fixed lines, and Kevin is traversing right across a frosty slab of deep snow, above the big roof, 100 meters above the glacier. The forecast is good for the next few days. This morning we woke together in sync, both of us calm. Today is the day. The anchor is solid, but protection on the traverse is forebodingly absent. I fight back thoughts of an avalanche and patiently wait for the rope to come tight. After this traverse retreat will quickly become a reckless option. Thankfully it's still early. The wall sheds its evening coat under the day's first rays, high above. Traversing together, I wonder if Kevin will find a safe belay, out of the way.

Kevin: I'm halfway through a 600-foot sideways wallow-fest when the shrapnel above begins to release. I find sparse pro and only occasional shelter before making it to the start of the milky smears we hope will give access to the upper dihedral. I find a belay under an overhang as the wall rains down on us, harder now. "Is this next pitch even doable?" I contemplate, as I bring Ryan across. I stick my tool into the névé above the Safehouse cave. It's sticky but looks like vertical snow for miles. If the debris slough stops we may have a chance. We brew up and wait.

Ryan: Sounds of tinkling, broken glass intermix with sliding snow. Sometimes something big comes down. The terrain out of the cave looks vertical, up endless white streaks, and I begin to calculate the

THE ENDLESS NEVÉ

L. FALLEY 2008

[Above] Looking down from a 700' section of steep, unprotected névé. *Ryan Jennings*

sanity of the dangerous simul-climbing sure to come. But I hesitate to think of retreat. I feel safe.

While some climbs in our past have had similarities, nothing has truly prepared me for this moment. The entire rack, my pack for four days, bivy gear, and two ropes dangle from me, while pickets clang against my knees. It's all useless. I hope the angle eases ahead. Salvation, it turns out, is much farther. Three and a half hours and 700 feet of vertical later, I search for a belay as Kevin comes into view. The rope, without a single piece between us, is distracting to look at, limply arching and pulling at its apex. Catching a glimpse of the wall above, I'm glad it will be Kevin's lead next—*once I find a damn piece of gear!*

KEVIN: We've been simul-climbing for some time and I'm thankful for two things: solid sticks and a solid partner. I briefly fanaticize we'll come across Andi Orgler's drilled copperhead, a rappel anchor he placed while bailing off an attempt on this face many summers ago. We know he'd like it removed. But now the wall is encased in white and finding the wire is surely impossible. Our lifeline, which feels more like a death line, stretches beyond sight. Steel spikes are the only connection to the vertical wall. *Focus!*...it echoes in my head.

"Well that went well," I proclaim, as I finally reach the belay. "I think you should lead the next one too." Ryan gives a blank nod in agreement, and we brew for the next hour. The mood is somber, despite my attempt at humor. Both of us know we're about to be fully committed, if not already. Our only way out is to continue up this Névé Highway. I silently pray we won't have to simul-solo like that again. We sit in awkward silence until Ryan announces, "Let's do this!"

RYAN: A rope length away, I start down then up. If no protection is found on this lead Kevin will be forced to remove the anchor and our ropes will arch free from he to me. There's an overlap above and right, which may take a piece. Nothing. Tackle's voice rings in my ears: "No cracks, guys! No cracks up there, I bet."

Prior to the trip, I'd calculated our chances for both success and survival. Our history, with 17 years climbing together, shows a much larger ratio of Coop falls to mine, and here we know the leader must not fall. I rationalize that with solid picks I can hold any slip he may make while following. Turning slightly outward, but refusing to look, I yell down to Cooper to remove the belay and begin following. I trust he will not fall today.

Once again we're untethered to the beast. I hang onto six-inch-thick, vertical névé. Calves scream as I focus on surmounting the bulge just ahead, hopeful the angle will ease. But quickly I'm disheartened. I stop completely and cry for a few minutes. The névé remains steep, and now it's thinner and less consistent. With family back home I have crossed the line of sane climbing, and I'm upset for being so selfish.

Left, right, up, back, down, left, then right again. I dance in the direction of the most solid snow. Still no pro and we've been climbing together for a long time. It's getting darker and sparks fly as I swing. Roughly 600 feet out I finally spy some rock up and left. The route goes right, but I need salvation. A large snow mushroom hangs above, but that threat is less frightening than to continue on. A belay! Cams and nuts behind a flake, my first ice screw, and tied-off ice tools, all equalized perfectly. I'm scared and have been for too long. I sink onto the anchor and feel a wild concoction of adrenal juices flood my beyond-spent carcass. I dream only of sleep.

KEVIN: Years roped up with Ryan instill enough confidence for me to unclip from the belay. I think of when we climbed Bridal Veil Falls in a single pitch and falling was not an option. *This is no different, right?* Continuing my mantra for the next three hours, I follow upward. It's dark by the time I get Ryan in my sights. Twenty hours in and I'm spent. I hope to hell there's a bivy.

Immediately I see the threatening mushroom directly above. There'll be no rest here. "Looks like only a pitch and we're in the corner," Ryan assures me. I grab the rack and head into the longest pitch of my life. I find good ice for 30 feet and my comfort rises, but then nothing but sn'ice and snow-covered rock, with protection every 100 feet or so. Finally, I reach the corner and the salvation of a protected bivy.

RYAN: I try not to dose off as Coop's headlamp drifts out of sight to the right. The night is dark and there's a constant hiss of spindrift and ice shards sprinkling down. Steep is still the angle. The death 'shroom lurks above. Eventually I flick on my light and rise to move. Calves come back to life and I sense he must be close to the corner.

Linked in simul-mode again, I climb into the dark. Debris bombards me, and I fear there'll be no bivy until the sun lights the sky. Eventually I find Kevin, burrowed into the corner with solid gear. We quickly make two one-person platforms. His is below, chopped into the slope with a do-not-roll-off edge. Mine burrows straight into the corner. I'm happy.

A few hours later, we rise in the warmth of the sun, below the corner we've studied so much. I quickly head into the maw. The corner curves up, out, and left in proportions I can't quite grasp, and so I don't look. After burrowing through snow, a steep slab propels me into an ugly wide crack stretching *too far*. Gear and helmet hang between my legs as I wiggle through the final constriction, a margin made thinner by my slightest exhale. Kevin ascends the rope on the outside, saving time.

[Right] Jennings starts up the Shredder, the first of many pitches in a long corner system. *Kevin Cooper*

KEVIN: Ryan has wrecked his outerwear freeing the Shredder pitch, and I'm served up much of the same on the next. Wide, crumbly cracks continue out of sight. The climbing is sustained and I fire in most of our rack in the first 100 feet. "I wish we had more wide gear!" I yell down as my crampons skitter off loose flakes, my last piece alarmingly distant. Finally, after getting our only Big Bro to stick, I fight through a few sketchy moves, find an anchor, and fix the rope. We're now deep in the belly and I can't think of a better place.

RYAN: I'm tired. Kev had to leave his pack hanging at the crux. The belay is cramped and I'm anxious to get on. We are 50 feet from the end of the rock section that had worried us from base camp. Soon we will join the beautiful smear of ice we have come for.

As the corner steepens, I climb deeper into the gut of a huge chimney system, topped by unconsolidated snow blobs. "It looks like shit!" I yell down. Fear builds and I push back by hammering a micro-nut into the overhanging wall on my right. One saving grace: The beautiful vein of ice I long for, hidden since our approach, extends over a small bulge 20 feet to my left. If I can traverse, we've made the ice! We're certain this incredible flow, the one we came for, will link us to the summit slopes.

After making the traverse, I haul my pack as Cooper jugs and the sun sets on another day. Time is nonexistent at this hanging belay. Moments of sleep intrude as we brew water. I wake Cooper and ask if he is continuing. I'm too tired to care about his response.

KEVIN: "Hell yes, I'm continuing!" The corner is locked in snow, but good sticks keep me moving. There's good pro for the first 40 feet, but eventually it craps out. I'm 170 feet out, in

need of a bivy, when yet another dreaded snow mushroom appears, cloaking the corner. I claw its side and uncover a cave. Peeling off my pack, I throw it into the slot and crawl inside, finding a three-inch crack in the back. We call this spot the Hideaway Bivy.

After sleeping for a couple of hours, we wake to the dreaded sun baking the next pitch. Temps have been warm, over 40°F during the day. As Ryan leads the morning's first pitch, ice melts from under his crampons. We would have been shut down a day later.

RYAN: A constant drip bounces off my bivy bag and I move to the back of the cave away from the sun. It's our enemy now. Far below it's melting our base camp, begging the glacier to swallow it whole. The cook tent just fell. "Damn it's hot out! Nobody's getting up shit!" I yell, flashing a childish grin down to Coop. There are hard moves out of the bivy cave and who knows what above that.

[Left] Looking out from the cramped nook of the Hideaway Bivy. *Ryan Jennings*

[Above] Cooper follows the quickly melting Névé's Nightmare pitch. *Ryan Jennings*

The ice is wet and losing its bond so I race up, only stalling at the slushy bulges, pro near nonexistent. This pitch, dubbed Névé's Nightmare, after Cooper's daughter Névé, will be the highlight of my climbing career. Above, I find a tight chimney and force my arm to the back, just barely reaching pro for the belay. Shivering deeply, I thank God as water rains on me.

KEVIN: On better ice now, my lead takes me to the top of the flow, and after 100 feet I spy Ryan's "exit cracks." He thinks they'll lead us to the diamond-shaped snow slope below the summit. I've always thought the corner we're in was the way. At the belay we agree: The main corner will be better than run-out dirt slabs and flaring cracks. Unfortunately our snow-choked corner gives way to pure rock, and Ryan's back to trundling large chunks of stone before reaching the next belay.

My lead is next. Steep mixed climbing on better rock leads me to a snow ramp, and I follow it left to a giant wall of shit rock. After 180 feet I'm lucky to find a solid chunk of granite in this shield. The granite blob, welded in, is split by a crack just fat enough for a ball nut and my smallest cam. When Ryan joins me, I can't tell him enough how great this belay is. He's pissed it took so long.

RYAN: Kevin's belay is near the overhanging black corner we saw from camp, reaching up to the ridge. I don't dare look at the anchor he keeps bragging about.

"It's bomber!" I blurt, spotting a solid crack splitting the dihedral. I aid 30 feet up the steep crack and then free climb to a short snowfield leading to the ridge. "We're home free!" I yell down. "Caaaw, Caaaaw!" resounds from below. The last piece of pro, a Pecker, seems fitting for the finale. Cooper follows, free climbing until he falls while pulling into easier terrain. He thinks it will go free at M7. We laugh at his cockiness and our energy, some 70 hours in now. Hanging at the ice screw belay just below the ridge, we brew up and take some celebratory photos, and then Kevin's off. "So…should I just go to the ridge and walk to the summit?" he asks, too soon. He calls down for the rack.

KEVIN: There's one more buttress guarding the way. I bypass it with a short downclimb and long traverse into a snowfield. Even though the summit is close I'm wrought with fatigue and uncertainty. When I turn back and see the northern lights appear, they give me clarity and energy to keep on. We reach the summit sometime after 4 a.m. A storm blankets the horizon. It all seems planned.

RYAN: The mandatory summit photos won't upload to Facebook yet—dammit! I start down the south ridge. Looking back up at Coop, I think of all the adventures and of all the love, and hate, we've doled out. Complete opposites, we've somehow managed greatness, yet again.

Midmorning finds us back at the base of the wall. Paul Roderick flies overhead as we sit exhausted on our packs. Tilting his wing, he salutes our efforts or thanks God we're alive. The gesture is grand to us. We know he and Tackle are anxious for our return, and we are grateful to know someone is thinking of us, someone who understands.

Back in base camp flakes begins to fall, and we spend two days in a storm before we can fly out. Boredom brings reflection, and we contemplate our success and the path that brought us here. Mugs' ideals of boldness, purity, and simplicity sang to us all those years ago, when Kevin and I started climbing together. Now we steep in pride, having held firm to those ideals.

[Above] Cooper and Jennings below Johnson's north face, after the descent. *Ryan Jennings*

SUMMARY: First ascent of Stairway to Heaven (4,000', WI4 AI5+ M6 A1), up the central north face of Mt. Johnson (8,460'), by Kevin Cooper and Ryan Jennings, May 1–May 4, 2014. Andi Orgler and Michael Rutter first attempted a direct route up the north face in July 1990 as a rock climb, but retreated due to blank rock.

ABOUT THE AUTHORS: *Ryan Jennings lives in Carbondale, Colorado, with his wife and two children. He looks forward to his children seeing the grace in mountain heights, scenic rivers, and far-off places. Kevin Cooper grew up in the California rat race and is thankful he found a small mountain community in Allenspark, Colorado. Two daughters leave him scrambling to find the balance between family time and free time, but, he says, he has a very understanding wife.*

ABOUT THE ARTIST: *Leighan Falley is an Alaskan-born pilot and climber known for her piles of expediton sketchbooks. Her Mt. Johnson illustrations were created in the Ruth Gorge. See more of her work at www.highcampartstudio.squarespace.com.*

KOREAN DIRECT

THE FIRST ASCENT OF GASHERBRUM V

AHN CHI-YOUNG

Insignificant against the blinding white backdrop of Gasherbrum V's south face, we stood like silhouettes atop a moraine, the wall before us in full view. The complex glacier leading up to the face reminded me of scaly dragon's tail. We had spotted a snaking line that would lead us to the jagged bergschrund at the foot of the wall. Once on the face, we would have to keep left to avoid a menacing serac, then move right in the upper mixed section before finishing with a direct line to the top.

Seong Nak-jong and I had never really considered a route on the south side of unclimbed Gasherbrum V until we were denied passage up the northeast face. We had started our first attempt on the 7,147-meter peak from Camp 1 on the South Gasherbrum Glacier, along the normal routes to Gasherbrums I and II. We trudged through thigh-deep snow to reach the northeast face, which was covered in loose ice and snow, and was nearly impossible to protect. Falling ice and spindrift poured down from above. We finally had no choice but to evacuate from our high point of 6,400 meters.

This unsuccessful attempt quashed our desire to climb. As the leader of our small team, the quandaries of a second

[Right] The line of Korean Direct on the 1,450-meter south face of Gasherbrum V, with the midway camp marked. The red dot marks the approximate high point (ca 6,700m) of the 2012 French attempt on the south face and southwest ridge, to the left of the Korean line. Another French party attempted the south face to the right of the Korean route in 1980, also reaching 6,700 meters. *Korean Direct Expedition*

[Above] Ahn Chi-young at about 6,000 meters on the south face. *Seong Nak-jong*

attempt weighed heavily on my mind. Not only were we physically weakened and our confidence shot, it was already mid-July and more snow was laying siege to the camps. We had been away from home for more than a month. The hard work and extra time required to relocate our base camp seemed less than appealing.

Wrestling with what to do, I finally understood that the summit counted for much less than I'd imagined. What really mattered was giving our absolute best effort. Only then could we prevail over our initial failure. When I shared these thoughts with Nak-jong and Choi Hyeong-woo, our base camp manager, they agreed to another attempt, this time from the south. We spent a long day moving camp down to 4,770 meters on the Baltoro Glacier, directly below the snaking glacier leading to the south face.

Unlocking the intricacies of the 3.5-kilometer approach up this glacier would be critical to saving strength for the actual climb. To minimize time and conserve energy, we decided to gamble and not rope up for this glacial approach. On July 23 we left base camp at 5 a.m. Our strategy paid off, and though the glacier was more difficult than we had anticipated, we reached the flat basin below the south face two hours quicker than planned and made it to the bergschrund (5,720m) about 10 a.m.

Chunks of avalanched snow filled the area around the bergschrund. We sheltered beneath a rock and took a short rest. After tying into our two 7mm ropes I started climbing, with Nak-jong following behind me. Surrounded by the steep walls of the enormous cirque, it felt like we were battling in an ancient coliseum, parrying and dodging with our axes. Hot sun bounced off the crusty snow and scorched our faces. Every step required two or three hard swings to set our picks. Avalanches boomed from the broken midsection of the face, and we pressed ourselves against the wall as wet snow showered around us. We kept moving left to get out from under the 300-meter-wide serac looming above.

My calves and thighs began to scream, and I resorted to sidestepping to relieve the fatigue. We had hoped to reach our bivy site by 5 p.m., but as evening approached we were only two-thirds of the way there. By dusk our water bottles were dry. Dehydration quickly took its toll, and around 10 p.m., still far from the ice cave where we planned to sleep, we rested briefly to melt snow and drink some water. Our bodies warmed and came back to life, and finally we reached the bivouac site, at 6,560 meters, at midnight.

The bivy site was worse than expected, with irregular formations of soft snow and ice, and miniature crevasses everywhere. Our thirst had to remain unquenched as we cut away at the ice floor to flatten a platform. The left corner of our tiny tent sagged into the open air of a gaping hole. We desperately needed water and crouched inside the small tent, diligently melting ice to stave off the cold and relax our hypothermic shivers. Too exhausted and parched to chew solid food, we added bits of porridge to our hot drinks. We had been on the move for 19 hours and had gained roughly 1,800 meters. We tied back into the rope before finally bedding down. Our cramped and tired bodies lay still, unaffected by the deep, cracking groans of the mountainside as the temperatures dropped through the night.

The next day, July 24, we began climbing again, but the avalanche danger and our deep fatigue prompted us to turn around and rest at our bivy site. That afternoon, while we were sipping tea, a palm-size stone crashed through the tent wall and landed on a mattress. I shrieked as a smaller stone penetrated the tent and badly bruised my knee. We moved our tent to a safer spot and tried to relax and regain our strength. At 3 o'clock the next morning we headed out again.

In the cold of the night the wall was silent and climbing conditions were prime. We advanced along the slanting, gash-like edge of the serac band until we could traverse above it roughly 200 meters, straight to the right, just below a wide, seemingly uncrossable bergschrund. Finally we discovered an ice column, no thicker than one's waist, that would lead us onto the upper wall and then the technical crux of the climb: a 300- to 400-meter section of chossy rock. The rockfall encountered here made us speechless. With just the slightest tug, rocks pulled free from the face, forcing us to search hard for mediocre protection. It took great effort and care to avoid dropping rocks on the belayer.

Though we were relieved to escape the mixed terrain, the final section of steep snow brought a new set of challenges. There were no rock outcrops for anchors, and the crusty snow lacked any integrity. We lost our footing repeatedly, both while

[Right] The 6,560-meter camp on Gasherbrum V's south face. The climbers spent two nights here during the ascent and one night on the way down. Behind: the northeast shoulder of Gasherbrum VI. *Seong Nak-jong*

[Above] The crux rock band above 6,600 meters. *Seong Nak-jong* [Below] Although dwarfed by neighboring Gasherbrum IV (just out of photo to the left) and by several nearby 8,000ers, the 7,000ers of the Gasherbrum group are impressive peaks, mostly unclimbed. Seen here from the west: (A) Gasherbrum VII (6,955m, unclimbed). (B) Gasherbrum Twins (6,882m, unclimbed). (C) Gasherbrum V (7,147m), first ascent in 2014 by the shadowed face hidden at right. (D) Gasherbrum VI (7,003m, claimed in 1986 but disputed). *Florian Ederer* [Next page] Seong Nak-jong (left) and Ahn Chi-young on the summit. *Seong Nak-jong*

climbing and standing at belays, and my heart raced over the avalanche danger.

Gasherbrum VI's summit finally came into view to the southeast, above the sub-peaks forming the cirque wall. I knew we were close, but dark, gloomy clouds were filling the western skies. Mist rose toward the summit and I prayed for the good weather to persist just a little longer. Step after tedious step, we pushed up the final slopes until finally we reached the top at 7:20 p.m. The summit consisted of a series of precarious cornices. We stood as high as we could safely go. To the north and east we glimpsed Gasherbrums I and II, veiled in clouds. Feeling the urgency, we quickly snapped photos and started downclimbing.

We retraced our footsteps toward the chossy rock section and then decided to rappel directly down the face, avoiding the awkward diagonal route we'd followed on the way up. Once committed to this route, we'd be unable to change our minds, especially in our wasted condition. Despite making numerous V-threads, our rack quickly diminished. We could see no sign of our ascent route through the surrounding darkness. We were completely lost, and I felt a sense of fear and harsh reality that I had never experienced so deeply in the mountains. The farther we descended, the more the surrounding walls seemed to press against us. We had only a snow picket and ice screw left for anchors—I cannot recall exactly. Then, at midnight, Nak-jong shouted from below: "I've spotted our footprints! Above the seracs!"

We returned to our ripped, collapsing tent at around 4 a.m., more than 24 hours after leaving. We hadn't had any water since late afternoon, and very little fuel remained in the canister, so we melted only enough ice to share one drink. After melting just a little more, we lay down and sleep took over.

The next morning we stayed tied in until the final snow wall, then down-soloed the final 300 meters to the bergschrund. By evening we were safely at the foot of the glacier. I found myself wondering how we might repair our ripped tent—how happy I was to worry about such a trivial matter! The sun slid into the night, and base camp came to life with the relief of laughter.

SUMMARY: First ascent of Gasherbrum V (7,147m) by Ahn Chi-young and Seong Nak-jong, via the south face, July 23–26, 2014: Korean Direct (1,450m above the bergschrund, WI4/5 M4). The pair reached the summit on July 25. The mountain had been attempted several times: a Japanese attempt from the east in 1978 that reached the 7,006-meter East III sub-peak; a French attempt in 1980 that reached 6,700 meters on the south face, to the right of the 2014 Korean line; a Korean attempt that reached 6,550 meters from the west in 2010; and a French attempt that reached 6,700 meters on the south face and southwest ridge in 2012.

ABOUT THE AUTHOR: *Born in 1977, Ahn Chi-young is a climbing guide and instructor. His alpine-style first ascent of Himjung (7,092m) in Nepal, with Kim Chang-ho, was featured in AAJ 2013.*

Translated from Korean by Peter Jensen-Choi.

WALL OF ICE

A TACTICAL TOUR DE FORCE ON THE WEST FACE OF SIULA CHICO, PERU

HÉLIAS MILLERIOUX

B enjamin Guigonnet, a guide from Nice, hatched the idea for our Peruvian expedition. His friend Stéphane Benoist had told him there was a huge dihedral still waiting to be climbed on the west face of Siula Chico in the Cordillera Huayhuash. In 2007, Jordi Corominas and Oriol Baro established the first and only route up the west face during Corominas' third year of attempts. He had first tried going up the central dihedral (which we ended up climbing), then made an attempt on the left side of the face, and finally succeeded on the right side. They climbed this line over six days, using a portaledge.

During the summer of 2013, Robin Revest and I shared an apartment in Chamonix with Ben for the guiding season. He was already planning an expedition to Siula Chico with Fred Degoulet, and Robin and I did not yet have any trips in the works for the coming year, so we proposed that we join them for this ambitious project.

With advice from Jordi and two other Spanish friends, brothers Simón and Martín Elías, we decided to make our attempt in early season, right after the spring rains, when the ice would be in the best possible shape. However, this strategy is a bit risky because the great flutings, runnels, and daggers of ice that form when the big faces purge themselves of their huge winter snow loads soon begin to melt in the warming temperatures. In order to climb these walls you have to time it just right, acclimatizing during the very end of the rains so you're ready to go during the first 10 days of the dry season. We were lucky in that the rainy season in 2014 was longer and wetter than normal, and when we saw the face for the first time it was even more iced up than it had been in Jordi and Oriol's photos.

We landed in Lima on April 24. It was a week later than we had planned, but I had to do some last-minute guiding in Chamonix to help pay for the trip. The four of us partied in Lima while waiting for the late-night bus to Huaraz—I think we drank a few too many Pisco Sours. When the bus arrived in Huaraz in the middle of the night, in a torrential rainstorm, we piled into a taxi toward the Huayhuash. In order make the most of our time, we had decided to leave immediately for an acclimatization hike and to check out Siula Chico via the Rasac Punta col. In the taxi, Ben suddenly realized he had left a pouch full of euros and some expensive electronic devices on the bus. We turned around and early in the morning discovered the empty bus back in Huaraz, missing all of Ben's cash and valuables. The trip was off to a great start.

We regrouped at our friend Zarela's house in Huaraz. Zarela is an extraordinary and very

[Previous page] Climbing as a team of four was crucial to the success of the French climbers, seen here on day three of the "ice big wall" of Siula Chico. *Robin Revest*

helpful woman, and I can't recommend La Casa de Zarela enough—you live well there. Over the next few days we acclimatized as planned, taking the bus to Pocpa and then hiking over Mancan Punta and up the Rasac Valley, past lush greenery and lakes full of trout. On April 28 we climbed to Rasac Punta at 5,129 meters, but the visibility wasn't great and from so far away we could see little other than the great size of Siula Chico's west face. We were back in Huaraz on the evening of the 29th. During this acclimatization trek the weather was relatively fair in the mornings, then it would rain until evening. On May 1 we went to Hatun Machay to climb for a few days. This is a beautiful place, with sport routes and bouldering at all grades, on a plateau at 4,200 meters. Once again, it rained every afternoon.

Back in town we finished our preparations. Our base camp would be near Laguna Sarapococha at 4,482 meters. We started the approach on May 6, and rain continued during the three-day trek—in fact it had rained every day of the two weeks we'd been in Peru, but each day it seemed to rain less and less. At base camp we thanked our *arriero*, who had loaded his mules with many kilos of gear and brought them all this way for the sake of a few Frenchmen who just wanted to waste their time and money in the Peruvian mountains. We were now at the foot of the mountains described in Joe Simpson's *Touching the Void*, a huge wall of 6,000-meter peaks: Yerupaja Sur, Siula Grande, Siula Chico, and Sarapo.

On May 10 we headed toward the west face of Siula Chico. It was tough going. The glacier was a labyrinth of crevasses, very tricky and dangerous. However, at last the weather was nice all day. The sun shone fiercely and the mountains purged themselves with big avalanches. We moved slowly—the packs were heavy and we were still acclimatizing. On this day we made it up to about 5,200 meters, and the following day we climbed to 5,400 meters and established our advanced base at the foot of Siula Chico.

The rainy season seemed to have truly ended, and the west face of Siula Chico was drying out very, very quickly. Day by day, we watched the face melt and fall apart. I would have preferred to rest and acclimatize at base camp for a few more days, but it was obvious that we needed to move if we didn't want to miss our chance. Our strategy would be to start each day extremely early and climb as much as possible during the night, before the sun rose. By noon, we needed to be somewhere sheltered from the falling ice and avalanches. While scouting we picked out potential bivy sites on the face almost by instinct. And we were not wrong—the sites we scoped were well sheltered and we

[Left] The author follows a steep M6+ corner on day two. The leader, Ben Guigonnet, used some aid, but the pitch was followed free. *Robin Revest*

[Above] Sunset at the exposed second bivouac on the west face. *Robin Revest*

didn't need portaledges, just tiny bivy tents. We packed lots of screws because of all the ice remaining on the face.

We planned to climb as a team of four—one big rope team. The leader would lead on double ropes, two of us would second, and then one would belay the leader on the next pitch while the other hauled our bag. The fourth climber would climb alongside the haulbag, belayed by one of the seconds on our third rope, while keeping the bag from getting hung up. We planned to change leaders every two or three pitches—the climbing is very difficult at this altitude and it would be exhausting for any of us to do more. We hoped to free all the pitches. Thinking about it now, this climb would have been very tough if there hadn't been four of us.

On May 14 we headed back up to our advanced base camp, ready to blast on May 15. That night it snowed. We sat out the day and allowed the face to purge itself of this fresh snow. The following night we gained the first ice runnels in two pitches. The climbing was not difficult, about 60 degrees, so we climbed side by side. At one point during the night a large projectile fell right past Robin, making a terrifying noise that pierced the quiet night air. Arriving at the first technical section of the wall, we formed one large rope team as planned and climbed to an amazing bivy site, chopping a narrow, flat ice ledge under the shelter of a rock overhang. The crux of the day was several pitches of sustained ice of about WI5 in difficulty, with one pitch of WI5+ or WI6, all of which Fred led. Fred and Ben set up the bivy site while Robin and I climbed two more pitches of ice up to a very steep dihedral. On this day, we climbed about 400 meters.

The rest of the day we hung out at our bivy, sitting on our Thermarest pads, our feet dangling over the void. As we sat safely under the shelter of the overhang, ice plunged from the face. The huge wall was decorated with overhanging umbrellas of ice, like the visors of ball caps, with massive stalactites hanging from them. We imagined ourselves on the famous north face of the Tête de Gramusat in Fressinière, and we were thankful for the training we'd done on the super-steep ice there all winter. The sun set, night arrived, and the falling ice stopped.

Early on May 17 we headed up to the base of the very steep and impressive dihedral where Robin and I had stopped the day before. Ben took the lead and spent a fair amount of time on this difficult pitch, using a few points of aid to get through blank spots without enough ice to climb. While following, we freed this pitch at around M6—and this at about 5,850 meters and with daypacks, which made it feel even harder. All four of us preferred leading on the face since the leader got to climb without a pack. Hauling the big bag at this altitude was exhausting.

Above the dihedral, Ben led another ice pitch at WI5+ and then turned over the lead, exhausted. I led two more pitches, one of WI6 and one WI5+, and then Fred led two more pitches to our second bivy at 5,980 meters. We had only climbed five pitches for the day—we aren't used to climbing so little. But seeking shelter from the coming avalanches and falling ice required us to cut the day short and, besides, we were pretty worked from the climbing. It took us a few hours to set up our bivy. During a break, a falling rock put a hole through Ben and Fred's tent.

Still in the dark, Robin set off the next day on mixed terrain. Then Fred brought us up a steep wall requiring two moves of dry-tooling at about M5 and more thin ice. It wasn't terribly difficult, but falling in that terrain would not have been good. Watching Fred climb such a delicate and dangerous pitch in the dark, with only the light from his headlamp, didn't exactly reassure the team.

The next pitch was a dead end. Above us was a hanging dagger, and Ben started toward it. He is really strong, but we feared he'd knock the dagger onto the rest of us. After many minutes he

[Photo] Siula Chico (6,265m) showing (1) Looking for the Void (2014) and (2) Baro-Corominas (2007). Corominas attempted the line of Looking for the Void in 2003, reaching the second bivy site shown, and then a line farther left in 2005. Center: Siula Grande (6,344m). Far left: Yerupaja Sur (6,515m). *Robin Revest*

retreated, frustrated to be off-route. I took off and led two pitches around the obstacle and onto a huge umbrella of ice. Ben wanted to redeem himself, and so he led the next pitch, an M5 traverse to our third bivy site. We set up our two tents on top of a huge cornice, at the base of the summit headwall at 6,170 meters, perhaps four pitches from the top.

That night the wind picked up and the temperature dropped. In the morning, when it would have been time to start climbing, the wind was blowing too hard for us to leave. We all huddled in one tent to try to stay warm. This had to be our summit day or we would run out of food and fuel. Ben wanted to redeem himself and lead the last two technical pitches. "*Allez!*" we said. He led a pitch of M5+ then a desperate and dicey M6+/M7. At the end of this section, he

placed a bird beak in a small seam and headed onto a thin smear of ice that fell apart under his picks and frontpoints. When it was our turn to climb, the little ice that had been there during Ben's lead was mostly gone and none of us succeeded in freeing the pitch.

Robin led up through the summit cornice in a long pitch of vertical snow, then up an arête of unconsolidated snow, and after four days of climbing we were on the summit. We all knew that despite our lack of experience in this range and our young age, this route would likely be one of the hardest we would ever climb. We headed back down to our bivy to rest a bit before descending the wall.

That night was epic. Violent winds and heavy snow whipped the dark face. We woke at midnight, packed up our bivy site, and began the descent. All of the rappels were incredibly steep and airy. We used the following technique: Two of us would rappel a single fixed line. At the end of the line, the two lower climbers would make a V-thread anchor. The two climbers still at the upper anchor would then drop the single rope so the lower climbers could rappel again. Then the upper climbers would rappel on their other two ropes, pull these ropes, and thread them through the V-thread the lower climbers had just left. Using this sequence, we were able to descend the nearly 900-meter face in three hours. True teamwork!

[Previous page] Ben Guigonnet starts day four with a pitch of M5+ at 6,200m. [Above] With a clever system for rapid rappels, the team's nighttime descent of the nearly 900m face took only three hours. *Robin Revest (both)*

During the night, we barely recognized the pitches we had climbed. "I climbed that? Me? Impossible…" At sunrise we reached the bergschrund in snow and fog. With a bit of luck, we found our tents and plunged into sleep in our wet down bags, completely exhausted and happy.

SUMMARY: First ascent of Looking for the Void, a direct route up the west face of 6,265-meter Siula Chico (865 meters, M7 WI6 R), by Frédéric Degoulet, 31, Benjamin Guigonnet, 26, Hélias Millerioux, 26, and Robin Revest, 23. The team climbed alpine-style between May 16 and 19, and descended early on May 20. Every pitch was led or followed free.

ABOUT THE AUTHOR: *Hélias Millerioux grew up in Paris, began to climb at age 14, and now guides in Chamonix. Later in 2014, he and two friends did the first ascent of Boktoh in Nepal (see Climbs and Expeditions).*

Translated from French by Todd Miller.

CHOSS ODYSSEY

ALPINE-STYLE AND ALL-FREE ON
BAFFIN'S BIG WALLS

BEN DITTO

"Rock!" The choss bomb exploded onto our haulbag and tag line. "You've got five meters left!" I yelled up to Sean. The ropes fed surprisingly quickly through my belay device, and when they came short Sean continued to tug. "I can't stop here," he yelled. I swore I could hear him laughing. "There's no gear and the rock is too loose. You'll have to start climbing!"

The thin lead lines traced a curve into an overhanging dihedral and up to Sean Villanueva O'Driscoll, the Irish-Belgian Beast, who was using his impeccable bridging skills to cop a no-hands. I tightened my shoes and started climbing. Ten meters up, I found a shoe-box-size stance where I could pull up the haulbag and clip it to me. I shouted, "Okay, man, you've got 10 meters of rope now." Ten meters higher the same scene replayed. Finally he settled into a broken belay stance, hauled the bag, and brought me up.

What had seemed from my belay like solid rock had proven to be dangling choss and decomposing kitty litter. The psyche and inspiration I'd felt at the base of this wall was quickly being replaced by a feeling of uncertainty and despair. I was confused—I wanted to bail—I had gravel in my underwear—I wanted to climb splitter cracks—I wanted to climb this huge line in a push—I didn't want to disappoint my partner or my captain Bob. At the belay the words came out as angry and frantic gibberish. Sean looked at me from behind his dust-covered beard like I was kidding. He asked me to calm down. I slumped onto the belay and looked around.

We were six pitches up the Great Cross Pillar in Sam Ford Fjord. High pressure was dominating the weather pattern for the first time all month. Polar Sun Spire, the Turret, and Broad Peak stood proudly across Walker Arm from our position on the 1,000-meter formation. This was a legendary place. We could be heroes. If only the rock would get better.

BAFFIN'S EASTERN COAST is well known for the huge walls that rise out of deep, ice-choked fjords, including the 1,400-meter Polar Sun Spire and 1,200-meter Walker Citadel looming over Sam Ford Fjord and Walker Arm. Baffin's fjords are iced over some eight months of the year, and prior to 2014 not many teams had ventured into the fjords during the ice-free months. Most climbs here have involved weeks of effort and extensive aid in subfreezing temperatures. A notable exception was the July 1992 expedition of Conrad Anker and Jonathan Turk, who piloted kayaks through broken sea ice and completed the first wall routes

[Photo] Sean Villanueva reaches for the warming sun during the first ascent of the Plank Wall above Gibbs Fjord. *Nicolas Favresse*

around Sam Ford Fjord. Their *AAJ* report reads like a multi-sport adventure race of snow machines, sea kayaks, rock climbing, and chess with pack ice.

To plan an expedition to this area during the summer months you need a team that has flexibility in their schedule and access to a sturdy boat. In 2010, Captain (and Reverend) Bob Shepton had invited Nico and Olivier Favresse, Sean Villanueva O'Driscoll, and me aboard his 10-meter sailboat, the *Dodo's Delight*, and over the next three months we climbed nine big-wall first ascents on the west coast of Greenland before sailing back to Scotland across the North Atlantic (*AAJ 2011*). Four years later, Bob had left his boat to winter at the shipyard in Aasiaat, on the west coast of Greenland, and he was looking for a climbing team and crew to join him for the summer of 2014. Sailing 400 miles from Greenland to Baffin Island seemed like an ideal way to access the big walls of the eastern fjords. I had wild dreams where global warming had reduced the icebergs to just the right size to fit in my glass. I envisioned our strong team climbing wall after wall and eating salmon nigiri on the beach below Polar Sun Spire. In a barrage of emails between 79-year-old Bob Shepton and our crew of thirty-somethings (whom Bob calls the Wild Bunch), a plan began to unfold.

We met in Aasiaat on July 5, my 39th birthday. This time everything seemed familiar—we knew where the portaledges would fit just right in the small boat, where Bob liked to store the condensed milk for his coffee, and which bunks were least likely to transfer mold to your sleeping bag. The Arctic sun illuminated late-night bouldering sessions on rocks we'd first climbed four years earlier. We hung the sails, topped off the water and gas tanks, and toasted our great fortune in being together for another summer of adventure.

Partnering with Bob and Belgians has been one of the highlights of my climbing career. Nico, Olivier, and Sean are famous for their climbing, but also for their mandolin, accordion, and flute music. Any time the psyche begins to ebb, out come the instruments. Through the years of our partnership I've learned to play the harmonica and the spoons, and even Bob gets in on the action with a bead-filled egg. On an expedition, handmade music has the effect of bellows breathing air into a fire. Music brings life into those spaces of expedition life that climbing can't satisfy—downtime isn't a downer anymore. As we sail around scouting climbing objectives, Bob is as giddy as a schoolboy, deeming some lines proud and denouncing others as too easy. At almost 80, he is an inspiration with his love for adventure and (mostly) good humor.

The online charts still showed sea ice intact around the Baffin settlement of Clyde River and the eastern fjords. Not wanting to get too soft while we waited for the main event, we started exploring the massive complex of fjords around Uumannaq, Greenland. During the next month we established five new lines on crumbling sea cliffs. [*See Climbs and Expeditions.*] We also climbed around 100 new boulder problems, gained weight on the unlimited cod and muscles we harvested, and saw dozens of whales as the weeks ticked past.

In early August reports finally showed that pack ice had slipped free of Baffin's coast. We had been in contact with a Canadian team that had been in Clyde River for a few days, also trying to reach Sam Ford Fjord by boat, and received word that after a few false starts their outfitter had managed transport them to a base camp near Polar Sun Spire. On August 5, we finalized our supplies in Uumannaq and steered west into Davis Strait.

AFTER FOUR DAYS OF SAILING and dodging pack ice and polar bears we reached Clyde River. Still unsure of exactly which fjord we intended to visit, we headed up the coast. As we sailed

[Previous page] Captain Bob Shepton and the Wild Bunch lived 10 weeks aboard their floating base camp, the Dodo's Delight. *Ben Ditto, except boat from above (Nicolas Favresse)*

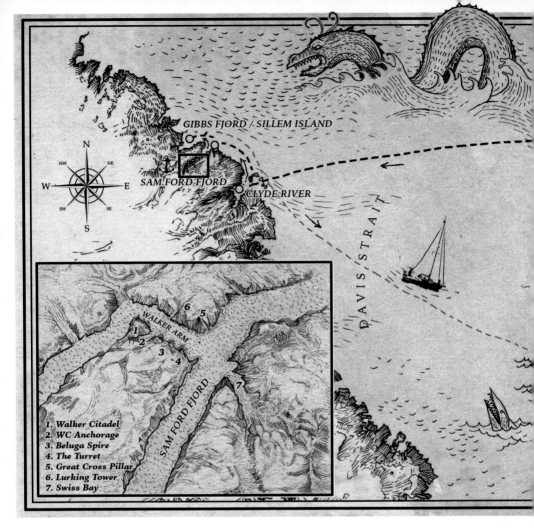

GIBBS FJORD / SILLEM ISLAND

SAM FORD FJORD

CLYDE RIVER

DAVIS STRAIT

N
NW NE
W E
SW SE
S

WALKER ARM

SAM FORD FJORD

6
5
1
2
3
4
7

1. Walker Citadel
2. WC Anchorage
3. Beluga Spire
4. The Turret
5. Great Cross Pillar
6. Lurking Tower
7. Swiss Bay

through the night on glassy seas, the sun began to dip below the horizon for the first time of the season, giving us a multi-hour show. After a 24-hour voyage, Olivier steered Dodo's Delight into Sam Ford Fjord and we began scanning cliffs for lines. On August 9, after a close call when the engine ran out of fuel as 30-knot winds pushed us toward shore, we dropped anchor in an inlet below Walker Citadel. This would be our home for the next two weeks.

Bad weather plagued us for several days. Snow started to pile up on the north-facing walls. Global warming seemed like a myth. We spent the days fishing for the fabled arctic char, hangboarding in a dry cave uphill from our anchorage, and motoring around the fjords to scope walls. We focused our attention on the sunnier aspects of Walker Citadel and got psyched on the 1,200-meter northeast and southeast pillars, which promised great alpine-style climbs if we ever got stable weather.

On August 15 we awoke to clear skies and were surprised by the sight of a large sailboat pulling into the fjord. The Novara was en route to the Northwest Passage but wanted to see the legendary walls first. That evening we joined the crew for chicken curry, all the wine we could drink, and an epic jam session. Outside, the sunset burned for hours in the clear Arctic evening. We rowed back to our own boat filled with energy, and impulsively decided to go climbing. It was 10 p.m., we were tipsy, and our skin was thin from bouldering, but the

SAM FORD FJORD

Lurking Tower: Up the Creek Without a Paddle (500m, E5 6a). Joins New Dog, Old Tricks (5.11 C3+, Haag-Libecki, 2014) after six pitches. Walk-off descent. Ditto-Villanueva, August 15–16

Walker Citadel, Superunknown Tower: Imaginary Line (1,200m, E3 5c). Red groove and crack system on right side of the tower. Rappel descent by Superunknown (Gagner-Lovelace, 1995). Ditto-Villanueva, August 21–22

Walker Citadel, Southeast Pillar (a.k.a. Drunken Pillar): Shepton's Shove (1,200m, E6 6b). Obvious arête line with crux pitches near the top. Walk-off to south and down gully. Favresse-Favresse, August 23–24

The Turret, East Face: Life on the Kedge (900m, E6 6b). Orange pillar right of huge chimney splitting the east face. Rappel descent by Swiss Route (south pillar). Favresse-Favresse, August 28–29

GIBBS FJORD

Plank Wall, north-facing wall (70°50'N, 71°43'W): Walking the Plank (900m, E4 6a). Climbs mostly left of prominent arête. Rappel descent. Favresse-Favresse, September 4–5

[Map] The 400-mile crossing of Davis Strait took four days each way. During the return voyage, the climber/sailors nearly ran out of water and battled a serious storm. *Jeremy Collins*

Map by Jeremy Collins

excitement was infectious. Nico and Olivier decided to have a go at the southeast pillar of Walker Citadel and set out on foot. Sean and I decided on a smaller objective across Walker Arm. Bob dropped us off at midnight.

We walked the base and scoped lines in the dwindling light, finally choosing a series of dihedrals on the right side. I started the first pitch in near darkness. Though the rock was far from perfect, cracks appeared in just the right places. We continued up steep, loose dihedrals through the pale night, hauling a small bag with the bare essentials. Sunrise greeted us with alpenglow on the symmetric massif of Polar Sun and Beluga spires, just across the fjord. Sean led out a 10-meter roof via a perfect hand crack for the crux. By the seventh pitch, thick cloud cover hid the summits, and a storm seemed imminent.

Partway up this pitch, I spotted a new, blue static line hanging down into the dihedral. One name kept ringing in my head like the sound of a hand drill: Libecki! Is there anywhere that guy hasn't been?! In May 2014, Mike and his partner had spent 12 days aiding a line that started farther to the right. [*See Climbs and Expeditions.*] We began to find two-bolt and cam anchors every 50 meters or so, and we stripped the gear to use later. Snow began to fall on the last pitches, but the rock got better and better until we were jamming a perfect fingers splitter up a steep slab. We topped out in a howling snowstorm after 12 all-free pitches.

[Above] The Walker Citadel (ca 1,200m), showing the approximate lines of (1) Shepton's Shove (Favresse-Favresse, 2014) on the southeast pillar (a.k.a. Drunken Pillar). (2) Superunknown (Gagner-Lovelace, 1995). (3) Imaginary Line (Ditto-Villanueva, 2014), with rappel descent by Superunknown. (4) Mahayana Wall (Helling-Libecki-Mitrovich, 1998). *Ben Ditto* [Below, left] Nicolas Favresse living Life on the Kedge, the first ascent of the 900m east face of the Turret. *Olivier Favresse* [Below, right] Olivier Favresse on the Drunken Pillar of Walker Citadel. The Favresse brothers made two attempts on the pillar before succeeding on a single-push ascent, climbing through a nighttime snowstorm with difficulties up to 5.12. *Nicolas Favresse*

From the summit we tried calling Bob and the others with our VHF radio. Before dropping us off the night before, he had been complaining about a sore appendix, and we wondered how he was getting along. There was no response. We decided not to eat any of our remaining food until we knew what was up. We walked down a huge gully to the shore, dug out a low cave in the talus, and lay on our ropes, rising occasionally to try the radio. The snow turned to rain. We had no means of protecting ourselves against bears and no way to tell time. I awoke from a nap to the sound of a horn, and Sean bolted upright so quickly he slammed his head on the roof of the cave. The storm had made it impossible for Bob to come looking for us sooner, and before long we all were back on Dodo's Delight.

During the same storm, Nico and Olivier climbed almost 20 pitches of Walker Citadel's southeast pillar before bailing. They were able to traverse off via a ledge system and descend a loose gully with only a few rappels. The weather stayed bad for another week, but on the 20th the skies cleared and Nico and Olivier set out for their second attempt on the Walker Citadel. However, they soon called for a pickup—the wind was too strong near the wall.

Sean and I woke early on August 21 to no wind and clear skies, and Bob ferried us in the dinghy to the base of the northeast buttress of the Superunknown Pillar on Walker Citadel. We put on our rock shoes directly at the waterline and began simul-climbing in huge blocks, with difficulties up to mid-5.10. We followed a huge, red dihedral system with decent rock to a scree-covered ledge about halfway up. Above this we continued on perfect cracks until, at three-quarters height, we realized the clear skies had disappeared. I put on more layers and started leading the next block. Sean joined me below an icy chimney and gave a wide grin. He loves this sort of thing—the wider, the looser, the sketchier…keep it coming. It was snowing heavily now and we put on our waterproofs. Two long, wet pitches later, I wrapped the ropes around a snow-covered rock on the summit of the Superunknown Pillar and belayed Sean to the top. We had been climbing about 12 hours.

The descent options seemed bleak. Our original plan had been to pioneer a way over to the Favresse brothers' rappel line, but in current conditions we could barely see the nearby walls. We had brought a topo of the Gagner-Lovelace aid route Superunknown (*AAJ 1996*), which showed two-bolt belays all the way down the 4,000-foot face. It was a questionable decision to head into irreversible terrain on a steep, blank wall, but finding the nearly 20-year-old line of bolts proved easier than expected, the line was steep and clean, and after five hours we met Nico and Oli, with the dinghy, at the base. Soon we were enjoying a civilized dinner in our floating apartment, wondering if it had even happened or if we had imagined it all.

A FEW DAYS LATER the Favresse brothers set out for their third attempt on the southeast pillar of Walker Citadel. The weather forecast looked solid for a few days. Sean and I packed up bivy and climbing gear, and Bob dropped us below the Great Cross Pillar, about an hour away from our anchorage. We had no protection against the polar bears except for a few flares, so we chopped out a sandy campsite about one pitch up the rambling initial wall. The next day we climbed and fixed the first five pitches of a new route. A pair of peregrine falcons swooped above our bivy ledge.

On the 1,200-meter southeast pillar, Nico and Olivier encountered difficulties up to moderate 5.12 as they climbed cracks, faces, and chimneys on generally solid rock. During the night, they were surprised by a snowstorm that once again coated the rock. They dug deep, and in the early morning the skies cleared. They topped out the southeast pillar in bright sunshine and enjoyed the feeling of hard-won success as they found a way down the mountain on foot. Back on Dodo's Delight, Bob informed them that he'd omitted the negative part of the weather forecast the day before to ensure they'd get the route done, exercising a "captain's prerogative." Thus the route name: Shepton's Shove. Olivier returned with a large dent in his helmet.

Back at Great Cross, Sean and I were disappointed to find that our idealized line was a pipe dream of overhanging and closed seams. Scrapping our big-wall plans, we scanned for another option and convinced ourselves that the steep, obvious dihedral system in the middle of the wall (well to the right of the existing climbs) would be the best choice for an alpine-style ascent when we returned. Stuck without radio contact, we waited several days at our camp on the ledge, sleeping with a flare between us in case a bear showed up, before the seas calmed enough to return to the mother ship.

Reunited with the rest of the team, we motored across Sam Ford Fjord to Swiss Bay, which was about the same distance from Great Cross but would allow radio contact. We rested another day and swam in the icy waters flowing from distant glaciers. With stable weather ahead, Nico and Olivier planned to try the unclimbed east face of the Turret, while Sean and I would go for broke on the Great Cross dihedral.

On August 28 we jugged five pitches back to the big ledge below the main wall of Great Cross with supplies for a long push. Sean started leading the dihedral, and it quickly became apparent the rock was horrendous. After climbing four and a half pitches of the worst choss of my life, with Sean stretching the rope and urging me on, he took a whipper on lead and I pulled the plug on our attempt. After five adventurous routes in Greenland and Baffin, with countless loose pitches, enough was enough. We cleaned our fixed lines and returned to camp.

While Sean and I felt the sting of defeat for the first time on this trip. Nico and Olivier managed the first ascent of the 900-meter east face of the Turret and open-bivied on top of their new route: Life on the Kedge. The next morning they rappeled the south pillar route (1987). They reported splitter cracks and sustained 5.11 and 5.12 climbing, with mixed rock quality. Olivier told me that at times it was just about bad enough to bail—I think he was just trying to make me feel better. This time Nico returned to the boat with a broken helmet. The captain was proud.

Sam Ford Fjord had delivered four new all-free routes in three weeks. Our vision of which lines seemed appealing and feasible had needed a bit of an adjustment. Obviously, everyone wants to find clean splitters up the biggest, blankest faces, but from what we saw those lines are best left to the wall rats. For free climbers there are abundant options on beautiful formations, but it takes a little luck, time, and patience to find them. Having a trio of badass Belgians doesn't hurt.

REGROUPING IN SWISS BAY, we took stock of our food and fuel. With two and a half weeks until our flights home from Greenland, there was plenty of time for more exploration, so on September 1 we sailed north, past the cliffs of Scott Island and into Gibbs Fjord. It felt like Indian Summer as we sailed to the south tip of Sillem Island. It wasn't yet truly dark at night, but we could see stars and the occasional aurora borealis for the first time all summer.

The southern wall of Gibbs Fjord hosts the most impressive walls and the best-looking rock, but at that time of year they were almost permanently in shade. The other side faces the sun, but the rock seemed loose. At this point we were all feeling a bit gun-shy about choss. Nico and Sean scoped an impressive but cold arête on the south side, and after a day of picking blueberries in the sun they headed out, planning to camp at the base with supplies for a few days. Olivier and I decided we couldn't motivate for the level of adventure these walls would require, and we gladly stayed with Bob aboard the Dodo.

Sillem Island felt like one of the most isolated places on Earth, and I reveled in the raw nature and beauty. Olivier and I went for a long walk on September 4, leaving the gun behind, and heading up a steep hill toward the top of the island. We could see massive icefalls cascading between big faces and into cold, dark water, and we could look across Gibbs Fjord to the wall

[Above] Nicolas Favresse follows a wide crack during the first ascent of Walking the Plank. *Sean Villanueva O'Driscoll* [Below, left] Olivier Favresse sheepishly displays his brother's helmet, broken when Olivier dropped a rock off the east face of the Turret. *Ben Ditto* [Below, right] Sean Villanueva stems past icy rock on the Superunknown Pillar. *Ben Ditto*

[Above] The Plank Wall. The 900m first ascent mostly followed the obvious arête. *Ben Ditto*

that Nico and Sean were climbing. The gray and gold rock near the top of the wall was just entering the sun for a few hours before a long, cold evening. We had left the summit, laughing and talking loudly, when Olivier stopped short and made a strange sound. I looked up and saw a bear, just 15 meters away, running the other direction.

Holy shit, a polar bear! was all I could come up with. We watched in awe, laughing nervously, as the bear covered about a mile in five minutes across rocky terrain. It stopped, sniffed the air for a while, and then started walking back in our direction. The laughing stopped. The bear came about halfway back before turning again and heading across the mountain. What was it doing up there? The only good answer was it had followed us up the mountain, hoping for an easy meal, but had been frightened off when we appeared, large and loud, above it. Bob, who was a bit disappointed that Olivier and I weren't climbing, concluded the bear must have been a "small female."

Nico and Sean started climbing early in the morning in cold and snowy conditions. Thin clouds covered the wall, coating the rock features in a snowy mist that only cleared for the last part of the climb. They topped out near dark after climbing 900 meters of clean cracks, with mostly solid rock and difficulties up to 5.11+, much of it covered in snow. The pair spent the night rappelling their route, Walking the Plank, as we slowly sailed back to pick them up.

Later that day we sailed out of Gibbs and into the large bay known as Refuge Harbor, toward the end of Scott Inlet. There are nice boulders here, and we talked of making the long walk into the Stewart Valley for a recon. But after a few cold, snowy days we made the tough decision to begin the journey home. We didn't know it yet, but our adventure was far from over: We would run out of water and battle a storm before making it back to Greenland. But after two and a half months and 10 first ascents the climbing was finished. Morale was low. But only for an hour or so. Then the epic jam session began.

ABOUT THE AUTHOR: *Ben Ditto is a professional photographer, alpinist, and rock climber. He lives in Bishop, California, with his wife, Katie Lambert, when he's not adventuring around the world.*

BELUGA SPIRE

THE ALL-FREE FIRST ASCENT

JOSHUA LAVIGNE

O ur team of four Canadians departed from Clyde River, Nunavut, with little certainty that we would reach our destination. We had decided against the traditional snowmobile approach to Sam Ford Fjord over sea ice because we wanted to free climb during the milder summer months. But we were denied access to the open ocean of Baffin Bay by a slow-moving flow of pack ice. Thankfully our Inuit guides were more persistent than postwar Polish alpinists and were deaf to the sounds of the crunching ice on the hull.

After hours of glacial progress we popped into the open ocean and speedily made our way to a base camp below the Turret, near the junction of Sam Ford Fjord and Walker Arm. Crosby Johnston, Paul McSorley, Tony Richardson, and I sat staring, smiling, and babbling about unclimbed walls, with the enormity of the place and the very palatable tastes of coastal, Arctic and alpine flavors flooding our senses.

With a favorable forecast, including highs of 20°C, we started gearing up for the big hunt: the north face of Beluga Spire, one of the last unclimbed big walls in Walker Arm. We packed our bags with enough food and bivouac gear to outlast an Arctic storm high on the wall, and added a couple of survival suits for the ride across the fjord in our 11-foot tin boat.

[Below] The north faces of Polar Sun Spire (left) and Beluga Spire, showing (1) Dave Turner solo attempt (2009) and (2) Harpoon (1,100m, VI 5.12) by the 2014 Canadian team. The Canadians descended by traversing south and then east behind Polar Sun Spire. *Ben Ditto*

[Above] Accessing Beluga Spire was a significant logistical challenge. We had rented an 11-foot boat with a 2 hp Yamaha engine, barely adequate to carry four climbers and gear. To retrieve the boat after we descended, we also had a two-person inflatable raft and custom ski-pole paddles. Luckily, during the retrieval mission, the tides and winds were in our favor. [Below] We climbed the wall as a team of four with two dynamic ropes; the second would follow with a belay while the others used Micro Traxions to self-belay or jug. Here, Paul jugs past the second-to-last pitch, which included a 30-meter runout in a squeeze chimney. Paul later described his position as "Olympian detachment from the world below." *Joshua Lavigne*

[Above, left] We started the route late on July 31 and climbed until our circadian rhythms encouraged us to sleep, as none of us brought a watch. We found small pieces of ice to melt for water and just enough ledges to fashion workable sleeping arrangements. [Above, right] Crosby led the first block of the Harpoon Headwall, a series of featured cracks and corners leading to the very apex of Beluga Spire. [Below] At night the red sunsets cast a smokey hue over North America's greatest walls, including the Walker Citadel at left. We summited late on August 2, and during the five-hour descent we traversed five kilometers of ridgeline and two more peaks to get back to camp. *Joshua Lavigne*

[Photo] After climbing Beluga the team wanted to establish a free climb up the Turret, and we knew it would take not only a creative eye but also a handful of bolts. The Precambrian granite and gneiss of Walker Arm is beautifully featured but rarely has continuous crack systems. We climbed about 450 meters over two days, placing 12 bolts for anchors and face climbing, before poor weather forced us down. Here, Tony tries to connect the dots on the unfinished west face. Afterward, on August 8, Crosby and I climbed a new line up the Turret's north pillar (5.12 A1) in 11 hours. Our style on the north pillar was born out of necessity but also to contrast with the style of the west face. *Joshua Lavigne*

[Above, left] The Turret from the northwest. (1) North pillar (1987). (2) Johnston-Lavigne (2014). (3) Nuvualik (1995). The unfinished Canadian line starts right of Nuvualik, and the south pillar (1987) is farther right. Life on the Kedge (Belgian, 2014) is opposite. [Above, right] We started up the north pillar in freezing conditions, and at first we couldn't use bare hands on the rock. Crosby, a renaissance man, wrapped the reflective lining from his backpack panel around his torso to retain heat. I cut the toes off my socks to make ankle warmers. [Below] Tony on a 5.11 pitch on the west face of the Turret. Deep in Baffin's fjords the weather is often up to 10°C warmer than in Clyde River, as it is more sheltered from ocean winds and currents. But if the wind blows from the northwest, be ready for chilly weather, as the Barnes Icecap is only 30 kilometers away.

Joshua Lavigne is a climber and IFMGA guide living in Canmore, Alberta.

SENDERO LUMINOSO

TWO YEARS OF EFFORT TO
FREE MT. HOOKER'S HARDEST ROUTE

DAVID ALLFREY

Open up, I'm coming in!" I squeeze under the rain fly of the portaledge next to Nik Berry and Mason Earle. The rain is turning to sleet and the thunder's getting closer. The three of us are hunkered down, 800 feet up the north face of Mt. Hooker in the Wind River Range of Wyoming. It's 2013, our first trip into the range, and we've just moved our ledge into the middle of the sheer headwall, right on the prow of this giant backcountry wall.

We count five to seven seconds between flashes and booms. Is five seconds a mile? Or is it seven seconds? We turn up the pop music and dig deeper into the bag of peanut M&Ms, wondering what to do. The rain is pounding. The inside of the portaledge lights up like a strobe. We barely sense the time between a boom erupting and then echoing within the massive cirque of 12,000-foot peaks surrounding Baptiste Lake.

"Holy crap! I'm out of here! See you guys in camp!" I squeeze back under the portaledge fly, clip into the fixed line, and drop away. Mason follows quickly. Nik sits in the ledge for a while longer, contemplating if the wall will dry enough for him to start rock climbing again. Another flash of thunder, quickly followed by a deafening boom. Mason and I are safe at the base, hiding in a massive cave. Nik reluctantly crawls from the ledge and begins his rappels.

THE NORTH FACE OF MT. HOOKER lies 20 miles deep in the rugged Wind Rivers. Several high alpine passes guard the wall, which erupts above Baptiste Lake at 10,500 feet. The face was first climbed in 1964 by Yosemite legend Royal Robbins and his team of Dick McCracken and Charlie Raymond, over an impressive four days in horribly cold temperatures. Unlike the sustained crack systems of Yosemite, Mt. Hooker is characterized by discontinuous cracks and flakes, making for difficult and inobvious lines. Robbins' team pieced together these broken features with 200 pitons and nearly no bolts. This marked the first wilderness Grade VI wall in the United States.

In 1990, two teams raced for the first free ascent of the north face. First, Stuart Richie, Mark Rolofson, and Annie Whitehouse made a three-week attempt, falling just 50 feet shy of their free-climbing goal. Just a couple of weeks later, Paul Piana, Galen Rowell, Todd Skinner, and Tim Toula completed the first free ascent via minor variations to the original 1964 route,

[Photo] Mason Earle leads the A3 Beauty, a 5.13d pitch on Sendero Luminoso. *Kyle Berkompas*

[Above] The north side of Mt. Hooker, showing Sendero Luminoso. The 2013 free ascent escaped right after seven pitches to end on Shady Lady. In 2014 the climbers freed the full line. *Pat Goodman*

which they called Jaded Lady (VI 5.12). Rowell recounted in the *AAJ* that Mt. Hooker's north face "had a serious alpine character." He claimed it was the coldest route he had done in North America, comparing it to climbing on Denali, minus the sunny days one might find in Alaska. I can attest that Hooker's north face is shrouded in shade the entire day and often beaten with a freezing wind.

For such an impressive wall, relatively few climbers make the trek to Hooker. But Steve Quinlan was obsessed with the wall, making several trips between 1986 and 1988 to establish Sendero Luminoso (VI 5.10 A4) completely solo. After this he teamed up with big-wall legend John Middendorf to establish the Third Eye (VI 5.10 A4, *AAJ 1994*) over three seasons.

There's no doubt Mt. Hooker's "Nose" is Sendero Luminoso, which takes an improbable and bold line straight up the prow of the formation. It follows the first four pitches of the 1978 Jim Dockery and Rick Bradshaw route Shady Lady (VI 5.11 A4), but where that route trends right into large corners, weaving in and out of the Robbins route, Sendero Luminoso quests out onto the steep, blank headwall for nearly 800 feet. On this monolithic wall, tiny and incipient seams require delicate piton craft and extensive bird-beaking. These seams connect over and over, in nearly perfect 120-foot pitches, each ending at a wonderful small ledge. The climbing is difficult with modern gear, and in the mid-1980s there's no doubt it would have been at the cutting edge of difficult aid routes.

I SPENT THE SPRING of 2013 training and preparing for a trip to Pakistan to attempt a new route on the Great Trango Tower. I had been invited by two Polish friends—guys with dozens of expeditions under their belt. It was to be a real dream trip. Then, in late June, a group of terrorists attacked the Nanga Parbat base camp. My trip became complicated and scary, and then fell apart entirely.

In the fallout I drove to the Sierra Nevada, where I ran into Mason Earle. Though we were only acquaintances, he soon invited me to join him and his partner, Nik Berry, out at Mt. Hooker. Just a few weeks later we met in Salt Lake City to start our drive to Wyoming.

Nik and I had never met, but we got along well from the get-go. I love to rock climb and be in the mountains—a lot. Climbing focuses my hyperactive brain and allows me to find clarity and meaning that I often struggle to see in real life. But Nik Berry—he loves to rock climb more than anyone I have ever met. When we got to Hooker, Nik was always the first one out of camp and the last one back, often staying on the wall for the final golden hour in the evening sun.

While hiking to the wall we realized we'd forgotten all of our topos for the existing routes on Hooker. When we began scoping lines our eyes were instinctively drawn to the large, clean, silver headwall on the nose of the north face. We spotted seams cutting across the face and knew this was the line we needed to climb. We got to work the next morning, thinking we were headed into uncharted territory.

NIK EXCITEDLY PULLS ON his climbing shoes and begins connecting obvious features: up a corner to a roof with small gear, then running it out to the belay ledge. One hundred feet later he finds an old bolt, rusty but well drilled. After phoning a friend on our sat phone we find out we're on the existing line Sendero Luminoso. Slightly disappointed, but not surprised, we push on for the headwall above. Mason casts out on the second pitch, the first of many 5.12 leads. He encounters an old bolt ladder we were unable to see from the ground. After free climbing along the line of bolts and rivets he reaches an old anchor. After updating the anchor it's my turn.

An old bolt ladder arches up the wall into slim corners, rooflets, and even thinner seams. Two hundred feet later, I've yet to find anything worthy of building an anchor, so I push over a roof made of puzzle-piece flakes stacked together. Pitons and beaks between blocks threaten to dislodge rock straight down onto Nik and Mason. I shout down warnings and climb carefully. There's a belay stance nestled in a large corner.

The next day, as I aid a thin crack system up and left, I fear that our chances of ever free-climbing this line are dying. The crack has finger locks here and there, but the higher I go the

[Left] David Allfrey leads out the A3+ seam—the A3 Beauty—that would later be free climbed at 5.13d. [Right] Mason Earle climbs pitch seven, one of four 5.13 pitches, while David Allfrey belays on the portaledge below. *Photos: Nik Berry*

thinner it gets. Beaks became the go-to protection, nailed into the slightly offset seam. I clip the anchor and yell my doubts to Mason.

At the same time Nik is three pitches below, swinging around on a fixed rope and exploring the blank face to the right of the old bolt ladder and the desperate thin seam I had climbed the previous day. He's excited because the rock is featured with thin patina face holds. With the rope fixed on my pitch, Mason begins jumaring and cleaning the gear up the beautiful A3 seam. Within moments he is fingering holds in the middle of the pitch, pushing on footholds, grabbing and pulling on edges, and gastoning the seam. He shouts up, "Dude! There are holds on this! I think this is going to go! It totally has holds!"

Nik follows, brushing and scrubbing the holds, chalking and ticking a few. Atop the pitch, we deploy the portaledge as the icy wind picks up to gale force. I'm rejuvenated by the idea that this beautiful seam could be free climbed. In honor of Leo Houlding's A1 Beauty pitch on El Cap's Prophet, and of trying to tackle the impossible, we dub the pitch the A3 Beauty.

For now we keep our focus on the 1,000 feet of climbing above our portaledge. Mason is first onto the sharp end the next day. The seam continues up the headwall and out of sight for another 500 feet. From the ground it had looked so blank. Now the angle appears less severe, with texture and features abounding. For Nik and Mason there are enough holds to provide hope.

THAT FIRST SEASON at Mt. Hooker we spent 18 days in the mountains: two days hiking, two rest days, and 14 days of climbing. The weather was difficult. Afternoon storms were regular, and the ice-wind demotivated and froze us. We established seven new free pitches before escaping to the right in a bizarre and accidental traverse, eventually joining Shady Lady to reach the summit. Most of the pitches were between 5.12c and 5.13d. (At the time Nik and Mason suspected the crux was 5.14a, but the following year, while releading the pitch, I broke a piece of rock in the seam, easing the grade slightly). After our new free linkup, we also repeated the entirety of Sendero Luminoso using a mix of free and aid techniques.

During that first trip I led many of the pitches first, aid climbing them and moving ropes up the wall. I soloed the two hardest aid pitches on the route: serious A4 nailing with beak tips barely hanging from terrible, closed seams, and all above ledges. I was worried they'd crumple me like a soda can if I fell. Mason and Nik worked hard down below, using the fixed ropes to unlock the secrets of a free route.

The three of us shared a vision for a big-wall free climb, and we worked together to realize that dream. Completing the entire aid route of Sendero Luminoso had been an important goal for me in its own right. At camp we debated the ethics of our tactics and decided we felt good about the style: aiding the route and then unlocking and freeing the pitches. While the rock was amazing quality, every pitch needed cleaning and deciphering. A true ground-up free attempt would have presented far too much deadly X-rated climbing.

After seeing all of Sendero Luminoso, we knew we had to return and complete our vision for the entire route, seeing the original line go free to the summit.

"OH, THESE THINGS ARE BOMBER, RIGHT?" Mason asks, hammering small beaks and pitons into the start of an A4 pitch. Dikes crisscross the wall to the left of the seam, and after a few pins Mason fearlessly steps out of the aiders to free climb leftward. After about two meters he places a small hook and drills a quarter-inch bolt. Calmly, he launches into thin, off-balance movements. It's not until later, when I free climb through this section, that I realize the climbing's very hard 5.12.

It's August 2014, and after the long hike in we've gotten straight to work. By the third

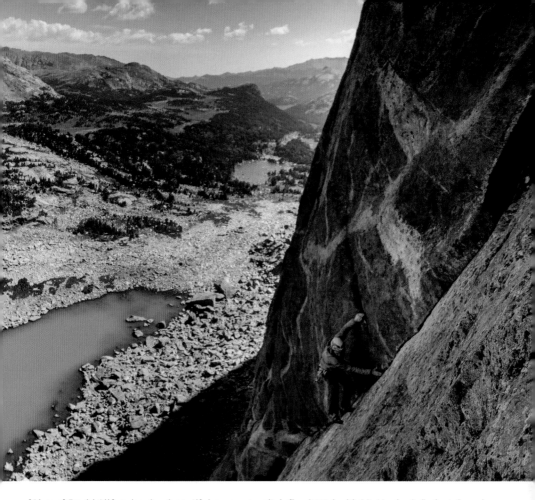

[Above] David Allfrey leads a beautiful corner on pitch five (5.11c) with Mt. Hooker's "private" pool, Baptiste Lake, below. *Kyle Berkompas*

day we've passed our free climbing high point from 2013, and now we're exploring a variation across the face to the left of an A4 pitch. Nik, Mason, and I each take turns pushing this pitch a little higher, hooking and drilling bolts on the dike-covered wall. Eventually Nik takes the lead and free climbs up to the high point. Like Mason he makes the 5.12+ climbing look easy. Once he drills another bolt up high, he lowers to the belay and Mason goes back up, adding one more bolt to the blankest section of face. The third 5.13 pitch on the route is ready to go.

Nearly 1,200 feet up the wall, the ninth pitch is the final difficulty. It looks wild but climbable, and we are sure there is a way to free the flared seam. Several hours of scrubbing grain and grit yield the fourth 5.13 pitch of the climb, an incredible and powerful lieback with a wild, head-high kick-through to get a foot onto a small, perfectly placed knob. "I'm headed down, I'll make dinner," I tell the guys before rapping off the wall to base camp.

OVER SMOKED HERRING BURRITOS, we resume the dreaded and difficult discussion about climbing ethics. At this point we knew the whole route would go free. The previous season we'd added only a single bolt to the A3 Beauty—a pitch that still requires fixed beaks and pitons for free climbing protection. Mason had led the second 5.13 pitch on scary, preplaced triple-zero cams and micro nuts. These tactics would not lend the route to being repeated in ground-up style.

Before our 2014 trip we had received a lot of excitement and enthusiasm from other climbers, expressing interest in repeating our route—and that was before we'd freed the entire line. In order for the route to be repeatable by anyone not interested in first climbing A3+ and then free climbing above poor, small beaks, we needed to add several more bolts.

Low on the route we had diverged from the original aid climb and established two long and excitingly bolted face pitches through immaculate thin patina. While these pitches had required bolting, they did not fall on the original route, allowing us to feel comfortable with our decision to add permanent protection. Now it was different.

"IT WENT TO VOICEMAIL AGAIN." After three days trying to call Steve Quinlan on our sat phone we make the difficult choice to add bolts to the route. We know the bolts will make the free route highly desirable and repeatable from the ground up—one of the hardest wilderness big-wall free climbs in North America, just as it was the hardest wilderness aid wall in 1964.

The next day we finish equipping the route and then take our first rest day, eight days into the trip. Mason's hoping to redpoint the A3 Beauty, and both he and Nik want to lead the whole route in a ground-to-summit effort. Rest days are spent fishing in the incredible Baptiste Lake, and thanks to the horses that packed in our gear we're fully stocked with food. As usual there's no one else around.

Nik and I wake early for the ground-up push. Mason is going to continue working out the A3 Beauty. By 7 a.m. the wind is howling full force and clouds are in the sky. Despite truly arctic temperatures and completely numbed-out fingers and toes, Nik climbs all the way to the top without falling, leading the most difficult pitches.

In our final days we both hope that Mason can finish preparing and rest up for his ground-up push. During this time, Nik and I repeat the wild and exciting Jaded Lady in a day. After a rest, Mason easily redpoints the crux A3 Beauty on our 12th morning, but the

weather begins to deteriorate that evening. Mason still wants to free the entire route, but with clouds and a bitter wind, he and Nik make a last-minute decision to jug past the crux pitch and free climb from there to the top, allowing Mason to redpoint all the pitches and realize his hard-earned summit.

"The weather looks like shit out here!" I say to the others as they lie in the tent the next morning. It's on me to jumar nearly 900 feet up the wall and

[Left] Mason Earle at the belay below the A3 Beauty, with a storm brewing in the Wind Rivers. *Kyle Berkompas*

[**Above**] NIk Berry eyes the crux of the second pitch (5.12b), the first of seven pitches rated 5.12 or harder. *Kyle Berkompas*

clean all our ropes and gear while the others pack camp. Clouds and rain swirl overhead. I lose sight of the ground in a light squall. Four hours later, everything is packed and we begin the long hike out.

A COUPLE OF MONTHS after returning home I finally connected with Steve Quinlan. We talked for over an hour about the Wind River Range, Mt. Hooker, and all his years of climbing there. I told Steve about the bolts we had added to protect 5.13 climbing. I felt good telling him that we had first repeated the route in ground-up style, aiding or free climbing the pitches as he had done. There was no doubt we had to stick our neck out in order to reach each anchor.

I was nervous to tell Steve about these details of the free route, but he offered his good graces and some sage words. He told me he didn't care if we had to add a few bolts. We weren't accountable to him. He had had his experience on the route. He said the next generation would climb and judge the route that we left behind, just as we did with his creation.

Lucky for us, whether aid or free, Sendero Luminoso is a hell of a line.

SUMMARY: First free ascent of Sendero Luminoso (VI 5.13d), with some variations, on the central prow of Mt. Hooker's north face in the Wind River Range of Wyoming. The 14-pitch route has four 5.13 leads, three of 5.12, and seven of 5.9 to 5.11. David Allfrey, Nik Berry, and Mason Earle completed the route in August 2014, with Berry and Earle leading every pitch free. [*See AAJ 2014 for Nik Berry's report about the first year.*]

ABOUT THE AUTHOR: *David Allfrey was raised in California and learned to climb in the Sierra Nevada. He now lives in Las Vegas but will always think of Yosemite as a second home.*

VOLCÁN AGUILERA

THE LAST GREAT VOLCANO
OF THE ANDES IS CLIMBED

NATALIA MARTÍNEZ

Volcanoes and glaciers have shaped the geography throughout Patagonia. Artistic masters in the opposing forces of orogeny and erosion, together they have created the most extraordinary landscapes.

The most pristine, remote, and untouched of the Patagonian volcanoes is Volcán Aguilera, which rises to 2,478 meters in the southern Chilean Andes, north of Fiordo Peel (50°24'01"S, 73°46'02"W). The closest city—El Calafate in Argentina—lies 100 kilometers directly to the east. Aguilera's raging past is revealed by footprints of tephra (volcanic ash) all around Patagonia. A large, explosive eruption about 3,600 years ago left a thick tephra layer still visible on the banks of Lago Argentino. This colossal eruption deeply transformed the upper basin of the Santa Cruz River in southern Argentina.

In 1933 the Salesian priest and tireless Patagonian explorer Alberto María De Agostini made the first ascent of Cerro Mayo, on the far western side of Lago Argentino, and from its summit he was the first human to glimpse vast portions of the Southern Patagonian Icefield. In its western reaches he spotted a prominent massif that he named Cerro Aguilera, after the first Chilean bishop in the Magallanes province of Chile. Bill Tilman was the first explorer to travel deep into the mountainous region observed by De Agostini. He visited the area in 1957, making a west-to-east traverse of the ice cap, wonderfully described in his book *Mischief in Patagonia*.

It wasn't until 1985 that Cerro Aguilera was first attempted. The young and ambitious British climber Matthew Hickman learned about Aguilera from Eduardo García, one of the best Chilean climbers of the time. With heaps of enthusiasm, Hickman's Cerro Aguilera expedition brought together British and Chileans, scientists and mountaineers. After a hard approach they reached the base of the mountain and explored its southern, eastern, and northern slopes, but they dismissed every line they saw, considering them either unclimbable or too dangerous. Plans for exploring the northwest face were dramatically frustrated by a two-week storm that kept them tent-bound at the southern end of the Altiplano Japón. Despite the weather, they conducted a great deal of exploration, among other things confirming the suspicion—due to its great prominence—that Cerro Aguilera was in fact a stratovolcano, thus to be renamed Volcán Aguilera.

[Photo] Traversing the South Patagonian Icefield. The peak on far right is Cerro Julie (2,284m), climbed by Americans in 1994. The peak on the left is unnamed and unclimbed. *Natalia Martínez*

In 1989 a Japanese-Chilean team, led by Eiho Otani and including Eduardo García, made a second attempt. They were unable even to approach the volcano, hampered by swamps and dense shrub. A 1993 British expedition led by James "Skip" Novak didn't get any further.

Novak's expedition aroused the interest of Dr. David Hillebrandt from the United Kingdom, who subsequently made four visits to the mountain, starting in 2003. With Hickman's advice, he made for the southwest face. Hillebrandt was able to solve the difficult approach through the Río Cari basin and achieved a high point on the peak, in 2004, of 1,300 meters. From this point, Hillebrandt could see a feasible route to the summit, but was forced to turn back due to lack of time and supplies.

In 2013 a Chilean expedition led by Abdo Fernández followed an approach similar to Hillebrandt's, but once again weather, rivers, and bog suffocated their attempt.

Our expedition in 2014 was part of the project Uncharted, initiated in 2011, combining mountain exploration, historical research, and mapping in the remotest regions of Patagonia. Last year we had the opportunity to make the second ascent of the iconic Monte Sarmiento, and we previously did the first ascents of Cerro Trono and Cerro Alas de Ángel in the Cordillera de Sarmiento (*AAJ 2014*).

After studying the logistics and difficulties of past expeditions to Aguilera, we decided to test a new and completely different approach. To this point, all attempts had approached from Fiordo Peel in the summertime. We traded the seemingly simple nine-kilometer approach from this fjord to the base of the volcano for a 47-kilometer traverse from Argentina over the Campo de Hielo Sur (South Patagonian Icefield). This required an untested approach to the ice cap, near the Spegazzini Glacier, that looked feasible based on satellite images and information

[Below] Previous attempts had tried to approach Volcán Aguilera (A) from nearby fjords. The 2014 team traversed the ice cap 47 kilometers to reach the peak. On the way back they climbed (B) Cerro Anacoreta, (C) Cerro Octante, (D) Cerro Spegazzini Este, and (E) Cerro Esperanza. *Uncharted Project*

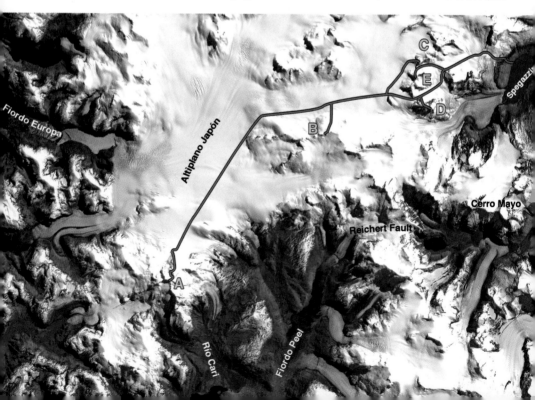

[Left] Crossing Lago Argentino to Spegazzini Arm. [Right] The author bushwhacking below snowline. The team carried loads up 1,300 vertical meters to reach the ice cap. *Camilo Rada*

from the local mountaineers Pedro Skvarca, Jose Pera, and Luciano Bernacchi. Despite being much longer, in our opinion this was a bet with greater—but still slim—chance of success. We felt that traversing the ice cap would be more predictable (and less expensive) than sailing to Fiordo Peel, and it would lead us directly to the north side of the mountain, where we were likely to climb. We chose winter in anticipation of better ice conditions.

So it was that we found ourselves sailing the calm waters of Lago Argentino, having departed Bahía Tranquila near El Calafate, and heading to our planned base camp in the Spegazzini Arm of the lake. We landed without difficulty on August 16 and found a beautiful forest of southern beech and canelo (winter's bark). The team comprised three Chileans (Camilo Rada, Ines Dusaillant, and Viviana Callahan), the U.S. citizen Evan Miles, and me from Argentina. Brimming with enthusiasm, we started exploring the way to the ice that same afternoon, the first steps in our long approach to Aguilera. We followed paths opened by "bagual" cows, untamed animals that have thrived in this territory that once belonged to the huemul, a native Patagonian deer.

The following four days were intense, as we portaged our 400 kilograms of equipment and supplies up 1,300 vertical meters of virgin forest, rock slabs, and crevasse fields to reach the Peineta Norte Glacier. On the fourth day we moved into our first camp on the ice cap, placed in a heavenly landscape. To the north was unclimbed and beautiful Cerro Heim, to the east and south massive Lago Argentino and the spires of the unclimbed Cerro Peineta, and to the west a range of superb summits, mostly unnamed and, of course, unclimbed.

Skinning through a previously unvisited valley, towing our sleds, we reached our second camp at the foot of Cerro Spegazzini, where we faced another big uncertainty: an 1,820-meter pass that we hoped would give us access to the main plateau of the Southern Icefield. It started easily but gradually steepened until a final 10-meter stretch of 50° snow, which seemed almost endless while pulling a sled loaded with more than 60 kilos. On top we suddenly arrived at the most lonely and pristine place you can imagine, the epitome of nowhere, incarnated in pure, endless, and immaculate white.

On the west side of the pass we descended a long, gentle slope for 15 kilometers, avoiding crevasses here and there, until reaching the Altiplano Japón, an expansive plateau at 1,000

[Above] The mountain on the left is Cerro Esperanza (2,502 meters), which the team climbed during its return from Aguilera. The peak on the right is unclimbed. *Ines Dusaillant* [Below] Volcán Aguilera (2,478 meters) from the north. The 1,480-meter first-ascent route followed the glacier left of the rock ridge, crossed the ridge just before it steepens sharply, and zigzagged up heavily crevassed slopes to the summit ridge. *Ines Dusaillant*

meters of elevation, named by a Japanese team that had attempted to cross the ice cap in the early '70s. This was the realm of the mysterious volcano, which finally made its appearance, towering over the horizon. Previously, all those who had enjoyed this view had been vying for the first longitudinal traverse of the Southern Icefield, a 400-kilometer challenge that left no time for rest, rendering them unable to answer this extraordinary mountain's provocative call.

After 47 kilometers, 10 days, and six camps, we had arrived. Our fabric castles were erected in a peerless landscape—no wonder it so deeply touched the hearts of early explorers. Even though we hadn't yet seen a full view of the mountain, we decided to attempt it the very next day, by the north face, closest to us. In fact, we spent the next two days gazing south, disillusioned and anxious, as heavy rain spattered the tents over our heads. The rain and a warm wind melted away our protective snow walls like a candle over flame. The soul of Patagonia is wild and unpredictable, and we could do little but wait.

August 29 was clear, and we left camp at 4:30 a.m. Crampons biting into snow, we advanced in the quiet darkness, gaining elevation quickly. We began on the east side of Aguilera's north ridge, climbing over a glacier to connect icy platforms and pass a number of serac bands. We topped a final platform and then moved to the right to face the first stretch of technical climbing, a steep slope between icy cauliflowers, funneling us to a narrow aisle between two prominent bergschrunds. The landscape seemed of Cyclopean proportions, and as the sun rose over the icefield Aguilera appeared majestically above us, and now we finally began to comprehend the sheer size and loneliness of our objective.

We continued westward, just below the upper bergschrund, until the north ridge, and then to the base of a prominent rock wall, where we hoped to find a way to the northwest face. Joyfully we discovered

[Above] Crossing the north ridge to the upper northwest face on Aguilera. *Natalia Martínez*

an easy pass, almost too good to be true. From this new vantage, however, we realized our planned route was dissected by multiple deep crevasses and broken seracs. We remained at high alert as we wound through this labyrinth. After traversing through several areas of ice and rock fall, we arrived below two humongous, frost-covered seracs, and encircling them we found the first of many massive bergschrunds that were to block our way. As in any labyrinth, retracing our steps became the only way to progress.

Visibility on the mountain had slowly worsened. But despite the adversities, we had everything we needed to continue—in particular, patience, the most valuable asset in Patagonia. One bergschrund seemed endless in either direction, but after a 200-meter traverse it narrowed and a fragile bridge gave access to a long, 60- to 65-degree slope. It looked like a perfect line to the ridge, but the cauliflowers above were protected by yet another bergschrund, perfectly invisible until we probed it. On to a new traverse, under, around, and over an ice mushroom, only to arrive at nowhere but yet another bergschrund—at least a bit higher than the last. Another traverse to the right brought us to a fragile clump of ice barely bridging a gap and, at last, to the summit ridge.

Following the ridge westward, we passed several false summits, including one negotiated in our best *Vertical Limit* style, with a leap. Finally, at 6 p.m., we reached the broad summit, amid freezing rain borne by strong wind, coating our gear and clothing with ice.

After a few moments of exuberant hugs it was time to head back. I began the descent with a feeling so grand it could hardly fit inside my tired body. Winding through my mind was the memory of each step we'd taken—from the original idea of climbing Aguilera to the research, permits, funding, food and equipment, all leading to this futile act of setting a foot on the summit. It was evident that the objective really was much more than a summit. It was the adventure we'd experienced with every step, every drop of sweat, each and every contagious laugh and fear overcome.

We slowly worked down through the labyrinthine turns as

[Photo] Working through the seemingly endless bergschrunds on the upper mountain. The round trip from camp took 25 hours. *Evan Miles*

snowflakes again turned to rain, creating a spooky atmosphere. Just before dawn we returned to the volcano's base, after 25 hours of effort and uncertainty. With smiles on our faces we sank into a deep, blissful sleep.

After 15 days our main goal had been accomplished. What now? Our fear was that King Wind would reclaim his domain while we were still so far from safety. Instead, Patagonia blessed us with weather as docile, meek, and submissive as you ever see. We took full advantage of the conditions, stopping along the way back to make four more first ascents: the peaks we propose to name Cerro Anacoreta (2,213m) and Cerro Octante (2,446m), as well as the 2,283-meter east peak of Cerro Spegazzini and finally Cerro Esperanza (2,502m).

Other interesting peaks in this immediate area await their first ascents, including Cerro Heim, Cerro Peineta, and the main summit of Spegazzini. South of Reichert Fault are many unclimbed and impressive mountains, especially on the western side of the ice cap. I hope those who read of our journey into the Southern Ice Field may feel the same drive as we did to explore and protect these unique and forgotten places.

SUMMARY: First ascent of Volcán Aguilera (2,478m) by the north face (Concierto de Rimayas, ca 1,480m), by Viviana Callahan, Ines Dusaillant, Natalia Martínez, Evan Miles, and Camilo Rada. The team also did the first ascents of Cerro Anacoreta (2,213m, northern slopes, proposed name); Cerro Octante (2,446m, from the west, proposed name); the northwest slopes of the 2,283m east peak of Cerro Spegazzini; and the north ridge of Cerro Esperanza (2,502m). The climbers were dropped off by boat on August 16, 2014, and picked up on September 9. The expedition was supported by a Gore-Tex Shipton/Tilman Grant.

ABOUT THE AUTHOR: *Natalia Martínez, 34, was born in Mendoza, Argentina, and works as a mountain guide and ski instructor, currently living in British Columbia, Canada. She is co-founder of the Uncharted project, which is working on a new map of the Southern Patagonia Ice Field. Like Uncharted's previous maps of Cordillera de Sarmiento and Cordillera de Darwin, this will be available free of charge. For information, write to natalia@unchart.org.*

ALPINE MENTORS

A VOLUNTEER PROGRAM TRAINS THE NEXT GENERATION OF ALPINISTS

STEVE HOUSE

Welcome everyone!" Bundled in a thick parka against the autumn chill, I toss my notebook on a picnic table in Ouray, Colorado, and address a group of ten climbers. They have come from all over the United States and even Europe for the first Alpine Mentors session. "Over the coming days we'll go sport climbing, trad climbing, and dry-tooling, learn some leader-rescue skills, and head up to the north face of Mt. Sneffels for an alpine climb. By the end of the week, we'll know which four of you are prime for mentorship."

I explain to the group that my fellow mentors, Vince Anderson and Bryan Gilmore, and I will debrief each climber with our impressions of their strengths and weaknesses as an alpinist.

[Below] Steven Van Sickle summits Sickle Spire (5,334m) during the Alpine Mentors expedition to India in October 2014. Behind is Brahmasar (ca 5,830m), the team's main objective. *Steve House*

And, finally, we'll select the four climbers with whom I'll spend many, many weeks over the coming two years. "Whatever happens, know that first and foremost I'm looking for people who are ready for mentorship and committed to alpinism," I say. "This isn't a climbing competition, this is the start of a team. A team that's going to spend a lot of time together. So, unless there are any questions, let's head up to the Pool Wall for some sport climbs."

And so began the first day of what would add up to 119 days of traveling and climbing together. Nine months earlier, on January 1, 2012, my wife, Eva House, and I had launched a website with an outline of our vision

[Above] Planning the Black Canyon trip. From left: Steven Van Sickle, Colin Simon, Marianne van der Steen, Bryan Gilmore, and Buster Jesik. *Steve House*

for a free, two-year climbing-mentorship program. From dozens of written applications I had invited ten climbers to Ouray. And from these we selected four climbers: Buster Jesik, 26, from Colorado; Colin Simon, 24, originally from California but a recent graduate of University of Colorado Boulder; Marianne van der Steen, 27, a Dutch woman who had committed to a month-long trip to the western United States in hopes of joining our project; and Steven Van Sickle, the oldest of the group at 28, a self-described "Air Force brat" who had been living in Ouray for seven years specifically for ice climbing.

OCTOBER 2012. BLACK CANYON OF THE GUNNISON, COLORADO.

"I RACKED EVERYTHING on one sling so I can hand all the gear to you at once—makes the transition faster." Colin and I are standing on a ledge below pitch five of Escape Artist. "Okay. Anything else?" he asks. "Keep placing good gear, keep moving. Stay in the flow; there's one more pitch in your block. Do you know where you're going? You're on belay."

"Yup. Climbing." And with that Colin moves down and right to the first good jam of the Lighting Bolt Crack, steps up twice, and places a solid cam.

Formalized mentorship programs for alpinists began in France in 1991. The Club Alpin Français program, which they call the Groupe Excellence, initially was directed by Luc Jourjon, assisted by half a dozen top guides, and has operated continually ever since on a two-year cycle, now with a mixed-gender group of ten young alpinists. The CAF funds the group, and as with similar groups elsewhere in Europe, the program pays a salary to instructors and all expenses for participants. Most of the programs share a two-year framework, with gradually increasing scale and complexity of objectives, leading to final expedition.

I first learned of such mentorship programs back in the 1990s, as a 20-something aspiring alpinist. At the time, I would have killed for such an opportunity. Luckily, I found mentorship the old-fashioned way, sharing many a rope with older partners. As my experience grew, I wondered if a more formal mentorship program might be possible in North America. In 2010, having survived a near-fatal climbing accident, I vowed to do something tangible for the sport and culture of alpinism. Mentorship seemed to have the power to bring really positive change to our geographically diverse North American climbing community.

WORLDWIDE MENTORSHIP PROGRAMS

GROUPE EXCELLENCE ALPINISME NATIONAL

France / Founded in 1991 / Cycle: 2 years

The oldest mentorship program for young alpinists, run by the federation of French alpine clubs (FFCAM). Each cycle trains 10 young alpinists, with a final expedition. BIG CLIMBS: first ascents on the Mooses Tooth and Bear Tooth in Alaska (2013); Piolet d'Or–winning expedition to Kyrgyzstan (1993).

SPANISH MOUNTAINEERING TEAM

Spain / Founded in 1997 / Cycle: 3 years

Run by Spanish Mountain Federation. Teams of six men and six women train in the Pyrenees and Alps, with expeditions to Nepal, Peru, and Pakistan. BIG CLIMBS: first ascent of Sakaton in Nepal (2014); northern ridge of Teng Kang Poche (2007).

DAV EXPEDITIONSKADER

Germany / Founded in 2000 / Cycle: 2.5 years

Funded primarily by the German Alpine Club (DAV), with other sponsors. Each cycle involves teams of six men and six women. Training camps lead up to group expedition. BIG CLIMBS: first ascents in India (2013); first all-female ascent of Cerro Torre's west face (2015).

NATURFREUNDE ALPINKADER

Austria / Founded in 2012 / Cycle: 3 years

Funded by Naturfreunde Österreich, a youth outdoor organization. First class did educational modules from sport climbing to winter mountaineering, followed by two years of training and an expedition to Peru in summer of 2014. BIG CLIMBS: many ascents in the Cordillera Blanca and Cordillera Huayhuash (2014).

SLOVENIAN YOUNG ALPINISTS GROUP

Slovenia / Founded in 2012 / Cycle: ca 3 years

Operating under the Alpine Association of Slovenia, the group consists of 10 young alpinists. Group members are encouraged to select their own objectives and are responsible for all aspects of expedition planning. BIG CLIMBS: east ridge of Ice Tooth in Tibet (2013).

NEW ZEALAND ALPINE TEAM

New Zealand / Founded in 2013 / Cycle: 3 years

Run by Expedition Climbers Club Inc., which hosts the Remarkables Ice and Mixed Festival each year. Established in hopes of reviving large-scale annual Kiwi expeditions. First team will do expedition to Peru in June 2016. BIG CLIMBS: first ascent of south face of Mt. Suter (NZ, 2014); North Pillar of Fitz Roy (2014).

— *Allie Levy*

The Alpine Mentors model we created differed from the European programs in several important ways: 1) We were entirely self-funded and self-organized; 2) we operated on an all-volunteer basis; and 3) we were open to climbers of any nationality. To make our program work, we needed to raise money for two key expense items: liability insurance to protect the mentors who volunteer to share their knowledge and experience, and meals, lodging, and travel expenses for mentors. Eva and I volunteered for all the administrative work, fund-raising, and operating what, by early 2013, had become a federally recognized 501(c)(3) non-profit.

By keeping the mentoring entirely volunteer and asking the "mentees" to pay for nothing but their own expenses (which would not be insignificant), we achieved a key legal benefit that I understood from my 25 years of working as a professional mountain guide. As long as no money was changing hands, we could freely access all public lands in the United States, from state forests to national parks, without having to acquire or buy into commercial operating permits, a requirement that would have kept us from getting off the ground at all.

Eva and I took an entrepreneurial stance toward the entire project. We'd try it, and if we couldn't raise money to fund our expenses, or if the market didn't demand this service, we'd shut down. Our first donor stepped out of a crowd in Tokyo. I'd just concluded a slideshow where I'd briefly mentioned this new idea, and an American businessman and climber asked a few questions and then handed me a fat envelope of Japanese yen. As I counted out the bills in my hotel room, it dawned on me that Alpine Mentors was now real. People, even strangers, would trust Eva and I to create this channel for enriching our common culture of climbing in the mountains. For the first time I allowed myself to feel some confidence that we might succeed.

In January 2013, Eva and I hit the floor at the Outdoor Retailer trade show in Salt Lake City. We had a program, we had four participants, and I had successfully run 30 days of mentored climbing around Ouray and Black Canyon of the Gunnison National Park. We went to 30 meetings over four days and came back with promises of financial support from Polartec, Patagonia, Outdoor Research, Grivel, Liberty Mountain, Asolo, MSR, and La Sportiva. If these companies all came through with their promised donations, we would be able to operate in the black for year one. Every one did.

MARCH 2013. CANMORE, ALBERTA.

FIFTY-SIX-YEAR-OLD SCOTT BACKES is reclined in an easy chair, wearing a fresh T-shirt for the first time in two days. It reads "Kiss or Kill." After every climb the mentors debrief the mentees by rope teams. This is where most of the reflection, discussion, and learning takes place. Many of these sessions go late into the night.

"When you're at the end of that second day of climbing, and your calves have already melted, and you've got 300 feet of black ice to get off the face, you kind of need to be able to simul-climb," he says to our small group, gathered in a condominium that has been loaned to us for two weeks by the parents of a climbing friend. "Being able to do that, with confidence, is going to make the difference between being alive and not being alive."

In the Canadian Rockies we spend two weeks climbing frozen waterfalls and all-day alpine routes. After a couple of ropes get stuck on the descent from Asteroid Alley on Mt. Andromeda, one of these days stretches more than 24 hours. As a group we quickly realize that the mentees are slow on moderate fifth-class climbing terrain. Difficult technical climbing is almost always slow, but the amount of time spent on Backes' "300 feet of black ice" is one area where the mentees could see dramatic improvements. As lead mentor, I begin laying plans to emphasize this skill during our next excursion.

[Below] Colin Simon belays Steven Van Sickle in the Canadian Rockies in spring 2013. *Steve House*

[Above] Steve House, Marianne van der Steen, Buster Jesik, and Steven Van Sickle (from left) make the most of an unplanned bivy in the Alps with a bottle of Italian *genepi* liqueur. *Colin Simon*

OCTOBER 2013. COURMAYEUR, ITALY.

THE COURMAYEUR GUIDE'S OFFICE sits on the town square, opposite the Catholic church. It is the second-oldest mountain guide's office in the world (the oldest being a short crow-flight away, in Chamonix). The head guide uncorks champagne and makes a speech welcoming us to the Alps, wishing us luck and assuring us we are in good hands. Over an extravagant spread of olives, thin-sliced sausages, and delicate cheeses, four of the most senior guides on Monte Bianco orient our young alpinists to the most storied mountain massif in the world. The guides unfold climbing topos and trace descent lines on a large 3D map of the range.

One week later, spindrift is whipping into a not-quite-sealed crevasse and settling gently upon all of us. Thinking we could cruise miles of moderate, exposed alpine terrain across the Rochefort Arête to the Canzio bivouac hut and on to the summit of the Grand Jorasses, we had left the valley on the first cable car. Sometime around midnight, lost amid blowing snow, I had pulled the plug, turned us around, and led the team back to a crevasse I'd spotted seven hours earlier. Colin and Buster make hot drinks and dinner. I pull out a light sleeping bag and a bivy sack; Buster has gone light and has only a foil emergency blanket. I snore, the others shiver, and at dawn we leave our little cave and head down. Lessons learned.

JUNE 2014. DENALI.

THE WIND WHIPS and fast-moving clouds obscure everything around us. I pace Marianne, kicking steps at a slow, even tempo across the hard-packed snow slope. Turning the corner, I see Buster and Colin reach the summit and wordlessly high-five. Raphael Slawinski, my co-mentor, and Steven Van Sickle must be on the north summit of Denali by now.

We are acclimatizing for a planned attempt on the Cassin Ridge. We move in the way top climbers move on Denali: on skis, mostly unroped, climbing to the 14,200-foot camp quickly, and then acclimatizing with light packs, never camping higher. This time it takes us almost ten hours to summit from the 14,200 camp, over three hours longer than what I'd consider a good time for the West Buttress, but conditions are snowy, the weather stormy. No one else is here.

Dr. Raphael Slawinski, a veteran of this mountain who had climbed with the group earlier, on our trip to Canada, is the perfect mentor. A tenured professor of physics, Raphael balances a healthy professional life with a marriage and a passion for climbing. As so often happens, our dinnertime discussion turns to these topics. Our relatively youthful charges are wrestling with how to find jobs that also allow them to climb.

From the beginning my aim had never been to train mountain guides (the American Mountain Guides Association exists to do that), nor was it to train the "best" climbers or the "next Steve House"—questions I was often asked. Mentorship and climbing, as I observed again and again, fundamentally are both discussions about being human. About expressing physically what you enjoy doing, while maintaining a balance with relationships and work. My first objective was to show them that climbers they look up to, like Raphael and me, are actually quite timid about taking risks. But we are also confident in important ways. Sometimes that means knowing I can simul-climb 300 feet of black ice in a few minutes. High on Denali in thick blowing clouds, it means knowing that I can navigate down to Denali Pass and then to the 17,200-foot camp in under an hour in a total whiteout. I've done it several times. For me it is a relatively casual situation; for someone who doesn't have that ability, the very same situation could prove fatal.

In dangerous situations you have to know in your head and in your heart that you will not fail. You build your safety net as you go, marking waypoints or placing cams, while hoping that you'll not need either. We have many types of safety nets, and we build in these redundancies to allow for survival and, in the end, for growth. The successful climber knows well the fine edge between recklessness and safety.

OCTOBER 2014. GARHWAL HIMALAYA.
THE MORNING AIR feels like water: deep, cool, still water. I feel it ripple across my shoulders as I cross the goat-cropped grass, look up, and stop. Above us are the three summits of the Brahmasar massif and our objective. Two years earlier, at the North Rim Campground in the Black Canyon, I'd posed the questions that have since defined everything we've done as a group: "Where do you each want to be in two years' time? What do you want to be able to climb?" The

[Photo] Moving up on Denali. *Steve House*

answer was unanimous: technical routes, at moderate altitude, alpine-style, in the Himalaya. At 5,850 meters, Brahmasar didn't even need a trekking permit, let alone a climbing permit or the dreaded liaison officer. The main summit was untouched. And the summits of B-2 and B-3 each had seen only a single ascent.

The door to mountaineering in the Himalaya was opened for me by the Slovenian Alpine Association. I was studying in Slovenia and was mentored by experienced climbers, who eventually invited me to join an expedition to Nanga Parbat. I turned 20 in base camp, and after I'd climbed to 6,400 meters and the expedition put two climbers on the summit, we still had a month before our flights home. I lit off across Baltistan and up the Hunza Valley, traveling, trekking, and taking in the mountains. The thing about climbing in the Himalaya is that it seems so complicated and expensive— almost impossible. Until you go there and see that it's not. That was my goal with this expedition: to show them how easy and cheap it can be.

After the first ascent of a 5,300-meter spire, by Steven and me, and some scouting of lines on the Brahmasar group, the group dearly wants to claim the first ascent of Brahmasar I. But an attempt by Buster, Colin, and Steven ends at just under 5,500 meters. (Marianne had opted out of the final expedition to India due to personal reasons.) They retreat to ABC

[Top] From left: Buster Jesik, Steven Van Sickle, Jim Elzinga, and Steve House at Brahmasar high camp. [Middle] Steven Van Sickle leads the way to base camp. [Bottom] The southwest face of Brahmasar. (1) The Jesik-Simon-Van Sickle attempt on unclimbed Brahmasar I (the tower above and right of their line). (2) Elzinga-House route to the summit of Brahmasar II. *All photos: Steve House*

with heavy hearts but the satisfaction that they couldn't have done much differently—or much better. As always we debrief their climb: Their decision to retreat followed a difficult bivy, compounded by hard climbing on dangerously loose rock, far from home. The unknown has outweighed these climbers' confidence, as it should have.

With Alpine Mentors I wish to pass on a view of mountaineering that strictly accepts the mountains as they are, with an ethic of climbing them by fair means and an appreciation for the most aesthetic route possible. I, and many others, have long held that climbing is not only a physical act, but also a spiritual pursuit. Walter Bonatti once said that each climb is a "victory over your own human frailty." Simple words that say much, for these struggles expose our values. And once our values are seen, we can mold them.

AUTUMN 2014. SEATTLE, WASHINGTON.

STEVE SWENSON HAD BEEN one of our volunteer mentors during our Canmore trip in the spring of 2013. Inspired by what he saw and experienced, Steve asked, "Would you be interested in having me organize a regional program based in Seattle?" In the fall of 2014, having selected its first group of mentees, Alpine Mentors Pacific Northwest began its inaugural two-year program with sessions in Seattle and Squamish, British Columbia. Eddie Espinosa, regional manager of the American Alpine Club, offered logistical support for Steve's efforts. The volunteer mentors have included Perry Beckham, Jim Donini, Colin Haley, Sarah Hart, Bob Rogoz, and Wayne Wallace.

The future of Alpine Mentors in North America lies in emphasizing regional groups, operating within the established group-development process, with a two-year cycle. Keeping things local not only reduces the time commitment for volunteers, but also the cost of running the program. With these efficiencies we can insure and operate more regional programs.

DECEMBER 2014. OURAY, COLORADO.

FORTY CLIMBERS CROWD the small upstairs room of Backstreet Bagels. With 20 posters and a social-media push, we've lured people from as far away as Portland, Oregon, to our first Alpine Mentors Ice Bash. Our tag line is: No clinics. Only climbing. Dirtbag lodging deals. Slideshow. Beer.

At the Ice Bash I want the mentees to have their own experience of mentoring less experienced climbers. They now have much to share. The Ice Bash also marks the graduation of our first class. After all we've gone through together, a ceremony to celebrate this transition seems important to all of us. After we hand them engraved wooden ice axes from Grivel as mementos, Buster, Colin, and Steven stand before the crowd to narrate a slideshow about their Alpine Mentors experiences, telling their story to their own tribe.

ABOUT THE AUTHOR: *Steve House lives in Ridgway, Colorado. Of Alpine Mentors, he says, "In my 44 years of life so far, this has been one of the biggest challenges I've ever undertaken. Overshadowing all else has been the deep knowledge and unbridled generosity of our climbing community. The biggest thank you goes to my wife and co-founder, Eva House. Without her business and marketing acumen, we would not have been able to create this project. We also owe big thanks to the volunteer mentors for our first cycle: Vince Anderson, Scott Backes, Jon Bracey, Jim Elzinga, Bryan Gilmore, David Göttler, Rob Owens, Ines Papert, Steve Swenson, and Raphael Slawinski." Visit www. alpinementors.org to learn more about the organization or make a tax-deductible donation. To get involved directly, email climb@alpinementors.org.*

SOUL GARDEN

A GIFT FROM SEAN LEARY

JIMMY HADEN

❝ *Right now your grief is this giant gaping hole with sharp edges, but as you move forward in life the edges soften and other beautiful things start to grow around it…flowers and trees of experiences. The hole never goes away, but it becomes gentler, a sort of a garden in your soul, a place you can visit when you want to be near your love."*

These are the words Sean Leary wrote to comfort a friend, who like Sean, had lost the love of his life. Now Sean is gone, and the hole in my heart is still sharp and jagged. But before Sean left us he gave me a seed to begin growing in my soul garden.

I first met Sean in Yosemite Valley. It was 1994. He was 19 and I was 21. He had long hair, pants with holes in the butt, and a big-ass grin. With carefree confidence in himself and others, he was always game for anything, no matter how big, how far, or how late in the day. Sean was a true force of nature: perpetually psyched, physically gifted, and completely uncompromising with anything that pulled him away from his dreams. This mindset would allow Sean to pull

off many unbelievable feats in the Valley, including climbing El Cap three times in a day, freeing El Cap and Half Dome in a day, and climbing the Nose in record speed. Sean would also take these skills into the greater ranges, establishing new routes on some of the biggest walls in the world.

Sean's Mt. Watkins project began in 2012, almost two decades after our first meeting. It was Sean's first time free climbing the classic south face route, with Jake Whittaker as his partner. While hanging on the wall, he was drawn to a nearby crack system, an old aid route called Tenaya's Terror (VI 5.9 A4, Bosque-Corbett, 1985). Sean was quick to check it out. The upper 800 feet of the route followed a continuous crack system, flowing from stemming corners to long sections of

[Previous page] Jimmy Haden leads a 5.11 offwidth on pitch 17 of Soul Garden, the new free route on Mt. Watkins started by the late Sean Leary. *Andrew Burr* **[Above]** Leary on the first ascent of the east face of La Espada, Torres del Paine, in 2001. *Jimmy Haden*

[Above] Sean Leary starts up Mt. Watkins on his and the author's 2013 effort. *Jimmy Haden*

offwidth, all capped by two steep and difficult pitches to the summit. Below this were two crux pitches and 1,000 feet of beautiful cracks and slabs running downward to the valley floor. Sean spent most of that summer in Tuolumne Meadows, and for training he would run to the summit of Watkins, rappel the upper 800 feet of the wall on a fixed rope, and climb out with a Mini Traxion. By the end of the summer he had freed the upper section and was convinced that if he could climb the crux pitch the rest would go free.

Sean called in the fall, "Hey, Jimmy, you should come check out this free route I've been working on Mt. Watkins." It was all I needed to hear. I packed my bags and raced down to Yosemite. The mission began the same way as most of our trips—out of Sean's famous doublewide trailer in El Portal. "The Trailer" was a well-known hang for many of the world's best climbers, regularly teaming up with Sean to storm the castles and make climbing history. Once both of us were over-caffeinated and frantically pacing around at hurricane force, we blew up to the Valley. We spent two days climbing on the wall. I was floored—amazing splitter cracks that just kept going on and on.

IN APRIL 2013, Sean and I hiked to the base and started working out the free line on the lower half of the wall, starting on an aid route called the Prism (VI 5.10 A3+, Franosch-Plunkett, 1992) to gain Tenaya's Terror. The climbing was fantastic. But more memorable for me were the fun times camping next to the river, eating gourmet steak burritos, and washing it down with "Jack O'Max"—that's Jack Daniels and Cytomax. Your head might hurt a little the next day, but your muscles will feel great.

Once the road to Tuolumne Meadows opened we refocused on the upper half of the wall and the crux of the route. We spent about 20 days together on the wall, figuring out the climbing and protection for the endless 5.12 pitches and mid-5.13 cruxes. We were getting real close and looking forward to completing it the next season.

IN MARCH 2014 I got a call that Sean was missing in Zion. I wasn't totally surprised. He had been pushing hard on wingsuit BASE jumping, opening many new jumps and quickly becoming one of North America's best flyers.

Sean had only started flying after the love of his life, Roberta Nunez, an amazing Brazilian climber, died in his arms after a horrible car accident. Flying though the air was the only thing that brought a smile back to his face and gave him the inspiration to keep living. In time, he'd planted other seeds, finding true love again with a beautiful woman named Annamieka, who was pregnant with their baby boy, Finn Stanley Leary. In so many ways, Sean was like a peregrine falcon, screaming across or up the wall at unimaginable speed—you might catch a glimpse of him just long enough to be in awe at the ability and skill...and then he's gone! *And now he was gone.* Flying had at first saved Sean but it ultimately took him; his body was discovered below a cliff in Zion.

While trying to process the loss of my best friend and climbing partner, my resolve to complete our Watkins route only grew. I was nervous because I now wanted to climb the route for both Sean and myself. I hoped I could focus my emotions enough to climb right at my limit and not let us both down.

Fortunately, my good friend Seth Carter had the ability, time, and psych to help me complete Sean's vision. Starting in late spring, Seth and I spent six days working on the upper half of the route and began stocking supplies for camping on the wall for a later push in June. Of course, we continued the tradition of challenging climbing by day followed by fun nights of camping on the summit.

On June 24 we hiked up beautiful Tenaya Canyon to the base of the wall. We began climbing early the next day. The forecast was for mostly clear skies, but it was hot and the route faces south. We planned to climb in the early morning or late afternoon to avoid direct sun. We hoped we had enough water.

The route begins on a low-angle sea of smooth, blank granite. A wandering slab pitch and the thin corner pitch that follows are a very calf-pumping way to begin the day. From there the route steepens into three 5.12 pitches—a wild chimney squeeze-slot, exposed changing corners, and a delicate layback. Seth had never been on these pitches, and he managed to climb them all onsight. We were moving well. From there the only two easy pitches of the route took us to the palatial Sheraton Watkins ledge and our first bivy.

The unforecasted rain began slowly that night with the faint pitter-patter that forces you to crawl deeper inside your sleeping bag, hoping it will simply fade away. This time it grew into a torrential downpour and then into a waterfall. We scrambled throughout the night to stay dry under a tarp that I had strung up on the side of the huge ledge. As the rain continued into the next day it was obvious that we weren't going anywhere. There was no more water problem, but reluctantly we had to ration our food for the unplanned rest day.

The next morning the sun dawned bright and began drying the rock above. We set off again, with a nice 5.11 corner off the ledge leading to the Golden Eagle Pitch. While on the wall we would often see a golden eagle circling around us. I hoped it was Sean with fresh new wings, keeping an eye on us and ripping through the sky like never before. The Golden Eagle Pitch climbs an amazing, gold-colored, left-arching feature for what seems like eternity. The thin, 5.12 liebacking with small gear on this lead is characteristic of the next 500 feet of hard climbing before reaching the crux. The majority of this route is just under vertical and the feet are relentlessly small. It's one serious leg pump.

That afternoon we arrived on a small ledge two pitches below the crux and set up our portaledge. We

[Above] Jimmy Hayden on the 15th pitch (5.11+). *Andrew Burr*

spent the next three days resting under our shade tarp until late afternoon, waiting for the sun to move off the wall and allow us to attempt the two thin, technical pitches of climbing above.

The crux pitch is a beautifully featured traverse that, with the exact sequence and perfectly placed feet, just barely allows passage. Sean and I spent a lot of time working on this 5.13b pitch, not sure if we could free climb these powerful yet delicate moves. It was the missing link between the lower and upper crack systems that made this route possible. This leads into a short section shared with the South Face Route—which happens to be the 5.13 crux of that climb. This crux is truly height-dependent; I watched Sean, who was 6 feet 1 inch, hike it many times with ease. For me it's an all-points-off sideways dyno, usually followed by some expletives. Tommy Caldwell, who is about my height, called this pitch 5.13c, so at least one my heroes thinks it's hard.

It took Seth and me two afternoons and many falls just to redpoint these crux pitches. We had been on the wall for five days now, and food and water were at a low.

On the sixth morning we blasted off early and headed for the summit. The 5.11 climbing, which continues for three pitches above the crux leads, felt relatively easy and refreshingly fast-moving. However, the final two pitches—5.12+ and 5.12—serve as an effective guard to the summit. The first lead follows an overhanging and leaning crack capped by a powerful, bouldery finish. Without relenting, the final pitch climbs a tricky face to a wildly exposed arête and glorious handjams leading right to the summit.

Once on top, I stood there smiling with tears in my eyes—the end of a bittersweet journey. I had completed my most challenging and meaningful climb to date. But more importantly I had realized Sean's vision and planted the first seed in my Soul Garden.

SUMMARY: The first ascent of Soul Garden (VI 5.13b) on the south face of Mt. Watkins, June 24–July 1, 2014, established by Seth Carter, Jimmy Haden, and Sean "Stanley" Leary (1975–2014). The 19-pitch route contains two pitches of 5.13 and nine of 5.12. The route starts on the Prism and shares two pitches with the South Face Route; however, it mostly follows Tenaya's Terror and new free variations to that route.

ABOUT THE AUTHOR: *Jimmy Haden lives in Lake Tahoe, California. He has climbed in the wild mountains of Patagonia, Alaska, and Madagascar, but he feels luckiest to have abundant new routes to climb on the beautiful granite walls of the Sierra Nevada.*

[Left] Seth Carter climbing pitch 18 with Watkins' summit above. *Andrew Burr*

SPEED

THE WHY AND HOW OF A NEW DENALI RECORD

KILIAN JORNET BURGADA

It was just getting light toward the east, always the coldest part of the day. I'd been walking for hours in the darkness, slowly, my shoulders painful under the weight of a heavy pack. My feet were frozen, crammed into an old pair of plastic Koflach boots that had been too small for years. My crampons bit without precision into the hard snow illuminated by my headlamp, the fingers of my hands clenched into fists inside my gloves, and the rope swinging behind me and slapping my calves. And the sun was not yet up.

Three days after summiting Mont Blanc, my partner and I returned to the heat of the valley. I was grateful for having reached the roof of the Alps. But something was gnawing at me. We sat in a bar in Les Houches, where the menu was decorated with a line that followed itself with no beginning and no end. It was an endless knot, a Tibetan symbol representing the interweaving paths of time and change that bind all existence. As we were driving back to Catalonia—I was still just the copilot, too young by a few years for my driver's license—I finally understood my unease. I had the satisfaction of having completed my objective, but I hadn't felt the pleasure of the journey.

SUMMIT
20,237', 15 MILES
9 HOURS 43 MINS

DENALI PASS
18,200', 13.3 MILES
7 HOURS 3 MINS

MEDICAL CAMP
14,200', 11.6 MILES
3 HOURS 25 MINS

MOTORCYCLE HILL
11,200', 8.8 MILES
1 HOUR 58 MINS

WEST BUTTRESS ROUTE WITH RESCUE GULLY CUTOFF

Many years later in Chamonix: "Did he do it or not?" I asked the French guide. "Yes, but he did not do it in *alpinisme*," the guide proclaimed, as if to end the discussion. *Les règles de l'art*, as defined by French guides, had rendered my friend's descent of the north face of the Aiguille de Peuterey illegitimate, since he had descended on skis, without using crampons or ice axes.

Such rules have always left a bad taste in my mouth. I am bored by the limitations of names, definitions, and etiquette. On the one hand we can be alpinists; we can climb mountains with ice axes, crampons, and ropes. Or else skiers, descending mountains with rectangular boards on our feet. Or climbers, ascending steep walls with only the strength of our arms. Or runners, repetitively putting one foot in front of the other like animals, even in the mountains. Or parapenters, those who have ignored humans' inability to fly. Or, on the other hand, we can look at things more simply. We can look at a particular mountain and ask: What tools do I have at my disposal for my own enjoyment?

AT THE BEGINNING of June 2014 I arrive in Talkeetna with three skilled friends: Seb Montaz, an excellent alpinist and extreme skier, and additionally a great filmmaker; Vivian Bruchez, an extreme skier in the tradition of Tardivel, Baud, Boivin, or Siffredi; and Jordi Tosas, a hyperactive first ascensionist with many solo ascents in big mountains all over the world. Our goal is to set a speed record on Denali. What is the reason for trying to set such a record? None. Why do we do the things we do, why do we risk our lives, wear ourselves out for days and years training to climb a particular peak? There is no rational answer. What moves us is emotion and passion. Going fast is not an end, but a consequence of going light, and going light is a consequence of

STATISTICS

ROUND-TRIP DISTANCE: 30 MILES

ELEVATION GAIN: 13,037 FEET

ROUND-TRIP TIME: 11 HOURS 48 MINS

PREVIOUS RECORD: 16 HOURS 46 MINS

START
ASE CAMP
,200'

[Photo] Times are from Jornet's GPS. Distances are approximate. *Alasdair Turner Photography*

my desire to be connected to nature, with the fewest layers separating me from my environment. So the record really isn't the reason behind the trip, but merely the excuse.

After a couple of days waiting out bad weather we finally fly onto the glacier. We load up our sleds, and soon we are settled into the medical camp (the 14,200-foot camp on the West Buttress Route). With our thirst for lightness—while we were shopping in Anchorage, Jordi discretely removed food from the shopping cart because he felt we were getting too weighed down—we are the only group in camp without a vestibule in which to cook. When there is heavy snowfall it is an ordeal to prepare our food and eat.

The fourth day the weather is exceptional (and is not going to last long), so we jump at the opportunity to climb the West Rib. The snow conditions are good and the ascent goes smoothly. In five hours we arrive at the Football Field. I decide to continue, and Jordi descends to camp. The first turns of the descent cost me, due to the altitude and the steepness, but skiing the West Rib, with the views out over the glaciers, is spectacular. The snowy first part leads into a mixed section, picking between rocky ridges with some snowless bits, but soon I arrive back at camp.

WITHOUT A DOUBT moving light and fast in the mountains is a paradox of opposites, between security and the lack of security. Traveling quickly allows one to spend much less time exposed to rockfall or seracs, to the cold, to bad weather. But it also demands much more technical precision and physical conditioning. The absence of extra gear means that a comfortable or safe bivouac is out of the question.

Going light in the mountains is not popular. Guides don't know what to say to their clients when they see someone descending Mont Blanc in running shoes or going light on the Innominata or Chardonnet. In 2013 I was climbing the Frendo Spur on the Aiguille du Midi with my girlfriend, and we underestimated the speed of an approaching storm, and three-quarters of the way up she injured her feet. When the storm came I did not hesitate to call for rescue. If I was alone, probably I would not have asked for help, but when I am with someone I prefer to make it safer. There was a lot of criticism afterward. This can happen in the Alps, where there is rescue available and an easy approach to the mountains. It's like a big training gym for alpinism, with 3G coverage throughout the massif and web services providing real-time conditions. You feel a bit more secure, and this is dangerous.

This is what I like about remote mountains where there is not cell coverage and you don't use a satellite phone. The exercise of decision-making is more challenging, more consequential, requiring you to absorb all the external elements. Denali is surprising because it is a big, remote mountain but it's really crowded and the camps have a lot of infrastructure. We carry a sat phone on Denali, but during the record attempt I will communicate with no one except the climbers I meet along the way. My team will not even know if I break the record—or fall into a crevasse—until I come back up to the medical camp afterward and tell them I'm okay.

[Above] Jornet climbing the Rescue Gully toward Denali's high camp. He wore or carried his lightweight skis throughout the ascent. *Summits of My Life*

THE DAY AFTER my first trip up to the summit we awake to heavy snowfall. We've been intending to climb the West Buttress next, for more acclimatization, but looking ahead we can see the weather report is fairly poor. There will be a two-day window of good weather, followed by a week of storm. What should we do? Wait for a new window while we continue to acclimatize or try for the record right away? We decide to go for it. In early afternoon the following day, Seb and I pack a small tent and some food and ski down to base camp.

After a few hours of sleep, we began our ski back up the glacier early the next morning. I'm carrying everything I will need for the day, including crampons, ice axe, insulated pants and two jackets, down mittens, one liter of water (I will refill at 14,200 feet), and a 300ml energy gel. The technique and fitness gained from more than 14 years of ski mountaineering competitions allows me to move quickly over easy ground. I can climb comfortably while still being able to converse with Seb. After three and a half hours I arrive at the medical camp. I drink a bit of water and begin to ascend the Rescue Gully [a shorter, steeper route to the 17,000-foot high camp on the West Buttress], in order to avoid all the crowds on the fixed lines. Now I have to carry my skis, but they weigh less than 800 grams.

By the time I come out of the gully, the light breeze of the morning has become a strong blast. Clouds cover the highest part of the mountain, and it has begun to snow. I put on my jacket and break trail in fresh snow up to 20 centimeters [nearly eight inches]. Two other people are above me, but their tracks disappear in the strong wind. I have to stop from time to time to warm up, swinging my arms and legs, as breaking trail isn't allowing me to move quickly enough. I have to fight for each step, thinking only of the summit. After a little more than 9 hours 43 minutes I finally arrive on top, but I can't see anything around me, just snow.

I take a bit of time to buckle my boots and then begin to ski down the summit ridge. The visibility is only a few meters, and I have to be careful not to go too fast, trying to remember the way I had ascended and not miss my tracks. Finally I arrive at the entrance to the Rescue Gully, and there I meet Vivian and we ski quickly together to the medical camp.

Still in poor visibility, I continue alone down the glaciers to base camp, leaning back hard to keep my tips up and absorb the changes in the snow and terrain. Through soft drizzle and fog, I see my orange tent a few meters ahead, just two hours after leaving the summit. While I am preparing dinner Jodi arrives, carrying three ice axes and a rope for us to use the next day. "Hey, congratulations! Tomorrow we are going to climb ice on Hunter, right?"

FOR ME, SPEED ASCENTS are not about being the fastest but about being out of my comfort zone—those moments when I am in limbo between the animal instinct to preserve life and the intellectual drive to approach one's limits, and perhaps even death, in order to understand life. In the mountains there is the possibility to choose one's own line, to decide to continue on or turn back, to take a risk or to avoid it. It is, in the end, the only place where I can apply my anarchistic beliefs without fearing the police.

But taking a risk is not like taking a leap into the void or playing the lottery. It is a spontaneous sum of decisions, taking into account our technical and physical skills, our experience, our mental state, the conditions of the route and the mountain, and with all of that being able to see the probability of success and recognize the level of commitment we want to assume. And sometimes our choices are wrong, and it is through our errors that we learn.

These attempts at records are, in the end, the excuse to learn something, to experience new mountains, and to see a new way of attaining the mountain—more directly, without aid or assistance, without téléferiques, without intermediate camps, without materiel that separates us from the land.

SUMMARY: Speed ascent and descent of Denali (6,168m) in Alaska by Kilian Jornet Burgada on June 7, 2014. Jornet followed the West Buttress Route with the Rescue Gully variation, reaching the summit in just over 9 hours 43 minutes. He then skied down the same route for a round-trip time of 11 hours 48 minutes. [*The online version of this article includes an account of Jornet's record-breaking ascent Aconcagua (6,962m) in December 2014.*]

ABOUT THE AUTHOR: *Born in 1987 in Catalonia, Spain, Kilian Jornet Burgada was raised in a mountain hut and began climbing at age three. He is a multi-time world champion in trail running and ski mountaineering races, and he holds the speed records for ascending and descending Mont Blanc and the Matterhorn.*

Translated from Spanish by Pam Ranger Roberts.

[Below] Jornet descended the 15-mile route in a little over two hours. *Summits of My Life*

[RECON]

CLOUD PEAK

WYOMING'S OFF-THE-RADAR GRANITE PARADISE

MARK JENKINS, DOUGALD MACDONALD, RAYMOND JACQUOT, ARNO ILGNER & MATT CUPAL

Sitting on our ropes on the summit, falling stars zooming around us, I'm afraid I might be freezing to death. I huddle as close as I can get to my partner, skinny Ken Duncan. We are bivying in the boulders, and I would give my left nut for just one layer of fleece. It's late August, but on a windy night at 13,000 feet you wouldn't know it. We have no tent, no sleeping bags, no bivy sacks, no stove, no jackets, no food, and no water. We have empty stomachs and windbreakers. Eventually I can't take it any longer, and I stand up and start running in place—which only manages to pump the cool blood in my extremities back to my heart. I'm cold as a stone. I snuggle back against Ken. He's shivering, but he's sleeping. Damn him!

We have just completed a new route on the prow of the Merlon, the southeast buttress of Cloud Peak, a massif of gorgeous granite that lies in the heart of the Bighorn Mountains of northern Wyoming. One shot, ground up, no beta, no bolts, no pins. It was harder than we expected and longer than we expected. When we pulled over the top it was dusk and we were so wasted we decided it was too risky to try to find our way off. We would just sit it out for the night.

Waiting in the darkness, shivering intensely, I can't believe I'm doing this again on the same bloody peak. A few years earlier, I'd gone into the Bighorns from the west side with Bryan Bornholdt. We bivied on the way in, got too cold after a couple of hours, and started moving again. We made the first ascent of a buttress on the northwest side of Cloud Peak, but then had to suffer through another frosty, sleepless bivy on our way out.

Now, cowering in the black cold, I promise myself I will never do this again. This is it! I'm wising up. Several weeks later, when the sun finally rises, splitting the eastern horizon like a golden axe, it takes over an hour to warm Ken and me enough to start rappelling. We stumble back into camp at noon, discover the wind has collapsed our tent, drink all our whiskey, drag our sleeping bags deep into the krummholz, and crash.

But of course I didn't wise up. Mountains brainwash you. Cloud Peak's towering granite walls, the shining snowfields, the isolation and consequent commitment—these are what you remember. It's a long hike to get there, so you don't see a soul on a single wall. You have a

[Previous page] High camp below the Merlon, the ca 1,250-foot buttress southeast of Cloud Peak. The big prow's climbing history is obscure, and at least two parties, in the 1990s and 2000s, mistakenly thought they were doing first ascents. *Bobby Model*

kingdom of rock all to yourself. There aren't many places like this left in the United States, where you will see more pikas and pine martens than people. Where you can choose a line and climb it and never see a sign that anyone else has ever done it.

Last year I went back to Cloud Peak, again, and did four long routes—probably new routes—in five days. Thirty new pitches, yes! The rock was (mostly) solid, the green meadows beautiful and beckoning below, the sky brilliantly blue. In all the wide world of climbing, from the months-long misery of 8,000-meter peaks to bouldering five feet off the ground in a chalky climbing gym, there is nothing better than unclimbed alpine rock. And this time there were no unplanned bivouacs.

– MARK JENKINS

GEOGRAPHY

CLOUD PEAK (13,166 feet/4,013m) is the highest summit of the Bighorns. Although popular with hikers and fishermen, the range has seen remarkably little attention from climbers, despite walls of solid granite soaring more than 1,500 feet. Yet over the years a few superb routes have been done—and there is much potential for more.

Uplifted in the Laramide orogeny that created the Rocky Mountains, and shaped by successions of glaciers, Cloud Peak rises more than 9,000 feet above the plains just to the east. The mountain is flat on top but very steep on all sides except the southwest, where a narrow ridgeline allows hikers to access the summit.

The cirque directly to the east has 1,000-foot walls on two sides and holds the Bighorns' largest remnant glacier, a half moon of snow and ice feeding meltwater into Glacier Lake. On the south side of this cirque is a rampart of granite extending to the east, culminating in an independent summit called the Merlon, with fine and difficult routes on its huge southeast face. A 900-foot buttress rises to Cloud's southern summit plateau, just west of the Merlon. The 1,500-foot west face of the peak, a broad cirque near the head of Wilderness Basin, is a complex of spires, slabs, and icy gullies. To the north the summit plateau sharpens into a jagged ridgeline leading over Innominate and Woolsey, two of Wyoming's most striking peaks.

The granite and gneiss making up the massif varies in quality but is often excellent, with

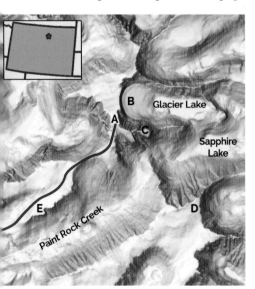

fine-grained cracks and numerous chicken heads and other alpine features. That these mountains are not crawling with climbers is a testament to their isolation: Cloud Peak's summit lies about 12 miles from the nearest trailhead, and the high camps are 7 to 11 miles in. The east face is so isolated that the first ascensionists approached by traversing over Cloud Peak's summit and downclimbing a snow couloir to the wall. (Horse packers can be hired to carry backpacks to Mistymoon Lake, 5 miles southwest of the peak, and partway in the east side as well.) The rock climbing season is short: mid-July to mid-September.

[Map] Cloud Peak's summit is about 12 miles from the road. (A) Cloud Peak, with the southwest ridge hiking route marked. (B) East face. (C) The Merlon. (D) Bomber Mountain. (E) Paint Rock Buttress.

[Left] High on Cloud Peak's southeast arête, a 1,200' route that may have been climbed as early as the 1970s but was never documented. *Mark Jenkins* [Right] Jenkins midway on Rust Never Sleeps (10 pitches, 5.11a, 2014), likely the first route up Cloud's south buttress. *Dougald MacDonald*

CLIMBING HISTORY

TECHNICAL CLIMBING in the northern Bighorns began in July 1933. An article in the following year's *AAJ* by W.B. Willcox, entitled "An American Tyrol," described an expedition into the valleys north of Cloud Peak that resulted in the first ascents of several high and difficult peaks, including Black Tooth, Woolsey, Hallelujah, and Innominate. These mountaineers did not attempt the steep walls of Cloud Peak, just to the south.

The first climbers to visit Cloud's east face probably were Keith Becker, Charlie Blackmon, and Bob Nessle, who approached from the west over the saddle between Cloud Peak and Bomber Mountain and circled around the Merlon. According to Ray Jacquot, who interviewed Becker, it was early September and the Cloud Peak Glacier presented black ice embedded with bits of black rock—a surface on which it was prudent not to fall, as Jacquot put it. They traversed the glacier along the foot of the east face but found little hope of a climbable line, even one involving direct aid. Instead they climbed the northernmost snow couloir leading to the summit plateau, thus likely completing the first climb out of the eastern cirque, but avoiding the major difficulties.

Fred Beckey, who, unsurprisingly, visited the Bighorns several times, also took a look at the east face but declared it was "too flawless of piton cracks for a decent route." Instead, he climbed a route up the eastern prow of the Merlon, with Joe Faint and Galen Rowell, in 1969. However, Beckey and his partners were not the first to climb the Merlon. That honor went to Wyoming climbers Dart Davis, Ray Jacquot, and Chuck Satterfield, who did the first ascent of the great tower in 1961, climbing the sharp eastern arête.

Throughout the 1960s and '70s, the only routes in the east cirque were snow and ice

FIRST ASCENT OF THE MERLON

BY RAYMOND G. JACQUOT

SOMETIME IN THE PERIOD from 1959 to 1961, I uncovered in the University of Wyoming Coe Library a 1906 USGS publication entitled *The Geology of the Big Horn Mountains*, by N.H. Darton. In this volume were some spectacular black and white photographs of the high country around Cloud Peak. Several of these revealed what we came to refer to as the southeast buttress of Cloud

go to the Bighorns to have a look at the Merlon. We met Dart in Buffalo and took his family Jeep up the four-wheel-drive road into Soldier Park, where the backpacking would begin. It turned out the clutch was nearly out of the Jeep, so we parked it a short distance west of Hunter Ranger Station and hoofed it to Soldier Park, then over the Ant Hills to Elk Lake, where we spent the first night.

The following day we packed up to the second lake above Mead Lake and had lunch. We then carried our technical climbing gear up around Emerald and Sapphire lakes to the base of the slabs

[Above] The first ascent team approaches the Merlon (the large, left-leaning tower) in 1961. The east face of Cloud Peak is visible behind and right. *Ray Jacquot*

Peak, although the top of the buttress is separated from the peak by a sharp notch. Sometime after our climb this feature became known as the Merlon.

In early July of 1961 I had just returned to Casper from a ten-day backpack trip to the Wind Rivers with Ken and Karen Endsley and Pat Johnson. I arrived in Casper to find Chuck Satterfield eager for a Fourth of July trip. He had been in touch with Dart Davis, who was home in Buffalo on leave from the U.S. Army. We decided to

leading to the east arête of the Merlon. We had to hurry to make it back to our camp by dark.

We rose early and went rapidly back around the lakes to the base of the climb and our gear cache. We left our ice axes at the base of the slabs for use on the return trip, and this turned out to be the first of several mistakes we were to make that day.

Once on the arête, the climbing initially was fairly easy, on broken rock for several pitches

was fairly easy, on broken rock for several pitches to the base of a vertical wall. Chuck led this elegantly, with good piton protection, utilizing a series of small, solid edges in the granite—it was a very exhilarating pitch (5.7). Another easy pitch took us to the base of a chimney just to the right (north) of the ridge crest. The chimney was steep but not difficult and landed us on the top of a pillar separated from the mass of the rock by a gap of three feet. After the step across this gap, a steep wall led to a belay on a sloping ledge beneath a small overhang. The final pitch dealt with the overhang and took us to the lower east summit. We passed a gap about 50 feet high on the west side and arrived on top about noon. We built a cairn and left a film-can register to note our first ascent.

At this point we made our second mistake of the day. Just west of the summit was another notch separating us from Cloud Peak itself. The west side of this notch was overhanging and monolithic, so continuing to the summit was out of the question. From the notch a couloir descended to the south, and it looked like one long rappel would put us on the snow. When we arrived at the snow we found it hard and not amenable to heeling down. Since we had left our ice axes behind, this dictated about five more rappels, each one requiring some hardware, sling material, and valuable time to rig. When we finally exited the couloir the light was fading. We had left much of our stock of pitons and slings in the couloir. We hurried to retrieve our ice axes and make our way back to camp.

The following day we packed out following a route across the east side of Bomber Mountain to Clear Creek, which led us back to Soldier Park. We got a good view of the east face of Bomber Mountain, which we were to address a decade later.

Editor's note: In July 1971, Jacquot and Art Bloom, Howard Bussey, Rex Hoff, and Bill Lindberg completed the first ascent of the east face of Bomber Mountain, just to the south of Cloud Peak.

couloirs, including an ascent by Robert Bliss and George Hurley, who, in 1973, climbed a "hidden couloir," likely the one that slants up to the north directly under the summit. In July 1974, Gary Poush and Dave Stiller made a spirited attempt on the big rock face left of this couloir and directly under Cloud Peak's summit. Approaching from the east, they climbed up the Cloud Peak Glacier and third-classed a few hundred feet of rock before roping up. "We did one or two easy fifth-class pitches up to a ledge system, where we spent a memorable night in the midst of a noisy and lengthy light show," Stiller said. After a stormy night, they climbed a couple of moderate pitches before traversing across ledges into the neighboring couloir and following it to the top. The rock face they attempted may still be unclimbed.

The west side of Cloud Peak got its first known technical routes in July 1970, when Rex Hoff and Gale Long climbed two full-length routes, following major weaknesses left and right along the face, the first of which involved some ice climbing and the second some aid.

Other early technical ascents were completed but not recorded, including some by Scott Heywood, now a fishing outfitter based in nearby Sheridan. "In the summer and fall of 1976 and summer of 1977, we did some routes on the prow and the east face," Heywood said. "We did not name these routes, nor report them, and the details are fuzzy for me. I think we did an obvious line on the Merlon, approximately 5.9, to the right of the other routes on the main face, plus a number of the other pinnacles in the area."

In the mid-1980s two climbers came to Cloud Peak determined to climb the first route directly up the east face. Arno Ilgner and Steve Petro camped on the summit before descending the northern couloir to the Cloud Peak Glacier, and then spent several days working on Shimmering Abstraction (V 5.11). Highly skilled and enjoying all the advances in equipment

[Above] Steve Bechtel on Super Fortress. The top seven pitches are 5.11. *Bobby Model*

of that decade, the two lifted Cloud Peak's standard of technical difficulty by two full number grades. The climbers placed about six bolts to protect face moves and also used pitons. Steve Bechtel, who made the second ascent with Mike Lilygren during the 1990s, said the route goes hammerless, but with an R rating, and that the 30-year-old bolts "should be considered suspect."

Other routes in the cirque have been attempted, including one by the late Craig Luebben and Annie Whitehouse. But no other full-length rock climbs are known. Climbers have focused greater attention on the slightly more accessible walls of the Merlon. Heywood and possibly others climbed routes on the lower-angle rock on the right side of this face, but Dennis Horning and Jeb Schenck were likely the first to probe the middle of the southeast face. Around 1975 they climbed about four pitches, aiming for the big chimney that drops from the summit, using bolts to protect run-out face climbing up to mid-5.10.

In the late 1980s, Matt Cupal and a partner picked the plum on the Merlon: the striking Nose-like prow that forms the left skyline when the formation is viewed from the east. Cupal remembers neither the date nor even his partner's name. But the route was so good that he went back on his honeymoon about five years later and did it again.

In 1994, Steve Bechtel, Mike Lilygren, and Bobby Model began working on the steep wall to the left of the Horning-Schenck attempt. They placed bolts to protect run-outs on the difficult upper pitches, along with bolted belay anchors. On their free push they climbed to within about 100 feet of the top before rain-soaked rock turned them away. Two years later they came back and freed the full route in a day.

"A mathematician would describe the steepness of the Merlon as increasing at an increasing rate," Model wrote in the *AAJ*. "The route starts as easy fifth class and gradually becomes more difficult. The top pitches [all] are 5.11, with four of the pitches at 5.11+.... The climbing was challenging and varied, ranging from hand jams to puzzles of razor-sharp crimps. The top portion [had] a vast array of water-sculptured chicken heads and huecos, spaced just far enough apart to make the climbing interesting." Their route, Super Fortress, has been repeated by at least two teams, who have verified its difficulty and quality.

Although the Merlon's southeast face had been climbed at least six years earlier, and attempted long before that, the 1996 team thought they were making the first ascent. "The funny thing was that although Dennis, Matt, Mike, Bobby, and I were all friends, we had no idea anyone had ever tried the southeast face before," Bechtel said.

This theme has been repeated numerous times in the Cloud Peak massif. In 2008, Ken Duncan and Mark Jenkins added their own line to the Merlon. Unaware that the prow had been climbed by Cupal and partner two decades earlier, they chose a line just a bit to the left of Cupal's, completing their 12-pitch route, No Climb for Old Men (5.11 A2), in a long day, with a very cold open bivouac on top.

In August 2014, Jenkins and Dougald MacDonald spent six nights below Cloud Peak and climbed several previously undocumented routes, including the 900-foot south buttress of Cloud Peak (Rust Never Sleeps, 5.11a). But one route they thought might be new probably was climbed in the 1970s by Scott Heywood and partners: the splendid, 1,200-foot southeast arête (5.8), just left of the Merlon. Such is the nature of Bighorn climbing.

POSSIBILITIES

THERE'S STILL ONLY one known rock route in the big eastern cirque. The wall to the left of Shimmering Abstraction is taller and steeper, and like the Ilgner-Petro line it likely would require some bolt protection. The north side of the Merlon promises at least one good 1,000-foot-plus line at its east end. The steep face above the cirque's northern couloirs also may offer a route.

There is still potential for routes on the southeast side of the Merlon—the Horning-Schenck line remains uncompleted, for one. The southwest-facing wall to the left of the Merlon's prow, about 1,000 feet high, is the steepest wall on Cloud Peak believed to be unclimbed. It has obvious, continuous crack systems. There is room for several more routes on the 900-foot south

[Below] The east face cirque above the Cloud Peak Glacier. Shimmering Abstraction (5.11, 1986), the only known rock route in the cirque, is marked. *Mark Jenkins*

CLOUD PEAK'S EAST FACE

BY ARNO ILGNER

IN THE MIX OF LIFE we can lose ourselves. I was lost in mid-1980s while I lived, worked, and climbed in Wyoming. At the time, we took pride in Wyoming climbers doing first ascents of Wyoming walls. One such wall was the east face of Cloud Peak. Steve Petro and I had climbed many first ascents at the local crags around Casper, and we teamed up with a fellow climber, Kirk Breuer, who had his pilot's license, to fly around Cloud and take photographs. We studied those photos intensely and wanted to make an attempt in 1984. That year, though, was full of chaos. Steve and I both lost our jobs and our wives, and I moved back to Tennessee. The east face would have to wait.

Steve did a recon of the best approach and got a close-up view of the face in 1985. Then, in August of 1986, I traveled back to Wyoming. The timing was right for us. We packed enough supplies

[Below] Steve Petro during the first ascent of Shimmering Abstraction (5.11). *Arno Ilgner*

for a week and hiked 12 miles, approaching from the west, to a bivy on the summit. Photographs had shown two couloirs on the north end of the east face. The northernmost one proved to be low angle, allowing us to descend to the base with enough climbing and bivy gear for the route.

We'd picked a line from our aerial photographs that started about 80 feet right of a prominent, left-angling black dike. Looking up, we saw smooth slabs that transitioned into small roofs as the wall steepened, finishing with slightly overhanging dihedrals. Our line followed weaknesses in the rock, and we felt confident we'd find adequate protection. We also felt confident that we could deal with any run-out sections. By the mid-1980s we had at our disposal pitons and bolts, as well as cams and shoes with sticky rubber. We also had elevated free climbing standards, standing on the shoulders of earlier climbers to find a possible route on the face.

The granite provided plenty of crisp, square-cut edges. The climbing was a little run-out, but moderate in difficulty. We found protection at regular intervals, drilling only about half a dozen protection bolts. We swapped leads as we made

our way up the steep slabs, free-climbing each pitch. I've often wondered why certain climbing partnerships work so well, and I've learned that nature requires balance. If I'd been just like Steve (or if Steve was like me), we probably wouldn't have made such a great team. Steve applied his analytical skills. "If we need to bolt belays," he told me, "we'll put the bolts vertically so the top bolt can give us protection for the next pitch." I applied my intuitive skills; I knew where the line of weakness went for the route. I could just go, even if there was a section that didn't have protection.

The first day we climbed a few pitches and descended to bivy on the glacier. The second day we carried our gear up the face and found some run-out 5.11 climbing at mid-height, but nothing super-serious. We climbed through small roofs to gain a big, grassy ledge system by the end of the day, where we set up our bivy. What a beautiful spot! Guys generally don't say much, but Steve and I shared the pleasure we felt from our day of climbing. We could feel the satisfaction of climbing well and the symbiosis of our team. The stars exploded into view in the dark Wyoming sky. We slept well.

Next morning the sun basked the wall in warmth. Clouds were building in the east, creating a reddish hue. We only had about 300 feet of climbing left, but needed to get going so we wouldn't be caught in the coming storm. The wall steepened, overhanging slightly in the last section. Protection was more abundant in the cracks of the dihedrals. I led the last pitch. Snow fell and the wind blew as Steve topped out and joined me. We tore down our base camp and gunned it for the car.

The climbing really wasn't that challenging for us. The real challenge, as always, was to find a way to enter the unknown, to take that first step. We could trust each other and the solid foundation that climbing provided for us. Many years have passed since then, but climbing is still my foundation. It helps me find my way when I feel lost in the chaos of life. How fortunate we are to have climbing. How fortunate we are to have unclimbed walls where we can enter the unknown.

SOUTH PROW OF THE MERLON

BY MATT CUPAL

WE DID THIS ROUTE way back in the distant past, probably my fourth year in college, which would have been 1988. I met a guy climbing in Vedauwoo (Wyoming), and we decided the Bighorns sounded remote and fun, so off we went. We hiked in from the east, from the Hunter Creek area, taking the Solitude Trail over the ridge and down into Mead Lake. From there we hiked up past Diamond and Sapphire lakes to the Merlon.

It's been a long time, but the route went at about 5.11a, taking a line slightly to the right of the tip of the south prow. We did it all free and all on clean gear, placing no bolts, starting about 6 a.m. It starts out with easy climbing up slabs. At about mid-height we moved into a right-facing corner system with some chimney climbing. Gear was generally good, though small, as is the nature of that rock. Most of the climbing was in the 5.9 to 5.10 range, except we did have one crux pitch midway up the wall that felt like 11a. I led that pitch, and the belay anchor at the top was just three good RPs above a steeply sloping ledge. I distinctly remember my partner having to hang as he got close to the belay, which was not a comfortable feeling at all, given my less than bomber gear.

The last pitch is burned in my memory. The belay was down in the middle of a large ledge. I climbed up and right on an easy, clean, unprotected face, aiming for a flake about 60 feet up. I managed to find a marginal stopper behind the flake, then moved up another 60 feet of easy but scary slab to the vertical summit rim. This was 10 feet of maybe 5.10 climbing, and I placed a solid No. 9 stopper in the middle. I faced the decision of free climbing and risking a fall onto a single piece or standing on the gear and reaching for holds above, but then risking popping the piece and taking an unthinkable ride. With trepidation, I chose to stand on the piece, and that created a terrible and inelegant beached-whale move, groping in wet moss, to flop onto the summit.

I topped out at 10 p.m. There was still a scratch of light in the sky. I had forgotten my headlamp (thank god I got done climbing before dark), so my partner set up all of the rappels. We must have gotten off route on the rappels because we spent way more time on ropes than we should have. It took us until 6 a.m. to get back to our tent.

I don't remember the name of my partner. I never climbed with him after that trip, and we had met not long before. I actually did the route twice, and the second time was easier to remember. My now ex-wife, Deb Cupal, and I went up there on our honeymoon in August 1996. We climbed a couple of small things and attempted some larger faces, then repeated the Merlon south prow. It took us two tries. On the first go we got to about two pitches below the large step and I got off-route—too far left—and got into really thin climbing. The second attempt went better. We had a nice snowstorm as we neared the top, but we got back to the ground with daylight left over.

buttress of Cloud Peak, with the steepest and best rock on the left side.

The broad, complex west face of Cloud has not had a new route (published) since 1970, although Jenkins and Bryan Bornholdt climbed a ca 1,000-foot 5.11 pillar guarding the northern edge of the cirque. Though continuous lines are not obvious on the west face, the wall is dotted with huge slabs of solid-looking rock and several major pinnacles.

The 600-foot formation protruding from Cloud Peak's southwest ridge, above Paint Rock Creek, is broken down low but steep and solid in the upper half, with many potential lines. The 2014 team climbed a six-pitch route (The Man Who Feared Marmots, 5.10+) in the middle of the face, which they dubbed Paint Rock Buttress. The eastern wall is overhanging and could yield a 5.12 or 5.13 route. This cliff is easily reached from a camp by Mistymoon Lake.

Given Cloud Peak's isolation and the silence surrounding past expeditions, it's very likely that some of these potential routes already have been climbed, with no trace left behind.

– DOUGALD MACDONALD

[Below] The south buttresses of (A) Cloud Peak and (B) the Merlon. (1) Rust Never Sleeps (10 pitches, 5.11a, Jenkins-MacDonald, 2014). (2) Southeast arête (1,200', 5.8, climbed in 2014 but first ascent unknown). (3) No Climb for Old Men (12 pitches, 5.11c R A2, Duncan-Jenkins, 2008). (4) South prow (5.11a, Cupal and partner, 1988). (5) Super Fortress (5.11+, Bechtel-Lilygren-Model, 1996). (6) Attempt (ca 1975) by Dennis Horning and Jeb Schenck. (7) Scott Heywood and partners (ca 5.9, 1970s, exact line unknown). (8) East prow (5.7, Davis-Jacquot-Satterfield, 1961). Lines on the Merlon are approximate. The steep, shadowed southwest face of the Merlon has no known routes. *Dougald MacDonald* [Previous page] Sunrise from the top of the Merlon. *Mark Jenkins*

CLIMBS & EXPEDITIONS

2015

[Photo] Tackling a steep ice pitch on Looking for the Void, Siula Chico (see p.38 for the feature story). The Cordillera Huayhuash had a very active season with many new routes (p. 196-201). *Hélias Millerioux*

UNITED STATES

WASHINGTON / NORTH CASCADES

MT. DESPAIR, NORTHEAST BUTTRESS, BIPOLAR BUTTRESS

HALF THE FUN is getting there—*that's usually true.* Reaching the unclimbed northeast buttress of Mt. Despair (7,927'), southwest of the Picket Range, would first require venturing up a brush-choked valley at which even seasoned Cascades aficionados balked. Correspondence with local dignitaries yielded little hope for straightforward access. Nevertheless, Rolf Larson and I decided to risk three precious days of fair weather on an end-of-July attempt.

The northeast buttress of Despair is an appealing line. It rises from low in the green and

[Below] The approximate line of Bipolar Buttress (3,700', 5.9, easy snow) on the northeast buttress of Mt. Despair, a remote peak in the North Cascades. *Eric Wehrly*

rugged Goodell Creek Valley. This promises a myriad of challenges, as does the serrated ridgeline itself, which finally gains the north ridge near the high glaciers. A friend and soi-disant Cascades dignitary pronounced this yet another "last great problem" of the Cascades, while the other side of his mouth dismissed it as worthless "table scraps." In the end these proved to be prescient words: This thoroughly enjoyable climb was like eating a gourmet meal off a dirty floor.

We are lucky that the Cascades, owing largely to the abundance of peaks, but also to their verdant and varyingly pleasant approaches, still offer new and interesting problems to solve. Many of our peers desired to climb the northeast buttress of Despair but either had difficulty convincing a partner to brave the approach or were turned back by it. For Rolf and I, the approach was half the fun and the return trip comprised the other half. Counting the climb, you might say we had fun greater than one.

On July 28, the morning after our approach, we began climbing up a massive, 1,300' open-book corner on the lower northeast buttress (5.6). After that we continued via scenic scrambling on the crest over many notches. These notches required increasingly committing rappels, followed by steeper and more technical climbing. Our pre-trip research suggested a particularly deep cleft (several hundred feet) near the summit of the upper buttress—this weighed on our psyches during the whole climb. Upon reaching this cleft, the opposite wall appeared very steep and the few viable lines looked loose and difficult to access. But we rapped in anyway and scoped it out. We settled on a right-trending ramp that kept the climbing reasonable and exciting (70m, 5.9). A shorter pitch followed, which led to moderate rambling. Eventually the buttress yielded a deluxe bivy site near a small col, where two glaciers meet.

The next morning we crossed the col and climbed a 70m pitch of steep rock to attain the upper north ridge. From there we continued up the final snow ridge to the summit, a remote and memorable place, with a unique perspective on the inimitable Picket Range. We descended by reaching a notch south of the summit and then headed down its west flank. We ultimately exited via Triumph Pass and the Thornton Lakes Trail to a stashed bike, where the lucky loser of roshambo commenced the eight-mile midnight ride to retrieve the car.

On a map, our adventure looks like a reasonable, horseshoe-shaped route. But make sure you plan for three physical days, two arduous stretches of hiking, and one experience far greater than the sum of its parts: Bipolar Buttress (3,700', 5.9, easy snow). 📷

– ERIC WEHRLY

LINCOLN PEAK, NORTHWEST FACE, WILKES-BOOTH

LINCOLN PEAK (9,080') is located among the "Black Buttes" and is a prominent subsidiary summit of Mt. Baker, less than a mile southwest of Colfax Peak. Steep on all sides, it is the gutted remains of a 500,000-year-old stratovolcano, otherwise known as choss. On March 13, 2015, Michal Rynkiewicz and I climbed a new route on the northwest face. We completed the route in 18.5 hours from the Heliotrope Ridge trailhead, during a one-day weather window. It would usually take at least a day to reach Lincoln Peak in winter, and not without serious avalanche concerns, but a nearly snowless winter in the Cascades created clear roads and all-time conditions.

I had not had my eye on the northwest face of Lincoln for very long. However, two ascents of the Polish Route on Colfax Peak that season, and a subsequent photo of the face, got me thinking. In early March 2010, Daniel Jeffrey and Tom Sjoleth had climbed the northwest side of Assassin Spire, a subsidiary summit of Mt. Lincoln, by their route Shooting Gallery (2,000', IV WI4, *AAJ 2010*) and published photos of unclimbed ice on Lincoln. If Colfax was in, I figured Assassin must be too, and possibly Lincoln as well.

Michal and I started our climb in the same location as the Assassin Spire route, where a pitch of WI4 begins right of the prominent hanging glacier. Above that, we simul-climbed along the west side of the upper amphitheater (a large basin between Lincoln Peak and Assassin Spire). Once on Lincoln's northwest wall, we climbed approximately four roped pitches on steeper ice, with snowfields up to 70° in between, followed by some rime-covered ridge climbing. After a brief stop at the summit, we descended the southwest face route. The descent was involved, with sections of snow and ice up to 65°. However, the immaculate conditions allowed for rapid downclimbing. We called our route the Wilkes-Booth (2,000', IV WI4).

— DANIEL COLTRANE

SUPERCAVE WALL, SOUTH FACE, THE TIGER

IN JULY, Colin Moorhead, Max Tepfer, and I completed a difficult new free climb on the Supercave Wall (a.k.a. M&M Wall) over the course of four days: the Tiger (1,000', IV 5.12b). This south-facing, semi-alpine wall is truly an amazing gem, located two miles north-northeast of Liberty Bell near Washington Pass, with only a 40-minute approach from Milepost 166 on Highway 20. The Supercave Wall has been mostly ignored since its first ascent in 1969 by Mead Hargis and Jim Langdon (5.8 A4). Only in 2009 did it receive its second route, the Ellen Pea (900', IV 5.11c), established by Erik Lawson and Arden Pete—one of the best routes in the Cascades. The face is remarkable for its huge caves and myriad pockets and quartz jugs.

[Left] The northwest aspect of Mt. Baker's "Black Buttes." Shooting Gallery (2,000', IV WI4, Jeffrey-Sjoleth, *AAJ 2010*) on Assassin Spire is shown at left. The Wilkes-Booth (2,000', IV WI4, Coltrane-Rynkiewicz, 2015) is shown on the right. *John Scurlock* [Right] Michal Rynkiewicz climbing the final, icy chimney up to the summit of Lincoln Peak. *Daniel Coltrane*

This was the first time I brought a drill and placed bolts in the mountains—we did some drilling on lead, some on rappel—yet despite our mostly top-down approach it still felt like we were onsighting some of the pitches on the final ground-up ascent. In all, there are 11 pitches, and all but one is 5.10 or harder. The climbing involves everything from fingers to offwidth. There are 12 protection bolts, and all the belays are bolted or off trees. Three of the protection bolts were added after all the pitches had been redpointed on gear alone because the protection was so poor for a ground-up attempt. There is also a direct variation to pitches six and seven, climbing directly out of the cave atop pitch five; I redpointed this 40m varation at 5.12+. The descent can be made by walking off or rappelling the route with two ropes.

I also freed a variation up to the fourth pitch on the Hargis-Landon route (at 5.12b) after starting on the Ellen Pea. The cracks and slabs above will likely go free.

– BLAKE HERRINGTON

OREGON / CASCADES

MT. THIELSEN, NORTH FACE; EAST FACE, BRAINLESS CHILD

MANY ALPINISTS suffer from an obsession or two. I am certainly no exception: My interest with Mt. Thielsen began in 1990. I thought there simply had to be a good winter route on the mountain. Fast-forward 20 years and I am obviously no longer a spring chicken. As a pilot and owner of a small plane, I had observed the north and east faces of Mt. Thielsen since 2010. This enabled me to see possible lines and just how quickly they came in and out of condition.

On my first trip to Mt. Thielsen, in February 2011 with Kevin Russell, we probed weaknesses all around the northeast buttress, north face, and northwest ridge. The mountain was very out of condition on that trip. My next trip, in Deccember 2011 with Tyler Adams and Bill Amos, ended similarly, but we did circumnavigate the entire mountain and saw firsthand the route on the east face that would become the final objective.

I made a third trip, solo, in January 2012 that resulted in a new line on the north face. (It butts into the McLaughlin Memorial route at the final headwall, but I didn't reach the summit due to a near catastrophe.) This line comprised an amazing 700' white streak of sn'ice and some vertical water ice. After this, my Thielsen obsession lay quenched and dormant for two long years but was inevitably rekindled by looking through old aerial photos. After two reconnaissance flights in early 2014, I was in full-blown relapse: The east face route looked in

[Above] Steve Elder starts the impressive second-pitch ice runnel of Brainless Child. *Tyler Adams*

the best shape I'd seen so far. A quick call to Tyler Adams and he was in.

We left the car at 1:30 a.m. on March 22. After an hour, we lost the boot track, donned snowshoes, and went straight up through the woods. We ditched snowshoes at the junction of the Pacific Crest Trail and then started laboriously post-holing under the west and north faces. Beneath the north face, the snow improved to crampon conditions. We reached the small saddle between the north and east faces at sunrise and the base of our planned route on the east face at 8 a.m.

The first pitch went well up a rocky buttress right of the ice, as the ice does not touch down (5.9). The next pitch climbed narrow rolling ice (WI3+) for 70m. Unfortunately, the next ice pitch was dripping like a waterfall due to the sun. I got one dubious ice screw in the soft, deteriorating ice, which had a 10m vertical section near the top (WI4+). The fourth lead looked easy from below—*how many times do I make that mistake!* But the ice turned out to be way worse than "not good." With huge relief, I found a good cam placement on the left side 10m up. Another 10m runout brought me to a horn, which I slung and then clipped with a couple screamers to weight down the sling; it reassured me up the final vertical section. Until now, the only thing I'd ever climbed with such difficult, rotten ice was Riptide on Mt. Patterson. The technique? Gently place an ice tool as high as possible and pull down till it kind of stops, do a quick weight test, close your eyes, and move up, then repeat. Ten meters of this brought me to a great rock belay above the ice (WI5+).

Two more pitches up a steep snow gully with a small, vertical ice step on each lead brought us to an easy snow couloir leading to the top. The final step below the upper couloir had such thin, rotten ice that I opted to climb the rock to the right, which was actually really fun with fair pro (5.8). Once in the upper couloir, we pretty much simul-climbed, just keeping a snow picket between us. Luckily, the gully was continuous all the way to the ridge just below the summit.

If Brainless Child (2,000', 5.9 WI5+ X) were in good condition, it could be recommended as a committing but safe WI4+ outing. The problem would lie in finding it in those conditions. The freeze-thaw from the sun is what makes the ice, but for good ice it really needs to be climbed when there's no sun on it. As it was, ice pummeled us all day. High up, we had one close call with rockfall. Generally, protection was marginal. I only placed three screws on the whole route, of which only one was good. Rock protection was good when available, which wasn't very often. Luckily, the belays were all pretty solid, although I belayed off my harness for all pitches except one. A huge thanks to Tyler for being an amazing partner on this quixotic quest. [*Editor's note: Tyler Adams passed away on October 12, 2014, in a flying accident. Steve Elder suggested an alternate name for their climb: "The Tyler Adams Memorial Route".*]

– STEVE ELDER

CALIFORNIA / YOSEMITE VALLEY

WIDOW'S TEARS, THE LURCH

OVER THE SUMMER, Jake Whittaker and I put up a new free route approximately 100 yards left of Widow's Tears amphitheater. We called the climb the Lurch (7 pitches, 5.12c/d), after one of the last moves on the route—by far the crux. The Lurch follows an obscure, unknown aid line that may be from the '90s, judging by the bolts at some anchors. Our line veers from the aid route in a few places to allow for free climbing and/or avoiding death. For example, a leftward traverse on the fourth pitch avoids monstrous and very precariously stacked, Volkswagen-size chunks of granite.

The aid route appears to climb to the major ledge 400' below the rim—our route stops short of this ledge by about 400'. You could keep going, but the quality of terrain diminishes

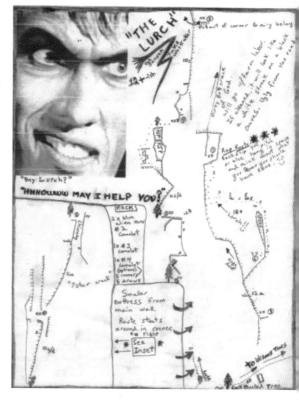

drastically, and it would take a silly amount of scrubbing and work—plus, this would leave a white streak on an otherwise black wall.

The Lurch is characterized by quality stone, quality climbing, and relative safety. It's a great route to throw oneself at if pushing the grade. And if you don't climb 12+, this might be a good one to see where you're at—you can really go for it at the cruxes. The seven pitches go at 10+, 11a/b, 12b, 11c/d, 10c, 12a, and 12c/d, and some are short for ease of belays and diminishing rope drag on the hard sections. Overall, the route is PG, but the cruxes are as G as G can be.

At the top of this no-summit, silly little route tucked into an obscure corner of the Ditch, climbers will be rewarded with a secluded, stunningly gorgeous perch where they can sit in peace, breathe, and take in the overall contentment that only accompanies climbing routes longer than a few pitches.

– BOB JENSEN

[Left] On the rugged approach to Lost Brother. The new routes Call of the Yeti and Bood & Coin both ascend the face on the left through the white rock scar. [Right] Richie Copeland leading up the white rock scar on Call of the Yeti. *Photos: Gabriel Mange*

LOST BROTHER, CALL OF THE YETI

LAST SPRING a team of jokesters with positive attitudes and some big-wall experience ganged up in Camp 4 for early morning libations. Richie Copeland was on the scene with his newly spray-painted chrome helmet and haulbag. A passerby couldn't help but crack a laugh for such blatant disregard for mainstream normality in climbing gear. Luke Smithwick, back from the Himalaya, turned up some music that made us shake our bodies a bit. I'm not sure if the convulsing was from the lack of caffeine, but it felt good.

Hours later, Luke, Richie, and I stumbled up the approach to Lost Brother. The woods and talus exuded a musky dew scent from the previous days of rain. Moss and leaves covered the rock and ground. The occasional views of El Capitan, the Three Brothers, Yosemite Falls, and the large monolith above kept us energized for the mission at hand. After an hour of battling our packs and cracking corny jokes we were at the base. We skirted to the west to gain a higher starting position.

The first pitch of Lost Brother ascends a splitter crack (5.7) that gains a large ledge, from which various routes start. From the left side of the ledge, the second pitch of our route starts in a finger-size crack that widens to four inches and involved a mix of free and easy aid. The next lead is mostly free, with some A1 climbing; this took us to a mildly sloping ledge where we set up camp for the evening. The next day we awoke to El Cap commanding the sunrise, which got us all dancing in our sleeping bags. What a blessing! Morning toast! From the ledge we climbed two pitches of A2, with some beaks, followed by a short rivet ladder that ends with some free climbing (5.8).

According to valley geologist Greg Stock, the last real action on Lost Brother was in 1857 during the valley's first recorded rockfall; the debris field from this slide reportedly covered 30 acres. We were the first to climb up this exposed, white rock scar—pitch six of our route goes through the center of the scar. The climbing is steep, exciting, physical, and fun, with various sized cracks (5.8 A2). From atop the headwall, moderate climbing (5.8 C1) gains the incredible summit. We used a handful of pins and installed 3/8" stainless bolts at the belays. The climb can be rappelled with two 70m ropes: Call of the Yeti (V 5.8 A2).

I dedicate this route to my friend Richie Copeland, a constant beacon of light and laughter. A month after this climb, Richie passed away while attempting another route in Yosemite Valley. [*Editor's note: This route is just left of Blood and Coin (see next report); the two routes share a portion of the first pitch off the initial ledge. Yosemitebigwall.com has an up-to-date photo showing the seven routes on Lost Brother.*]

– GABRIEL MANGE

LOST BROTHER, BLOOD & COIN

HAVING STARED AT Lost Brother for weeks on end, soloing routes on El Cap, I finally ventured over in May. Lost Brother hadn't seen a new route in a decade; however, I quickly found a line following a stark white flake that splits the upper wall; it seems to draw the eye from almost every vantage point on El Cap. After filling my iPod with a full set of Game of Thrones audiobooks, I set off to rope-solo the route.

I started by climbing an approach pitch shared by the existing routes to gain a big ledge, then traversed left to a corner system. Easy climbing (5.7 C1) brought me to a series of broken ledges left of the large slab climbed by Prowd (IV 5.5 A3) and right of Back in the Day (IV 5.10). From here, I climbed a full rope length on beak tips up a thin seam (A3) and through a small roof to gain an obvious triangular ledge. Above the ledge, I gained a bottoming seam that had looked good from my scope on the park road; however, it didn't pan out. To continue, I drilled a 90' rivet ladder up bulletproof rock that managed to destroy nine quarter-inch bits. This seemed an appropriate consequence for my roadside hubris.

After that unfortunate section, the route returned to solid cracks and roof systems, leading up and left via a mix of easy free and aid to reach the base of the white flake crowning the route. After a clean C1 section and some manteling onto broken ledges, I gained a stellar bivy ledge in the middle of the white scar. From here, a long pitch follows a thin and fragile flake to the end of the vertical climbing (A2), and another 280' of moderate climbing (5.8 C1) leads to the summit of Lost Brother.

Blood & Coin (V 5.7 A3) is primarily A2 nailing in thin seams or clean climbing with small gear in splitter cracks. The route took 11 days, spread out over two months, with seven nights total on the wall. Aside from pitches 3 and 4, I anticipate much of this route would go free with a strong attempt. All anchors contain at least two 3/8" bolts. Standout pitches include pitch 3—180' of mostly beak placements on a vertical wall—and pitches 8 and 9, the thin, splitter corner and flake system that makes up the obvious white scar. You can bivy atop pitches 3 and 8 without a portaledge, but the other ledges are not recommended.

Coincidentally, Gabriel Mange, Luke Smithwick, and Richie Copeland established Call of the Yeti (V 5.8 A2) on Lost Brother around the same time. [*See previous report.*] With these two new routes, I hope that Lost Brother will become less lost in the coming years.

– KEVIN DEWEESE

SENTINEL ROCK, NORTHEAST FACE, SHORT HAUL BAIT

FROM JUNE 4–5, Cheyne Lempe and Everett Phillips completed a new route up Sentinel Rock: Short Haul Bait (V 5.8 A2+). The route climbs seams, chimneys, and corners on the left edge of Sentinel's sheer northeast face for approximately 1,000'. Much loose rock and vegetation was encountered, and the duo placed four belay bolts, one lead bolt, and a rivet. The ascent took 35 hours from base to summit.

– WITH INFORMATION FROM **CHEYNE LEMPE**

GLACIER POINT APRON, JERICHO WALL, JERICHO

I'D STARED AT the obscure shady buttress on the left side of the Glacier Point Apron for three years while new-routing on Liberty Cap. So Steve Bosque and I decided to hike up in the summer of 2013 and check out the options for a new route. We chose a direct line up the 1,200' face, piecing together what would become a very moderate and fun route, almost devoid of the brutal Valley sun. We fixed ropes to the fifth pitch, where there was a very large sloping ledge to accommodate our gear. We could see signs of previous attempts by the left side of this ledge; they seemed to terminate where some tattered ropes were anchored.

We committed to a summit push during the onset of the massive Rim Fire. This proved to be a bad decision. Horrible, smoky conditions made it so we could barely see each other. For three days we awoke to our bivy covered in a thick blanket of ash. Finally, we decided to fix all of our ropes down to the ledge and come back to finish the route a few weeks later in October. During that time the government shutdown occurred, further delaying our summit bid. We named our high point the Government Shutdown Bivy.

Upon returning, we finished the remaining pitches and summited this independent buttress (which we've nicknamed Jericho Wall), in awe of what a cool route we had stumbled upon. The climbing is mostly clean, and 95 percent of the limited nailing is beaks, which are always fun. Rappelling the route is smooth and quick, as we equipped belays with stainless-steel hardware all the way down. We called the climb Jericho (V 5.8 A2+).

Kevin Deweese and Ryan Riggings completed the second ascent of Jericho two months later, and in January 2014, Kevin established a harder, three-pitch direct start to the route, which he called Horns of Jericho (A2/3). This route deserves future visits due to its moderate climbing in a part of Yosemite Valley that is very overlooked. 🖼 🔍

– **JOSH MUCCI**

THE HOURGLASS WALL, BLUE COLLAR

CLIMBING AROUND Yosemite Valley has been tremendously rewarding over the past few years, as obscure walls have delivered excellent new routes and solitary experiences. In the spring, Steve Bosque, Josh Mucci, and I established another of these routes, this one on the left flank of the Hourglass Wall, located right (east) of the Ribbon Falls Wall. The only other route on this wall, found a couple of hundred feet to the right of ours, is Indecision Time (VI 5.7 A4), authored by Eric Kohl; it climbs the namesake Hourglass feature to the aptly named Sherwood Forest summit (*AAJ 1994*).

Upon initial inspection, the first pitch did not present an obvious line; this was the crux in reaching the impeccable splitter cracks above. All three of us took turns establishing the first pitch, which involved every trick in the book: counter-balanced placements on loose flakes, upward driven knifeblades barely a millimeter deep, horizontal full-body stretches to hand-placed and wobbly Bugaboos, and intricate hooking. Steep and bulletproof stone proved to be the norm—it would continue for nine more long pitches.

The pitches leading up to the midway ledge, which we called the Horticulturist Bivy, involved a mix of moderate hooking, a big pendulum to ultra-thin beaking, and also clean climbing up splitter cracks on cams. The only questionable rock on the route was a band of diorite found just above this ledge. Extreme caution was needed to navigate this loose section, complete with shifting pillars and blocks.

Above the diorite, perfect cracks awaited to the summit. Some were climbed all clean and some with a few pins; however, the final 250' ascended a perfect wide crack, which gobbled all of our big gear. We finished the climb on May 20 and descended the same route: Blue Collar (V A3). The route was climbed completely via aid. Many of the pitches will go free, but how many and at what grade will be for those that follow to determine.

Overall, this route was a gem—just hard enough to keep it interesting while following some of the best features one could hope for in a new route. The name of the route seemed fitting, as the nature of "blue collar" climbing demanded that our route pushes were made only on the weekends, after which our ropes were left fixed, in order to return to our 9-to-5 jobs. Adding up the many weekends we spent approaching the wall, ascending our lines, unpacking gear, pushing the route higher, repacking our gear, descending our lines, and reversing the approach would have us spending approximately 11 days on the route in total.

We equipped the route for rappel from the summit with bolted stainless the whole way down. Fixing a rope on pitch 7–8 is necessary for retreat, as there's a large roof to pass.

– KEVIN DEWEESE

HIGHER CATHEDRAL ROCK, NORTH FACE, THE CONSTANT GARDENER

CHEYNE LEMPE and Ethan Pringle established the Constant Gardener (V 5.11+ R A3) on the north face of Higher Cathedral Rock, from September 12–13. The approximately 1,000' climb ascends 600' of new terrain before joining the Chouinard-Kamps-Pratt Route (*AAJ 1961*). Lempe and Pringle placed one bolt and tried to free climb as much as possible, but they were thwarted by vegetation-filled cracks.

– *INFORMATION FROM* CHEYNE LEMPE

CALIFORNIA / HIGH SIERRA

LAUREL MOUNTAIN, EAST FACE, HAI'NANU

IN LOCAL PAIUTE LEGEND, a young boy named Hai'nanu disrespected Tuvaimawiye'e (what we now call Convict Lake) and challenged its power. The lake swelled up and chased Hai'nanu high into the mountains. After climbing to the top of the highest peaks, Hai'nanu was just barely able to escape by jumping through a hole in the sky.

Over July 21–26, Kristoffer Wickstrom and I established a new route on the previously unclimbed "Sevehah Cliff," a prominent collection of cliffs and spires between the Northeast Gully and the Pinner Couloir, on the east face of Laurel Mountain (11,812'). Hai'nanu (7 pitches, 5.10 A2+) follows weaknesses up the right side of the main wall of the Sevehah Cliff and then a long ridge to the summit.

Laurel Mountain is one of the most accessible big mountains in the Sierra. After only two miles of largely flat trail walking, Kristoffer and I detoured toward a 400' apron of easy scrambling, which leads to the base of the Sevehah Cliff. Our route began in a right-facing corner, where there is a distinct junction of black and white rock.

Kristoffer led the first pitch and found moderate but hard-to-protect climbing up to a sloping ledge. The second pitch leaves the dihedral and climbs an obvious crack to the right. The rest of the climb continues in the same fashion: follow a dihedral until there's a natural jog right into another crack. Kristoffer rope-soloed pitch five, which turned out to be the aid crux of the route and involved thin nailing with beaks in a large corner easily visible from the valley below. Above this pitch, we climbed two moderate, right-trending pitches up a gully to reach a large notch and the top of the wall proper.

Once on the crest of the east ridge, nearly 3,000' of easy terrain (mostly Class III with some harder steps) leads to the summit. Along the way we passed five very loose but easy towers we dubbed the Pillars of Jenga. From Laurel's summit, the most appropriate descent would be to fly off, jumping through a hole in the sky.

Despite Mt. Laurel's reputation for loose rock, we found the most technical climbing on our route to be fairly solid. In total, we spent four days fixing to the top of pitch five (returning to the ground each night), and on the fifth day we tossed our lines from the top of the wall to make the final push to the summit (gathering our gear afterward). We climbed the main wall in seven pitches before mostly simul-climbing the east ridge. We placed three anchor bolts on the route (one each at the top of pitches one, four, and five).

– PRESTON RHEA

[Left] The Juggernaut, showing (1) Arch Rival (III 5.10, Barnes-Greenberg, 2013). (2) Crimson Gem (III 5.10, Barnes-Greenberg, 2013). (3) Dihedral Route (III 5.10, Clevenger-Dougherty-Farrell-Rowell, *AAJ 1975*). (4) Beckey Route (III 5.10, Beckey-Black-Roberts, *AAJ 1974*). (5) Unfinished project. (6) Irresistible Force (III 5.10+, Ferman-Nettle, 2000). (7) Hidden Agenda (III 5.11-, Barnes-Greenberg, 2013; *out of view*). *Jim Barnes*

JUGGERNAUT, NEW ROUTES

MY INFATUATION with the Juggernaut began years ago. Dave Nettle and I were high on the Incredible Hulk, waiting out a summer thundershower. As the rain eased and the clouds lifted, I noticed the profile of the Juggernaut to the west. I later asked Dave about it; naturally, he'd put up a route on its beautiful north face. Each visit to the Hulk's summit ridge increased my desire to visit this remote part of the Sawtooth Range.

In July 2013, I wrangled Nate Greenberg to join me. We made our way in past Little Slide Canyon and into the upper reaches of Robinson Creek. We had Dave's topos for the three established routes: the original route (Beckey-Black-Roberts, *AAJ 1974*), the Dihedral Route (Clevenger-Dougherty-Farrell-Rowell, *AAJ 1975*), and Irresistible Force (Ferman-Nettle, 2000). The Dihedral Route, a beautiful left-facing corner that splits the north face, immediately caught our eye. The climbing was outstanding, and the descent, we discovered, is an easy walk-off. The next day we tackled Irresistible Force, a sandbagged 5.10+. We were smitten. Here was an amazing cliff with tons of potential. Though the cracks are often lined with lichen, the rock is generally very good. Any intrepid climber could see the diamond in the rough.

[Photo] Nate Greenberg leading pitch three of the Dihedral Route (III 5.10) on the Juggernaut. *Jim Barnes*

Over the next several weeks, Nate and I stared at our photos, brainstorming potential lines. In August we finally returned, excited about the prospect of picking some plums. Over the next three days, we established three routes and started a fourth project (out the obvious, huge corner left of Irresistible Force). All of the routes are five to six pitches, with most of the climbing in the 5.9 to 5.10 range. We only placed one bolt and a pin for an anchor; all the climbing went clean. Staying with the superhero theme, we named our routes Crimson Gem (III 5.10), Arch Rival (III 5.10+)—both on the north face, left of the Dihedral Route—and Hidden Agenda (III 5.11-), which climbs the right side of the formation.

As the Hulk gets busier, formations like the Juggernaut seem more appealing. While it is justifiably overshadowed (the approach is longer, the routes are shorter), Juggy boasts great camping, easy-access water, no crowds, and moderate climbing on good stone. A motivated team could climb two or more routes in a day. 📷 🔍

– JIM BARNES

MT. CHAMBERLIN AREA, CRABTREE CRAGS, NEW ROUTES

ON SEPTEMBER 9, Scott Sinner and I hiked 12 miles from Whitney Portal to the base of Mt. Chamberlin (sometimes spelled Mt. Chamberlain). Going from sea level to over 13,000' with a 60lb pack knocked me down a peg, and I slept for 14 hours. We camped on the eastern shore of the upper, and largest, Crabtree Lake, and just a few hundred yards from the base of the main north face of Chamberlin. The next morning we decided to take a look at the handsome wall just west of Chamberlin's north face. This wall is east-facing, approximately 700' tall, and is located just right (west) of the regular descent gully from Chamberlin. The wall is called the Crabtree Crags by Bart O'Brien in *AAJ 1993*.

[Above] The east face of the Crabtree Crags, located above the Upper Crabtree Lake, showing the Portzline-Sinner (700', III 5.10-). The one other reported route on these formations is the Harden-O'Brien Route (*AAJ 1993*), which likely starts a few hundred feet right of the line shown. [Below] Scott Sinner leading the seventh pitch of Skinny Girls (1,000', IV 5.11 C1), on an unnamed 1,000' wall above the Lower Crabtree Lake. *Photos: Dustin Portzline*

Two obvious crack systems split the east face of the Crabtree Crags, and with no obvious signs of travel on either, we chose the left-hand line. A hand- to fist-size crack leads up a few long pitches to an alcove, where the crack pinches down to a short fingers section. Several rope lengths of fun, moderate romping lead to the top of the formation. Well protected and with lots of blue-collar 5.9 crack climbing between a few short cruxes, this route makes a nice warm-up for Chamberlin suitors: Portzline-Sinner (700', III 5.10-). From the report in *AAJ 1993*, I would guess the Harden-O'Brien route is located a few hundred feet down and right of our route, at the northeast toe of the wall.

The following morning, September 11, we awoke early and stumbled in the frigid dawn to attempt Asleep at the Wheel (V 5.12-, *AAJ 2002*), a masterpiece by Mike Pennings and Jimmy Haden on Mt. Chamberlin. We bailed after a few pitches but were impressed by the immaculate rock quality and purity of the line. Tails between our legs, we packed up and walked west down the valley, following the outlet of Upper Crabtree Lake downstream for about one mile. Once at

Lower Crabtree Lake, a north-facing wall just above caught our attention. A single laser-cut crack splits the right edge of this clean buttress. "Look at that hand crack!" Scott exclaimed. But as we hiked toward the base of the wall, the features exploded in scale: What I'd thought was a stem box in the first pitch was actually a 15'-wide slot, and the splitter we first noticed was, well, bigger than hands. We reconnoitered the first pitch (5.10) and left the rope hanging to give us a warm-up the following morning.

Our hand crack turned out to be a flaring squeeze chimney. The sting of committing groveling (5.9 R/X) was only soothed by impressive rock quality and occasional knobs. Above we found more excellent, varied climbing up dikes and cracks. A short, steep boulder problem out of an alcove (5.11-) set us up below a crisp tips splitter, unseen from below. Scott grabbed the rack and gave 'er, free climbing until his skin split and he was forced to aid 8' around a suspect block (5.11 C1). The next pitch was a long, steep corner, with a 50' section on lower quality rock that required aid (5.10 C1). Engaging climbing for a few more pitches took us to horizontal ground.

We ended our climb at the tip of the formation, but the terrain continues gradually upward beyond it. We traversed off to the east (climber's left of the route), contouring on a broad bench and then descending steep fourth-class slabs. The route could likely go free at 5.12, or the aid sections could be bypassed by an attractive crack system just right. We placed and removed one piton. We named our route Skinny Girls (1,000', IV 5.11 C1) after our girlfriends, who would have fit in the squeeze chimney better than we did. It is a highly recommended outing in a pristine setting.

— DUSTIN PORTZLINE

MT. BARNARD, EAST PILLAR, THE GOOD, THE BAD, THE AWESOME

ON AUGUST 10, Greg Horvath and I established a new route on the east pillar of Mt. Barnard (13,680'), which is ca 3 miles north of the Mt. Whitney massif. I first eyed the route a year earlier during an ascent of the east pillar on which Mike Maiden and I failed to locate the Rowell-Auger (*AAJ 1973*) and instead established a line with six new pitches up to 5.9.

The Good, The Bad, The Awesome (1,500', IV 5.11) follows a prominent right-facing dihedral system beginning about 20' above the lowest point of the wall. After 800' it intersects the northeast arête. We climbed mostly in the corner itself and once reaching the arête climbed splitter finger cracks up to 5.11. While the rock quality ranges from poor to excellent, the climbing predominantly consists of enjoyable 5.10 cracks. We climbed the route onsight, swapping leads, and found perfect belay ledges every 60m to 70m.

— DOUG TOMCZIK

BASTILLE BUTTRESS, SOUTH FACE, SMALL TOWN THROW DOWN

MYLES MOSER AND I began climbing a new route on Bastille Buttress in October. Located on the south side of Lone Pine Peak, the Bastille is a whale of granite soaring about 2,000' and with only two established routes: the Beckey Route (Beckey-Brown-Haas, *AAJ 1972*) and Papillon (Schneider-Slate, 1987). With the help of many local climbers, we humped several loads of equipment, including a portaledge, to the base. Our goal was to start at the toe of the wall and follow dikes to a finish on the true headwall, which was still untouched.

The logistics for this route were different from our normal routine, for several reasons. First, we had two buddies, Andrew Soleman and Neil Woodruff, who wanted to partake in the adventure, but because of work conflicts could only commit to the first few days. Thus we decided to fix the first 1,000' or so, until they had to depart, then push capsule-style to the top. Next, the wall is a massive slab. Normally, we go for crack systems and only bolt the blank sections in between, but we knew this was going to involve a lot of bolting. Plus, the Bastille is deceivingly foreshortened from the ground. When Beckey and his partners climbed it, they thought it would only be seven pitches—they summited on the 17th pitch!

We placed a total of 105 bolts, including bolted anchors, and climbed 11 new pitches before linking into the last two pitches of the Beckey Route. Most of the pitches were 200' or longer, and 10 of the 13 pitches are between 5.10 and 5.12. The granite was stellar and required no cleaning other than a crack on the first pitch. We encountered slabs, troughs, dikes, and black swirls on this sustained calf-killer. Unfortunately, a bolt ladder was required through the steepest part of the wall; although we were disappointed about this at first, it proved to be quiet fun once finished. It's 5.12 to reach the ladder and will more than likely go free at a harder grade now that the protection is in.

Because of all the support we received from the local climbing community, we called it Small Town Throw Down (13 pitches, V 5.12 AO). A special hats off goes to the duo SoulMan and Sinner, who started the second ascent before we were even off the wall! 📷 🔍

– AMY JO NESS

FLATIRON BUTTE, EAST FACE

OVER A WEEKEND in mid-June, Caitlin Taylor and I established a new route and first free ascent on the remote Flatiron Butte (ca 11,600'), a seldom-visited wall somewhat lost to history. In recent years the area has come to be known as Shangri La. On June 14 we made the first ascent of Parasitic Nematode (IV 5.10+), which climbs a right-leaning crack and corner system on the right side of the east face. The route contains about 500' of sustained climbing up steep cracks and corners before joining the northeast ridge (Beckey-Nolting, *AAJ 1981*). There are no fixed belays or bolts on this route; a standard rack with the addition of a few offset cams will suffice.

The next day we ventured up the central part of the face, hoping to free climb Et Tu,

[Left] Flatiron Butte, showing known routes: (1) Brutus of Wyde Memorial Route (V 5.11a, Musiyenko-Taylor, 2014), the free version of Et Tu, Brute! (V A2 5.9+, Binder-Harris-Holland-Hove, 2001). (2) Parasitic Nematode (IV 5.10+, Musiyenko-Taylor, 2014), which joins the northeast ridge. (3) Northeast ridge (Beckey-Nolting, *AAJ 1981*). *Vitaliy Musiyenko*

Brute! (V A2 5.9+, Binder-Harris-Holland-Hove, 2001). This ca 1,500' route follows natural crack and corner systems and contains some bolted belays from the first-ascent team. Near the upper pitches, which were previously aided, I led a super-fun two-pitch variation. The first pitch features a double roof and a slightly overhanging crack that widens from ring locks to fist jams—the enduro crux. The technical crux follows with a wide overhang where large cams are highly recommended. Even though it looks like the route tops out above this, difficulties up to 5.8 continue before the summit. Overall, the route seemed like a step up in difficulty from the southwest face of Conness, but without any step down in quality. I dubbed the free version Brutus of Wyde Memorial Route (V 5.11a), named for the late Bruce Binder.

As a side note, I carried out over 40lbs of garbage from this "secret area," no doubt left by climbers—including sleeping bags, bivy sacks, rope tarps, and a ripped-up haulbag.

– VITALIY MUSIYENKO

BUBBS CREEK WALL, SOUTH FACE, THE EMPEROR

EXPLORING NEW LINES on peaks deep in the backcountry rarely makes someone a stronger climber, right? At least I didn't think so. Having read about Bubbs Creek Wall from multiple Internet threads, I wanted to see it for myself. This wall had five established routes along with some free variations, all put up by true all-star teams of backcountry, first-ascent smashers. I first made the nine-mile hike in July to look for a new line on the east or west faces, though these walls turned out to be full of vegetation. Thoughts of a line on the south face, splitting down the middle between the Samurai Warrior and What's Up Bubb, crossed my mind, but chances of that seemed slim to none. I looked anyway.

All hopes for a new line seemed like delusions after I aided one pitch and encountered a blank face above. However, with a second day on the wall, my partner and I discovered a stance to drill from on that blank face, and then another. By the end of the trip we had completed three new pitches and an ascent of Aquaman (*AAJ 1984*). The following week I came back and climbed two more pitches; another trip produced four more. Every time I returned to climb, I went home humbled

[Above] Pitch 10 of the Emperor, the Railroad Dike (5.11a). *Vitaliy Musiyenko*

and physically and mentally drained by the continuous difficulties and endlessness of the wall.

Each pitch seemed highly improbable, but simply being on such a beautiful wall yielded great satisfaction. The climbing was beautiful and varied, from technical faces to burly liebacks, stems, and awesome dikes. I was soon able to redpoint a couple of the pitches, but many required direct aid. With such a grim beginning, I could have abandoned this madness, but I couldn't keep it off my mind. When I was at work I would stare at the photos of the wall and ponder the

[Below] Bubbs Creek Wall, south face, showing: (1) Crystal Banzai (VI 5.11 A3, Joe-Leversee, *AAJ 1987*). (2) Samurai Warrior (V 5.11 A1, Nettle-Thau, *AAJ 1998*)—Brandon Thau and Peter Croft completed a free ascent of this line in 2005 via a 5.12a variation that they dubbed Ronin. (3) The Emperor (2014, V 5.11d A1). (4) What's Up Bubb (VI 5.9 A3, Brown-Mayo, 2000)—Luke Stefurak and Casey Zak completed a free ascent of this line in 2014 via a few variations at 5.12a and dubbed the line Sensei. (5) Beckey Route (IV 5.8 A2, Beckey-Cundiff-Losleben-McGoey, *AAJ 1976*). (6) Aquaman (IV 5.10+, Leversee-McConachie, *AAJ 1984*, doesn't reach summit). *Vitaliy Musiyenko*

overhanging corners. *Is it possible to get to them? Would the giant roof allow a free passage?* Over time, individual pitches went from impossible on top-rope to doable on lead.

After about 20 days of work on the route, using a variety of tactics, my seventh partner, Luke Stefurak, and I completed the climb ground-up, including the final six pitches to the top of the formation. Out of 16 pitches, I led 13. [*The last 400' are shared with the recently free climbed route What's Up Bubb.*] Even though free climbing on the Emperor (16 pitches, V 5.11d A1) initially seemed too difficult for me, the first eight pitches now go free—5.11c, 5.11a, 5.11d, 5.11c, 5.11c, 5.11a, 5.11a, and 5.11b. Additionally, pitch 9 has been followed free, pitch 10 goes at 5.11a, pitch 11 goes at 5.10a, pitch 12 was followed clean at solid 5.11, and pitch 13 will go at 5.11a and was also followed free. The only big question mark is a tough 15' section on pitch 14. I hope to free climb the rest of this outrageously sustained route next season. 📷 🔍

— VITALIY MUSIYENKO

CASTLE DOME, SOUTHEAST ARÊTE

CASTLE DOME (10,800'), in Kings Canyon, has been on my list of places to visit for quite a while, with good-looking rock, a high adventure factor, giant approach, and only one recorded climb: Silmarillion (IV 5.10), established by Mark Menge and Jack Roberts (*AAJ 1979*).

In mid-July, Caitlin Taylor and I made the beautiful, 13-mile one-way approach to the dome over a three-day weekend. After setting up a scenic camp in the meadow below the rock, we set our sights on the southeast arête, which forms the right-hand skyline of the dome.

The ensuing seven-pitch climb provided an aesthetic line in an incredible setting. The southeast arête (1,100', IV 5.10 PG13) offers good variety—fun face, big jugs, pulling over wild roofs, and a few cracks—all at moderate difficulties. Later in the summer the route saw its first repeat ascent, with the climbers noting its potential to become a new, moderate Sierra classic. 📷

– VITALIY MUSIYENKO

THE SPHINX, NORTHEAST BUTTRESS, COTTON MOUTH KHAFRA

As FULL-TIME DESK JOCKEYS, Daniel Jeffcoach and I did not have an extra day for an approach that gains 4,000' over seven miles. We did not want to carry much water either. We thought our new route on the Sphinx (9,146') would go quickly and be no more than 600'. [*The Sphinx has two other routes, much shorter and easier in difficulty. See R.J. Secor's guide to the High Sierra.*]

After downclimbing a 1,000' slab on the approach, we realized our one liter of water was to be much less than desired. Not willing to bail, we started up the northeast buttress. The first pitch began with solid 5.10 climbing. The rest of the climbing was often spicy, but Daniel provided excellent stress relief. After many hours of waterless climbing, sustained in the 5.9–5.10 range, with a 5.11 crux, we eventually reached the top of our 1,500'-plus new route in the fading light. We had drilled one bolt to back up an anchor comprised of a single half-decent cam. We would've placed a few more but had no time to waste. We had barely enough daylight to scramble down to our packs and come up with a clever name for our route: Cotton Mouth Khafra (IV 5.11a). 📷 🔍

– VITALIY MUSIYENKO

[Photo] A pristine camp below Castle Dome. The southeast arête takes the right skyline of the formation. Silmarillion (IV 5.10, Menge-Roberts, *AAJ 1979*) ascends a dihedral up the central wall. *Vitaliy Musiyenko*

TOKOPAH VALLEY, NEW ROUTES

TOKOPAH VALLEY is an overlooked gem tucked within the west side of Sequoia National Park. While it's known primarily for the 1,000' Watchtower, towering over Tokopah Falls, the north side of the valley holds several beautiful granite formations with a variety of climbs that will please crack, slab, and even sport climbers. The only thing missing is people. Although a mere handful of climbs have been reported since the early 1980s, climbers have been steadily exploring the domes and cliffs. Many of these adventurous souls have been seasonal employees who came and went without leaving much more than an occasional bolt or rusty piece of fixed gear, making the climbing history in the valley patchy at best. The climbing, scenery, and rock quality are on par with the best in the Sierra.

Over the last few years some classic routes have been pioneered and some older routes rediscovered. In November 2013, Matt Schutz and I went to Upper Tokopah Dome (a.k.a. Santa Cruz Dome) and established a beautiful route we dubbed Tan In November (4 pitches, 5.9). Later, in December, Jonathan Zerlang and I made the first ascent of a pleasant moderate route on Tokopah Wall, directly across from the Watchtower: Snow Boots (7 pitches, 5.8).

After hearing stories of incredible rock in a picturesque setting within two hours of the road, Vitaliy Musiyenko, Tom Ruddy, and Hunter Bonilla joined me at the Tokopah Domes in January 2014. Vitaliy likes to suffer, so our first objective was an obvious 500' offwidth splitting the west face of Lower Tokopah Dome. It ended up being pain-free and provided us with the first recorded ascent of the Boardwalk Chimney (3 pitches, 5.8). That same morning, Tom and Hunter beat us to the summit while establishing Welcome to Wal-Mart (4 pitches, 5.10d).

In April, not yet satiated, Vitaliy and I returned to Tokopah and finished a line on Upper Tokopah Dome that he and Tom had started on the previous trip. Usually It's Sunny (5 pitches, 5.10d) starts near the toe of the dome, right of the big corner of Funky Neurosis/Southwest Face (*AAJ 1990*). While it is usually sunny in the Sierra, we got snowed and rained on during this trip. Over the following two and a half days, Vitaliy and I returned to Lower Tokopah Dome to put up Beauty and the Beast (5 pitches, 5.11a).

Still haunted by an incomplete and improbable-looking route that Tom Ruddy and Hunter Bonilla had started on Lower Tokopah Dome, Tom, Vitaliy, and Brian Prince visited the valley yet again in May to complete the crown jewel of the new dome climbs: Tokopah Reality (5 pitches, 5.11). Two offwidth pitches gain a nice ledge underneath the massive arching roof on the southwest side of the dome. From here an incredible, overhanging hand crack goes up the corner and traverses out a flake, almost forcing the leader to cut his feet and campus in order to reach the finishing mantel onto a small ledge. A couple more fun pitches up chicken heads lead directly to the summit.

Late in June, Rob Brown and I made the last trip of the season, traveling to Silliman Point, a rock northwest of the Tokopah Domes, sitting on a ridge across from Mt. Silliman. We climbed seven fun pitches up a recess and onto the ridge, passing cracks, blocks, and highly featured granite along the way. Although we saw no signs of previous passage, we later learned that the first ascent had been made by Skip Gaynard and a friend in 1973: West Recess (7 pitches, 5.7). All of these climbs were climbed ground-up, though several of them took a bit of work before they were redpointed. 📄 📷 🔍

– DANIEL JEFFCOACH

[Next page] Tom Ruddy leading out a very steep flake on Tokopah Reality (5 pitches, 5.11), one of many new routes on the granite domes of Tokopah Valley. *Brian Prince*

[Above] Jon Glassberg following pitch 4 (5.10c) of the 11-pitch new route Bromancing the Stone (1,200', IV 5.10d) in Red Rocks. *Chris Weidner*

BRIDGE MOUNTAIN, EAST FACE, BROMANCING THE STONE

ON JANUARY 8, 2015, Jon Glassberg and I climbed a long new route on the east face of the East Peak of Bridge Mountain. The first six pitches climb a wide crack system visible on the left side of this multi-colored wall and can be seen from the 13-mile loop road, between Icebox and Juniper canyons. The easiest approach ascends the middle of three broad gullies beneath the east side of Bridge Mountain, starting from a small pullout on the right, less than a mile before the Pine Creek trailhead.

We found two bolted anchors on the first three pitches (5.6–5.9 cracks and chimneys) and then a bail anchor about 12m up the fourth pitch, suggesting a prior attempt on the route. The fourth pitch heads up a gaping chimney, which narrows to a squeeze, and finally a finger and hand crack (5.10c). From there, four more pitches of cracks and chimneys gain the crux ninth pitch, which climbs a roof crack to a slab (5.10d). Two more pitches gain the top of the ridge and complete Bromancing the Stone (1,200', IV 5.10d).

To descend, stay as close to the ridge crest as possible, careful not to veer into Icebox Canyon. We made one single-rope rappel off a tree (perhaps not necessary) then followed cairns, in the dark, down a delightfully improbable path that was never harder than fourth class. Either traverse the long hillside back to the base of the route or continue straight down a gully to the loop road (2–3 hours). 📷

– CHRIS WEIDNER

ARIZONA / SEDONA

TIM TOULA SPIRE, A BETTER WAY TO DIE

JAKE DAYLEY and I made the first ascent of a spire in Mormon Canyon, on the north side of the drainage, directly across from Earth Angel. The route follows a crack system on the west face before traversing to the southwest aspect of the summit block. We placed one bolt at the belay for pitch two and a two-bolt rappel anchor on the summit: A Better Way To Die (2 pitches, 190', 5.10+ R/X). The climbing is funky, thin, burly, and committing. Props to Jake, who forgot his harness that day in October but still agreed to climb with a bowline tied around his waist. We named the spire after Tim Toula and the route after Tim's 1995 guidebook to the area, which is famously sparse on information, for those who like a taste of the unknown. "T.N.T." has left an indelible mark on Sedona climbing with his prolific and bold first ascents. He knows how to "bust a move," even if the rock is crumbling and the gear is bad. We follow in his footsteps with trepidation and respect! We want this spire to be a tribute to a mentor, inspiration, and friend.

[Photo] Jake Tipton atop Tim Toula Spire after climbing A Better Way To Die (2 pitches, 190', 5.10+ R/X). *Jake Daley*

— JAKE TIPTON

IDAHO / SAWTOOTH RANGE

ELEPHANT'S PERCH, BOOMER'S STORY

ON THE LAST weekend in June I met up with Ian Cavanaugh and Peter Hekan to take care of some unfinished business at the Elephant's Perch. It was my third trip in twice as many years, and we finally managed to free climb Boomer's Story (V 5.13-). Big thanks to Brad Heller and Jason Klophaus for their support on previous attempts.

Boomer's Story is located between the Beckey and Mountaineer's routes, and features the typically awesome rock quality and crack climbing found up at the Perch. The pitches stack up like so: 5.8, 5.13-, 5.11, 5.12-, 5.11-, 5.10-, 5.9, 5.8, 5.7, 5.7. The first five pitches have the best

[Photo] Ari Menitove engaging the crux (5.13-) of Boomer's Story. *Ian Cavanaugh*

rock and most engaging climbing, and the second-pitch crux requires pretty sustained and techy stemming technique that almost exploded my thighs and calves. It's the kind of corner that makes the angels sing in harmony.

We free climbed the route from the ground up, after aiding the crux pitch first to rehearse it on top-rope. Amazingly, it required hardly any cleaning. We left two pitons to protect the tricky opening moves, but I imagine they could be removed easily if someone were to actually fall on them.

— ARI MENITOVE

TEMPLE OF SINAWAVA: DATURA (FIRST FREE ASCENT), DR. SPACEMAN

LAST MARCH, I spent my spring break in Zion National Park with Mike Brumbaugh and Andy Raether. Not caring about grades, crowds, or really anything other than having a good time on a sandstone big wall, we set out to find something that piqued our interest. We came away with two free ascents of adventurous routes: Datura (900', 5.12 R, originally climbed solo by Jim Beyer at 5.9 A2, *AAJ 1981*) and Dr. Spaceman (900', 5.12 PG), a mostly new route that climbs adjacent to an older aid route. Both routes are located near the start of the Narrows on the Temple of Sinawava—Datura climbs a gaping chimney on the center-left side of this wall, and Dr. Spaceman is located about 150' to the right.

— ROB PIZEM

WATCHMAN, CENTRAL PILLAR, FIRST FREE ASCENT

JASON NELSON AND I free climbed the Central Pillar/Watchman Direct on the Watchman on October 30. Bryan Bird and Zach Lee had previously freed most of the route, up to a feature called the Red Clam, at 5.11. For us, the remaining three pitches went free at 5.10+. We climbed the route onsight in a day, descending via the south ridge after 14 pitches (420m, V 5.11c). 📷 🔍 ▤

– STEFFAN GREGORY

UTAH / UINTA MOUNTAINS

REIDS PEAK, NORTHEAST FACE

ON OCTOBER 4, Scott Adamson, Angela VanWiemeersch, and I established a new ice and mixed line, The One Who Knocks (550', WI6 M5 R/X), on the northeast face of Reids Peak (11,708') in the Uinta Mountains of northeastern Utah. Although visible from the Mirror Lake Highway, the line is difficult to see and has a short window of accessibility when there's enough snow to form melt-freeze ice in the chimney but before there's too much snow and the road closes for winter. The shadow of Bald Mountain (11,942') keeps the ice itself out of the sun. It's about an hour uphill hike to reach the climb

With a week of snow in the Uintas, then rapidly warming temps, we found the right mix of conditions, with fully formed ice on three out of four pitches. We each took one of the harder leads, and in the alpine spirit we continued from the top of the route up the northeast ridge to the summit of Reids Peak before descending. Although much of the route was ice, our ice screws functioned merely as decoration. This is a unique route for Utah. So far, there are not many alpine ice and mixed routes, and ones of this length and difficulty are pretty rare.

[Above] Angela VanWiemeersch leads the third pitch of The One Who Knocks. *Nathan Smith*

Not having had enough, Scott and Angela decided to try for another line in the fading light while I bowed out. After reclimbing the first pitch of The One Who Knocks, they found two pitches of thin ice and mixed climbing. They left two pitons and slings atop the route and rappelled: Golden Spike (345', WI4 M5 R). Again, rock gear and no ice screws. 📷 ▤ 🔍

– NATHAN SMITH

MONTANA

BARRONETTE PEAK, SOUTHEAST FACE, SICK BIRD

THE YEAR 1998 marked my first year of ice climbing. That's when I first laid eyes on the approximately 3,000' southeast face of Barronette Peak (10,354')—all covered with snow, ice pillars, rock gullies, and cliff bands—located in north Yellowstone, outside of Cooke City.

In November 2002, Jim Earl and Jeff Hollenbaugh made the first ascent of this huge face: Jim and Jeff's Excellent Adventure (1,500', 5.8 WI5). However, there was one plumb line that still remained unclimbed, to the left of Jim and Jeff's. The route starts on an established pitch of ice at the foot of the face called South of Summit. From there it follows the major weakness up and right, with pitches of ice and mixed climbing in the upper gully.

Justin Griffin and I made the first ascent up this line of ancient volcanic rock, ice, and snow, from base to summit, on February 20, 2015. Over its nearly 3,000' of gain I would estimate a total of about 600' of "real" climbing—the rest was pure snow wallowing. We encountered a lot of unprotectable ice and rock in the crux sections, with difficulties up to M7. It snowed lightly during the morning hours of our ascent, and we got blasted from spindrift and small natural avalanches. This route is a giant avalanche path, and unless the conditions are perfect it's not worth the risk—hence my excitement after 17 years of waiting to finally climb this thing! Our car-to-car time was 11 hours. We named the route Sick Bird (2,800', WI5 M7) after our good friend Ross "Sick Bird" Lynn. Ross was an avid admirer of this beautiful corner of Yellowstone and all the adventure it holds. 📷

– WHIT MAGRO

BEARTOOTH MOUNTAINS, LAST CALL

ON OCTOBER 17 Chris Guyer and I went on an early morning recon run in the northern part of the central Beartooths. About five miles in we discovered a brilliant vein of ice dripping down a prominent north-facing wall. On October 19, Tanner Callender, Chris, and I started up toward the ice at 4 a.m., reaching the base of the wall by early morning.

We climbed moderate mixed terrain for several pitches before getting to the base of a large headwall where there were several drips of unreachable ice. At this point we traversed up a snow ramp to gain the ridgeline. Once on the ridge, a small traverse led us to the approximately 1,000' vein of ice we'd spied the day prior. In order to move quickly, we simul-climbed the next 500' of ice, which was mostly moderate with short, technical mixed sections. The final three leads contained more sustained and technical thin-ice climbing, and the route finishes in a tight corner system with lots of exposure. At many times the ice was only a foot wide.

We finished in the dark and then tried a walk-off from the summit plateau. After going the wrong way, we wandered a snaking ridgeline for several hours before finding a good descent route back to the trail. We arrived at the car psyched and tired around 2 a.m. We named our route Last Call. It has about 2,000' of vertical gain from base to summit, and we broke up the climbing into 13 pitches. 📷

– AARON MULKEY

[Previous page] Justin Griffin leads the final pitch of Sick Bird (2,800', WI5 M7) on the southeast face of Barronette Peak, located in north Yellowstone. *Whit Magro*

STORM POINT, SOUTHEAST FACE, HIGHWAY TO HEAVEN

IN JULY, Nobuyuki "Yuki" Fujita and I climbed a possible new route on the southeast face of Storm Point in Cascade Canyon: Highway to Heaven (11 pitches, 5.8). Our climb is located far to the right of the Guides Wall and what guidebook author Leigh Ortenburger calls the "central bowl" and southeast ridge of Storm Point, where most reported development has taken place.

"New," of course, is a loaded term in the Tetons; there's been a lot of unreported climbing activity on Storm Point over the years. We found two fixed pins along the upper part of our route, though most of the terrain we climbed seemed new. In any case, the climb provides a great alternative to the crowded Guide's Wall around the corner. We descended via some scrambling and double-rope rappels. 📷 🔍

– RON WATTERS

[Photo] Blake McCord following the crux pitch of the West Face Dihedral. *Matt Spohn*

FREMONT PEAK, WEST FACE DIHEDRAL, FIRST FREE ASCENT

FROM JULY 16–24, Steve Richert, Blake McCord, and I—all Type 1 diabetics— spent time in the Titcomb Basin of the Wind River Range, hoping to establish first ascents and first free ascents. We packed in with horses to Island Lake, then shuttled loads by foot to a base camp below the west face of Fremont Peak. We spent the rest of the day eyeing the enormous wall with binoculars.

Over the next two days we tried to put up a new route, without success, on the westernmost flank of Fremont's maze-like west face. The attempted route followed a beautiful dihedral and wide crack system, which led to a massive ridgeline where we eventually bailed. We found excellent rock and the climbing tended to be difficult. In all we put up seven pitches, with difficulties up to 5.11 A1+, and placed four bolts and one piton.

Feeling a bit overwhelmed by the magnitude of the west face, we opted for some fun days off, scaling small faces and long slabs. After a few days we set our sights on completing the first free ascent of

[Above] Titcomb Basin in the alpenglow, with light painting the complex west side of Fremont Peak (right) all the way down to Mt. Helen (far left). See the *AAJ* website for detailed route lines and topos of the various new routes. *Mark Evans*

the West Face Dihedral, established solo by Chris Landry (*AAJ 1978*). This follows a prominent left-leaning corner system left of the West Buttress (Beckey-Lahr-Martinson, *AAJ 1977*).

On the morning of July 23, Blake McCord and I started up the route. We found spectacular climbing that was marred only by some seepage. I onsighted the crux aid pitch, a dihedral split by a very thin seam that moved through two overhangs, the second of which was the crux. Blake and I both felt the grade to be solid 5.12. In all, we climbed about nine pitches—a first free ascent of a big wall by some crazy Type 1 diabetics! 📷 🔍

— MATT SPOHN

MT. HELEN, TOWER ONE; FREMONT PEAK, RED TOWER

IT WAS AN UNSEASONABLY COLD, wet month in the Winds, according to the locals. And, indeed, during our four-week stay in Titcomb Basin (mid-August to mid-September), we saw only seven days of sunny, somewhat stable weather. And only half of that time allowed for climbing, as we were forced to sit and wait while fresh snow slowly melted and the walls barely dried.

Following 10 days of protracted base-camp festering, we three could stand the stasis no longer. Ignoring the warning "red sky in morning," Mark Evans, Oli Shaw, and I opened three new pitches on our primary objective, the 1,500' west face of Tower One on Mt. Helen. Rain, hail, and then graupel sent us back down to camp. Two days later, on August 29, we blasted early from our deluxe cave bivouac below the face, and we succeeded in establishing a fine, nine-pitch rock climb.

Strange Bravado (IV/V 5.10 A0) is located right of West Face Left (V 5.11a, Collins-Keough, 1981) and left of West Face Center (V 5.10 A2, Beckey-Lahr-Mortenson, *AAJ 1977*) [*see AAJ 2012 for the older route lines*]. It follows a conspicuous left-facing corner system past a series of ledges at half-height. From there it solves the problem of the steep upper headwall via a cunning yet reasonably moderate line. Both of my partners dispatched their respective pitches with some brilliant onsight free climbing. However, a short and wet section of squeeze

chimney (that we dubbed the Ric Flair) forced the route's only point of aid. In drier conditions the line would easily go free, adding to this impressive backcountry wall a long, quality, well-protected—and pre-trundled—free route.

During another brief window—about three weeks into our trip—Mark and I (Oli was under the weather that day) opened a casual, three-pitch route on the south face of Red Tower, the prominent pinnacle on Fremont's southwest buttress (right side of the sprawling west face). Red Iguana (500', II 5.8) meanders for three pitches past obvious weaknesses to the looker's right of the six-pitch Red Tower Arête (*AAJ 2012*), then continues to the pointy summit.

In our third and final break in the weather we climbed new ground to half height on Fremont's West Pillar, on the impressive face left of West Face Dihedral (Landry, *AAJ 1978*, free climbed by McCord-Spohn, *AAJ 2015*). At this point we had only days remaining in our trip. Despite ominous signs of approaching moisture on the horizon, we went for it, only to find suffering in high winds, verglased rock, and bitter, humid cold. Upon discovering that all three of our full one-liter water bottles were frozen, Mark, Oli, and I finally decided to call it. Hopefully we've paid our dues in Titcomb, and when we return next summer it'll go!

[Above] Oli Shaw belaying Shingo Ohkawa on pitch 7 of Strange Bravado, on the 1,500' west face of Mt. Helen. *Mark Evans*

– SHINGO OHKAWA

MT. HOOKER, NORTHEAST FACE, HOOK, LINE, AND SINKER

IN AUGUST, Whit Magro and I completed a free version of the Boissenault-Larson Route (VI 5.11 A4, 1979) on the northeast face of Mt. Hooker, which we called Hook, Line, and Sinker (1,800', V 5.12). We started from the Big Sandy trailhead using horses. The horses dropped us at Mae's Lake (otherwise a four-hour walk), and from there we made the two-hour hump over Hailey Pass to Baptiste Lake.

Whit originally had tried the line with Hermes Lynn earlier in the summer. After Whit and I completed two additional days of work on it, we did an all-free ascent of the 12-pitch route. The climb begins near the obvious left-trending ramp/flake just left of the nose of the wall (the free version of Sendero Luminoso also starts on this feature). Going ground-up, we cleaned and then redpointed the first six pitches and climbed the remaining pitches onsight. Our one-day ascent took about 11 hours, with both the leader and follower taking no falls.

Many sections of the climb that appeared difficult proved to be only 5.11-, due to a veritable potpourri of incut edges. A good portion of the terrain differs from the original aid line, and our route shares the crux pitches (seven and eight) with the Free Eye (V 5.12, Goodman-Miyamoto-Sharratt, *AAJ 2011*). [*Free Eye is a free variation to the lower portion of the Third Eye (VI 5.10 A4, Middendorf-Quinlan, AAJ 1994) and the upper part of the Boissonneault-Larson. All of the Free Eye's pitches were redpointed or onsighted but not climbed in a continuous free ascent.*] About one-third of the terrain we covered appears to be new.

Since this route was so good and proved surprisingly moderate, our goal was to create a high-quality free line that would be fun to repeat (not a "headpoint" route that's a pain in the ass for everybody but the first-ascent team). By adding six bolts to our free variations, and also replacing a couple of old button-head bolts, I think we succeeded. 📷 📄

– JOSH WHARTON

LITTLE SANDY VALLEY, NEW ROUTES

IN JULY, Ben Rosenberg and I traveled to the Little Sandy Valley with no fixed plans other than to do some exploring. In part due to laziness and in part due to the attractiveness of walls low in the valley, we did not make it very far.

We first climbed Pricker Buttress (1,500', 7 pitches, IV 5.9 R) up the right side of Lower Sandy Buttress (a.k.a. Point 11,427'). The highlight of the route was a pricker-bush-filled offwidth leading near the top. Overall, the rock on the Lower Sandy Buttress was more reminiscent of the Tetons' metamorphic rock than the granite of the Wind Rivers. [*This route likely climbs just right of the East Face (Beckey-Stevenson, AAJ 1968).*]

We spent the second day climbing Wyoming State Bird (1,200', 8 pitches, IV 5.10+ R) on the east buttress of Point 11,720'. The route followed a very obtuse, sometimes vegetated dihedral about 300' right of Symbiosis (Duncan-Keith-McCarthy, 1993). After the dihedral ended on the east face, we traversed right into another dihedral system around the other side of the northeast arête and followed that to the summit. This route was surprisingly sustained and entertaining.

The most remarkable part of the experience was the lack of people. After three days in the valley, the only footprints we saw on the trail out were the same ones we'd left on the hike in. 📷

– BENJAMIN COLLETT

[Below] The Little Sandy Valley as viewed from the hike in. Little Sandy Buttress (Point 11,427') is the prominent feature on the left. *Benjamin Collett*

CLOUD PEAK; BOMBER MOUNTAIN; PAINT ROCK BUTTRESS

MARK JENKINS AND I spent six nights in mid-August at the head of Paint Rock Creek, just south of Cloud Peak (13,166'), and climbed several probable new routes. Three of these are described in the feature article about Cloud Peak in this edition: The Man Who Feared Marmots (ca 550', II 5.10+) on "Paint Rock Buttress;" the southeast arête of Cloud Peak (1,200', III 5.8, possibly climbed in the 1970s); and Rust Never Sleeps (10 pitches, III 5.11-), possibly the first route up the 900' south buttress of Cloud Peak.

On August 19, our last full day in the area, we first climbed Bomber Mountain (ca 12,840'), then descended south to a break in the peak's eastern cirque wall, which we downclimbed for more than an hour, plus one rappel, to reach the base of the east face, four hours after leaving camp. We then scrambled about 800' of slabs and steps (some fifth class) to reach a headwall, which we climbed in six pitches: two excellent leads bookended by loose chimneys and corners, where stacks of blocks were poised like unexploded bombs. We can't recommend our route, UXO (1,300', III 5.10 R), but it was satisfying to climb such a large and remote alpine wall. [*Editor's note: In July 1971, Art Bloom, Howard Bussey, Rex Hoff, Ray Jacquot, and Bill Lindberg climbed the "central arête of the east face," following a prominent chimney line to the right of the 2014 route, then traversing left to finish on a pillar with a few moves of aid (15 pitches, 5.7 A2), AAJ 1972.*]

– DOUGALD MACDONALD

NEW ICE AND MIXED CLIMBS

THE GROWING POPULARITY of ice climbing was a source of increasing frustration before I discovered the potential for mixed first ascents in the San Juan Mountains. In January–February 2015, Grant Kleeves and I dedicated ourselves to trying a new route every weekend—easy for me, on break from seasonal work, but psychologically taxing for the gainfully employed Grant.

We started on January 24 by climbing a deep gash to the right of the Calling (700', WI4 M4) on the south-facing Outward Bound Wall in Eureka. We found five pitches of interesting climbing on ice and rock, hidden in the depths of a chimney system. At a certain angle this line appears to have been sliced into the rock by the Kleever (700', WI4 M6). Expect loose rock, an obligatory squeeze chimney, and no fixed gear to mark the way.

On January 31 we tried the rightmost of several prominent chimneys dividing the "21 & Up Buttress" on the south side of Camp Bird Road. An initial pitch with moderate climbing led to treed slopes and a snow gully stretching up to the base of a pair of chimneys. We steered clear of the flared squeeze on the left and chose the more sensibly sized chimney to the right. After 350' this system ended, so we made an exposed traverse into the left chimney. This chimney then widened and split into two separate cracks. We finished on the right-hand of these, which ends in a strenuous left-facing corner. In honor of Bird Brain Boulevard, we named this looser version Thick Skull Thoroughfare (1,000', M6).

Our nerves were beginning to fray, so for our third weekend we recruited Drew Smith and Lance Sullins to join us for a leapfrogging, party-of-four adventure in the Sneffels Range.

On February 6 we skied into the basin beneath the imposing north face of Peak 13,134' (a.k.a. "Dark Horse" or "Sneffels 9") and bivied. The next morning we began up the prominent left-trending weakness, believing it to be unclimbed. We enjoyed the usual San Juan choss, thin ice, and unstable snow for over 1,000' to the top. Afterward, we were impressed to learn that Jared Vilhauer and Dave Ahrens had made the first ascent of this line in October 2006: Ski Line (1,600', 5.8 R WI3 M5, *AAJ 2007*). Despite pleasant temperatures, we are guiltily calling our climb the first winter ascent of the face and what may be the second ascent overall.

For the final escapade, Drew Smith replaced Grant, and we returned to Camp Bird Road on February 10. We decided on a distinct right-angling weakness to the left of Tasty Talks (1,400', 5.8 M5 R, *AAJ 2013*), on the buttress of the same name. We were rewarded with the best route of the bunch. It featured engaging climbing on good rock for the first four pitches. Higher up, the line regressed into the usual choss, but potential variations to the left could produce a sustained, high-quality route. Bring good fist-crack skills for your visit to Dr. Toboggan (900', 5.9+ M5). All routes were climbed ground-up, free, and without bolts. 📷 🔍

– JACK CRAMER

[Above] Jack Cramer following the chimney of Dr. Toboggan (900', 5.9+ M5) on the "Tasty Talks" buttress, Camp Bird Road. The route climbs a distinct right-angling weakness to the left of Tasty Talks (1,400', 5.8 M5 R). *Drew Smith*

COLORADO / BLACK CANYON OF THE GUNNISON

SOUTH RIM, EVENT HORIZON (NEW VARIATION)

THIS MISSION STARTED in April when Josh Wharton invited me to the Black Canyon's South Chasm View Wall to have a look at freeing an old, obscure aid route called Harpua (V 5.11 A1, Gunther-Schoepflin, 1994). The line starts just right of the infamous Black Hole (VI 5.12b, Copp-Donson, 2001) and left of Bull Girl (VI 5.11 A4, Warren-Williams, 1996). [*Bull Girl was free-climbed by Topher Donahue and Jared Ogden and dubbed Burlgirl (V 5.12- X, AAJ 2003).*] That day we free climbed a couple of pitches and cleaned a third. Above the third pitch we bailed onto Black Hole. Subsequently, we figured out that much of Black Hole actually climbs Harpua, so in a way we were still on route after all.

I returned in the heat of August with Stephanie Bergner, and we freed the third pitch at 5.12- and then another easier pitch of new climbing. On the fifth pitch we set off across a face toward another unclimbed crack system. I drilled one bolt and then we bailed for lack of time. Stephanie and I came back in September, and we climbed the entire route wall-style over two and half days, placing one more bolt, though we did not manage to free the route. Wanting to finish what we started, Josh Wharton and I returned on October 18 to free the entire line in 11 hours. Originally done in 15 pitches, Josh and I did it in 12 pitches. The route contains many pitches of 5.11 with two of 5.12.

In many ways, Event Horizon (1,500', 5.12) is a series of variations. The route more or less links the first three pitches of Harpua to four pitches of new climbing. After the seventh pitch, the route follows Black Hole to the upper meadows and then ends on the standard Astro Dog finish. The name arose from getting pulled into the Black Hole despite trying to find an independent line to the upper meadow. 📷 🔍

– CHRIS KALOUS

GREAT WHITE WALL, ANY COLOR YOU LIKE AS LONG AS IT'S BLACK

IN OCTOBER, Mike Brumbaugh and Rob Pizem climbed a new route on the Great White Wall, located on the eastern side of Fisherman's Gully: Any Color You Like As Long As It's Black (12 pitches, 5.11+ PG). The Great White Wall has three other known routes. In 1989 Rob Schmidt and Rich Strang climbed Great White Wall (IV 5.10+). And in 2002, the wall saw two new routes: Super Wuss (IV 5.11-, Cochran-Wharton, *AAJ 2003*), which climbs the large red arête left of Great White Wall, and Death Camas Dihedrals (IV 5.10+ R/X, Donson-Murphy, *AAJ 2003*), which climbs a line of steep corners and arêtes.

Brumbaugh and Pizem's new route is located right of the route Great White Wall. It was established top-down and cleaned on rappel. They found two older bolts on the route but believe a previous ascent is improbable, given the amount of loose rock. A few bolts were added for protection and belays. They redpointed the route on October 6.

– *INFORMATION PROVIDED BY* ROB PIZEM

COLORADO / FRONT RANGE

MT. EVANS MASSIF, BLACK WALL, SILHOUETTE BUTTRESS

IN OCTOBER, Ben Collett and I added two new routes to the Silhouette Buttress (ca 13,000') on the Mt. Evans massif, both located left of last year's route Silhouette (*AAJ 2014*). After trying many different options to approach this buttress once the road up Mt. Evans is closed, we discovered the best option this fall: a meandering bushwhack though a willow-filled bog, heading eastward from Guanella Pass. The approach takes between two and three hours by foot.

On October 2, Ben and I climbed the prominent right-facing corner and chimney system up the center of the buttress. A huge roof above the belay was festooned with icicles and verglas. This involved strenuous dry tooling on good hooks in cracks and blocks, with excellent protection from hand-sized Camalots. The crux was rounding the roof and delicately powering up on lock-offs in one- to two-inch verglas. This section was very similar to the crux on the Vail climb Flying Fortress. Above the crux roof, the protection got much worse. I got two pieces in about 60' of climbing—it was some of the most challenging thin-ice climbing I have ever done. The 140' second pitch began with a weird and difficult series of chimney moves followed by easier climbing to the top: Shooting Star (2 pitches, 250', WI7 M9). It's

[Left] The routes on the Silhouette Buttress (ca 13,000'), from right to left: Silhouette (3 pitches, 480', WI6+ M9 R), Shooting Star (2 pitches, 250', WI7 M9), The Ghost (1 pitch, 165', WI6 M10 R). The top of Monochrome (III WI4 M5) ascends the ice in lower left, and the gully out of view right of the buttress contains the route Black and White (WI4 M5). See Ben Collett's article in *AAJ 2014* for more information and photos. *Will Mayo* [Right] Will Mayo works through the steep crux of Shooting Star. *Ben Collett*

possible that future ascents may find either better rock protection without the verglas, or better ice protection with more ice.

On October 11 we returned to climb a ghostly icicle dangling from the roof left of Shooting Star. From the belay I climbed up a thin smear of ice to a preplaced bong, then stepped carefully right into a groove below the overhang, where a suitcase-size block offered protection. Big, awkward, and committing moves brought me up the overhang and ice dagger, all while dealing with small protection. After summoning some courage, I turned the icicle and committed to an off-finger-size crack above the ceiling. There are some hooks in constrictions at the start, but mainly the crack requires torqueing the head of the tool in the crack. Above the crux, the remainder of the pitch climbs thin ice smears, with quartz-riddled horizontal cracks that offer solid but sparse rock protection. This route may have ice pouring out of the crack above the initial icicle, as it did on my subsequent ascents; this makes the route less technically demanding but also considerably more run-out. Either way, the route is a rare and precious traditional mixed testpiece: The Ghost (165', WI6 M10 R).

Silhouette and Shooting Star were both done ground-up, onsight. However, the Ghost was cleaned on rappel to dislodge loose blocks, and some pitons were preplaced. The entire buttress has no protections bolts—please, let's keep it that way! 📷 🔍

– WILL MAYO

SHOSHONI PEAK, FINNACLE RIDGE

PAUL GAGNER AND I climbed a long, stepped ridge on the southeast aspect of Shoshoni Peak (12,967') on July 19. This ridge defines the left side of the big gash on Shoshoni's south face. We climbed six pitches (5.9-), plus a long section of scrambling in the middle, to reach a prominent spire that we called the Finnacle. After reversing the top pitch, we downclimbed and rappelled a gully to the east to the big, snow-filled gash. It's very possible this ridge has been climbed before, but it's never been reported and we saw no evidence from prior ascents. 📷

– DOUGALD MACDONALD

PEAK 12,878', NORTH FACE, STALKER

IN EARLY OCTOBER, Jonathan "JD" Merritt and I climbed a long ice and mixed route on the north side of Peak 12,878', a sub-peak just northeast of Shoshoni Peak (12,967') in the central Indian Peaks. I first scouted the route after a deep two-day freeze in mid-September. On October 2, Phil Wortmann and I tried to make an attempt, but with gale-force winds, snow, and intense cold we never geared up. With a forecast for two days of melt-freeze conditions following, I hoped this moderate-looking route would reach perfect condition.

JD and I started our five-mile hike around 6 a.m. on October 5 out of the Long Lake Trailhead. We battled over the Continental Divide via Pawnee Pass in strong winds and fog, and then descended around 1,000' into the west-side basin to reach the base of our intended line. With a low cloud ceiling obscuring the peaks it was impossible to see the route, but we submitted to faith and the climbing unfolded flawlessly for the next 1,100'.

After climbing 100' of steep snow to the base, I snatched the first lead, which had impeccable mixed climbing up a series of steep corners with ice no more than a few inches thick or wide. Above this, JD begged to lead an incredible ice smear. The smear led to easier climbing and past a thick, yellow ice roof shaped by strong updrafts.

[Photo] JD Merritt en route on Stalker (1,100', WI4 M5), a long ice and mixed climb on the west side of the Continental Divide, in the Indian Peaks. *Erik Rieger*

We simulclimbed the middle of the route (600' of continuous low-angle ice with some short steps up to WI3) in one long "pitch." To our surprise, the most technical climbing came in the final 400'. First, a fantastic, iced-up, Chamonix-style corner, then a steep groove and corner system up compact, rime-covered granite leading directly to the summit plateau. We topped out on the summit of Peak 12,878' around 3 p.m., a mile southwest of Pawnee Pass. In all, I walked about 30 miles to find this route in condition: Stalker (1,100', WI4 M5). The double meaning of the route name comes from the film of the same name by Andrei Tarkovsky. Make sure to seek this one out in early season before the Brainard Lake road closes. 📷

– ERIK RIEGER

LONGS PEAK, EAST FACE, BONGALONG, FIRST KNOWN FREE ASCENT

BONGALONG (600', 5.5 A1) was established by Jerry Brown and Rod Smythe in 1966. The route begins one-third of the way up lower Lambs Slide, just left of Alexander's Chimney. Thinking it would be low-hanging fruit, Jake Miller and I decided to try free climbing it in August. We climbed about 600' up mostly hand-sized cracks, with nothing harder than 5.8—pretty casual, especially for a possible first free ascent on Longs. 📷 📄

– JASON HAAS

NEW MEXICO

CAPULIN CANYON, MANY NEW CRACK CLIMBS

CAPULIN CANYON lies in the heart of the Dome Wilderness, a pristine section of the Jemez Mountains in New Mexico's Bandelier National Monument, famous for its Ancestral Puebloan cliff dwellings. However, no cliff dwellings exist in this area. The welded tuff composing these cliff bands is often bulletproof, and the normal welded-tuff features you'd expect to see, such as huecos and pockets, are all but missing here. Instead, the rock has fractured to form splitter cracks and corners, riddling the cliff line for a several-mile stretch.

First visits to Capulin Canyon by exploratory rock climbers may have begun sometime in the '80s. In the early '90s, brief visits to Capulin by the likes of Doug Pandorf, Lee Sheftel, and Jean Delataillade created a handful of lines. However, the 1996 Dome Wilderness Fire drastically changed the access and appearance. The canyon lay quiet for 15 years or so, until Josh Smith, an ambitious local climber, rediscovered the area in 2010. Since then, Josh, with help from a small band of scruffy climbers—such as George Perkins, Jason Halladay, and me—have opened up a plethora of newly minted crack climbs, many of which are awaiting a second or third ascent. With nary a bolt-protected move, the routes range from 50' single-pitch lines to multi-pitch routes that top out at 200' or higher; the average seems to be around 90' to 100'. Grades range from 5.10- to 5.12, with a few token 5.9 and 5.13- lines. Overall, Capulin Canyon has a distinct flavor and texture that distinguishes it from desert-style sandstone crack climbing and makes this a unique and memorable place to climb.

There are currently four crags. The Main Wall contains the longest lines, with several 170' pitches, many of which are broken into two where a natural ledge exists. The Upper Wall has the greatest variety and a good density of routes. Capulet Canyon is the only crag that faces west, and it boasts a high density of four-star lines. The other walls face south and get strong sun exposure; however, the complexity of the corners and alcoves allows one to seek lines in the sun

[Photo] Josh Smith on the steep hands section of Tip of the Toe (5.12-) at the Upper Wall in Capulin Canyon. *Fred Berman*

or shade most of the day. The canyon can be accessed from either Albuquerque or Santa Fe, with the trailhead located on Dome Trail Road. The climbing is best October–May, and there is open camping throughout the area; however, the road is often closed January–February due to snowpack; contact the Jemez Ranger District before making a trip during this time. 📷 📄 🔍

— AARON MILLER

ORGAN MOUNTAINS, COMPLETE SOUTH-TO-NORTH TRAVERSE

FROM APRIL 25–27, Glen Melin, Jon Tylka, and I made the first recorded traverse of the Organ Mountains skyline, climbing from south to north. The Organ Mountains form the rugged barrier between the Tularosa Basin and the Mesilla Valley in southern New Mexico, rising more than 5,000' from the valley floor. The highest point is Organ Needle (8,990'), and from there the rounded peaks of the South Organ Mountains roll toward Texas, while the jagged peaks of the Needles/Squaretops, High Horns, Low Horns, and Rabbit Ears march northward to San Augustine Pass and range's terminus in the north.

After a storm forced Jon Tylka and Aaron Hobson to abort an attempt in July 2011, Jon, Glen, and I were determined to complete the endeavor in an unsupported push. We planned to start on the west side of the range at Modoc Mine, climb the initial 4,000' to Organ Needle, then traverse north along the ridgeline to the last major peak, North Rabbit Ear, before descending to the valley floor on the east side of the range at Aguirre Springs. The total traverse would encompass 22 peaks, 10 miles of climbing, and 9,000' of cumulative elevation gain.

We began the traverse in excellent spring weather on the morning of April 25. Faced with a forecasted windstorm, we had a 36-hour window to reach Aguirre Springs. Beginning with a fourth-class scramble to the summit of the Retaining Wall, we then worked north along the ridgeline, following third-class to moderate fifth-class routes to the top of each major peak. During the first day we completed the Organ Needle/Squaretop and High Horns complexes, summiting the Retaining Wall, Organ Needle, Squaretop, Little Squaretop, Squaretop Massif, the Wedge, Lost Peak, Third Peak, Dingleberry, Wildcat, Razorback, and the Spire. Unfortunately, the windstorm arrived earlier than expected, with 70mph-plus wind gusts, which forced us to bivy for seven hours in the saddle between the High Horns and Low Horns.

With the wind unabated on the morning of April 26, we elected to continue climbing through terrible conditions. By 1 a.m. on Sunday, April 27, we had completed the Low Horns and Rabbit Ears in a brown-out dust storm, summiting the Low Horns, Rabbit Ears Massif, South Rabbit Ear, Middle Rabbit Ear, and North Rabbit Ear. At 3 a.m. we finally arrived at the Aguirre Springs, after 34 hours of climbing.

While the traverse is technically rated only 5.8, its greatest challenges are in route-finding and overcoming the harsh high-desert environment. With very little human traffic, there are no established trails, and moving between peaks involved dodging cholla, agave, sotol, yucca, and rattlesnakes. Additionally, completing the traverse required complete self-sufficiency and speed, as there are no water sources along the route. Favorable conditions and a now clearly defined route should allow for a traverse in less than 24 hours by future climbers.

Jon suggested the route's name based on a quote from Dick Ingraham, father of Organ Mountains mountaineering, who stated that the Organ Saint is "by definition, a person so enamored of the harsh beauty of the Organs that, far from minding the length of the approaches and the hostility of the terrain, he actually lies down with the cholla and blesses the rattlesnakes." If you like to suffer, you'll love the Organ Saint Traverse. 📷 📄 🔍

— NATHAN FRY

ALASKA

ANGEL, EAST FACE; DIKE PEAK, WEST FACE; HYDRA PEAK, NORTHEAST FACE

AFTER SEEING CLINT HELANDER'S incredible article in the *AAJ 2013*, unselfishly revealing the secrets of the Revelations, Kris Irwin, Darren Vonk, and I flew into the range on April 2. We didn't have to look far upon arriving to find good objectives.

On April 4 we climbed the Angel (9,265') by a new route: the John Lauchlan Memorial Award Route (1,200m, AI4+ M5). Our line followed two ice streaks up a weakness on the east face before joining a long ridge to the summit. Most of the route consisted of moderate climbing, with a short vertical ice crux. We continued along the upper ridge and arrived at the summit that same day. Our choice of descent left something to be desired as we rapped through a hanging glacier that we later witnessed collapsing.

In subarctic temperatures, we got a late start on our next objective, a fine-looking line up the west face of the farthest right pinnacle of the Four Horsemen (ca 8,400'). We climbed six technical pitches and found amazing thin, sticky coastal ice. We could not believe the tiny blobs of ice that would stick to rock here in the far western reaches of the Alaska Range, unlike our drier home range of the Canadian Rockies. However, steep snow climbing and our late start eventually stopped us. We have left this beautiful line for those who will visit later.

On the flight in we had spotted a spectacular thin-ice line on the west face of unclimbed Dike Peak (7,800'). This route went without a hitch as we had the Rockies Ice Specialist Kris Irwin along to lead two thin pitches (WI5) that opened passage to the moderate upper mountain. A dreamy line of single-swing névé led us to a huge gully that followed the black dike the peak is named for. After passing an impressive chockstone, we reached the summit. It was the first ascent of the mountain as far as we know: Powered by Beans (1,000m, AI5 M5).

With two routes down we figured we were ready for our main objective, the unclimbed central gully on the west face of Pyramid Peak (8,572'). This 1,500m wall had drawn us to the range. A team of four European climbers visiting two weeks earlier did the first ascent of Pyramid via a highly technical mixed line: the Odyssey. [*See Jerome Sullivan's report in this AAJ.*] The obvious central plum line remained unclimbed. On our first attempt we climbed 10 pitches. The most difficult leads involved vertical snow steps, while the thin ice climbing was, again, very enjoyable. We hadn't truly expected to make the summit in a day, so when it began snowing ever so lightly and the gully began to unload spindrift, we were happy to bail from our go-look-see.

Looking to tack on a "casual" day, we headed to the northeast face of Hydra Peak (7,800'). The route to the summit consisted of only five pitches of technical climbing. Mind-blowing thin ice climbing was interspersed with a drytooling roof or two. This was all topped off by a spectacular ridge walk where we could look out over the flatlands on the western side of the range. We hoped to see folks frolicking on the distant Pacific coast, but settled for the Casual Route (600m, AI4 M6).

[Photo] Darren Vonk leading the ice crux on the east face of the Angel.
Ian Welsted

[Left] Dike Peak's west face, showing Powered by Beans (1,000m, AI5 M5), which climbs thin ice runnels and névé for most of its length. The climbers descended the right skyline to lower-angled slabs. [Right] West face of Pyramid Peak, showing the Canadian attempt (10 pitches) on the left. (Clint Helander, Jason Stuckey, and Aaron Thrasher also attempted this line, in 2013, climbing six pitches.) The Odyssey (1,100m, 6b A1 M7 90°) climbs the right side of the wall. [Bottom] Darren Vonk leading around the large chockstone on Dike Peak. *Photos: Ian Welsted*

We jokingly decided the criteria for our final climb must include a less-than-one-hour-uphill ski approach from base camp, a walking descent down a safe snow gully, and a start no earlier than 10 a.m. On our second attempt on Pyramid Peak, we stood at the base and witnessed a full-height avalanche triggered by a cornice collapse—it obliterated the route. Anyone in the gully wouldn't have lasted long. Perhaps it was late in the season, with warming temps, or it could have been that we had a fixed idea of a route that had to be done without adequately assessing its hazards. We should have stuck to our casual rules. 🔘

– IAN WELSTED, *CANADA*

PYRAMID PEAK, WEST FACE, THE ODYSSEY; MT. BOUCANSAUD, EAST FACE, THE ILIAD

[Above] Mt. Boucansaud's east face. The Iliad climbs the prominent ice and snow gully in left center. *Jerome Sullivan*

AFTER CLINT HELANDER showed me some amazing photos of unclimbed summits and projects in the Revelations, Lise Billon, Jeremy Stagnetto (both France), Pedro Angel Galan Diaz (Spain), and I flew into the area on March 17. Pyramid Peak (8,572') immediately fascinated us; it was unclimbed and had a very steep and imposing west face.

The winter in Alaska had been unusually warm and dry, and we were quite worried about the conditions we would find. Fortunately, the unusual weather seemed to play in our favor as we encountered more ice than reported by previous expeditions.

Our first aim was to climb a fairly direct line to the summit of Pyramid Peak, but after two days of effort, having climbed past thin and unprotectable ice smears, we finally dead-ended only 200m off the ground. More often than not the cracks were closed off, and finding a logical line proved complicated. Clint had tried an obvious line to the left in the large gully, but it is protected by large, overhanging snow mushrooms and a huge roof at the top. [*See previous report by Ian Welsted about an attempt on the gully line.*]

To boost our spirits we decided to climb an evident line on an unclimbed peak, which we later called Mt. Boucansaud (Pt. 7,500', located on the east shoulder of Mt. Patmos and named in honor of Jean-Marc Boucansaud). Leaving on March 23, we climbed a striking ice smear on the east face of the peak in 20 hours camp to camp. The climb was mostly straightforward alpine ice climbing with two amazing crux pitches of thin water ice: the Iliad (900m, TD+).

After this, we spotted another thin ice line on the right side of Pyramid's west face and decided to try it. We started climbing on March 27 and bivied three times on the wall. We were unable to start climbing until late morning every day due to very cold temperatures. The route had various hard pitches of mixed climbing, vertical snow, and only a few pitches of

[Above] Ice smears don't get much better than this one, found on the Odyssey (1,100m, 6b A1 M7 90°), the first route up Pyramid Peak. *Jerome Sullivan*

easy snow climbing. The crux pitches included an overhanging chimney with bulging snow mushrooms and a sketchy traverse to reach a very steep corner. The climbing was often in the M5-6 range, including much thin ice. In all we climbed 18 pitches and 300m of ridgeline to reach the summit on March 30.

From the summit, we descended the northwest face via nine rappels to reach a big couloir, which led us back to the glacier. We called the route the Odyssey (1,100m, 6b A1 M7 90°). Protection along the route was quite scarce, and many of the pitches were run-out. We flew out of the range on April 2. 📷

— JEROME SULLIVAN, *FRANCE*

[Bottom] Fred Beckey (left) and Clint Helander. *Clint Helander*

MT. TITANIC, WEST FACE

FRED BECKEY SHIFTED conspicuously in his chair, looking over his shoulder as if someone were about to steal his most prized possession: Before me lay the "Black Book," a file of tattered photographs of unknown mountains scrawled with hand-drawn lines. I had long heard rumors of such a folder, packed with scrupulously kept notes on unclimbed objectives. I gleaned the information as if it contained heavily guarded nuclear launch codes.

At age 91 Fred Beckey still dreamt of first ascents. The peaks he visited in Alaska's Revelation Mountains several decades ago are no exception. Sitting alongside, I helped him identify the few peaks he hadn't yet labeled. One photograph showed a sprawling granite wall simply labeled "unclimbed," but I recognized it immediately. "What do you think of the west face of Titanic?" he asked. "Looks like good granite."

Beckey made the only ascent of Mt. Titanic (ca 9,300') in 1981 by its east face (Beckey-Hogan-McCarty-Tillery, *AAJ 1983*), three years before I was born. Mt. Titanic had always been at the front of my own "black book," and I felt more than a little guilty when I admitted to him that I had intentions on the craggy monolith. The west face had inspired me since my first trip to the Revelations in 2008. From atop many peaks to the south, I vowed that one day I would venture north for a look. If Beckey thought it worthy, there was no question.

On April 17, Graham Zimmerman and I flew to Titanic on a halcyon day. Our pilot, Conor McManamin, dropped us off in a small hanging glacial valley in the northern Revelations, above and east of the south fork of Big River. We set up a base camp beneath the southwest ridge of Jezebel Peak (9,620'), which was climbed by Ryan Hokanson and Kirby Spangler while Beckey sauntered around at their base camp (*AAJ 2001*). From camp we scouted various objectives, but the west face of Titanic beckoned.

[Above] The unclimbed, ca 3,700' north face of Titanic (ca 9,300') on the far left and the west face on the right, separated by the large gash in the center. Clint Helander and Graham Zimmerman's route up the west face (3,500', 5.8 M6 50°) climbs the path of least resistance from atop the crescent-shaped snow ramp on the lower right. The Beckey-Hogan-McCarty-Tillery route (1981) climbs the east face on the opposite side. *Clint Helander*

We awoke in the dark cold of April 21 to a glorious display of the aurora borealis dancing above Titanic. We took it as a sign and trudged away from camp at 4:30 a.m. with daypacks. Scaling teetering moraines, we made the 2.5-mile approach to the shadowed face in predawn light. Down low the rock quality was poor, but we weren't concerned. On the upper buttress, gorgeous white granite caps everything below.

For 1,300' we kicked steps up a prominent, crescent-shaped snow couloir before the real climbing began. At the top of the couloir we downclimbed several meters over a notch and I led a long section of simul-climbing over mixed snow, rock, and ice in a gully. Above, we encountered another 1,000' or so of high-quality mixed climbing. Graham started things off on the upper mountain by scratching up a brilliant chimney (M6), and then we swapped leads on generally excellent granite, often hand-jamming without gloves while our crampons scratched for purchase.

In the evening we found ourselves near the top of the face after many pitches of engaging climbing. After a quick brew stop on the upper snowfield, we strolled up the final ridge to the summit and reveled in the evening light. This was the second ascent of Titanic: the west face

(3,500', 5.8 M6 50°). From the summit, we downclimbed the north side to the northeast face and then rappelled over a cold, shadowy, and serac-laden icefall. A long slog under the northeast face and over a steep pass led us down a glacier under the northwest face of Jezebel Peak. After 5 miles of foot travel, a brutal crawl around Jezebel's southwest ridge landed us at camp at 2 a.m. Utterly exhausted from our 22.5-hour push, we imagined Fred Beckey would be proud.

A few months after our climb, a call from ol' Fred led to inquiry about another Revelations peak. After discussing our route on Titanic, I asked if he was planning a trip. He sputtered, "I don't know about this year, I'm getting pretty ancient. Maybe next year." 📷

– CLINT HELANDER

KICHATNA MOUNTAINS

[Above] The Erdmann-Roskelley Northeast Face (4,000', IV M3 70°) on Augustin Peak. The first ascent by the west face climbed the opposite side of the mountain. *Ben Erdmann*

TRIDENT GLACIER AREA, SNICKLEFRITZ; AUGUSTIN PEAK, NORTHEAST FACE

ON APRIL 8 Jess Roskelley and I flew into the Trident Glacier, a triple-forked glacier in the northern Kichatna Mountains. Augustin Peak (ca 8,600') is the tallest summit in the area and forms the head of the glacier. When we landed, we found the region drowning in winter weather cycles, with daily storms and unconsolidated snow on the faces. At this time the year before we had found solid blue ice in the Kichatnas; however, the wide-swing freeze-thaw cycle had not yet set in.

On April 9 we launched up a route on the southeast side of the ridge that divides the middle and north forks of the Trident Glacier. We found the mostly mixed climb in rotten condition and climbed the route with one bivy just below the summit ridge. After gaining the ridge crest, we descended from a col atop the ridge. We called the route SnickleFritz (1,500', 5.9 A2 M5 80°).

Back in camp, the weather stayed socked in for 10 days. During this time we explored on skis each fork of the glacier and the adjoining passes. Jess joked that we were a bit like Shackleton, "except with lots of good food, global communication, and minimal hardship."

On April 20 we left in the middle of the night for the cold shadow of Augustin Peak's northeast face, hoping to avoid danger from a serac band in the middle of the face. Once gaining the entry ramp on the left side of the face, we bivied for a few hours with one sleeping bag between us. When the sun emerged we began simul-climbing and continued in this

[Above] Ben Erdmann following the final snow slopes up Augustin Peak. *Jess Roskelley*

style for the entire route, reaching the summit at 2:30 p.m. We descended our line of ascent by downclimbing and several rappels, and we arrived back at base camp in the last hour of daylight. We named our route the Erdmann-Roskelley Northeast Face (4,000', IV M3 70°). The climbing was classic and enjoyable. It's possible this marks only the second ascent of Augustin Peak, following the first ascent by the west face (Graber-Long-Schunk, *AAJ 1978*). 📷 🔍

– BEN ERDMANN

CENTRAL ALASKA RANGE

IDIOT PEAK, WEST FACE, DOWN THE RABBIT HOLE

"DOES EVERYONE HAVE a good feeling about this?" Scott said, before we descended south 2,000' into the Valley of Death of the Tokositna Glacier. Scott Adamson, Andy Knight, and I were hoping to climb a new route up the center of the west face of Idiot Peak (ca 10,700'), a sub-peak located just south of Mt. Huntington's south ridge. Down the rabbit hole we plunged, and after navigating some seracs, steep ice, and crevasses, we slept at a small, sheltered bivy.

[Editor's note: Jay Smith and Paul Teare are the only other climbers known to have used this descent/approach, once in 1990 and again in 1991, en route to the Phantom Wall. The so-called Valley of Death is threatened by steep icefalls on three sides. Idiot Peak was first climbed in 2005 by Will Mayo and Chris Thomas, who climbed the Harvard Route's access couloir and traversed under the Phantom Wall to reach the steep northwest face. Their route is called Mini-Intellectual (AAJ 2006), and it starts north of (climber's left) and 1,500' higher than Down the Rabbit Hole.]

We awoke at 4 a.m. and traversed right (south) 500' to a long snow slope (ca 6,500') that led to the main, rocky west face of Idiot Peak. After soloing 1,000'–2,000' of 60° to 80° snow with short ice steps, we arrived at the technical climbing, where ribbons of water ice and mixed climbing stretched for five pitches (WI5+ M6). After reaching a good ledge we were greeted by a 30' ice column. Scott quickly discovered the column was completely detached. Avoiding the ice, he made a short tension traverse and began free climbing up rock to the right. A 10' section of A2 climbing was required to avoid a fall onto a single Pecker and gain better gear. Above this, he resumed free climbing.

After a full pitch up hard glacial ice (WI3+) and a quick brew, we continued rightward. Three pitches of steep ice and mixed climbing in a blocky chimney eventually brought us to the Thank God Mushroom Bivy around midnight, one pitch below the summit ridge. We slept in the next morning, and one more mixed pitch led to the south ridge, where the traversing began. After navigating around a big gendarme, we stayed mostly below the corniced ridge crest. Five pitches of snow wallowing and ice traverses led us to the corniced summit, where a mere tap of the ice tool on top would have to suffice: Down the Rabbit Hole (4,200', V WI5+ M6 A2).

[Above] Scott Adamson climbs around the detached ice column on Down the Rabbit Hole. *Aaron Child*

From the summit we climbed one pitch around the north side of the peak to reach the col between Huntington and Idiot. More rappels down ice on the west side led to a section of sketchy broken rock. We rappelled through the broken rock to the base of a major snow slope left of Idiot Peak. From there we traversed left 500' and then up 800' on 70° snow to reach yet another technical pitch leading to a large ledge that traverses under the Phantom Wall. We bivied in a rocky cave just below this pitch. The next morning we climbed up and then traversed under the Phantom Wall to reach the top of the Harvard Route's access couloir. We rappelled down the couloir and reached the glacier and camp again on April 23, after four days away. ◙

— AARON CHILD

MT. HUNTINGTON, WEST FACE, SCORCHED GRANITE

As I TURNED MY HEAD upward, I heard Josh Wharton shouting encouragement: "Dream line!" The shaded corner of gray granite in the center of Mt. Huntington's west face rose above me toward the cobalt sky. This climb originated months before, in Vail's dank limestone amphitheater, when I ran into Mark Westman. He sent me a photo a few weeks later, and I was astonished that the striking line of ice—a compelling swath of terrain between Polarchrome and the Colton-Leach, leading to the French Ridge—had never been climbed. A weather window appeared the second week in May, and Josh Wharton and I quickly packed our bags and flew ourselves to Alaska in my small plane.

After soloing the first 800' of the Colton-Leach route, we branched left onto our new variation and climbed a few pitches of steep, high-quality ice and mixed to the prominent

[Left] The Colton-Leach route climbs the large ice gully; the obvious, icy corner branching left is Scorched Granite. [Right] Josh Wharton follows plastic alpine ice on Scorched Granite. *Will Mayo*

horizontal ledge splitting the west face. Once on it, we traversed leftward into the base of a couloir, and then continued up moderate mixed terrain to the French Ridge. The ridge was in ideal shape with styrofoam-like névé and patches of alpine ice for solid screws. We reached the summit at 5:30 p.m., basking in the warm evening sun. The descent along the upper Harvard Route was straightforward, and we finished rappelling the west face couloir as the late-evening shadow engulfed us. We were back in camp at 11:30 p.m., merely 13 and a half hours after leaving.

As Josh likes to say, so much of alpine climbing is about luck, so half the battle is simply showing up. Sometimes, you just get lucky: Scorched Granite (4,200', M7 AI6; about 800-1,000' of new terrain). 📷 📄

– WILL MAYO

RADIO CONTROL TOWER, SOUTHWEST BUTTRESS, IT'S INCLUDED

IN JUNE, Alan Rousseau and I flew into the Southeast Fork of the Kahiltna Glacier and decided to get creative. This led us up a new route on the very rocky southwest buttress of Radio Control Tower (8,670'), located just east of Kahiltna Base Camp. The route was an interesting outing with some harder pitches and a lot of exploration required to reach the top of the buttress: It's Included (1,000', 5.10+ AI3 M7).

[*Editor's note: Previously unreported, in May 2013, Alan Rousseau and Aaron Kurland made the first recorded ascent of the west face of Radio Control Tower, climbing a prominent gully and snow-ramp system just left of the southwest buttress. They called the seven-pitch climb Spindrift Couloir (1,000', AI3 M5). Given the proximity of Radio Control Tower to the Kahiltna Base Camp it's possible other routes have gone unreported.*] 📷

– MARK PUGLIESE

MT. FRANCES, NORTH BUTTRESS, SCRATCH AND SNIFF

IN MAY, Andres Marin and I traced a line up a rocky buttress on the north side of Mt. Frances. Although significantly shorter than any line we had hoped to climb, this was a worthy consolation when conditions prevented other attempts. We simul-climbed up a right-trending snow ledge that led to a weakness in the first steep rock band. Andres started things off with an amazing 65m pitch up a steep corner and then a wide, left-facing chimney. Above that, almost every pitch contained a technical 5m to 15m crux of engaging M5/6 climbing. After about nine hours we topped out on the pointed, ca 9,000 summit of the north buttress. Several rappels on rock gear led to an easy descent down an adjacent ice gully, where 11 rappels got us back to camp. Our new route, Scratch and Sniff (1,200', IV M6 5.8) on "Stubbs' Buttress" (named in honor of Talkeetna's world-famous cat mayor), contained 12 pitches of incredible climbing on a previously untouched feature, less than two hours from Kahiltna Base Camp. 📷 ▤ 🔍

– CLINT HELANDER

DENALI, SOLO WINTER ASCENT

LONNIE DUPRE reached the summit of Denali on January 11, 2015. This was his fourth attempt to become the first person to solo the mountain in January. Dupre was flown to base camp on the Southeast Fork of the Kahiltna Glacier on December 18. He climbed the standard route up the West Buttress. Dupre made it safely down to Kahiltna Base Camp on January 14 and was flown back to Talkeetna on January 15.

– CLIMBING.COM

MT. DAN BEARD, SOUTH FACE (VARIANT) AND EAST FACE (REPEAT); PEAK 11,300', NORTHEAST BUTTRESS (NEW ROUTES)

I HAD VISITED ALASKA several times, but this time Junji Wada and I—"Team Wasabi"—had the extreme luxury of not seeing anyone during our seven-week stay on the glacier (April 21–June 6). This was a real treat that gave us significant time to face each other, nature, earth, and the mountains around the Don Sheldon Amphitheater more directly. Without any noise, we chose unclimbed lines in this severe and beautiful place by pure sensation.

We completed four climbs in all, which we called the "Wasabi Quartet," three of them likely new. On April 28 we began with the Wasabi Prelude (V 60°), which wove up a possible new variation on the south face of Mt. Dan Beard (10,260'). [*Editor's note: The south face of Mt. Dan Beard was first climbed in 1974 (Boardman-O'Donovan, AAJ 1975) and many variations have been reported on its south face over the years.*] The line took us approximately seven hours from base camp. We started up the right (east) side of the south face. The climb was comprised of a snow and ice gully with some climbing through a rock band. Near the top we climbed the right side of a rock headwall, crawling through a chimney to reach an icy plateau leading to the summit. We descended the same route.

On May 9 we progressed to the Wasabi Concerto (AI4+ M5+ R) on Peak 11,300', climbing the northeast buttress in 18.5 hours. The route faces directly east and is plainly visible from the Don Sheldon Amphitheater. The lower couloir was choked with rotten ice, rock, and dry snow. When the sun rose and shone upon the upper wall, avalanches began to release periodically through the couloir. The upper rock wall contained six pitches of wide cracks, slabs, chockstones, loose rocks, and ice—a very enjoyable mixed passage. The last part was snow and ice climbing all the way to "Point KJ" (ca 10,500'), which is the highest point along the northeast buttress of Peak 11,300'. We bivouacked on the summit of Point KJ and

[Above] The east face of Peak 11,300', showing the routes Wasabi Concerto (left) and Wasabi Sonatine (right). *Kei Taniguchi*

descended our route the next day with downclimbing and eight rappels.

On May 13 we wove our way up the east face of Dan Beard in 12 hours (WI4 AI5 M5). Avoiding seracs, we found a way up a V-shaped couloir on the far right (north) side of the east face. Trending left, an ice gully led to distinct sections of rock and snow and then up to the icy northeast ridge. On the very top part we needed to cross a huge crevasse, which we did by climbing a steep pitch of ice—the "Alaskan way" we quite enjoy. To descend, we revisited the Wasabi Prelude on the south face and descended under a full moon. [*Editor's note: It's likely that Taniguchi and Wada climbed or intersected the route Sideburn Rib (Hughes-Scott, AAJ 2008). The central wall just left (south) of this line is still unclimbed and very seriously threatened by objective hazards. The southeast ridge has been climbed to the summit (Kerr-Woolums, AAJ 1980).*]

To complete the quartet, we climbed the Wasabi Sonatine (WI4 M4) in 10 hours, ascending the east side of the northeast buttress of Peak 11,300', north (right) of Wasabi Concerto. The route we climbed is invisible from almost anywhere and we researched it heavily, making several reconnaissance trips. These were needed to help us understand the avalanche intervals. The route proved to be a very beautiful ice line up a couloir with rocks on either side. From the top of the ice couloir, we continued along the ridgeline for five fun pitches of

[Right] Junji Wada leading an M4 pitch on the upper part of Wasabi Sonatine, Peak 11,300'. *Kei Taniguchi*

mixed climbing. Again, we topped out at a logical high point above the route rather than the main summit—this one we called "P3."

[*Editor's note: Taniguchi and Wada describe the northeast buttress of Peak 11,300' as having four distinct summits. They dubbed these unofficially, from right to left (north to south), as Point 1, Point 2, Point 3, and Point KJ. A very sharp, corniced, and knife-edged ridge separates Point KJ and the northeast buttress from the main mass of Peak 11,300', making the buttress almost a distinct entity.*] 📷 🔍

– **KEI TANIGUCHI**, *JAPAN, ADDITIONAL INFORMATION FROM* **MARK WESTMAN** *AND* **VIVIAN SCOTT**

DRAGON'S SPINE, TWO TOWERS

IN JULY, James Gustafson and I returned to the Pika Glacier of Little Switzerland, hoping to complete a traverse of the Dragon's Spine [*The Dragon's Spine is a long ridgeline that culminates in a 7,490' summit. It lies three miles down glacier (north-northwest) from the Trolls and other formations.*] This trip resulted in more stepping stones. We first added a new starting pitch to Green Couch, a short route we put up last year (*AAJ 2014*). About a week later, in a 48-hour "sunny" period, from July 19–20, we made a 36-hour push on our intended traverse. We did not even come close to finishing the traverse but did top out on the first major tower, completing a new route in the process. We climbed about 20 pitches—a mix of slabs, steep cracks, and scrambling—and bivied once: Two Towers (IV 5.10). We descended climber's right, from a notch below the tower, via many rappels. 📷 🔍

– ZACH CLANTON

HAYES RANGE

MT. HAYES, NORTHEAST FACE TO SOUTH BUTTRESS, THICKER THAN THIEVES

BY CHANCE I teamed up with Jason Stuckey, a Fairbanks climber, and upcoming alpinist Angela VanWiemeersch to climb the east face of Mt. Hayes (13,832'). Jason's picture of a thin line of ice plastered in the back of a wide chimney had lit the same fire in all three of us. It was the perfect recipe for a grand adventure. We met in Delta Junction in mid-April. Our pilot, Jim Cummings, had to shuttle us to the mountain one at a time in his tiny Super Cub. On the Trident Glacier we finally glassed the route in person. The 6,000' climb was a major garbage chute and well beyond our level of acceptable risk. Lacking any bold Euro-blood to take on seracs, falling ice, etc., we decided to take a less steep but safer line on the southeast (far left) end of the wall.

On April 22 we left camp at first light, and by 7 a.m. had crossed the bergschrund. An easy 1,800' of couloir climbing brought us to a short rock band. One pitch of fun, easily protected 5.8 climbing led us to a steep snowfield, which then led to a pitch of boilerplate alpine ice. Above that loomed another steep rock band. A blind, engaging traverse (M5 R) provided the only reasonable path. Luckily this deposited us on another snow and ice slope, and a few more pitches (up to AI4) brought us to the knife-edge ridge atop the wall. Well past dark, we searched for a bivy from behind the feeble beams of our headlamps. The whole affair looked quite bleak until I noticed an overhung cornice, which allowed us to shovel a plush camp in the most unlikely of locations.

[Above] The new route Thicker Than Thieves (7,300', VI 5.8 AI4 M5), which climbs Mt. Hayes' northeast face to the upper south buttress, first reaching the south summit (left) and then main summit (right). The final part of the descent is shown by the dashed line. *Jason Stuckey*

The next morning, feeling a bit hammered, we began traversing the knife-edge ridge toward the south summit of Mt. Hayes. The typical Hayes Range winds concerned us, growing more powerful as we wound through an incredible maze of crevasses, cornices, snow bridges, and seracs. Our progress was much slower than anticipated. Still far below the south summit, but with night fast approaching, we found another bivy site among the seracs and drifted off to sleep with a spectacular vista.

We awoke on the third day with a strong desire to finish our route and get off the mountain—and back to our whiskey supply. Quickly reaching the south summit, we joined the

[Bottom] Angela VanWiemeersch and John Giraldo climbing toward the south summit of Mt. Hayes. *Jason Stuckey*

South Buttress and headed toward the main summit. [*The South Buttress has been incorrectly dubbed the "south ridge" in past AAJs. See AAJ 2011 for a photo of the South Buttress*]. By 2 p.m. we were taking cheesy summit photos, completely psyched to be on top of Mt. Hayes.

Unfortunately a 7,000' descent still separated us from our whiskey. A building storm chased us off the summit and down the east ridge. Some highly involved route-finding ensued, and we finally made it back to the whiskey at 5 a.m., having completed Thicker Than Thieves (7,300', VI 5.8 AI4 M5). It is worth noting that Sam Johnson, an Alaskan climber, made the same descent solo (*AAJ 2014*), a fact that was the source of some consternation during our own downclimb—he obviously possesses that elusive, bold Euro-blood.

[*Editor's note: This marks the first time the south buttress of Mt. Hayes has been reached from the Trident Glacier, rather than the Susitna or Turkey glaciers. In all, the trio climbed around 3,000' of new terrain on the northeast aspect of the mountain before reaching the south summit of Mt. Hayes and then continuing up the South Buttress. From the south summit they gained another 1,300' over 4 miles to reach Mt. Hayes' main summit, and then descended its east ridge back to the Trident Glacier, completing an approximately 15,000' traverse of the peak.*] 📷 🔍

– JOHN GIRALDO, *WITH ADDITIONAL INFORMATION FROM* JASON STUCKEY *AND* JEFF BENOWITZ

CHUGACH MOUNTAINS

PEAK 4,360', FIRST ASCENT; WHITECROWN, FIRST ASCENT

IN MARCH Carrie Wang and I climbed two peaks comprising the "last of the Western Chugach Mountains." The Western Chugach includes all peaks with at least 500' of prominence south of the Knik River Valley and west of the west fork of Twentymile River. We first made a base camp at Bagg Pass on the eastern edge of the Western Chugach Mountains. On March 21 we skinned up Peak 4,360', and the following day we skinned partway up and then climbed Whitecrown (6,390') via a spur on its southeast ridge. These were reportedly the last two unclimbed peaks in the Western Chugach.

On July 16, Carrie and I climbed Far Out Peak (5,750') and Pass Out Peak (5,940') from the flats to the northeast. My summiting of these two peaks marked the first time anyone had climbed all 166 peaks in the Western Chugach. 📷

– WAYNE L. TODD

MT. MUIR, NORTH FACE

On April 28, Nathan Lane and I launched my 16-foot inflatable Achilles boat in Whittier, hoping to make the first ascent of Mt. Muir (7,605') via Harriman Fiord. On April 29 we motored into Harriman and were not disappointed. From our first look at Muir in person, we immediately knew it was possible. However, we noticed an obvious problem with our intended route: a massive icefall on the Colony Glacier, regularly puking ice downward. We made camp on the southwest shore of Surprise Inlet that day and just stared up at the route in question for some time. Thinking it best to take a quick hike up the Serpentine Glacier for a better look, we found a 2,500' snowfield with possible access to the glacier.

The next morning we loaded our packs, donned neoprene boots, and started the half-mile boulder traverse up toward the Serpentine. From the shore we angled up toward a narrow avy chute that we climbed to reach skin-able terrain. After 500' of gain, the angle lessened and

our skis came off our backs to zigzag up a 2,000' snow slope. Once on the Colony Glacier we were relieved to see a fairly easy and flat ski across it toward a little glacier flowing down the northeast side of Muir. This was our first glimpse of the mountain up close, and we instantly felt a little put off by the huge seracs dangling from the north face, where we hoped to find a route.

As we skied closer, I noticed a possible route up the left end of the face. We skied up to a camp safely tucked below the face. We fell asleep to hard wind gusts and icy condensation shaking down the tent walls and left camp just after 6 a.m. on May 1. The climbing on the glacier below the face was steep, and we encountered firm alpine ice that made front-pointing and two-tooling necessary. Once in the couloir the ice was even firmer, and as the angle steepened we slowed down to place our tools well. The angle stayed at a consistent 60° until the last 60', where it steepened quite a bit. The entire face was about 800' long, and we were able to simul-climb the first 500' before belaying. At the top, I was stoked to see the last 500' to the summit was a mere walk-up. Close to the summit I plunged chest-deep into a hidden crevasse but was able to climb out. After I pointed Nate around the crevasse, we reached

the summit of Mt. Muir within minutes. It was 10:30 a.m. and the entire Prince William Sound unfolded below. [*Editor's note: Mt. Muir had been attempted previously and noted by climbers for its mountaineering potential as early as the 1930s, though weather and crevasse issues have thwarted other known attempts.*]

Due to the warm air, we didn't linger on the summit long and quickly descended our line of ascent. By 1:30 p.m. we were back at the tent and giving each other our first true congratulatory hug. That afternoon we trudged down the Serpentine Glacier and finally hit the shoreline right around high tide. The beauty of a sea-to-summit climb is being able to say you completely earned every foot of that mountain. 📷 🔍

– RYAN FISHER

FAIRWEATHER RANGE

PEAK 8,290' AND OTHER FIRST ASCENTS

IN APRIL AND MAY, Kieran Parsons and I made the first ascents of three summits between Mt. Abbe (8,250') and Mt. Bertha (10,204') in Glacier Bay National Park in southeast Alaska. The most exciting of these was Peak 8,290', which sports a pyramid of clean granite leading to its summit. After landing in the southern part of the range, we originally planned to attempt the unclimbed east ridge of Mt. Crillon (12,726')—a challenge put forth by Bradford Washburn in the *AAJ 1941*—but heavy snowfall, high winds, and unseasonably warm temperatures made the approach to the ridge too avalanche-threatened. Hence, we made a 20km traverse north on

[**Below**] West side of Peak 8,290' from Peak 7,400'. The pillar is about 1,500' high. Paul Knott and Kieran Parsons made the first ascent of the peak by its southeast ridge (right skyline). *Paul Knott*

the Brady Icefield to an area north of Mt. Bertha, where we climbed to a col at ca 6,190' and a high bowl overlooking the Johns Hopkins Glacier. [*Editor's note: See AAJ 2010 for Paul Knott's report on the first ascents of Mt. Bertha's south face and northwest ridge. Also, see the AAJ 2010 online-only report where Knott describes the difficult access to the Johns Hopkins Glacier.*]

On May 6 we made the first ascents of two snow summits on the south side of the bowl: Peak 7,507' via its snowy northern arête and Peak 7,274' via its west ridge. The view from these peaks convinced us that the snowy southeast face of Peak 8,290' was not viable due to a threatening ice cliff and wet avalanches. So early on May 7 we set off on the 2km-long southeast ridge of Peak 8,290' from a camp by the ca 6,190' col. We noted the potential for time-consuming difficulties along this ridge, and beyond Point 6,706' we found ourselves tackling a series of knife-edged, corniced snow mushrooms and rime towers. It took us three hours to negotiate a few hundred meters of ridgeline. Above, an easier snow arête brought us to the base of the granite pyramid. The only way up this was on steep rock, but the granite was superb, providing secure climbing with juggy holds and plentiful protection. We climbed close to the crest for three pitches (5.7).

From the top we could see the plentiful untapped climbing potential in this knot of granite peaks. The west side of Peak 8,290' sports a steep and continuous 1,500' pillar, and other summits in the Mt. Abbe group sport similar monolithic pillars up to 2,500'. Warming temperatures created an involved descent, and we reached our tent in mist and light snow at 6:30 p.m. Luckily, by the next afternoon the weather had cleared and our pilot, Paul Swanstrom, was able to pick us up directly from our ca 4,184' cache below the ridge. 📷 🗒

– PAUL KNOTT, *NEW ZEALAND*

COAST MOUNTAINS

WEST WITCHES' TIT, WEST RIDGE, NO REST FOR THE WICKED

JOHN FRIEH AND I landed below the Devils Thumb on May 27 and set up camp below the east ridge. Leaving camp at 3 a.m. on May 28, we headed westward over the glacier, below the south side of the massif. After rappelling the lower rock rib that rises up toward the east and west Witches' Tits, we continued along the glacier to a steep snow ramp that reaches the col below the west ridge of the West Witches' Tit.

John and I swapped leads up the west ridge, finding steep ice, snow, and mixed climbing until reaching a crux squeeze chimney with brittle ice deep inside the cleft, which I led. Difficult terrain continued above and we pulled on gear as necessary to keep moving. Near the summit we found rappel anchors from a prior ascent (Belcourt-Rackliff, *AAJ 1996*). Shortly afterward, around midnight, we reached the top, having completed No Rest for the Wicked (1,500' AI6 M7 A0). We used the old rappel anchors, which took us down the southwest face of the West Witches' Tit.

We reached the glacier again at 8 a.m. and began making our way back to camp. Our pilot expected us in camp by noon on May 29. We were late. Through fog we heard the helicopter scan in vain, then retreat to Petersburg. After refueling and making a return flight, he spotted us and landed before we reached camp. Weather was approaching and we were informed it was our only chance out. Without hesitation we piled in with our crampons still on and ice tools in hand. 📷 🔍 🗒

– JESS ROSKELLEY

[Above] Erik Bonnett and Max Fisher with pilot Drake Olson upon arrival. Kooshdakhaa Spire is the prominent granite tower in the center. *Max Fisher*

KOOSHDAKHAA SPIRE, FIRST ASCENT

BETWEEN MAY 25 and June 14, Erik Bonnett and I climbed about 45 pitches of rock, ice, and snow in a relatively unknown glacial area on the border of southeast Alaska and northern British Columbia, bearing similarities to the Kichatna Spires. We then traveled over many kilometers of glacier and packrafted down the Chilkat River to civilization.

We flew into the area with Drake Olson out of Haines, intent on making the first ascent of what we've called Kooshdakhaa Spire (2,200m), the southern summit and most prominent feature of a complex granite mountain. The neighboring mountain range in northern British Columbia goes by the name Kooshdakhaa, so this made sense to us.

I noticed the spire during three trips into the area as a NOLS instructor, entering from the British Columbia side. I know of only one other expedition to the range, by NOLS instructors headed up by Dave Anderson (*AAJ 2004*). They attempted a 300m spire north of the one we climbed; however, they were turned around by poor rock quality.

After Drake departed we spent 15 days in the area, staging climbs from a base camp on the moraine below Kooshdakhaa Spire. We climbed the spire via a sustained couloir on its north side, reaching a col and then the summit: North Couloir (600m, AI3 M3). We also climbed a gully on the opposite side of the spire: South Couloir (350m, AI3 M3).

Our main objective, the steep, 700m, north-facing granite wall on Kooshdakhaa Spire, turned us away on both of our alpine-style attempts, after we encountered tricky routefinding, poor rock, and difficult climbing (up to 5.11) about two-thirds of the way up the wall. The lower climb generally followed sustained and continuous splitter cracks up great rock.

We also attempted a couloir to the north of Kooshdakhaa Spire, on another granite feature; however, we were forced to descend about one pitch from the top. The route contained physical mixed climbing up to M5.

After climbing, we walked 25km across the glacier over two days and began rafting toward the Chilkat River through small tributaries. Upon reaching the upper Chilkat River we paddled two short sections of Class III whitewater in our packrafts before dropping to the Chilkat River Valley, where we paddled more Class III whitewater. To our knowledge we were the first people to paddle the Upper Chilkat in packrafts and the second team to paddle the 60km of river from the glacier to Haines. Toward the river's exit we encountered a thriving game area full of wolves, bears, and moose, inciting much nervousness—it was the most scared I was on the trip!

The name Kooshdakhaa is derived from the lore of the Tlingit and Tsimshian Indians of southeast Alaska. Loosely translated, Kooshdakhaa means "land otter man," a mythical shape-shifting creature capable of assuming both human and otter-like forms. In many stories, the Kooshdakhaa saves a lost individual by distracting him with curiously otter-like illusions of family and friends as he is transformed into a fellow Kooshdakhaa, thus allowing him to survive in the cold. Naturally, this is counted as a mixed blessing. Kooshdakhaa legends are not always pleasant. It is said the Kooshdakhaa will imitate the cries of a baby or the screams of a woman to lure victims to a river. Once there, the Kooshdakhaa either kills the person and tears him to shreds or turns him into another Kooshdakhaa.

– MAX FISHER

[Left] Max Fisher following a perfect, steep thin-hands crack on the third pitch of an attempt on Kooshdakhaa Spire's north face. [Right] Max Fisher packrafting out from the glacier via the Upper Chilkat River. *Photos: Erik Bonnett*

CANADA

WADDINGTON RANGE, VARIOUS ASCENTS

In late July, Brette Harrington, Hannah Preston, Andrew Rennie, and I spent two weeks base-camped out of Sunny Knob. On our first day, Harrington and I established a direct variation to the upper part of Serra 2's approximately 1,500m south ridge. Most of the route consisted of easy but quality scrambling (5.7), but we climbed several more difficult pitches (5.11 A1) on the steepest section. The climbing would go free at 5.12, but we aided the crux due to our backpacks and limited gear. We descended southeast and down the Stilletto Icefall to Sunny Knob. Straight No Chaser (TD+ 5.11 A1) climbs approximately 400m of new ground.

A few days later Harrington, Preston, and Rennie made the first ascent of Dentiform's south ridge, beginning from the Tiedemann Glacier, southeast of Sunny Knob. They encountered long sections of loose rock and climbing in the 5.9 range. From the top they rappelled to Upper Tellot Glacier and spent the night at Plummer Hut before descending back to Sunny Knob. It is possible that a faster party, or a party prepared to bivouac, may be able to continue this route beyond Dentiform to the summit of Stiletto Peak.

During this same time, I made solo ascents of Serra 5 and Asperity Mountain in an 18-hour push from base camp. The couloirs leading to the Asperity–Serra 5 col were severely threatened by rockfall so I climbed numerous variations. I first climbed the rock buttress right of Carl's Couloir. Above a bergscrund I joined rock left of the upper couloir. Upon reaching the col I quickly bagged Serra 5 via its northwest corner in excellent mixed conditions. This was the first solo ascent of the mountain. After returning to the col, I spent the next couple of hours climbing Asperity. Once down at the col, with the sun off the snow, I tediously downclimbed the couloirs. The rock variation to Carl's Couloir was later called Serra Marco (400m, 5.10a) by Preston and Rennie. However, I decided not to label my Asperity line as a new route, since it was just a crisscrossing variation to avoid objective hazards (1,600m, TD+ 5.10a WI3).

Rennie and Preston later reclimbed my variation and then made the first free ascent of Thunderbird, on the spectacular south buttress of Serra 5, eliminating a section of A1 with free climbing to 5.10+. Harrington and I also made an attempt on the southeast face of Grand Cappuccino tower, climbing eight fantastic pitches of steep granite to 5.12a. We were turned back by an exfoliating wide crack a pitch below the summit of the tower.

– MARC-ANDRÉ LECLERC, *CANADA*

RETHEL MOUNTAIN, RETHEL HEADWALL

The El Niño weather pattern created very unusual conditions in western Canada during the 2014–15 winter season. Powder skiing did not happen and the lower-elevation waterfalls all fell down. Following my nose higher than usual, I discovered atypical perfect winter-climbing conditions on the prominent north-northeast-facing alpine wall of Rethel Mountain (7,060'). This wall is located just above Wedgemount Lake, immediately north of the Blackcomb ski resort. The über-prolific cragsman Robin Barley climbed the main rock buttress lines several decades ago, in summer conditions, but I doubt there has been much or any traffic since. I'm not sure of a previous name for this cliff besides the Wedgemount Lake Bluffs, so I've proposed the Rethel Headwall. It's a Canadian tradition, and it always sounds cooler when it's a headwall.

On March 3 and 4, 2015, Tony Richardson and Kye Petersen joined me for back-to-back first ascents up two of the nicest-looking and least cornice-threatened lines. Both involve 140m of vertical gain from the base of the wall to the rim and involve all the joys of winter climbing: steep ice, thin ice, sn'ice, névé, snow mushrooms, drytooling, and frozen turf. They aren't "hard" routes, but folks gunning for repeat ascents will want solid skills and a headspace for slightly bold climbing. Both routes maxed out around WI4+ and M5+, with the plus added to denote the seriousness for the leader: Intolerant Tearin' (140m, M5+), No Cupcakes (140m, WI4+). The rock on the Rethel is relatively good but compact alpine granite, so can be hard to protect. If the right conditions arise, these lines should be high on the list for any coastal ice climber—they are definitely jewels and it couldn't be a more scenic spot.

— JASON KRUK, *CANADA*

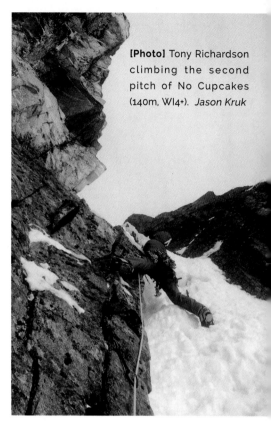

[Photo] Tony Richardson climbing the second pitch of No Cupcakes (140m, WI4+). *Jason Kruk*

SQUAMISH, THE CHIEF, PARALLELS WALL

THE LEFTMOST END of the Chief's north walls is braided with splitter cracks, coarse-grained corners, and ledge systems. Apart from a couple of seeps down low, the Parallels Wall dries out quickly after storms.

In 2011, Eric Huges and I redpointed the first of two new routes on the Parallels Wall: Inside Passage (350m, 5.11a), located about 100m left of Alaska Highway. This 12-pitch route originally was conceived as a more moderate way to reach Astro Ledge than Alaska Highway (a notoriously strenuous 5.11+), though it now goes to the top of the wall and is a worthwhile route in its own right. The route begins up a series of steep, blocky corners just past Alaska Highway on "Strato Ledge." Most of the pitches average 30m and fall in the 5.9–5.10 range. The technical crux, a steep, thin corner, comes on pitch six; however, I'm sure many climbers will appreciate a few #5 and #6 Camalots for the strenuous 50m offwidth on pitch eight. The start of Inside Passage can also be linked with the seldom-climbed and classic North North Arete to stay mostly in 5.9 country to the top.

I completed a second route just left of Inside Passage in 2011, which I redpointed with Crosby Johnston (starting on the route New Life), and then I revisited the climb in 2013 with Eric Hughes to free a direct start. Finally, in 2014, Jason Kruk joined me for the completion of the integral route: Parallel Universe (450m, 5.12b). The name refers to the fact that most pitches follow sustained, parallel-sided cracks. The third-pitch crux finger crack, which we dubbed "Parallelojam," is a particular joy (45m, 5.12b). Many of the individual pitches had

old, rusty evidence of previous attempts, but this is the first known free ascent of a complete line. The 11-pitch route begins at the base of the Saturn V Tower with 100m of 5.11 climbing right off the ground. From there it gains a steep headwall with two 5.12 pitches and a number of others in the 5.9–5.11 range. Many of the pitches contain difficult, heartbreaker moves near the end of the climbing. Both routes can be descended easily by walking off climber's right on a good trail to the Zodiac summit. 📷 🔍

– **PAUL CORDY**, *CANADA*

YAK PEAK, SOUTH FACE, CARDIYAK RHYTHM

YAK PEAK (2,039m) is the highest point along the Zopkios Ridge, which also includes Nak and Thar peaks. From the highway, Yak appears as a beautiful, clean slab of south-facing granite that steadily increases in steepness before the summit. It has been compared to the granite domes of Tuolumne Meadows in California.

Rob Birtles and I began talking about new-route possibilities on Yak Peak three years ago. Many routes on the face have serious runouts because they were established ground-up. Yak Crack (12 pitches, 5.9-) has multiple, loose, and run-out corners, and Reality Check (13 pitches, 5.10+, Cox-Wolkoff, 1992) has an infamous and unnerving 35m runout on 5.10+ climbing, which has sent experienced climbers to the hospital. Not wanting to create a climb that risks life and limb, we chose a combination top-down/ground-up approach.

Rob and I started sussing out a line in August 2011, and we quickly installed 12 anchors along our route to facilitate quick escape, given Yak's unpredictable weather. The first three and last three pitches of our 17-pitch route were climbed ground-up, as we were able to sufficiently bolt those sections on lead. The rest was established top-down, and we redpointed the harder pitches to figure out the best balance of gear and bolts.

On September 6, Rob, Gary Wolkoff, and I made a 12-hour push to the summit. CardiYak Rhythm (17 pitches, 5.11b) weaves a cunning line up the center of the south face of Yak Peak, between Reality Check and Hole In My Heaven. It links numerous clean corners and breaches a series of overlaps through gradually steepening terrain to the summit slabs. All the pitches have been redpointed, but the climb still awaits a true ground-up free ascent. The route can be climbed at 5.10c A0—enjoy! 📄 📷 🔍

– **LYLE KNIGHT**, *CANADA*

MT. SIR DONALD, NORTH FACE, SASHIMI DON

In July 2012, Dylan Johnson and I made a brief stop at Rogers Pass to climb the classic Northwest Arête of Mt. Sir Donald (3,284m). I was blown away by the quality climbing, so when I saw David P. Jones' new guidebook to Rogers Pass, I did not hesitate to buy it. The cover is a photo of Mt. Sir Donald's north face, and it showed a very obvious unclimbed gash that looked like a good candidate for a mixed climb.

In mid-June 2014, Sarah Hart and I drove to the interior of BC. Our "Plan A" was the unclimbed gash on Sir Donald. On June 17 we hiked up the Asulkan Brook Valley to a bivy at the Uto–Sir Donald Col. On June 18 we woke up very early and left our bivy around 2:30 a.m., downclimbed to the Uto Glacier, and traversed to the base of our line. There had been only about four hours of darkness and the snow wasn't very refrozen, but it was just barely enough.

The first half of the route climbs a couloir up the center-left side of the north face. It then goes partway up an obvious right-angling ramp/gash, before branching left onto a rocky rib near the end (mostly mixed), and finally joining the northeast buttress for 75m to the summit. I estimate we simulclimbed about three-quarters of the route, and pitched out the rest. We climbed one distinct crux pitch (M5 R). Most of the route contained 60° ice and névé, with an occasional step of 70-85° ice and plenty of easy mixed climbing on good quartzite (up to M4).

We headed down the south ridge, which felt like the right choice in wintery conditions.

[Below] Mt. Sir Donald, north face, showing the new route Sashimi Don (left) and the Beckey-Chouinard, 1961 (right); the latter was climbed primarily as a rock route in summer conditions. The left skyline comprises the northeast buttress (Cox-DeBeyer-Sellers, 1996); the striking ridge on the right is the classic northwest ridge (Bartleet-Fynn, 1909). *Felix Parham*

It was past 6 p.m. when we finally took off our harnesses in the basin below Sir Donald's west face. Sarah carried our climbing gear down to the dry trail while I hoofed back up to the Uto–Sir Donald col to retrieve our bivy gear, and then we hiked out to the car. We named our route Sashimi Don (900m, M5 R 60-85°). 📷

— COLIN HALEY, *USA*

PURCELL MOUNTAINS / BUGABOOS

NORTH HOWSER TOWER, WEST FACE, DODGING DEANNA

ON JULY 28, Tony McLane and Nathan McDonald climbed a new route on North Howser Tower's west face: Dodging Deanna (V 5.10). The pair started up the Shooting Gallery and then crossed Seventh Rifle (Jones-Rowell-Qamar, 1971) to gain new ground. The 10 pitches of new climbing follow a large prow between Real Mescalito (Johnston-Lavigne, *AAJ 2008*) and Spicy Red Beans and Rice (Greene-Tague, *AAJ 1998*). They did not use any bolts or pitons, and the route took 19 hours from the Pigeon-Howser Col, including the descent to Applebee Campground.

— *GRIPPED.COM*

SOUTH HOWSER TOWER, NORTHEAST FACE, ETHEREAL

AFTER REACHING the Kain Hut around midnight on October 10 and sleeping in past our alpine start, Tim McAllister and I hiked out toward the Howser Towers intent on some winter-conditions climbing. Sighting excellent conditions, we chose a line to the left of Perma

[Left] Jennifer Olson starts up a ribbon of sn'ice on the third pitch of Ethereral. [Right] South Howser Tower, northeast face, showing the mixed routes: (1) Ethereal (McAllister-Olson, 2014). (2) Perma Grin (Isaac-Semple-Webster, *AAJ 2003*). (3) Big Hose (Krakauer, *AAJ 1979*). *Tim McAllister*

Grin (*AAJ 2003*) and the Big Hose (*AAJ 1979*) on the northeast face of South Howser Tower. Climbing through the 'schrund provided a pumpy start through steep icicles to a Styrofoam-like ice ramp. From there we found ribbons of sn'ice interspersed with mixed climbing up a prominent, left-facing corner system. Near the top we veered left out of the corner to continue up a lower-angled snow and ice ramp. From the summit we descended the standard rappel route. Our route, Ethereal (1,000', D+ WI4 M6 R), has eight pitches with excellent thin ice and mixed climbing. It shares some terrain with the Thompson-Turk (5.10 R, 1990). 🖸

— JENNIFER OLSON, *CANADA*

WIDE AWAKE TOWER, ELECTRIC FUNERAL

In August, Jon Walsh and Michelle Kadatz flew into East Creek Basin and climbed a new route on Wide Awake Tower. The tower is located in the seldom-visited Pigeon Feathers group, and the new, nine-pitch route Electric Funeral (300m, 5.11+) mostly climbs splitter cracks to the right of the original route, Wide Awake (V 5.10+ A2, *AAJ 2000*), right of the tower's main (southeast) prow.

— *FROM INFORMATION BY* JON WALSH, *CANADA*

PURCELL MOUNTAINS / LEANING TOWER GROUP

SHARKSHEAD TOWER, EAST FACE

On August 6, Joanne Mauthner, Jeffrey Bury, and I climbed a new route on the east face of Sharkshead Tower in the Leaning Tower Group. We climbed glacial ice to gain the rock, and from there it was six 30m pitches to the north summit. The hardest pitch was 5.9, and all the climbing was on very clean, fun, and solid granite. From the north summit we traversed to the higher south summit, then descended by rappelling the gully down the east face, which separates the two summits. We accessed the tower out of Dewar Creek. 🖸

— KIRK MAUTHNER, *CANADA*

HALL PEAK, EAST FACE, FREE VARIATION

In summer 2014, Katie Bono, Hannah Preston, and I went to explore the Leaning Towers. Following logging roads outside of Kimberly, BC, we set off on our adventure. Burdened with 80lb packs, we traveled along a horse trail for 10km. This was the easy part—soon we were bushwhacking on steep, rough terrain. After several days of being pinned down by rain and fog in the forest we were able to reach the base of Hall Peak. A promising line on the east face caught our attention, and we devoted our weather window to it.

At sunrise we eagerly kicked steps up a snow slope, and then did some acrobatic movements to gain the rock over a moat at the base. The crack systems were delightful, taking excellent gear, though some required cleaning with a nut tool in the more challenging sections. The rock was featured, providing frequent reprieve from jamming. Swapping leads, we free-climbed about 12 pitches to reach the summit ridge and breathtaking views of the surrounding peaks. The descent was fairly straightforward: We scrambled down the northwest ridge, did several rappels, and downclimbed exposed and icy snow slopes.

The next day a storm moved in and we decided to pack out. We later found out that our

[Above] Hall Peak, east face showing: (1) McComb-Myers-Twomey, 1975 (this was free climbed with some variations in 2014 and dubbed Quarter Life Crisis (IV 5.10, Bono-Kadatz-Preston). (2) Direct East Buttress (Morriss-Ramos, 2014). (3) Upper Ramp (Leary-Reimmondo, *AAJ 2014*). Post Credit Cookie (Morriss-Ramos, 2014) climbs the short wall on the far right, topping out on the lower north ridge. To the left of Hall Peak is the Pulpit, and Sharkshead is located out of frame further left. The tops of Block and Wall Tower can be seen far right. *Ryan Leary*

route consisted of several variations to the original route (5.9 A2, McComb-Myers-Twomey, 1975) up this face. We've named our free variation Quarter Life Crisis (IV 5.10). The Leaning Towers is a beautiful place and seems to be a mecca for unexplored lines. 📷

– MICHELLE KADATZ, *CANADA*

HALL PEAK, EAST FACE, NEW ROUTES

IN AUGUST, Winter Ramos and I ventured into the Leaning Towers, a remote and rarely visited bleb of granite just south of the world-famous Bugaboos. After two friends, Ryan Leary and Evan Reimondo, put up a new route on the east face of Hall Peak (*AAJ 2014*), Ryan told me the best line in the range was still unclimbed: a direct route up the east buttress of Hall Peak (3,040m). [*This buttress is located just left of the McComb-Myers-Twomey Route (1975).*]

A two-day approach was made much easier with the help of Kootenay Raft Company's horse packers, who carried our gear for the first 12km. Once in, Winter and I spent a day scouting the descent off Hall Peak, took photos, and recovered from two days of brutal hiking. On August 6 we roped up for our attempt. From the ground, the crux of the route appeared to be a roof two pitches off the ground; however, Winter snuck to the right just below the roof on airy 5.8 edges. From there we followed our noses pitch after pitch. The crux turned out to be a 5.9+ jam crack on pitch nine. After summiting a tall gendarme on the east buttress, we began following the ridgeline on lower-angle, less difficult climbing, where shorter pitches led us to the summit. Our 17-pitch route was comprised of great granite and diorite, and we only encountered a few loose blocks: Direct East Buttress (2,000', IV 5.9+).

With more food and time available, we examined some of the cracks along the northeast side of Hall Peak. On August 8 we climbed a prominent 500' corner. Atop the wall we traversed 100' left and rappelled: Post Credit Cookie (4 pitches, 5.10a). 📷 🔍

– MATTHEW MORRISS, *USA*

CANADIAN ROCKIES

STORM CREEK HEADWALL, NEW ROUTES

ON NOVEMBER 8, Jon Walsh and Marc-André Leclerc (both Canada) completed the first ascent of a traditionally protected mixed route on the Storm Creek Headwall: the Plum (120m, WI6 M7). Storm Creek Headwall is similar to the Stanley Headwall, located just to the west. The route is on a prow to the right of the Peach (110m, WI5 M8) and climbs steep rock and thin ice smears for three pitches.

Walsh returned to the area on January 23, 2015, with Jon Simms and together completed the first ascent of Kahveology (160m, WI5 M8). The four-pitch mixed route finishes on the final ice pillar (WI5) of the route Check Your Head. Unlike the Plum, this route required four bolts to protect the M8 first pitch, and bolted anchors were installed atop each pitch.

— FROM INFORMATION BY **JON WALSH**, *CANADA*

CAPRICORN PEAK, NORTHEAST FACE

IN MID-NOVEMBER I completed a couple of big, new mixed routes on the lower northeast face of Capricorn Peak. This mountain is just north of and behind Mt. Patterson along the Icefields Parkway. The routes are both about 300m long, with mixed climbing and very thin ice climbing. They do not reach the summit, topping out at the ridgeline.

I completed the first route on November 16 with Steve Holeczi and Eamonn Walsh. The

[Left] Jon Walsh starts up a thin ice runnel on the second pitch of Kahveology on the Storm Creek Headwall. *Jon Simms* **[Right]** Jay Mills leading the final pitch of Space Goat, a new route on the northeast face of Capricorn Peak. *Rob Owens*

[Above] After hand-drilling a bolt and fiddling in a small cam, Chris Brazeau makes his way up pitch 17 of the Accomplice. The new route climbs the right side of Mt. Stephen's nearly 4,000' northeast face. The sheer wall in the background is unattempted and unclimbed. *Jon Simms*

route appeared to have the fattest ice on the cliff, and we named it Big Ears Teddy (300m, WI4 R M4 X). On November 20 I climbed a second route, with Rob Owens, and we named it Space Goat (320m, WI5+ X M5). Space Goat had one of the thinnest and most run-out ice pitches either of us had ever climbed—hard to grade and certainly adventurous! Both routes require an extensive rock rack, including pitons, Peckers, and short ice screws. No bolts were used. We rappelled back down both routes using V-threads and piton anchors.

It takes about two hours to reach the wall. Space Goat is the farthest right line, and Big Ears Teddy is located just left. These routes hadn't been tried before, although climbers had scoped them for years. They often appear quite thin, but there is some ice every season. 📄 📷

— JAY MILLS, *CANADA*

MT. STEPHEN, NORTHEAST FACE, THE ACCOMPLICE

OVER THREE DAYS in August, Jon Simms and I established a new route on the northeast face of Mt. Stephen (10,495') in Yoho National Park. Our goal was the massive, unclimbed, and eye-catching wall known locally as the "Great Wall of China" or "Apocalyptic Wall." Arriving at the base we felt way underequipped and tiny. I was content with the hike in and "have a look" approach, but Simms was fired up and bino-ing the wall for other opportunities.

He convinced me to continue having a look, so we forged up a weakness on the right side of the face with ridiculously large packs. Much loose rock was encountered, with the occasional stretch of solid limestone, and we were rewarded for persevering with an amazing bivy cave. The next day we climbed through more choss and reached harder climbing. Thankfully, the rock quality improved on the steeper rock, and the crux of that day was getting through the first steep pitch, which required hand-drilling six bolts and smoking several cigarettes. (We hand-drilled 18 bolts total, all on lead.) After several more steep pitches up mostly good quality rock we arrived at another amazing bivy: a flat ledge with a huge roof and a trickle of water.

We started the third day with a 300' leftward traverse to a corner system we had eyed from the base. This wall is remarkable for its striations, going from limestone to quartzite to infusions of the two, embedded with fossils and crystals throughout. The corner system was comprised of the quartzite band and provided some of the best climbing on the route, with two pitches of steep stemming and jamming up excellent rock. The crux of the route came a few pitches higher on immaculate, steep limestone. A couple more 5.11 pitches and some simul-climbing brought us to the end of the difficulties, where we dropped everything and ran for the summit (a separate, lower summit from Mt. Stephen proper).

The descent was heinous, with almost 7,000' feet of heel-bruising, ankle-twisting, knee-bashing scree and steps—in the dark—back to the highway. Jonny finished it off with a three-mile run at 3 a.m. to pick up our car, while I smoked our last cig, hiding in the bushes. While that's a whole 'nother story—it is how the route got its name: the Accomplice (3,600', VI 5.11+). 📷 🔍

– CHRIS BRAZEAU, *CANADA*

MT. LAWRENCE GRASSI, CANMORE WALL NEW WINTER ROUTES

THIS PAST WINTER a few friends and I did something unusual. Rather than further support the petro-state of Alberta by driving the six-hour round-trip to the Ice Fields Parkway or four hours of off-roading into the Ghost, we approached the mountains right above home. Canmore has a plethora of limestone cliffs crowding it. We started joking that we were busy in Canmonix.

Recently, the mixed game in town has regressed to hanging upside-down on drilled pockets and clipping bolts. In contrast, if one goes mountain climbing up the steep, alpine faces above town when they are covered in snow, there are new lines full of excitement and adventure. It helps that the approaches to the north face of Mt. Lawrence Grassi (2,685m) and the Canmore Wall (a large face between Ship's Prow and Ha Ling Peak) are quite short.

Partway up Lawrence Grassi is a 10m-diameter hole through the cliff; this feature was

[Below] Raphael Slawinski makes way through The Hole. *Ian Welsted*

first on my list. By traversing above this hole the previous summer with Sam Eastman, then traversing through it from the other side with Raphael Slawinski in winter, I finally figured out how to make a direct ascent with David Lussier and Jay Mills in December. The result is The Hole (300m, M6). This nine-pitch route is memorable for the experience of climbing through one of the most interesting natural features in the Bow Valley.

Next up on the tick list was to finish a route just left of The Hole that had been attempted and named almost a decade earlier: Town Gash. Rob Owens and Sean Issac had started up the most obvious gash on the north face of Mt. Lawrence Grassi, just left of the gully taken by the Hole. On my only attempt, with Sam Eastman and Raphael Slawinski, we quickly got past the previous high point, after two mixed pitches, and then Raph got to work bolting the steepness above. He has returned another three times as of this writing, equipping it for the future send.

Maybe it was my schedule, the prevailing avalanche conditions, or my general dislike for projecting, but by February 2015 my focus had moved to the Canmore Wall. My partner, Alik Berg, had climbed 19 El Cap routes, up to A5, so he was simply fooling himself into thinking he wasn't ready for the big faces of the Rockies in the winter. He asked to warm up on something smaller. We hiked uphill for two hours from the Peaks of Grassi subdivision to the base of the summer rock route Kurihara (430m, 5.10d). From there we'd aim for a weakness to the left of that route on the upper wall.

On our first try we encountered the leading edge of a five-day storm and made it up to some technical, cruxy dry-tooling in a finger-crack-size corner. From the wall, I tried to hype our efforts by tweetering #CanmoreWall, a scant month after Obama and Ellen jumped on the #DawnWall bandwagon. But in spite of my best efforts at generating social media buzz, only one of the multitudes of alpine climbers in Canmore responded to the call. I knew it was cheating, but I invited the "Real Rockies Ringer" along. On our next attempt, Raphael Slawinski camped out on the nonexistent feet to make it through the crux, Alik trundled death blocks visible from the coffee shops of Main Street, and I chimneyed up the gully we had been aiming for once it got dark. With the lights of Canmonix glowing below we topped out on Perpetual Spring (350m, M7).

Reflecting on a nearly nonexistent winter, this style of winter drytooling on fresh limestone might become more prevalent, especially as the tar sands continue to expand and we all enjoy living in the fishbowl. 📷 🔍

– IAN WELSTED, *CANADA*

ACROPOLE DES DRAVEURS, SENS UNIQUE, FIRST WINTER ASCENT

SENS UNIQUE (200m, 5.10+, Bérubé-Frick, 1974) is a particularly remote route that follows an imposing rock pillar up Acropole des Draveurs. The route is in the Charlevoix region and is well known as an ice-climbing destination because of the mega-classic ice route La Pomme d'Or (330m, WI5). Even in the regular rock climbing season, Sens Unique is rarely done due to a long, strenuous approach and poor rock quality on the third pitch.

Yannick Girard and I climbed this route on February 7, in "normal" Northeastern winter conditions: high winds, spindrift snow, and temperatures between -19° and -28°C. Many of the useful cracks became filled with ice. And the overall difficulty was increased by a 25km ski approach. Paths of deer, moose, hare, and huge gray wolf tracks decorated the astonishing frozen scene. After the ski approach, it took four hours of steep climbing up an icy gully and then dense bush fighting to reach the base of the wall.

We climbed until dark and "slept" at an open bivy on the route. The following morning we finished the climb, rappelled, and skied out to complete the adventure in a 48-hour round trip. We both experienced temporary hypothermia and frostbitten fingertips and toes. Climbing Sens Unique in winter (200m, M6+ R A1 [in winter conditions]) revealed once again that Québec is not only a terrific hard-core training ground, but also that the difficulty levels, extreme cold, and remoteness make this a world-class climbing destination in itself. For Yannick and me, it was another opportunity to fulfill our wild alpine dreams here among the gentle rolling hills of eastern Canada. [o]

– LOUIS ROUSSEAU, *QUÉBEC*

BAFFIN ISLAND / SAM FORD FJORD

LURKING TOWER, SOUTHEAST BUTTRESS, NEW DOG OLD TRICKS

IN MAY, Jonas Haag and I made the first ascent of Lurking Tower over 13 days by the route New Dog, Old Tricks (3,000', VI 5.11 C3+). This was my sixth trip to Baffin Island and my partner's first big wall—ever. We chose a beautiful tower on the northeast side of the Walker Arm. I had stared at this tower from the other side of the fjord for more than a month in 1998 while climbing Mahayana Wall on the Walker Citadel (*AAJ 1999*).

Almost half of the route looked to be comprised of thin, splitter cracks up golden granite and the rest of mysterious, red-granite corners— some of these corners would end up providing journeys through mottled sections of mayhem, up black-and-white, narwhal-skin-colored rock. I got to lead every pitch and haul the bags. Jonas learned to jug and clean, which is no easy task. After a week on the wall, climbing capsule style with two portaledge camps, we fixed ropes high and then blasted to the summit in a 35-hour push. A total of 17 pitches led us to an easy hike to the summit. We climbed the route hammerless and all clean, which was really pretty cool for a first ascent on an Arctic wall. (I did place some anchor bolts.)

On our way out, we learned a bear had ambushed two Inuit hunters near us and they'd barely survived. One hunter was dragged out of the tent with his head in a polar bear's jaws. [≡] [o]

– MIKE LIBECKI, *USA*

[Photo] (1) New Dog Old Tricks (Haag-Libecki, May 2014). (2) Up the Creek Without a Paddle (Ditto-Villanueva, August 2014, see p. 48). *Mike Libecki*

GREENLAND

UUMMANNAQ REGION: BIG-WALL FREE ASCENTS

IN THE SUMMER of 2014 I made another Tilman-type sailing and climbing expedition with my 10-meter boat Dodo's Delight. My crew and climbers were the "Wild Bunch" from 2010: Ben Ditto, Nicolas and Olivier Favresse, and Sean Villanueva. In early July they joined the boat in Aasiaat.

We moved north to explore the area around Uummannaq. On Ikerasak Island the team climbed two new routes on the peak that overlooks the village of Ikerasak. On July 13, Ben and Oli climbed the 400m left ridge to create Married Men's Way (E3 5c or 5.10a), a very good alpine rock route, while at the same time Nico and Sean climbed along the right-hand arête of the main face to give the more exciting Crocodiles have Teeth (400m, E5 6a or 5.11b/c). This gave consistently good climbing, finishing via two pitches up an overhanging crack. The area also had good bouldering.

We found our next big wall to the north, on the southeast corner of Qaquglugssuit. The climbers did two routes on the buttress forming the east side, which we named Goliath (70°41'N, 51°13'W), as it was big, bold, brazen, and blocky. On the 17th, Ben and Nico climbed the left side of the buttress via Standard Deviation (500m, E4 6a or 5.11), where a band of rather loose, black rock soon after the start really concentrated the mind. At the same time Oli and Sean

[Photo] Bouldering on Ikerasak Island with Ikerasak Peak behind. Married Men's Way takes the prow facing the camera. Crocodiles Have Teeth follows a series of excellent cracks just behind the steepest arête forming the edge of the face to the right. *Nicolas Favresse*

climbed Slingshot (E3 5c or 5.10) on the right side of the buttress. We then took the boat around to the north side of this island, where we discovered walls with tremendous potential for long, medium-grade routes on what appeared to be mainly good rock. However, they were not steep or serious enough for this team.

We traveled back south to the peninsula called Drygalskis Halvo and a formation on the northwest coast that the team named Funky Tower (70°35'N, 51°16'W). Ben and Sean climbed it by a steep, variable, and formidable route with much loose rock, especially on the rightward-slanting ramp that gained the summit ridge. They named it No Place for People, a.k.a. Sunshine and Roses (500m, E6 6b or 5.12a). I had anchored the boat in a cove to the northeast, where there was much good fishing and bouldering.

All the climbs were completed onsight and free, without recourse to pitons or bolts. As usual, the climbing was backed by musical jam sessions, but as the walls were climbed in single long pushes, instruments were not taken on the climbs, as they had been during the team's multi-day ascents in 2010. After a good deal more bouldering in the west bay of Uummannaq, waiting for the ice to clear from the east coast of Baffin Island, we set off for a three-day passage across the Davis Strait. The team's adventures on Baffin are described by Ben in a feature article beginning on page 46. 📷 📄 🔍

Ben in a feature article beginning on page 46.

— BOB SHEPTON, *U.K.*

[Top] Funky Tower with the 500m line of No Place for People, a.k.a. Sunshine and Roses. *Bob Shepton* [Bottom] The 500m Goliath Buttress on Qaquglugssuit. (1) Standard Deviation. (2) Slingshot. *Ben Ditto*

EAST GREENLAND / LIVERPOOL LAND

NORTH LIVERPOOL LAND ASCENTS AND SKI DESCENTS

ON APRIL 25 a group of experienced alpinists—Geoff Bonney, Peter Chadwick, my wife Sandy Gregson, Michael Smith, and me (all U.K.), along with Alexandre Buisse (France) and Tony Hoare (Canada)—flew to Constable Pynt in East Greenland. With logistical support from Tangent Expeditions, we then traveled ca 80km north by snowmobile to the North Liverpool Land Icecap. I had first visited this area six years earlier (*AAJ 2009*), and many peaks still awaited first ascents. During the cold and uncomfortable snowmobile journey we sighted a polar bear and two well-grown cubs, a salutary reminder of why we carried firearms, flares, and pepper spray. After a drop-off a few kilometers from our intended base camp, an abrupt bout of heavy pulk hauling across the small icecap took us to a level glacier shelf at ca 525m (71°21.656'N, 22°07.378'W), where we camped. We then split into three teams to explore the area.

Alex and Tony, both pro photographers, had sponsor obligations to fulfill, with Alex bravely skiing with a bionic knee brace, having ruptured a ligament in an avalanche above Courmayeur just a few weeks earlier. They skied up and down Mt. Thistle (1,040m) via the northeast glacier and made the first ascent of Mt. Hulya I (830m) by the Marmotte (northwest) Ridge at PD+. They also climbed 3 P.M. Attack Nunatak (528m) and made a ski descent. It should have been called Noon Nunatak, but the pair was late leaving camp. Alex and Tony also climbed to Snow White Col (788m) by its 200m north face (60°); this was the start of an attempt on the traverse of the Seven Dwarfs, abandoned due to poor rock.

Michael and Peter, first-timers in Greenland, whizzed about on Nordic skis, making a number of ascents. They later hauled northward to establish a new camp, from which they accessed a number of tops, some of them first ascents. Geoff, Sandy, and I made a first ascent of the fine northwest spur of Kuldefjeld (Cold Mountain, 980m), a 450m PD+/AD- that we named Charlotte Road. We descended the northeast face. This peak lies between Mt. Mighty and the Seven Dwarfs.

Geoff, aged 75, took a rain check while Sandy and I skied east to attempt a traverse on the Neild Bugt Glacier, starting with Hvithorn (White Horn). After climbing the west arête we were surprised to find ourselves on top of an exposed, isolated summit, cut off from Hvithorn by an almost vertical gap a rope length deep. We named this summit Varmtind (Warm Peak, 750m).

With Geoff on the move again, we spent a day skiing up Carlsberg Dome (845m), and

[Bottom] North side of the Mt. Mighty–Seven Dwarfs Group. (A) Mt. Mighty. (B) Kuldefjeld. The Seven Dwarfs: (C) Grumpy, (D) Sneezy, (E) Bashful, (F) Happy, (G) Dopey, (H) Doc, (I) Sleepy. (J) Tower of Silence. (1) Australian Route (2012). (2) Northeast face descent (2014). (3) Charlotte Road (2014). (4) Attempt via Snow White Col (2014). (5) Australian attempt on tower (2012). *Alexandre Buisse*

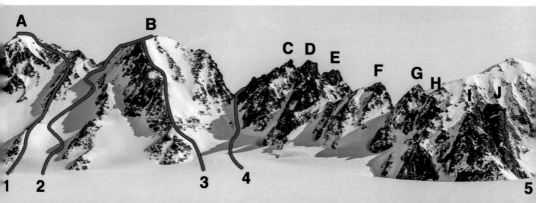

then along the ridge east to repeat Kagoo Peak, first climbed in 2012 (*AAJ 2013*).

From all summits reached we saw a wealth of striking unclimbed and unnamed peaks. The granite and gneiss of the area are compact, but have a fair share of loose material. The big rock tower—Tower of Silence—at the west end of the Seven Dwarfs remains unclimbed. Thanks to the Alpine Club Climbing Fund for financial support. 🖸

– JIM GREGSON, *U.K.*

KIRKEN, SOUTHWEST FACE

IN 2013 I SAILED single-handed across the Atlantic from the U.K. to Newport, Rhode Island, and then to Nanortalik in South Greenland. There, I was joined by Harald Fichtinger (Austria) and we explored Greenland's east coast between 61° and 63°N, with only the two of us as crew. At 61°08.1'N, 42°56.7'W, we attempted the main peak of the Kangerdluluk mountains, which we dubbed the Dru. However, we soon abandoned the climb due to very poor rock. It may have been possible to access the summit from the back (north and west), but this would have involved a long trek across a glacier, and we had no ice equipment. We consoled ourselves with the first ascent of a nice 13-pitch route (5c) in Umanaq Bay at 62°52.2'N, 41°34.6'W.

We left the boat in Iceland for the winter and in 2014 sailed to Liverpool Land. We wanted to climb Kirken, which we only knew from a picture in a book. Kirken (Church Mountain) is wrongly positioned on the popular Saga map, where it is given a height of 1,209m. However, it was named by William Scoresby Jr., and there is no doubt to which peak he was referring: "...another mountain at latitude 71°04'—Church Mount—has two vertical summit towers with gable-formed tops closely studded with pinnacles." We first had to find a safe bay to anchor, because we had no crew to look after the yacht when we headed into the mountains. We also had to carry a rifle in case of a polar bear encounter, and we had to make sure we could still access the boat in case a bear destroyed the dinghy, as happened to another party this year in Greenland. Our anchor bay—uncharted—was to the north. On the first day we headed toward Peak 1,209m, still believing this to be Kirken, as marked on the map, but once we arrived on the ridge we realized it was not the right summit.

Next day we found the right approach, climbing the southwest face via a steep snow gully and a six-pitch climb over solid granite, with difficulties up to 6b. We measured the summit coordinates as 71°07.4'N, 21°48.8'W, and the altitude as 1,108m (the peak is unnamed on the Saga map but has a spot height of 1,082m). We then sailed back to Iceland, where Harald disembarked and I continued single-handed to Scotland. 🖸

– RALPH VILLIGER, *SWITZERLAND*

EAST GREENLAND / RENLAND

SHARK'S TOOTH, THE GREAT SHARK HUNT; EL GÜPFI, OASIS; DADERBRUM, NORTHWEST COULOIR TO SOUTHWEST RIDGE

CHRISTIAN LEDERGERBER, SILVAN SCHÜPBACH (both Swiss), and I planned to climb the striking 900m northeast face of the Shark's Tooth (1,555m) in the best possible style: by fair means, clean, and completely free. This proved to be a rather bold, committing, and taxing adventure.

On August 5 we set off from the village of Ittoqqotoormiit in kayaks to cross Scoresby Sund. We had very little kayaking experience, having just learned basic paddle strokes and

[Above] The view across Kangerdluluk Fjord to the little-known, unclimbed summits of Graah's Fjeld. [Bottom right] The unclimbed Kangerdluluk Dru. The Austrian-Swiss pair reached the top of the vertically oriented snow patch below the left skyline (east) ridge, and then climbed two more pitches toward the crest before retreating due to bad rock. [Bottom left] Kirken from the sea. The Austrian-Swiss pair climbed the right-hand and highest of the two prominent summits by the slanting face seen in profile to the left. *All photos: Ralph Villiger*

[Above] The Shark's Tooth and the line of the Great Shark Hunt (900m, 7b+). The Russian route Dance on Tiptoes climbs the snow couloir to the right, then the ridge above to the summit. *Matteo Della Bordella* [Below] Matteo Della Bordella negotiates tricky face climbing between two crack systems on the Great Shark Hunt. *Silvan Schüpbach*

rescue techniques in April. On the first day it became evident that paddling in Scoresby Sund had little in common with training on a lake. Overloaded kayaks, ocean swell, and choppy waves really tested our ability to remain upright. Fortunately, conditions improved. Spotting musk ox, seals, and a polar bear, as well as passing close to cracking icebergs, proved a profound experience. After a seven-day paddle and a two-day walk, we established base camp below the Shark's Tooth. For the moment, our big unknown—kayaking—was over. Now it was business as usual.

The Shark's Tooth was first climbed in 2011 by Mikhail Mikhailov and Alexander Ruchkin via the northwest ridge (*AAJ 2012*), and its northeast face looked stunning. It's incredible to find such a wall still virgin these days. It strengthened our desire to climb it free—opening an aid climb almost would have seemed like failure.

After the initial easy and mossy slabs we got to the real deal. Unfortunately, the rock was not of the best quality, and the aspect of the wall meant the climbing was cold and demanding. We gave it everything we had. Many times we were about to give up and say "take;" many times we had no idea how we were going to link crack systems free. But no one fell. On the

[Above] Silvan Schüpbach, Matteo Della Bordella, and Christian Ledergerber (left to right) during their seven-day kayak approach across Scoresby Sund. *Matteo Della Bordella*

evening of the second day we made a spectacular portaledge bivouac in the middle of the face, and next day, on much improved rock, climbed nine excellent pitches to the top, completing the first ascent onsight. We slept on the summit of our dreams, and the following day rappelled the Russian route. We named the 25-pitch route the Great Shark Hunt (900m, 7b+). Repeaters will find only two bolts on the route: one used for hanging the portaledge, and the other to protect the second climbers on a 30m traverse.

Although we were entirely satisfied, we still had some time left at base camp, and we didn't rest much. Soon we were heading up the Edward Bailey Glacier as far as the entrance to the Alpine Bowl. Here, in 2012, Christian and Silvan had put up a fine rock route called Die Ideallinie on the north-northwest face of a formation called El Güpfi (originally dubbed the Gherkin by an Irish team that attempted it in 2008; see *AAJ 2013*). This time Silvan and I climbed a line on the right side, which we named Oasis (600m, 7a) because of the warm, pleasant conditions during the climb. The main difficulties are concentrated on the initial pitches; the upper part gives pleasant climbing in cracks and dihedrals. One bolt was left on the second anchor, but the rest is clean because we rappelled and downclimbed somewhat farther to the right.

Christian and I also climbed a large, striking mountain closer to the Shark's Tooth. We estimated its height at 2,200m. In a 14-hour round trip from camp we followed the easiest line, with classic snow, ice, and mixed terrain for ca 1,800m, finishing up a snow arête. We propose the name Daderbrum—the northwest face could be an interesting objective for future parties.

As we started our journey home, the weather became colder, wetter, and windier. On three days we were unable to move due to storms, and during the rest it was either misty or raining. We finally reached a hut 25km from Ittoqqortoormiit, where we met our final surprise. At 6 a.m. Christian heard snuffling sounds outside the hut. It took him only seconds to realize: polar bear! Trapped in a sleeping bag he started to yell, hoping it would scare away the animal. The bear forced open two doors, and by the time it was standing in the middle of the room we were all making as much noise as possible. This had the desired effect, and the bear turned around and walked out. No doubt she'd been curious about the smell from our feet—she didn't deserve such a bad welcome. That same day we arrived in Ittoqqortoormiit. 🗎

– MATTEO DELLA BORDELLA, *ITALY, WITH CHRISTIAN LEDERGERBER AND SILVAN SCHÜPBACH*

EAST GREENLAND / SCHWEIZERLAND

FOX JAW CIRQUE

ON JULY 10, Sion Brocklehurst, Robert Durran, Pat Ingram, Simon Smith, and I were dropped at the head of Tasiilaq Fjord. We began the first of three arduous hauls up the Tasillaq Kuua (valley) to the foot of Fox Jaw Cirque, where climbing potential was first discovered in 1998 by Americans Dave Briggs and Mike Libecki.

Our team climbed three new routes on the formation variously known as Milk Tooth or Baby Molar. Simon and Sion also put up a new route on Left Rabbit Ear with stunning crack climbing, from tough fingertips to stomach-churning offwidth burls: Rampant (400m, nine pitches, E4 6a or 5.11+). [*This route appears to lie immediately right of the 2007 American-Canadian line called Naeterqaabin-Jebbananee (550m, 13 pitches, IV 5.10).*] Team members attempted new lines on Cavity Ridge and the Molar, and also climbed 10 pitches of Beers in Paradise (2007) during two attempts, the first of which ended when Simon pulled off a large block on lead and took an 8m whipper, fracturing his heel.

During our three-week visit bluebird sky days were plentiful and building clouds rarely produced anything apart from apprehension. We experienced two days of rain, but the valley wind meant the rock was quick to dry. When not climbing we explored farther up-valley for possible objectives. However, many of the glaciers looked very crevassed and made approaching the rock difficult and time-consuming. 🗎 🗎

– CATH ALLDRED, *WITH SIMON SMITH, U.K.*

CAPE FAREWELL REGION

EGGERS ISLAND, DANCE WITH SEALS;
IGDLUKASIP TUNUA FJORD, KEEPING THE FAITH

IN THE SECOND HALF OF AUGUST, Liam Fleming and I paddled kayaks from Nanortalik around Cape Farewell and back, attempting rock routes on suitable peaks along the way. Cape Farewell is the southernmost tip of Greenland and one of the windiest places on earth. We knew rounding it would be the crux of the trip.

Two days and four flights after leaving the U.K. we collected two kayaks in Nanortalik and began the process of loading them with 23 days of food, camping equipment, two 50m ropes, and full climbing gear. We left at lunchtime on August 14 and paddled east for several days, passing a 1,000-year-old Viking settlement and an inquisitive minke whale before reaching the fjord of Narssap Sarqa. Opposite the settlement of Frederiksdal, we stopped to climb the 900m Ikigaitqaqot. This gave a fine mountaineering day—a lovely ridge scramble with a rope and small rack, and stunning views.

After rounding Cape Christian and waiting out a storm on a rocky shore, we passed Cape Farewell and eventually found a small, sheltered landing site on the eastern tip of Eggers Island. The following day we climbed a new rock route on a slabby, south-facing wall on the flanks of Quvperitqaqa (681m), which we named Dance with Seals (eight pitches, HVS 5a).

During our return journey we paddled up Igdlukasip Tunua Fjord and climbed the west flank of the south ridge of Natsingnat (1,080m). It was misty to start, and upon climbing out of the cloud we realized the face was rather bigger than we'd thought. After 12 pitches we reached the top, completing Keeping the Faith (E1 5b). There was some good climbing, but also the usual loose rock one would expect on a big mountain face.

As we began the last section of the journey, the weather was bitterly cold, with snow on the tops. We returned to Nanortalik after 21 days, having covered 270km in challenging conditions. Fourteen days had involved paddling, on another four we had been stormbound, and on three we climbed. The trip was supported with grants from the BMC, Welsh Sports Association, and the Gino Watkins Memorial Fund. 🄰 🄴

– OLLY SANDERS, *U.K.*

[Above] The eight-pitch Dance with Seals (HVS 5a) on Eggers Island. [Below] East of the settlement of Augpilatoq, looking south across the fjord and into a valley on Pamiagdluk. *Olly Sanders*

MEXICO

[Above] The northwest face of Las Guacamayas, showing the new route Confabulación Cósmica (400m, 13 pitches, IV 5.12a). The wall is located in the Parque Nacional Cumbres de Monterrey in northeastern Mexico. *Luis Carlos García*

LAS GUACAMAYAS, NORTHWEST FACE, CONFABULACIÓN CÓSMICA

THE PARQUE NACIONAL Cumbres de Monterrey is a large area of limestone big walls in northeastern Mexico. The park is located in the Sierra Madre Oriental, in the state of Nuevo León, and is accessed from the city of Monterrey. [*See AAJ 2002 and AAJ 2003 for further information about logistics, recent developments, and climbing potential in the area, best known to climbers for the Cañon de la Huasteca.*]

About a year ago I was lucky enough to obtain a picture of an unclimbed wall in the area (25°36'18.28"N, 100°29'51.29"W), just up the road from the sport climbing area Guitarritas. I quickly started to investigate this overhanging, orange-colored wall and found out the access was easy by car.

On February 18, Joel Guadarrama G., Rodrigo Garza Maldonado, Mariano Torres Robles, and I set out for the wall, making a one-hour approach from the road. We soon found out that it was located on private land known as El Caracol, and it was necessary to ask Victor Mata for permission to camp below the wall. After carrying loads to the base, we started up the wall in late February, climbing a couple of pitches a day, fixing rope, and bolting ground-up. The terrain started easy and grew harder as we made our way up the wall. After 40 hours of bolting over three weeks and eight days of climbing (utilizing one bivy atop the sixth pitch), we reached the top on March 8 and then rappelled the route.

After some rest days, Mariano and I came back to redpoint the route in approximately 8 hours on March 13. We called the climb Confabulación Cósmica (400m, 13 pitches, IV 5.12a). The climb is sustained in the 5.10-5.11 grades, contains many hanging belays, and is best climbed in a day. Overall a great climb, with excellent virgin limestone—it was an adventure to climb it. 📷 🔍

— LUIS CARLOS GARCÍA AYALA, *MEXICO*

EL GIGANTE, AMAPOLA EXPRESS

In May, Giuseppe "Beppe" Torre, Rudy Salinas (both Mexico), Rodrigo Fica (Chile), Jesus Ibarz, and I (both Catalan) opened a new route on El Gigante in Mexico. We spent 10 days on the wall, first fixing lines from the ground, then climbing capsule style to the top. We free climbed many of the pitches on the ascent and successfully redpointed four additional pitches after topping out the wall. The sixth pitch remains to be free climbed on lead, as we were only able top-rope it (7c+). We called the climb Amapola Express (860m, 7c A0).

The line mostly follows the left side of the wall, first through big roofs then following superb dihedrals and cracks to the top. The first half of the climb is fragile and extremely loose, but we cleaned it and now the climb is much more enjoyable. The rock on the second part is really solid, and it feels like climbing on El Cap; it's rhyolite, so it's like climbing on good granite but with a smoother texture. The route is partly protected with bolts on the hard-to-protect pitches (approximately 60 not including anchors), but we climbed clean on the cracks

[Above] Following one of the lower pitches on Amapola Express (860m, 7c A0). *Oriol Anglada*

and the sections where we were able to use gear. The route Yawira Batú (Buil-García, *AAJ 2000*) crosses our line about 450m up the wall, as does Man on Fire (Bluementhal-Catlin-Tolle-Longoria-Scott, *AAJ 2004*) on the upper part; we undoubtedly shared one pitch on the upper wall with Tehué (Almada-Buil, *AAJ 2014*). 📷 🔍

— ORIOL ANGLADA, *CATALAN*

PIEDRA BOLADA, WEST FACE, RASTAMURI

From April 8 to 27, Sergio "Tiny" Almada (Mexico) and I climbed in Candameña Canyon in Parque Nacional Cascada de Basaseachic, likely making the first ascent of a 1,000m wall. The west-southwest-facing wall is situated directly across from the well-known El Gigante and is nearly as tall. The first 300m appear to be covered in plants and loose rock; however, we found a continuous, steep line without much vegetation.

Once in the park we hooked up with Valentin, a local man who showed us how to reach a base camp as easily as possible. We were then joined by Isidro, another local who helped us carry some loads, and also by Oscar Cisneros, who would help us with logistics and morale.

We began our approach on the afternoon of April 8 and reached the base of the wall

[Above] Tiny Almada finds clean free climbing near the top of Rastamuri. *Oscar Cisneros*

after a six-hour hike and a bivy along the way. On April 9, Tiny and I started up the first pitch while Oscar brought water from the river, located about 80m below the start of our route (some sections of this wall start directly from water level). We fixed the first three pitches (one 5.10 and two of A4) and, having realized the lower section would prove slow and difficult, we decided to take food and water for 15 days. With 84 liters of water, our haulbags now weighed 120kg!

On April 12, Tiny and I took off again. During our first 10 days on the wall we climbed approximately 600m, and at times we were happy to progress 50m a day. The lower section of the face did not have many cracks, and the ones we found were either seams or crumbly. In this initial section of the climb we breached five large roofs, climbed numerous aid pitches up to A4, and did free climbing up to 5.11 with runouts up to 5.10+. Our equipment was very heavy to haul and slowed us down significantly.

After 600m of climbing we reached the first natural ledge and began to see the light at the end of the tunnel: The climbing looked like it would go free, and there were far more cracks to offer protection. From this point we managed to free climb about 100m a day, and this proved to be great fun! On April 25 we reached a second natural ledge near the top of the wall. Seeing us there, Oscar abseiled down from the top to take some photos, and he slept on the ledge with us that night. From the ledge, we climbed another three pitches and finished the route on April 26 after spending 14 days on the wall. We slept on the summit that night and awoke to the strange sight of El Gigante looking slightly lower than our camp.

We've called our 24-pitch route Rastamuri (1,030m, VI 5.11+ A4). We placed 59 bolts, including 40 for belay anchors and the rest only where they're completely necessary.

— CECILIA BUIL, *SPAIN*

COLOMBIA

SEASON SUMMARY

THE SIERRA NEVADA DEL COCUY saw three new rock routes of moderate length and difficulty, all climbed in January 2015. The first was established on the slabby, high-altitude south face of Güicán Peak (4,890m) by Angélica Gutierrez and Luis Pardo: the South Face Direct (200m, 5.9). The second route was climbed by Rafael Naranjo, Juan Camilo Ramirez, and Alexander Torres. It weaves up the broken-looking Cardenillo Wall (4,680m) and tops out on the ridgeline: Matto Tracción (250m, 5.10c). At the far southern end of the range, on Campanillas Negro (4,875m), Ruben Arguello, Ricardo Cardozo, and Ricardo Rubio climbed a variation to the upper part of the route Gárgolas (5.10d, Cárdenas-Pardo, 2011), which they called El Mojón (5.10d).

Two new routes were established on volcanoes in the Cordillera Central. In January 2015, Sebastián Lopez and Eduardo Lascano climbed Laberintos (D 65°), a circuitous route up the steep icefall of the Pijao Glacier on the northeast side of Nevado del Tolima (5,250m). In February, the team of Heber Achicué, Alejandro Sánchez, Carlos Higuera, David Martínez, and José Cano climbed a new route to the south summit (5,085m) of Volcán Nevado del Huila (5,364m). This is the highest volcano in Colombia, and the new route, Achicué (AD 60°), weaves through the lower rock bands on the southeast side to gain a glacier and the south summit. 📷 🔍

– FROM INFORMATION BY **LUIS PARDO**, COLOMBIA

[Left] Campanillas Negro, showing Gárgolas (5.10d, Cárdenas-Pardo, 2011) and the new variation branching right, El Mojón (5.10d, Arguello-Cardozo-Rubio, 2015). *Luis Pardo* [Right] A close-up view of the new route Matto Tracción (250m, 5.10c) on the Cardenillo Wall. *Alex Torres*

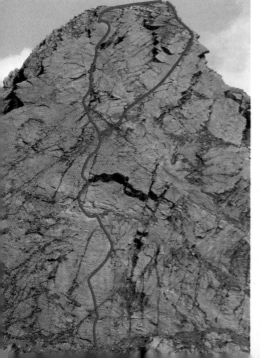

BRAZIL

PEDRA CARA, EAST FACE

AT THE BEGINNING of November, Josef Ficek, Lukas Kozlik, Filip Martinek, David Michovsky, and I traveled to Rio de Janeiro, and from there we moved north 700km by bus to Pancas in the state of Espirito Santo. Pancas contains a huge array of dark quartzite walls with endless possibilities for first ascents up to 700m.

We set up our tents at Fabio Eggert's climber camp, just below the impressive Pedra Cara. We first made an attempt on the north face of Pedra Camelo, a 700m wall with only one existing route, up a chimney system. We started our line on the left side of the wall with two pitches of face climbing (5 and 7b+) and then continued up an obvious corner for two more pitches. However, atop the corner, the rock quality got dramatically worse and we couldn't climb free. We've left this project for other climbers.

For our second objective we chose a line up the east face of Pedra Cara. After six days of work we finally finished this difficult new route, which mostly follows an obvious corner system for its 12 pitches. Most of the route is moderate (up to 6c) except for two pitches (7b+ and 7c) of hard slab climbing on crumbly rock. To protect the climb we used a mix of gear and bolts. We called the route Obrigado Amigos (650m, 7c).

There's a great future in this area, which offers many unclimbed towers and possibilities for new routes. However, you will always be searching for good rock. Fabio maintains a book with first ascent records, though he only speaks Portuguese. 📷 🔍

— **ONDREJ BENES**, *CZECH REPUBLIC*

[Photo] Face climbing on the 7c crux pitch of Obrigado Amigos (650m, 7c). *Ondrej Benes*

PERU

NEVADO QUILLUJIRCA

NEVADO QUILLUJIRCA (5,040M) is located in the Rurec Valley—sometimes called the "Little Yosemite" of the Andes. On July 15, Rafael Cáceres, Esteban Mena Yañez, Nicolás Navarrete, and Carla Perez (Ecuador) climbed a new 250m start to the Italian route El Sueño De Los Excluidos (Iannilli-DiDonato, *AAJ 2011*) on the southeast face of Nevado Quillujirca. The variation joins the existing route at a prominent vegetated shelf, from which the Ecuadorians continued for 500m to the top; it appears they climbed new terrain on the final third of the route. [*Editor's note: The Italians noted their route was over 1,300m in length, which appears to be an overestimate. Additonally, the upper part of the Italian route, on the upper southeast face, was first climbed by Americans Kent McClannan and Cameron Tague and called Mission Control (IV 5.11+ A2+, AAJ 2000); their route was the first known technical ascent of the peak and climbs the right side of the southeast face.*]

[Above] The south and southeast faces of Nevado Quillujirca (5,040m). (1) La Teora de la Gota de Agua (Iannilli-DiDonato, *AAJ 2011, no summit*). (2) Cáceres-Mena-Navarrete-Perez, 2014 (*attempt*). (3) El Sueño De Los Excluidos (Iannilli-DiDonato, *AAJ 2011*). (4) Cáceres-Mena-Navarrete-Perez, 2014 (5 pitches, 5.11d). (5) Mission Control (McClannan-Tague, *AAJ 2000*). *Esteban Mena Yañez*

It took the team two days to bring their gear up to the wall, and over the next three days they established five pitches on the lower wall (5.11d, 5.7, 5.11a, 5.10, 5.10). Some belays have bolts or pitons (where necessary), and the second pitch has three protection bolts due to continuous face climbing. On their fourth day they started climbing at 5 a.m. from a bivouac on the vegetated shelf and reached the summit by 2 p.m. The team simul-climbed the entire upper part, which has maximum difficulties of 5.10. A GPS reading indicated about 800m of elevation gain from base to summit. The Ecuadorians descended a ridge to the west, reaching the vegetated ledge in about 40 minutes, followed by another two hours of rappelling to the base.

The team also attempted a route on the upper south face of the mountain, consisting of 5.11+/5.12- crack climbing with face climbing cruxes between the cracks. Overall, the Ecuadorian team said the valley offers good potential for new-routing on great rock; the only problem is the cracks are often filled with vegetation.

– SERGIO RAMÍREZ CARRASCAL, *PERU*, WITH INFORMATION FROM ESTEBAN MENA YAÑEZ
AND SEVI BOHÓRQUEZ, *PERU*

[Above] The heavily fluted northwest face of Jurau B (5,727m), showing the line of El Inca, El Cachaco y el Azteca (300m, AD 60–90°). *Beto Pinto*

JURAU B, NORTHWEST FACE TO NORTHEAST RIDGE (NO SUMMIT)

HAVING HEARD that Jurau B (5,727m), located directly below Siula Grande's northeast face, was still unclimbed, Daniel Araiza (Mexico), Florian Burger (Austria), and I set out to attempt the peak in early July. From camp we headed toward the northwest face at midnight on July 13. We reached the base at 3 a.m., finding many steep snow mushrooms near the bergschrund. Above, we followed snow and ice flutings (60–80°) to gain the upper northeast ridge, which we reached at 6:30 a.m. From there we traversed south along the ridge toward the summit; however, we found it to be blocked by a dangerous 10m snow mushroom. We called our route El Inca, El Cachaco y el Azteca (300m, AD 60–90°) and rappelled the route, reaching the base at 10 a.m.

   [*Editor's note: In AAJ 2007 an Italian team reported making the first ascent of the unclimbed peak labeled Pt. 5,740m on the Peruvian map, which they called "Siula Antecima." And in AAJ 2008 it was noted that this peak was Jurau B (5,727m). However, with new information it is now clear the Italians climbed Jurau A (5,617m). The primarily ice-covered Jurau B lies between the primarily rocky Jurau A and Siula Grande's northeast face, and is believed to be unclimbed. The 2014 ascent reached the summit ridge but not the summit.*]

— BETO PINTO, *PERU*

JURAURAJU, NORTHWEST FACE; JURAU, WEST FACE (NO SUMMIT)

DAVIDE CASSOL AND I left Italy on May 26 to travel to the eastern part of the Cordillera Huayhuash and attempt new routes. Once in Huaraz we purchased food for a month and then enlisted nine mules and two horses to transport nearly 300kg of gear to a base camp at Sarapococha, below Lake Jurau (ca 4,300m). We were joined by super-cook Pio Polo (Peru). After a three-day trek we reached base camp on June 1, which we shared with Tito Arosio, Saro Costa, and Luca Vallata.

   The next few weeks were comprised of amazingly intense days where toil and adventure held sway. During our initial acclimatization we explored the area and made an ascent of Cerro Gran Vista (5,152m), located just west of Sarapococha. On June 5 we set our sights on the unclimbed northwest face of Jurauraju (5,335m), located southeast of Jurau Lake, below the Jurau Glacier. The mountain contains beautiful, gray, high-quality limestone. Our route Laurapaq (800m, UIAA V+) climbs just right of a prominent arête and gully feature. It is entirely on rock and quite moderate.

On June 9 we traveled east from camp onto the Jurau Glacier to attempt the west face of Jurau (5,674m, a.k.a. Jurau D), a pointy summit located between Carnicero (5,960m) and Huaraca (5,537m). Our new route La Siesta del Bodacious (600m, WI4+ M4) climbs mostly snow and ice up a direct line just left of the summit pyramid. Upon reaching the top of the wall and the north ridge, we continued around to the east side of the peak and up its east ridge route (*AAJ 1967*). We stopped 80m below the true summit due to huge, dangerous-looking cornices. This proved to be a wise move, as the following day we saw a cornice collapse on the ridge, causing a large avalanche 200m left of our new route. To descend, we rappelled our route using V-threads and a couple pieces of rock protection.

[*Editor's note: Jurau was first ascended in 1961 by its north ridge (AAJ 1962) and then again in 1966 by its east ridge. Only one other route has been reported on the western side of Jurau: the west face (500m, TD– 60-90°, Barker-Preston, AAJ 1989), a difficult route that may climb a weakness up the southern (right) end of the west face.*]

Following this climb we had five days of bad weather. Our next goal was a new route on the south face of Yerupaja Sur (6,515m), but we found prohibitive snow conditions, with powder snow up to 90°. Davide took three falls held by a snow picket before we turned around.

[Below] Getting the best of both worlds: Davide Cassol leads a section of thick water ice on Jurau's west face [*see page 198 for route line*] and jams a splitter limestone crack on Laurapaq (800m, UIAA V+), one of two new rock climbs on Jurauraju. *Photos: Carlo Cosi*

On June 20 we headed back to the northwest face of Jurauraju and climbed another route, which we called La Zuppa di Pio (650m, UIAA IV+), dedicated to our travel companion and chef, Pio. Again, this face provided a climb on excellent rock with moderate difficulty, and plenty of opportunity for lucid dreaming. 📷 🔍 ▶

— CARLO COSI, *ITALY*

QUESILLO, WEST FACE (NO SUMMIT); OTHER ATTEMPTS

IN JUNE Saro Costa, Luca Vallata, and I (all from Italy) explored the southern part of the Cordillera Huayhuash, where we attempted four peaks and succeeded on one climb (though we didn't reach the summit). We set up base camp close to Sarapococha, near Jurau Lake, which sits just below the west side of Quesillo (5,600m), Huaraca (5,537m), Jurau (5,674m), and other peaks.

After acclimatizing, Costa and I attempted a direct route up the unclimbed southeast face of Tsacra Grande (5,774m), which lies in the southwestern part of the range in the Segya Valley. After exiting the main central gully, which ascends the first half of the face (AI4+ M6), and then continuing up the snowy upper portion of the mountain, our attempt ended approximately 150m below the summit due to classic and dangerous Andean snow conditions. From our high point we quickly abseiled down our line of ascent. [*Editor's note: A Dutch team reported an attempt on the east face of Tsacra Grande in 1986 and also retreated 150m below the summit (AAJ 1987); however, since they described beginning from the col near Tsacra Chico Oeste, they may have climbed the existing east ridge route (AAJ 1965), which follows a weakness on the right side of the east face before joining the upper ridge.*]

We rested for a few days and then the three of us set off for a new route on the west face of Quesillo (5,600m). Over two days we climbed the wall via a prominent, left-angling snow ramp that splits the rocky face: El Malefico Sefkow (800m, ED2 AI5 M5+ A1). However, we did not reach the true summit because huge cornices on the summit ridge turned us back. We descended the north ridge (Lindauer-Salger, 1964) to the Huaraca-Quesillo Col. [*Editor's note: Many AAJ reports cite similarly dangerous corniced terrain on the path to Huayhuash summits, and many "new routes" have not reached their summits. On Quesillo, this was noted most recently in 2007 by a four-person British team on the first ascent of the peak's east ridge; their route stopped just below the top (AAJ 2008). Quesillo's summit was likely last reached in 2006 by Carlos Buhler and Brad Johnson, after their new route up its northeast face (AAJ 2007).*]

After a few days of bad weather we all set off for the massive west face of Siula Grande (6,344m) to try and repeat the difficult Noches de Juerga (Jost-Mlinar-Monasterio-Zerovnik, *AAJ 2002*), the only route that seemed in condition. Unfortunately, the condition of the face, coupled with high temperatures, stopped our attempt at ca 5,700m.

The day before leaving base camp we tried to make a quick raid up the west face of Huaraca (5,537m), but we were stopped at mid-height; the route turned out to be much more challenging than expected, and we didn't have enough gear for aid climbing. This small but very steep face remains unclimbed. [*Editor's note: The same British expedition that climbed the east ridge of Quesillo in 2007 also made the first ascents of the north ridge and northeast face of Huaraca, after first reaching the col between Huaraca and Jurau; both routes (graded D) reached the summit (AAJ 2008).*]

[Photo] Steep and thin mixed on Huaraca's west face. The team was unprepared for such difficult terrain and retreated midway up the wall (see route line on the next page). *Tito Arosio*

[Above] The view from Lake Jurau showing routes climbed or attempted in 2014. The prominent peak on the far right is Quesillo, with El Malefico Sefkow (800m, ED2 AI5 M5+ A1). The sharp peak in the center is Huaraca, with the west face attempt and high point [*see report about both these climbs on previous page*]. To the left is Jurau, with La Siesta del Bodacious (600m, WI4+ M4) [*see page 195*]. Carnicero is the dominant snowy peak on the far left. *Carlo Cosi* [Below] The attempted route on the unclimbed east face of Tsacra Grande, with the high point shown. *Tito Arosio*

From our experience in the range, it seems that the lesser-known and shorter mountains still offer big opportunity for new and interesting routes. It also seems, as others have said, that global warming has had a major effect on these mountains. For example, the Simpson-Yates route on Siula Grande appears as though it may no longer be in condition due to a newly formed serac in the middle of the wall. 📷 🔍

– TITO AROSIO, *ITALY*

CORDILLERA CENTRAL

NEVADO TATAJAYCO, NORTHWEST RIDGE

ON MARCH 22 Alberto Hung (Peru) and I climbed Nevado Tatajayco (5,342m) by a new route up the northwest ridge: A Puro Huevo (D UIAA V M3 60°). We descended the west side. Nevado Tatajayco is located in the middle of Quiullacocha Valley. Peruvian mountaineers first climbed the peak in 2003 by easy glacial slopes on the west side; this route has been repeated twice: by English climbers in 2011 and by Peruvian climbers in 2012. Thus we believe our ascent was the fourth overall. This part of the Cordillera Central is also known as the Cordillera Pariacaca because Nevado Pariacaca (5,750m, a.k.a. Tulluqutu) is the highest mountain in the area. It is rarely visited by foreign climbers, despite beautiful landscapes, many 5,000m peaks, and impressive glacial valleys. 📷 🔍

– STEVE MEDER, *FRANCE*

TUNSHO SUR, SOUTH FACE

TUNSHO SUR (5,420m), thought to be previously unclimbed, is one of the three summits of Tunsho (5,730m), located in the picturesque Reserva Paisajistica Nor Yauyos-Cochas, alongside other peaks such as the mythical Nevado Pariacaca (5,750m) and Nevado Antachaire (5,700m). Tunsho's main summit and second-highest summit, Tunsho Central (5,565m), were first reached by a German expedition (*AAJ 1968*). In October 2011, Rolando Morales and I reached Tunsho Central's summit by a new route, Chinita (MD+ 90°), on the southeast side. [*Editor's note: Due to problems with earlier maps, some reports incorrectly stated the 2011 ascent took place on Tunsho Sur. Tunsho Central is also sometimes referred to as Tunsho Oeste. The elevations given above are the best modern approximations and differ from those provided by the Germans. Additionally, the peak has been spelled "Tunshu."*]

In June, Guy Fonck and I decided to try Tunsho Sur, which had been previously attempted by its south face. We set out at 1 a.m. on June 7 from our base camp (ca 4,520m), and within a few hours we reached the glacier. We reached the south face around 6 a.m. Starting up very loose snow, we soon realized the 'schrund was over 5m wide. At a narrower spot, I made an anchor using ice screws and then leaped across the crevasse, landing on a hard ice ledge on the other side. The rest of the climb consisted of loose snow, and we reached the summit at 9:30 a.m. We took a GPS reading of 5,520m, which is close to the elevation indicated on the map. On the descent we used four rappels down the route, two of which were not very secure due to loose snow. But everything went to plan and by 3 p.m. we were back at base camp. Our new route Mel & Lies (200m, 70°) is named after our girlfriends. 📷 🔍

– BETO PINTO, *PERU, WITH ADDITIONAL INFORMATION FROM* SEVI BOHÓRQUEZ

CORDILLERA URUBAMBA

NEVADO CHICON, SOUTHWEST FACE AND TRAVERSE

IN EARLY JUNE, Phillip Moser and Chris Romeike (both Germany) started their ascent of Nevado Chicon (5,526m, a.k.a. Ch'iqun) from the small village of Munaychay (ca 3,300m), located in the Chicon Valley, above Urubamba. They made two trips with loads to an advanced base camp (ca 4,900m) on the moraine under the central glacier on the west side of the Chicon massif.

After one day at high camp they began their attempt to reach the central peak (5,490m) via a shadowed snow and ice couloir that rises almost to the height of the summit. They climbed 400m of steep ice steps and snowfields up this southwest-facing couloir to join a narrow ridge leading toward the central summit. After climbing much loose rock and snow along the ridge, they reached the central summit around 7:30 p.m. It was late and they decided to bivouac slightly north of the peak (ca 5,486m).

With the sunrise they continued traversing north along the loose and dangerous ridge to reach the north (main) summit of Nevado Chicon around 10:30 a.m. They descended the north side of the peak and then traversed around the massif by crossing the northern glacier. They named their route Via del Corazon (550m, TD+ WI4 M5). 📷 🔍

– SERGIO RAMÍREZ CARRASCAL, *PERU, WITH INFORMATION FROM* PHILLIP MOSER

NEVADO SAHUASIRAY, SOUTHWEST FACE

NEVADO SAHUASIRAY (5,818m) and its neighbor Nevado Chicon are an impressive sight, towering almost 3,000m above the cities of Urubamba and Calca. The first ascent of Sahuasiray was by an Italian expedition, which climbed the southeast face/east ridge and stood on both summits, the northern one being approximately 50m higher (*AAJ 1964*). Since then, the only known attempt was by the southwest ridge (*AAJ 1972*). I previously thought Sahuasiray was the highest in the Cordillera Urubamba; however, my recent GPS reading on Nevado Veronica (5,911m GPS) suggests that peak may be higher.

Erich Nordt Orihuela, Eduardo Baca, and I left Cusco on April 8 to attempt the southwest face of Sahuasiray. In Huaran we met an arriero to help with gear. The trek up to the herding community of Cancha Cancha went quickly; however, the community leader forced the arriero to unload our gear from his horse in the village. It then took us two hours from the village to reach a camp under two large rocks. On April 9 we carried our gear to the top of a rock buttress (ca 5,300m) and made camp. From here, we had to go down to go up—we found easy access onto the glacier from camp down a snow chute.

Erich and I left camp at midnight after Eduardo opted out. Once on the southwest aspect of the peak, the snow became knee-deep and the crevasses complicated. A couple of hundred meters below the summit, we reached a large, wide crevasse. It was about 5:45 a.m. and Erich did not have the energy to keep going; he decided to wait while I went to the summit. I

[Next page, top] The north (main) summit of Nevado Chicon (5,526m) on the left and the slightly lower central peak (5,490m) on the right, with the German route of ascent and traverse between the two peaks shown. *Phillip Moser* [Middle] Sunrise from Nevado Sahuasiray's southwest face, with the peaks Salcantay (back left, in the Cordillera Vilcabamba), Veronica (back right), Chicon (front left), and Sirijuani (front right). *Nathan Heald* [Bottom] An overview of the route up the southwest face of Nevado Sahuasiray (5,818m). Nevado Chainopuerto is on the left. *Nathan Heald*

[Above] Nevado Sirijuani (5,400m) from Cuncanicocha. The northwest face route climbs the prominent glacier. *Erich Nordt*

followed the crevasse left, toward a ridge, where a convenient snow bridge allowed me to cross with ease. This was followed by about 200m of snow climbing (60–70°). I reached the summit at 7:24 a.m. (AD/D). After retracing my steps, Erich and I continued back down our route to camp. A seven-hour slog brought us back to the road in Huaran.

– NATHAN HEALD, *PERU*

NEVADO SIRIJUANI, NORTHWEST FACE

AFTER STARTING from the town of Quiswarani (ca 4,000m) on Januray 5, Eduardo Baca, Yjeguel Camasa, Jorge "Coqui" Galvez (all Peru), and I climbed the northwest face (AD 70°) of Nevado Sirijuani (5,400m) on January 7. The crux of the route involved a 150m ice wall (60–70°) under a large but stable serac. [*Editor's note: Nevado Sirijuani has a few other known routes: A Scottish team climbed the northeast ridge and southeast face in 1964 (Alpine Journal 1965), and the east face was climbed by an Italian team (AAJ 1977).*]

– NATHAN HEALD, *PERU*

CORDILLERA VILCANOTA

NEVADO COLQUE CRUZ, SOUTH FACE

IN APRIL I went with Luis Crispin to explore the south face of Nevado Colque Cruz (6,102m, a.k.a. Alcamarinayoc) at the northern end of the Cordillera Vilcanota. We made it to ca 5,900m before a large slab avalanche cut loose and we retreated. In July we tried again, but we were not able to pass our previous high point. As a consolation on that trip, we climbed Nevado Chumpe (6,110m) by its northwest ridge to get a better view of our objective.

I returned in late September with Luis Crispin and Edwin Espinoza for another attempt. Just getting to the first camp involves climbing through an unstable moraine I've affectionately called the "gravel pit." We left for our climb at 11:30 p.m. on September 24 and made our way through the now-familiar crevasses beneath the wall. There was more snow than expected, because the rainy season had begun a week earlier and dumped loose, wet snow on the mountain.

When we reached the crux ice wall, Luis turned back due to an ankle injury he had sustained on Yerupaja. As he made his way down alone, we watched an avalanche almost hit him far below us; however, he was okay and we continued. Edwin and I climbed up and left across the ice wall toward its apex. Most of this wall is 60–70° until the final, steep 5m. Above the icefall, we simul-climbed for 300m on good snow (60°) until reaching a bergschrund below

[Above] Nevado Colque Cruz, as seen from Nevado Chumpe, showing the line of ascent on the south face (500m, D). *Nathan Heald*

the final summit block. From here we traversed right (east) across the south face to gain a lower-angle ramp. We arrived at the summit at 10:25 a.m. just as the clouds began to blow in from the jungle to the north (500m, D). From the top, we downclimbed and rappelled from V-threads on the icy south face. We reached the tent around 4 p.m. and hiked out the next day.

Nevado Colque Cruz is known to have been climbed seven times, first by Germans in 1953, by the Japanese in 1965, a Canadian–New Zealand–Australian team in 1974, by Germans in 1984, by Italians in 1987, and most recently by a British team up the mountain's technical southwest face (*AAJ 2007*). In 2005, Dave Wilkinson explored the south face but judged it out of condition and made an ascent of nearby Nevado Ichu Ananta instead (*AAJ 2005*). 📷 🔍

– NATHAN HEALD, *PERU*

CORDILLERA VILCABAMBA

NEVADOS HUMANTAY (NORTH SUMMIT), NORTH FACE

THE NEVADOS HUMANTAY (5,403m GPS, also spelled "Huamantay") are a chain of peaks extending northwest from the west ridge of Nevado Salcantay (6,279m), with three summits (south, central, and north), all about 5,400m. They are surrounded by cloud forest and technical climbing on all sides. I haven't found reference to these peaks in past accounts of the range. On July 9, Michael Church (USA), Macario Crispin (Peru), Michael Hauss (USA), and I climbed the north face of the north summit (AD 5.7 70°). 📷 🔍 📄

– NATHAN HEALD, *PERU*

CERRO JATUNJASA, SOUTHWEST RIDGE

IN OCTOBER, Luis Crispin, Edwin Espinoza, Alexis Trudel (Canada), and I climbed Cerro Jatunjasa (5,350m, a.k.a. Incachiriasca) by its southwest ridge (350m, PD). Cerro Jatunjasa appears to have been climbed twice by the north face, in 1970 by a German expedition and then again by Conny Amelunxen and Karen Perry (*AAJ 2004*). 📷 📄

– NATHAN HEALD, *PERU*

BOLIVIA

PEAK 5,600, SOUTHWEST RIDGE; CHEAROCO, SOUTHWEST FACE

DURING JULY I TEAMED UP with New Zealand expat Gregg Beisly for our annual exploration of the cordilleras Real and Occidental. Gregg lives with his family in Bolivia and works with a youth leadership program in the shantytown of El Alto, above La Paz.

Conditions were the harshest I have met in over 20 years of climbing in the Bolivian Andes; the weather was unusually unstable and stormy, with deep snow, consistently high winds, and extreme cold. Our initial plans to climb long, technical new routes therefore had to be replaced by faster, more traditional alpine assaults.

After a climb of the southwest ridge and south face of Pomerape [*see report later in this section*], Gregg and I drove to Estancia Kelluani, ca 100km northwest of La Paz, and the same day walked up the Kelluani Valley for 10km to place a low camp (4,600m) below the Chearoco Massif.

The next day, July 25, we made the first known ascent of Peak 5,600m, which we reached via a side valley northwest of camp. Crossing the glacier, we climbed the steep, rocky southwest buttress for 200m to an upper glacier. We continued up the southwest ridge for 500m to the highest of three tops. Descending our route, we regained camp in a nine-hour round trip. [*In 1978 a team of Italians report climbing "five summits on the ridge running west from Chearoco and separating the Chearoco and Kelluani valleys." It has been impossible to ascertain the exact location of any of the peaks they climbed.*]

On July 27, from a high camp at 5,100m, we climbed Chearoco (6,104m). We first traversed north-northwest to reach the southwest face. This gave excellent, steady climbing for 400m (50°) to emerge onto the bitterly cold and windswept southwest ridge, below a small but distinct summit. From here we slowly traversed the entire upper shoulder of the mountain,

[Below] Looking northeast from the Kelluani Valley. (A) Peak 5,600m. The 2014 ascent followed the left skyline. (B) Unnamed peak, ca 5,500m. (C) Chearoco, with the standard route up glaciated slopes facing the camera. *Gregg Beisly*

[Above] Chearoco from the southwest. (1) Southwest face (possibly first climbed by Argentinians Burrieza and Crispo in 1993; climbed in 2014 at AD+). (2) Original route (AD+, Horeschowsky-Hortinagel, 1928). (3) Southwest spur (AD+, Ferrari-Gemli-Gugiatti-Lanfranconi-Marmori-Vitale-Zappelli, 1978). (4) South face (normal route, AD, first ascent uncertain but climbed by Italians in 1978). (5) Southeast ridge (AD+, Floodpage-Hunter-Quicke, 1962, west access; the route originally was climbed from the east.) The normal finish to routes 1–4, once climbers reach the snow basin below the summit, is the line shown. This can be cut by a large bergschrund, particularly later in the season. In that case it's possible to climb the left (southwest) ridge or head right to join the top of the southeast ridge. *Gregg Beisly*

wading in waist-deep snow, cutting under seracs, and avoiding a series of crevasses, to reach the southeast ridge. After a small break, taking shelter in the lee of a howling wind, we gathered sufficient energy to climb the steep 20m névé step to the razor-sharp summit pyramid. The route was AD+. [*Chearoco is a broad massif with the south summit 20–30m higher than the north top. The southwest face—either the route reported here or a similar line—is believed to have seen previous ascents.*]

As Chearoco is one of the Cordillera Real's highest mountains and sits close to the middle of the range, its summit serves up unparalleled views of the entire chain, Lake Titicaca, and the verdant eastern valleys. The south face (first ascent unknown but climbed in 1978 by Italians) is the most frequently climbed route today. Until two years ago the Chearoco area had attracted few mountaineers. The Omasuyo locals, who live on the western flanks of the mountain, have a fierce reputation and have consistently harassed, stoned, and robbed visitors, including Bolivians. In the mid-1990s I was harassed and fired upon. However, a recently arrived Catholic priest and climber, Father Antonio Zavatarelli, who is contributing to the development of sport climbing in the Penas area, has seemingly convinced the Omasuyos to become more congenial hosts, opening up this important area to trekking and mountaineering. During our brief stay we found the locals welcoming and helpful, without any shots fired. 🖸

– **ERIK MONASTERIO**, *NEW ZEALAND*

WARAWARANI I, SOUTHWEST FACE

ON OCTOBER 10, Artem Bylinksi (Russian), Juvenal Condori, Rodrigo Lobo (both Bolivian), and Davide Vitale (Belgian) reached Penas, drove to the road head at Jalluwaya, and then walked three hours to Laguna Warawarani, where they camped. Leaving next day a little after 1 a.m, and climbing as two pairs, they made the first ascent of the southwest face of Warawarani I (5,542m).

[Above] The southwest face of Warawarani I from Laguna Warawarani, showing the line of Alaxpacha Warawara Thaki (Condori-Lobo, 2014). Bylinski and Vitale climbed variants to the right in the upper half. The four climbers descended the far side. *Juvenal Condori*

Although this face may have provided a relatively pleasant outing in the past, climate change and glacial retreat have left very unstable rock. Climbing first on the face, Condori and Lobo ascended 15 pitches over mixed terrain, with soft snow covered by a thin crust. Large blocks shifted under their feet and fell, leaving them fearing for their two friends climbing below. For this reason, Bylinski and Vitale made significant variants to the Condori-Lobo line. The first party reached the summit about half an hour before the others, grading the 600m route TD- M4. Bylinski and Vitale gave a grade of D+/TD- 65° 5.6 M4 R. Warawarani means place of many stars, so the team called their route Alaxpacha Warawara Thaki, which roughly means "reach the sky, by the route of stars."

The four started down the northeast ridge, were forced onto the east face, and then downclimbed to the top of a gully. After a 60m rappel they were able to traverse north into a couloir, which they downclimbed in wet snow. They then ascended the glacier northwest to a col and descended the far side southwest to the lake, arriving in camp at 4:30 p.m.

Editor's note: Warawarani had no known prior ascent other than the one on August 12, 1975, when it was climbed by Italians Santino Caligari, Melchiorre and Giovanni Foresti, and Giuseppe Ferrari. They climbed the east face, but their line is unknown. In September 1998, Florence Barrault, François-Xavier Grillon, Olivier Guidet, and Gregoire Volluet (France) started from the Morokho Khota Valley and climbed what they called Warawarani North via the 700m southeast ridge, which they found straightforward at F. This appears to be Peak 5,604m on the watershed ridge well to the north-northeast of Warawarani I, and not part of the Warawarani Group. There are four peaks in the group, with IV (ca 5,480m) not climbed until July 1996 (from the east, PD) by an Anglo-Bolivian team (AAJ 1997). 📷

– SUPPLIED BY DENYS SANJINES, BOLIVIA, TRANSLATED BY CHRISTIAN ROMERO, CHILE

PICO ITALIA–HUAYNA POTOSI TRAVERSE; PICO MILLUNI EAST RIDGE, SOLO ASCENT

In May, David Mayta and Robert Rauch made a rare and rapid traverse over Pico Italia (ca 5,750m) and Huayna Potosi (6,088m). They started from the Casablanca Base Camp (ca 4,700m) by Zongo Lake, and 12 hours later were on the main summit of Huayna Potosi, having climbed the southeast ridge of Pico Italia at night. Descending the north side of Italia they found a nasty pitch of M4, followed by a corniced and mixed ridge. One pitch on the south ridge of Huayna Potosi took two hours, shoveling away 1m of sugar snow, and then climbing with two snow stakes instead of axes. Rauch also made possibly the first solo ascent of the east ridge of Pico Milluni (5,500m), climbing over all five summits. 📷

– LINDSAY GRIFFIN, *FROM INFORMATION SUPPLIED BY ROBERT RAUCH, BOLIVIA*

HUAYNA POTOSI, SOUTH SUMMIT, WEST FACE, VIA DEL TRIANGULO, VARIANT

ON AUGUST 25, Pacifico Machaca and I drove to the west side of Huayna Potosi and then walked two hours to the lake below the west face. Here, we examined possibilities for a new mixed route on this stunning wall. Carrying neither tent nor sleeping bag, we sought shelter for the night among the rocks. A strong wind blew and we didn't sleep a wink.

At 3 a.m. we set out for the face, but since the line we had in mind began with a rock section, we had to wait for sunrise at 6:30 a.m. in order to start. The first pitch, with delicate climbing and thin cracks, took longer than anticipated. The third pitch, which had only small holds, was badly protected. We continued up another slab with thin cracks, and then a delicate ice-covered wall, where screws penetrated

[Above] Delicate rock climbing in the lower part of the west face of Huayna Potosi. *Juvenal Condori*

no more than 4cm—the best protection we could get. Higher, I reached a couloir and managed to place a good anchor in soft ice. The climbing now became more mixed, with loose rock. We were not even halfway up the face when the sun began to disappear. We continued into another couloir, where there was a strenuous 90° icefall. Determined to complete the route, and above all safely, we continued climbing through the night on sustained 75–80° snow and ice, interspersed with sections of delicate rock.

By the time the sun rose again we were exhausted, but at 10 a.m. on August 27 we reached the south summit (ca 5,960m). We descended southeast to pick up the normal route. The avalanche risk was high and we saw evidence of three wind-slab avalanches. At 2 p.m. we finally arrived at the standard base camp. We named our line Andinismo Creativo Boliviano (800m, ED VI/5+ M5 6a+, *see photo on page 211 for route line*).

Editor's note: The new Bolivian route begins well to the right of the 1971 Via del Triangulo, attributed to Hans Haztler and Alain Mesili. It slants up left then climbs ground close to but right of the 1971 line before joining it for the upper section of the face and then finishing directly to the summit. In the 1970s this right-hand section of the west face was mostly snow and ice; Mesili graded his route D- (70°) and noted it became steeper and harder near the top. An ascent was made very early in the 2004 season by Pierre Bogino and Alexis Loireau, who found delicate ice and mixed terrain (IV/5 90°).

– JUVENAL CONDORI, *BOLIVIA, TRANSLATED BY CHRISTIAN ROMERO, CHILE*

HUAYNA POTOSI AND ILLIMANI, HISTORICAL AMERICAN ASCENTS

FROM JUNE 17–20, 1974, Americans Roman Laba and John Thackray climbed the northwest ridge of Huayna Potosi. The *AAJ 1975* feature describing this climb is erroneous in recording it as the northeast ridge. The only reference to an earlier ascent of the northwest ridge attributes it to Hans Ertl in 1972. This is not only unconfirmed but is extremely unlikely for a number of reasons, not least because Ertl had given up climbing before then. Laba and Thackray's climb is the first confirmed ascent of the northwest ridge.

Laba climbed two more routes on Huayna Potosi: the west ridge in 1969 with John Hudson, a first ascent (and always correctly identified as such), and a 1976 repeat, with John Roskelley and Jim States, of the 1970 American Route on the west face.

Laba and Thackray also made the first ascent of Illimani's south face in 1974. Recent *AAJs* have reported new routes on the south face but repeatedly failed in photodiagrams to note the first route. This ascent took place in early July 1974 when Laba and Thackray climbed a line more or less in the center of the face. As their approach to the face and the climb itself were carried out in very poor visibility, the line cannot be identified exactly, but it started on the left side of the broad buttress in the center of the face. It is likely unrepeated. [*See updated photo with all known route lines on Illimani's south face at the AAJ website.*] 📷

– LINDSAY GRIFFIN, *AFTER DISCUSSION WITH ROMAN LABA AND JOHN THACKRAY*

PICO TRIANGULAR, SOUTH FACE, WORMHOLE

ON JUNE 19, Gregg Beisly, Robert Rauch, and I climbed what we believe to be a new route in the Zongo Pass area. Although the feature we climbed has several routes, it may not have a real name, and we started calling it Pico Triangular due to its obvious shape as viewed from the wholly irrelevant and mildly annoying police checkpoint at Milluni. It is a 5,600m subsidiary

[Next page, top] Huayna Potosi from the northwest. (A) Pico Mesili. (B) Main (north) summit. (C) South summit. (1) Northeast ridge from Pico Mesili (first ascent unknown). (2) Northwest Ridge (1974). (3) West-northwest face (claimed 1979). (4) West Ridge (1969). Several routes are not shown between 4 and 5, including the 1970 American Route. (5) Argentinian-Spanish Route (1990). *Gregg Beisly*

[Middle] The west face of Huayna Potosi in unusually snowy condition, the day before the Bolivian ascent in 2014. (A) Main summit. (B) South summit (ca 5,960m). (1) West ridge (900m, D+, Hudson-Laba, 1969). (2) Slovenian Route (900m, D+, Jereb-Pogacar, 1983). (3) American Route (900m, D-, Harthorne-Harvard-Janney-Thompson, 1970). (4) Primorska Route (900m, TD+, Cernilogar-Humar-Sveticic-Trusnovec, 1983). (5) French Route (900m, D, Afanassieff-Afanassieff, 1978). (6) Via del Triangulo (800m, IV/5, Haztler-Mesili, 1971). (7) Andinismo Creativo Boliviano (800m, ED1 IV/M4 6a+, Condori-Machaca, 2014). (8) Argentinian-Spanish Route (800m, D+ 80°, Enriquez-Godo-Godo-Pagani, 1990). The older west-face routes are now considerably harder than their original grades due to lack of snow and ice, and although (4) was feasible in the 1980s, the state of the large serac today makes crossing it highly inadvisable. *Juvenal Condori*

[Bottom] Looking north toward Huayna Potosi. (A) Pico Triangular. (1) Southwest ridge (D-, likely first climbed in 1963). (2) Baked (D+, Baker-Beisly, 2011). (3) Happy Meal (TD, Cusik-Stock, 1999). (4) Wormhole (TD/TD+, 2014). (B) Huayna Potosi. (C) Pico Italia. (5) Monasterio Route (D, Monasterio-Monasterio, 1998). (6) Normal route (AD). (7) Southeast face (AD+). *Gregg Beisly*

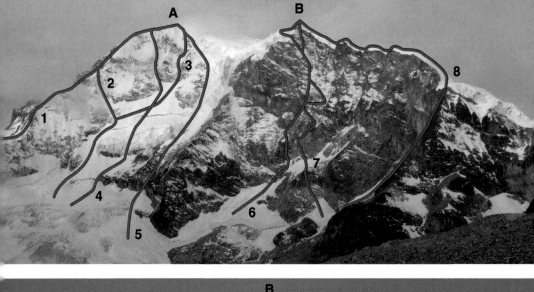

peak of Huayna Potosi, just to the south of Pico Italia.

After three hours of walking we arrived at the base of a deep cleft toward the right side of the south face. I was expecting a dry chimney, but Robert found a slender drip of ice, 5–7cm wide and likewise deep, through steep, loose terrain. Each pitch above offered interesting climbing. A passage of ice underneath a large chockstone, where everyone except me had to trail their packs to squeeze through, gave the route its name: the Wormhole. We did about 12 pitches, with the upper ones giving some particularly fun ice in a corner. We graded the 500m route TD/TD+ WI4 M4, and the consensus was that this was one of the best routes any of us had climbed in Bolivia.

We would have enjoyed lingering in the sunlight on the summit of our small peak, but we needed to move quickly down the southwest ridge, as there was less than an hour before dark. We rapped a few times, but mostly weaved our way through loose granite blocks. I was relieved to see the col, from which we had only about 300m of 50° snow to descend, plus several kilometers of hiking to the car. However, I then pulled on a desk-sized block that rotated under minimal pressure. The block hit me in the chest as it went into the void, and I fell roughly 6m. Since there are no helicopters or other rescue services in Bolivia, there was only one choice: Continue on. Darkness fell. We did not want to cross beneath seracs again, so we aimed directly toward the car and fortunately found it without problems. On arrival I gave a spectacular demonstration of dry-heaving from exhaustion—15 minutes later we were discussing future plans. 📷

– CHRIS CLARKE, BOLIVIA

PICO MILLUNI (5,500M), EAST SIDE, VARIOUS ROUTES

THE EASTERN ASPECT of Pico Milluni features rather nice rock, and the following routes, which end on one of Milluni's summits, are likely new. In May my wife, Sal, and I climbed the main summit by the central, northeast-facing buttress. The first three pitches finish on a small tower, which we downclimbed easily on the far side; we then scrambled up 50m to where three more fantastic pitches led directly to the summit. The crux (5c) was the first pitch of the route. Later in the month, and on the higher of the south peaks, my son, Aedan, and I put up a quality four-pitch route at 5a. Aedan called it the Black Condor, because near the top we were buzzed several times by one of these enormous birds. On the lower of the two south peaks, Jesus Churata and I climbed a direct five-pitch line to the summit, which Jesus named Ruta de los Vikingos (6a+) after his unit in the Bolivian Navy. The upper three pitches, above a scree terrace, are particularly fun and exposed.

In January 2012, in the middle of the wet season, Sal and I climbed the northeast face to the left of the central buttress mentioned above. We climbed a long snow slope followed by mixed climbing to reach Milluni's middle summit, immediately south of the main top (AD-). 📷

– GREGG BEISLY, BOLIVIA

PICO MILLUNI (5,500M), SOUTH FACE, YA PUES!

FOR THE PAST THREE YEARS, while traveling to Zongo Pass for rock climbing, I have looked at the south face of Pico Milluni and thought that in the right conditions it must hold interesting mixed lines. Despite its easy access and a number of obvious possibilities, climbers appear to have largely ignored this face in recent years. For various reasons, mainly involving too many other projects, I never went. Finally, on June 5, Roberto Rauch and I left La Paz at 6 a.m., and after picking up Gregg Beisly in El Alto, drove to within an hour and a half's hike of the south

[Above] The southwest face of Pico Milluni. (1) North Pillar. (2) Ya Pues! (3) Central Couloir, Mesili-Sanchez finish. (4) Central Couloir, Gelmi-Ferrari exit. *Gregg Beisly*

face. As far as we know, two variations were climbed in the prominent central couloir during the 1970s, when the face held far more snow, and a line predominantly on rock was completed up the left central buttress.

We chose a funnel of steepening hard snow and easy mixed ground between these two, which we climbed unroped for about 300m to a belay stance beneath the crux mixed section. This involved 20m of very thin ice in a vertical corner, which Gregg led to a small snowfield. Above, we followed a classic narrow mixed gully for a few pitches until its exit onto a more open snow and rock face. Another few pitches led to the summit ridge at a prominent notch. Finally in the sun, we followed the ridge for 600–700m of easy but fun climbing on very good rock, similar in character and quality to the Upper Exum on the Grand Teton. We believe our line is new and have called it Ya Pues! (600m to ridge, D+/TD- M5 AI3). Ya Pues is an expression commonly used in La Paz to mean "come on already," "just do it," or "knock it off."

Editor's note: In his various guidebooks Alan Mesili reports that the central couloir was climbed in 1972 by Italians Angelo Gelmi and Giuseppe Ferrari, and by Ernesto Sanchez and himself. The Italians climbed to the low point in the summit ridge (AD+), while Mesili suggests he and Sanchez veered left and climbed almost direct to the summit (D 55°). Mesili also reports that he repeated the route solo in April 1974. Three years later it was skied by Dominique Chapuis, in the same season that he made the second ascent of the Afanassieff Route on the west face of Huayna Potosi. The left (north) pillar on the face was climbed in 1981 by Frenchmen Yves Astier and Olivier Mandrenes. Although reports suggest that the late Stanley Shepard soloed the first ascent of the south ridge in 1979, his description makes it far more likely he was on the higher Pico Italia. 📷

– CHRIS CLARKE, *BOLIVIA*

[Photo] The south spur of the west ridge of Pico Norte. Three climbers can be seen on the crest of the spur at one-third height. *Amedeo Rosso*

ILLIMANI, PICO NORTE (6,403M), SOUTH SPUR ATTEMPT

IN JUNE, Italians Marco Erbetta, Enrico Rosso, and Father Antonio Zavattarelli, the latter a missionary in Penas, made an unsuccessful attempt on the south spur of Pico Norte's west ridge. From a camp below the mountain the team spent a day trying to access the south spur directly, but were turned back by large seracs. They then climbed to the Nido de Condores at 5,450m on the normal route (west ridge) leading to Pico Sur, Illimani's main summit.

On June 8, Erbetta, Rosso, and Zavattarelli continued up the ridge to a point where they were able to descend a couple of hundred meters left onto the glacier basin below the central and north summits. They camped below the south spur and the following morning climbed two-thirds of this elegant, sharp snow arête to an altitude of 5,900m, where they were forced to retreat. Conditions proved too dangerous, with unconsolidated snow on one flank and wind slab on the other. If they'd succeeded on the south spur, their plan had been to continue along the ridge from Pico Norte, over the central and main summits, then down the normal route.

– LINDSAY GRIFFIN, *FROM INFORMATION PROVIDED BY ENRICO ROSSO*

QUIMSA CRUZ

ACHUMA GROUP, NEW ROCK CLIMBS

GIORGIO CASALOTI (Italy), Paolo Cogliati (Italy), Patricio Payrola (Argentina), Grover Teran (Bolivia), and I explored the Achuma Group and put up a couple of new rock routes. From the village of Asiento de Araca (where, as normal in Bolivia, it is appropriate to obtain the consent of locals before venturing up their mining roads), we drove to El Rosario mine (4,000m) and then walked up an abandoned mining trail to a lake we named Laguna Castaya, where we set up base camp at 4,550m. Needles, pyramids, and large granite slabs dominate the amphitheater, mostly facing south. Potential routes are a maximum of 300m. Many cracks here can be vegetated and have to be cleaned well to offer protection. Or you can just run it out.

– DENYS SANJINES, *BOLIVIA, TRANSLATED BY CHRISTIAN ROMERO*

CORDILLERA OCCIDENTAL

POMERAPE, SOUTHWEST RIDGE WITH SOUTH FACE VARIATION

IN JULY, Gregg Beisly, Max Jimenez Llusco, and I climbed a possible new variation on Pomerape (a.k.a. Pomerata, 6,282m) in the Cordillera Occidental. Starting from the village of Sajama (four hours' drive southwest of La Paz) on the 19th, we walked up to the 5,350m col between Parinacota and Pomerape, intending to climb the southwest ridge. However, due to very unstable rock and considerable objective danger, we bailed to the right at around one-third height and climbed the south flank, possibly creating a new variant. We reached the summit in temperatures of –30° C, approximately nine hours after setting off. We descended directly down the south face. [*The southwest ridge and south ridge, both rated PD in good conditions, are established routes. In 1993 a team of Chileans ascended the "previously unclimbed south face" above the col; they found this steep and icy, and eventually had to bivouac on the summit.*]

– ERIK MONASTERIO, *NEW ZEALAND*

ARGENTINA-CHILE

PIRÁMIDE ALEJANDRO LEWIS

PIRÁMIDE ALEJANDRO LEWIS (4,800m) is a fine, rocky pyramid in the Nevado de Cachi, named after a deceased climber. From Las Pailas, the approach is made by hiking up the Quebrada de la Hoyada. In November, Matias Cruz and Facundo Juárez Zapiola opened a new route on the peak: Trankahuasi (200m, 5+/6b+). Their route follows a diagonal crack on the left side of the south wall for four pitches and finishes by the upper west face. Zapiola and Patricio Payrola ascended another line on the south wall in 2011, located right of the new route (200m, 6a).

– **MARCELO SCANU**, *ARGENTINA*

ANSILTA 7, NICO MADE, ALEGRIA

IN OCTOBER, Wenny Sanchez and I climbed a new route in a remote part of Argentina's Central Andes: the Cordillera de Ansilta. The area is reached from the town of Barreal, in San Juan Province, and then by following harsh and rugged high-desert terrain westward along the Río Blanco. From Barreal it is about 30km to Estancia del Rio Blanco. From there it took us two days and about 12 total hours to hike 18km, starting at ca 2,000m, to reach a base camp at ca 4,300m.

Our climb ascends a very beautiful granite needle on the eastern side of Ansilta 7 (5,780m), starting just off the moraine below the Glaciar la Fría. Ansilta 7 is a large, glaciated mountain, and this needle is one of many possibilities in a recently discovered area that somewhat resembles Frey, outside of Bariloche. The route mostly followed steep, clean cracks up compact, brown granite. We called the needle Nico Made (ca 4,600m) and the route Alegria (230m, 6c), which means "joy." Eight rappels bring you back down the route. The other walls and needles

[Above] Nico Made tower, showing the first ascent route Alegria (230m, 6c). *Gabriel Fava*

range from 100–400m in height. [*See http://bit.ly/1s0SDUk for a map and overview of the mountain, including a selection of walls and spires for future new routing.*] 📷 🔍

– **GABRIEL FAVA**, *ARGENTINA*

CERRO PIRAMIDAL DEL POTRERO ESCONDIDO, SOUTH FACE

CERRO PIRAMIDAL DEL POTRERO ESCONDIDO (5,386m) is located in the Central Andes, outside of Mendoza. On September 16, Lucas Amuchástegui, Juan Bautista Alonso, and Pablo Laumann (all Argentina) departed from Punta de Vacas to reach Río Chorrillos and begin their approach to the peak. The next day they trekked westward up the Quebrada de Chorrillos. On the third day they reached a 400m section of technical climbing that gains the upper valley. (This is approximatley two-thirds way up the valley.) They climbed three pitches and fixed ropes due to lack of time. On the fourth day they managed to climb through the rock band and make camp at ca 3,800m.

[Above] The south face of Cerro Piramidal del Potrero Escondido (5,386m). Alto Guiso (500m, D 75° AI3 M3/4) climbs the obvious ramp to the summit. It took the team five days to reach the base of the mountain and begin their climb. *Glauco Muratti*

On the fifth day they continued gaining elevation up the valley and found a camp below the glacier under the south side of the peak at ca 4,200m. On day six they departed at 6:20 a.m. and began traversing a glacier (ranging from 30–60°) and passed a bergschrund. The section above contained deep snow and steepened to 75° on the final pitch. They reached the summit at 6:30 p.m and arrived safe at camp at 4:30 a.m. after getting lost on the descent.

In two days, the group hiked back out 40km to Punta de Vacas. They named the route Alto Guiso (500m, D 75° AI3 M3/4). The mountain had two previous ascents, one in 1965 from the west and one in 2005 from Quebrada del Potrero Escondido. 📷 🔍

— MARCELO SCANU, *ARGENTINA*

CERRO ALBARDÓN DEL POTRERO ESCONDIDO, SOUTHEAST FACE

CERRO ALBARDÓN DEL POTRERO ESCONDIDO (5,112m) is part of the Cordón del Potrero Escondido Los Clonquis, outside of Mendoza. In November, Adrián Petrocelli and Glauco Muratti (both Argentina) departed from Punta de Vacas to make the first ascent. They made four camps as they approached up the Quebrada Potrero Escondido. The lack of winter snowfall and hot conditions made travel difficult. While one would normally expect south-facing couloirs to contain large avalanche cones at their base, the climbers found black névé and rotten water ice. The pair reached the summit on November 20. The last section was easy 40° snow. They descended the same route and returned to Punta de Vacas in two days. 📷 🔍

— MARCELO SCANU, *ARGENTINA*

TORRES DEL CAMPANARIO, NEW ROUTES

TORRES DEL CAMPANARIO (ca 5,090m) is a nice set of towers outside of Mendoza in the Cordillera Frontal of Argentina's Central Andes. It has granite very similar to the walls in southern Patagonia. In March, a number of fine new lines were opened in this relatively

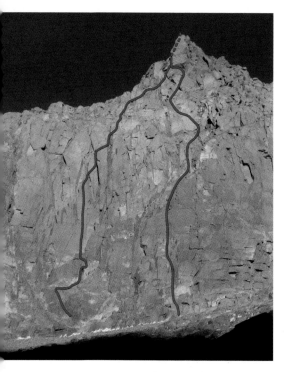

[Above] An unnamed wall in the Torres Del Campanario, showing the new routes Che Gil Otario (left, 350m, 7a) and Dias de Insomnio (305m, 6c+ A0). *Diego Nakamura*

unknown area. The approach is not easy, with a steep snow and scree field to reach Paso Tucson (ca 4,600m), a high pass that provides access down into the alpine cirque where the towers are located.

In early March, a team of four Argentineans visited one of the largest walls, erecting a camp at ca 4,300m. After scoping things out, Diego Nakamura and Lucas Alzamora opened Dias de Insomnio (305m, 6c+ A0), and Carloncho Guerra and Macarena Zanotti opened an adjacent route to the left they called Che Gil Otario (350m, 7a). Climbing at the same time, the two groups united on the summit of one of the three lesser, eastern summits but did not continue to the highest one.

Later in March, Luciano Fiorenza and Pablo Pontoriero were active in the same zone. They first opened a beautiful crack climb on a tower comprised of orange-colored granite, which is located in the approach valley to Torres del Campanario, near Laguna Arenales. They called it Aguja El Topo (180m, 6c). Afterward, they traveled over Paso Tuscon and ascended Cerro Krakus (ca 4,900m) by a tricky glacier to study new-route options on the adjacent Torres del Campanario. On March 17 they climbed No Hay Pìcaro Sin Suerte (300m, 6b). The route is said to climb excellent granite and reaches the highest summit of Torres del Campanario. ▶

– MARCELO SCANU, *ARGENTINA*

CAJON DE ARENALES, AGUJA EL MARINERO, NEW ROUTE

IN LATE OCTOBER, Wenny Sanchez and I climbed a new route on Aguja El Marinero (ca 3,300m). This fine wall is located in Cajon de Arenales in the Mendoza Range, outside of Tunuyan, a granite canyon that has seen much recent development on its 200–400m walls. Our new route Liberate y Baila (200m, 7a) climbs a direct line up the center of Marinero's south face, mostly following splitter cracks and corners. [*For more information on Cajon de Arenales check out AAJ 2009.*] 📷 🔍

– GABRIEL FAVA, *ARGENTINA*

CERRO NEGRO PABELLÓN

CERRO NEGRO PABELLÓN (6,086m, 33°26'59.9"S, 69°42'09.7"W) is a rarely visited peak in the Cordón de las Delicias; it is the highest of the Cordillera Frontal, near Mendoza. The mountain had three previous ascents: first by Mendoza climbers in 1953 (although it's unclear

if they climbed to the highest summit or the slightly lower east summit, ca 6,060m), then by a Japanese team in 1969, and once more by climbers from Mendoza in 1984.

From November 15–23, Lucas Gómez, Guillermo Ferri, Mauro Schmiedt, and Diego Cavassa (all Argentina) opened a new access route to the mountain from Portillo Argentino, which is 96km long, with a cumulative gain of 8,081m. The mountain had previously been approached from Río Tunuyán. Once at the peak the climbers made camp at ca 3,920m. From there the group split in two: Gómez and Ferri ascended an unclimbed peak, calling it Cerro Bautismo (5,039m); Schmiedt and Cavassa made two more camps as they approached the summit of Cerro Negro Pabellón. On November 20 they departed at 6:30 a.m. and reached the summit at 1:55 p.m. by a variant to the Japanese route (northwest ridge). They reached their camp again at 7:30 p.m. 📷 🔍

– MARCELO SCANU, *ARGENTINA*

CERRO MARMOLEJO, NEW ICE CLIMBS

In mid-July I met Cecilia Buil (Spain) in Chile, our plan being to climb some new routes on Cerro Marmolejo (6,109m), located at the head of Cajon del Maipo, a long, mountainous valley near Santiago. We first wanted to climb the route established by Harry Berger and Albert Leichtfried in 2006, Senda Real (6 pitches, WI7+). However with extreme cold and blizzard conditions persisting, a long approach, and little time at our disposal, we could only complete two pitches on this hard icefall. [*See AAJ 2006 and www.escalando.cl/marmolejo.htm for more information about Senda Real and other climbs on this high-elevation wall.*]

After this we shifted our attention to the rocky bastion that supports the Marmolejo Glacier, 1,000m lower in elevation (the climbs are ca 4,000m). From our base camp, a number of icefalls on the east side of the mountain could be reached by just a couple of hours on foot. There were often high winds and storms during our 15-day stay, but we made good use of two weather windows. The icefalls face northwest and on sunny days this means you have only one hour before rocks and ice begin to tumble down.

First we established a variation to a route completed by Jose "Josito" Romay and me

[Below] The wall below Marmolejo Glacier as seen in October during a "fatter" year. The icefalls were thinner when Torretta and Buil visited in July; however, temperatures were colder and more conducive to climbing. La Gioconda (160m, WI6) is the line on the right. *Cecilia Buil*

[Above] Gran Torre del Cortaderal from the Cortaderal Glacier. The route (MD 5.9 55°) climbs the snow gully and skyline of the highest summit above the climbers pictured. *Ulises Espinosa*

in 2012 called Le Patou; that route tops out on a large ledge, as does our new variation Le Bombardier (30m, WI6-) which lies just right of it. Next we established La Gioconda (160m, WI6), which is the most obvious line on the wall, the biggest, and most beautiful. It can be broken up into two sections due to a dividing ledge. The first, in the shade, climbs extremely hard ice, while the second receives the afternoon sun and climbs porous, stalactite ice. We needed three days to climb the five-pitch route.

We also attempted a route we dubbed Mega Couloir, which climbs up to the Marmolejo Glacier past two vertical-to-overhanging pitches at the end. The first part is hidden from sight, deep in the rock, and after a snowstorm it runs like water with spindrift. Additionally, a local named Nicolás Gutiérrez opened a new route (180m, WI5) during our trip; it is located in a gully on the left side of the wall. 📷 🔍

— ANNA TORRETTA, *ITALY*

GRAN TORRE DEL CORTADERAL, CORONA DEL DIABLO

In November 2013, Christian Quezada, Ricardo Hernandez, Ulises Espinosa, and I (all members of the Grupo de Alta Montaña de los Perros Alpinos), traveled to the University and Cortaderal glaciers, which are located south of Santiago and comprise the second largest glacial zone in Chile. (The Patagonian Ice Cap is the largest.) The area is composed of more than seven independent glaciers, covering an area approximately 70km long and 5km wide.

Absurd access restrictions have been imposed by the private hydroelectric companies Pacific-Hydro, Hydro-Chile, and Maitenes, which make it very difficult to enter the area. Therefore, most of the mountains have had few ascents, and possibilities for opening new routes are high. The remoteness of the area only adds to the difficult logistics, and the slender, challenging mountains make the climbs a tremendous undertaking.

Due to the lack of legal foot access, we approached the area by helicopter. We spent approximately a month on the glacier, operating out of two base camps, the first on the University Glacier and the second on the Cortaderal Glacier. We climbed new routes on the following peaks (most summits had only two or three prior ascents and the vertical gain from the glacier to these summits ranges from approximately 700m to 1,500m): Pilar Meridional, west face (AD 5.7 65°); Nor-Este Torreón (secondary summit of Corona del Diablo), Goulotte West (D+ 5.8 60°–90°); Nevado Cisne, southeast ridge (AD 60°–70°); Pilar Occidental, Playboy Rabbit Goulotte (AD 5.7 55°–60°); Gran Torre del Cortaderal, (MD 5.9 55°); Nevado Penitentes, south ridge (AD 60°); and Corona del Diablo (AD 5.8 70°). [*See Gastón San Román's report about the first ascents of some of these summits in AAJ 1965.*] 📷

– ELVIS ACEVEDO, *CHILE*

CERRO GENERAL CARRERA, NORTH FACE; CERRO MANUEL RODRÍGUEZ

In November, Ulises Espinosa (Chile) and I went to the Las Leñas Valley, where in six days we completed the first ascent of Cerro General Carrera (both its west [3,198m GPS] and central summit [3,313m GPS]), and Cerro Manuel Rodríguez (4,026m). We also explored the relatively unknown Cajón de Espinoza.

We climbed Cerro General Carrera in a day from our base camp by its north face, which is composed of snow slopes and very bad rock (900m, AD- 60° 5.7). We descend by its south face, crossing the mountain and both of its summits. To climb Cerro Manuel Rodríguez, we first established an advanced base camp in Cajón de Espinoza. The next day we ascended easy snow slopes (50°) until reaching a final, loose rock tower, which we climbed to its highest point (1,100m, AD- 60° 5.7).

Previously, Las Leñas Valley was closed for decades to mountaineers due to private ownership. However, in 2010 the government declared the road into Las Leñas Valley national property for public use and downed the gates preventing access. There now awaits an entire area full of canyons and mountains; many are nameless and unclimbed. 📷 🔍

– ELVIS ACEVEDO, *CHILE*

CERRO DE LOS PANTANOS, TORRE BLANCA DE ECTELION

Diego Nakamura and partners have climbed many spires in the Sosneado Group over the past few years. The zone lies on the east flank of Cerro de los Pantanos, southeast of Cerro el Palomo (4,850m), along the Chile-Argentina border. In March, Lucas Alzamora and Diego Nakamura ascended the last virgin spire: Torre Blanca de Ectelion. They christened their route Chaparral (10 pitches, 475m, 6b). The route climbs a long rib just right of a prominent, steep gully. It is mostly 5+/6, but also contains a few meters of 6b climbing. They descended from the summit by a scree slope. This was their fourth attempt on the spire, with three previous attempts up a route left of the gully.

– MARCELO SCANU, *ARGENTINA*

[Photo] Torre Blanca de Ectelion, showing Chaparral (10 pitches, 475m, 6b) on the right and the previously attempted line on the left. *Diego Nakamura*

EL HERMANO, CENIZAS A CENIZAS

IN SUMMER 2011, Mike Ybarra cornered me inside the tourist-laden Yosemite Lodge cafeteria and asked if I wanted to open a new route with him in northern Patagonia. Controversial landowner and conservationist Doug Tompkins had given him a picture of what looked like a taller, more feral brother of El Cap. By the time the expedition finally took place in February 2014, a lot had changed: Mike died soloing in the Sierra in 2012, and Gil Weiss, another one of our original expedition partners, perished in Peru only a few weeks after Mike (*AAJ 2013*).

Instead I went to Chile with two Yosemite friends, Niels Tietze and Althea Rogers. With little knowledge of the wall or approach—beyond what Tompkins had seen from his airplane years ago—we shuttled from Chaiten an hour south to Lago Yelcho, a salmon-filled, glacial lake that guards the entrance to Valle Correntoso. Our local connection arranged a motorboat to take us across the lake. A mile into our 15-mile approach, we came across a year-round ranch and asked to rent a horse. They graciously agreed to take us to another ranch 3 miles up. The second rancher agreed to take us as far as his horses could go the next day. After unexpectedly traveling by horse for 10 miles, we said goodbye to the locals and began hacking our way through thick, temperate rainforest to the base of our less-than-vertical but taller El Capitan sibling.

We forged trail through stubborn bamboo barricades and over elevated, decomposing tree lattices for about 4 miles to a "clearing" where we set up our advanced base camp. To gain

[Left] El Hermano, showing the only route in the valley: Cenizas a Cenizas (4,000', 5.10 R A3). It took the team nine days to reach the base of the wall and six days total to climb and descend the route. [Right] Althea Rogers nears the summit of El Hermano on the fourth day of the climb. Unclimbed walls adorn the background. *Photos: Libby Sauter*

the wall required another mile of hiking with 1,800' of elevation gain. The rock is located in a large, lush drainage called Cañadón Huillín (43°07'08.39"S, 72°12'33.37"W). As far as we know, only Damian Benegas (Argentina) had hiked through the area, a decade prior, but no one had done any climbing. In total, our slog to the base of the wall took nine days.

Our first push ended in failure on the first day, owing to the heavily vegetated cracks and an impending ark-worthy storm. We rappelled, leaving lines fixed, and slept on the ground. We jugged up the next day to our high point about 900' up. This time we came prepared with our green thumbs—and a trowel! Above our fixed lines, Althea took the first leads, taking us up to and beyond a nice natural ledge through very slimy, wet, and vegetated corners. Fixing lines above, we rappelled back down to the ledge and bivied that night. From our new high point 1,500' up, we encountered progressively less plant life and occasionally sparkling-clean crack and corner systems. After sleeping on another natural bivy ledge on the fourth day, we blasted to the summit, climbing another 2,000' of chimneys and splitters before a scramble to the top.

With meticulous cleaning, the route would likely go free at around 5.12. We climbed it about half free. We placed only one bolt on the 4,000' climb (to protect 5.10+ slab climbing above a ledge on the second pitch.) We rappelled the route over two days, leaving single nuts and slings for anchors. We called the wall El Hermano and the route Cenizas a Cenizas (4,000', 18 pitches, 5.10 R A3), which means "ashes to ashes." The name came from all the ash we found on the summit from the recent eruptions of Chaiten, in honor of Niels' two brothers, whose ashes he released on the summit, and for the memory of Gil and Mike.

We attempted an additional peak in the Valle Correntoso, chossaneering and climbing up to "jungle 5.9," but turned around with approximately 600' of glowing white, slabby alpine rock remaining to the summit. Massive potential for 4,000' first ascents still exists in this valley if you've got a green thumb and a strong back. [o]

— LIBBY SAUTER, *USA*

COF

AT T ...OLS instructors organized an
expe ...olmillo. This range (northeast
of Sa ...ific Ocean, this valley collects
all tl ...dition shuttling food up the
mou ...vind.

...plit in two groups. We climbed
two ...Colmillo (1,896m) and Cerro
Ded ...n, Matt Beehler, and I headed
for t ...Colmillo. It took us two hours
to re ...ridge. Our descent was made
by d ...el got us back to camp. [o] [Q]

— PEDRO BINFA, *CHILE*

AV ...R

IN ...I spent a week in the Avellano
Mou... ...Ice Cap and northeast of the
shores of Lake General Carrera. We focused our attention on the Avellano Towers, an area of granite spires at the head of the Avellano River. The lack of accurate mapping, coupled with

various approaches to the towers, have led to fragmented descriptions of the region.

Our group approached from the small town of Bahia Murta, using the approach employed by John Bragg, Wes Bunch, Angela Hawse, and Brenton Regan in 2005, and used again by Jim Donini and Thom Engelbach in 2008. This leads to a valley west of these striking granite peaks. [See AAJ 2004, 2006, and 2008 for details on this approach and established climbs.]

After putting base camp between two lakes below the spires, we climbed to a bivy site in a col south of the smaller, tooth-shaped tower to the south of Avenali Tower, aptly nicknamed the Tooth. The following day we climbed the east ridge of the Tooth. This tower had previously been climbed, as we found abseil tat on the summit, but it's suspected the prior ascent was via easy, broken terrain to the north. There was no evidence of ascent on the route we've called Tooth Arête (300m, 5.10). After descending we bivied again at the col.

The next day John Crook and I set out to climb the east ridge of the tower just north of Avenali Tower and south of a summit assumed to have been climbed by Dave Anderson and party (AAJ 2004). We first dropped from the col between the Tooth and Avenali Tower, then crossed under the northeast face of Avenali Tower before gaining the east ridge of the unnamed tower just to its north. The ridge was easy for several hundred meters until it narrowed to form a classic knife-edge. Many steep pitches (5.10–5.11-) gained one of the twin summits of this tower. The climb took about 10 hours from the bivy. We descended the ridge, which took 7 hours and involved a complex mixture of abseiling and downclimbing. This was a high-quality route, ascending mostly very good granite to a fantastically sharp and pointy summit. We called the formation Crown Tower and the climb Crown Jewels (800m, 5.11-).

John Crook also scrambled to the top of the two highest summits south of the Tooth (both 5.6); the left had abseil cord indicating a prior ascent while the right-hand one did not. [image]

– DAVID BROWN, *U.K.*

LA PIRÁMIDE, NEW ROUTES

IN FEBRUARY 2015, Matt Van Biene, Coleman "Troutman" Blakeslee, Tad McCrea, and I climbed at La Pirámide (a.k.a. Cerro Colorado), a cliff discovered by Jim Donini and others in 2009 [see AAJ 2014 for Donini's introductory report]. While at the cliff we established four new routes.

The Magic Spatula (150m, III 5.11c) is the most significant line that we established. It climbs four long, quality pitches up the face to the right of the main prow, followed by a short fifth pitch that scrambles to the top of the cliff. There are two-bolt anchors at the top of each pitch, except for the fifth, which tops out on easy terrain. From the top it's a 30-minute walk down the backside. Matt and I first established the climb, and then our group of four made the first free ascent. [See this report on the AAJ website for detailed information about the three other shorter routes, how to approach La Pirámide, and various access concerns.] [image] [image]

– AUSTIN SIADAK, *USA*

CERRO SAN LORENZO, AGUJA ANTIPASTO, ROMANCE EXPLOSION

IN EARLY NOVEMBER, Rob Smith and I traveled to Cerro San Lorenzo (3,706m), Patagonia's second-tallest peak. While the Chaltén massif to the south is about ease of access to amazing climbing, San Lorenzo is about big adventure, with difficult unclimbed walls. [See AAJ 2009 for

[Next page] Matt Van Biene climbing the crux pitch of the Magic Spatula (150m, III 5.11c), one of the few routes on La Pirámide to reach the top of the cliff. *Austin Siadak*

[Above] Aguja Antipasto (left) showing Romance Explosion. The unclimbed 1,100–1,300m wall to the right is part of Cerro San Lorenzo. *Colin Haley*

more information about San Lorenzo.]

On November 10 we hired a pickup from Gobernador Gregores into Perito Moreno National Park and got dropped off at the end of the road. It then took three days to haul all our gear and food into base camp, an old hut known as Puesto San Lorenzo. During our three-week stay, we did not see a single other human, although we did see tons of guanacos and fresh puma tracks nearly every day in the lowlands. We could only see the mountain a handful of days, and on clear days the summit remained cloaked in a lenticular cloud. There are no trails and we waded no fewer than 19 river crossings. It rained nearly every day.

For me, the most appealing objective is a massive rock tower at the far southern end of San Lorenzo's south ridge. It may be the most difficult unclimbed feature in Patagonia. The east-northeast face of this formation is ca 1,000–1,300m. There are two summits, of which the west is higher. November 20 was the first of two periods of good weather, and we made an attempt on this large tower. From a bivy on the flat glacier below, we gained about 600m of elevation in terrible snow to reach the bergschrund, arriving just as sunlight hit the east aspect. Unfortunately, our chosen line started up a large east-facing gully system and it was too hot to climb such a terrain trap. We proceeded to pass the best weather day of our trip by taking naps in the tent. We watched an enormous number of avalanches that day, reassuring us we'd made the right decision.

The forecast was for significantly worse weather the following day, and we were running low on food, but we decided we ought to try to climb something. We turned our sights to the sharp spire just below and east of the main tower. It is dwarfed by the larger spire but would look proud in most other surroundings. We left our glacier bivy at 2 a.m. and kicked steps up a roughly 500m approach buttress. We climbed the spire via what can be roughly described as the east ridge—really more of a face than a ridge until the last few pitches. The middle of our route follows an ice gully, which was unfortunately decomposing into slush, so we were forced to climb harder rock variations. The last three pitches to the summit were only 5.7–5.9 but also the crux of the route due to poor rock. It was cold, windy, and cloudy the entire day. The summit of the spire was spectacularly sharp, and we tagged it one at a time. The descent took some time, as we rappelled all but 50m. We finished shortly after dark and made it back to our bivy roughly 22 hours after leaving. We climbed 14 pitches on the ascent and made 12 rappels. We named our route Romance Explosion (500m, 5.10 M5 R A0) and the spire Aguja Antipasto.

We owe big thanks to Rolo Garibotti and Seba Perroni, who helped us with logistics and weather forecasts throughout our trip. 📄 📷

– COLIN HALEY, *USA*

SOUTHERN PATAGONIA / CHALTÉN MASSIF

RESCUE UPDATE AND SEASON SUMMARY

THE 2014–2015 SEASON was marred by the death of Pablo Argiz, the pilot of a helicopter that crashed while attempting to rescue an injured climber. Argiz crashed because he misjudged the capabilities of his own helicopter; however, he was attempting to help a climber who fell into a crevasse while traveling unroped on a glacier, and the climber's partner was unable to carry out a simple crevasse-rescue maneuver. Earlier in the season, another rescue involved two very inexperienced climbers who, for their very first alpine climb, ventured drastically beyond their experience and abilities onto the west face of Cerro Torre.

The climbing in the Chaltén Massif is of serious wilderness character. Rescues are carried out on a Good Samaritan basis, and individuals risk their own lives in the process. Wall rescues are not currently possible (other than self-rescue, not a single wall rescue has ever been successful in the area). All this requires that climbers choose objectives that correspond with their skill level. Adequate risk management is essential, and it's imperative to be self-sufficient.

Although the local rescuers are volunteers, in the last five years the team has started billing for many rescues. The proceeds have been used to purchase equipment and pay for training. Starting next season, it appears likely they will start billing for all rescues and that rescue insurance will become mandatory in the park and surrounding area. The cost of rescues varies greatly depending on their complexity, but the minimum coverage currently being discussed is US$12,000. Should this come to pass, it will be possible to buy the coverage on-site,

[Left] Punta Herron and Torre Egger, showing the integral Tobogán (950m, 6b AI4 M6), which links the Tobogan and Spigolo de Bimbi routes with the Huber-Scnarf. [Right] The northeast face of Aguja Poincenot with Invisible Line (400m, 5.11+ A1). Many other routes ascending these towers are not shown. See www.pataclimb.com for the all the routes. *Photos: Rolando Garibotti*

through an Argentine insurance company, for an estimated US$125 for three months. On top of training and equipment, the local rescue team will use the proceeds to buy insurance coverage for volunteer rescuers, including "worker's comp" (currently they have none), and have a fund available to pay for helicopter time without delay from insurers (crucial hours, often days).

Although this season had a number of fairly lengthy, good weather periods, it was an "alpine" season, with a decent amount of snow and difficult conditions. Colin Haley (USA) had an incredibly successful season, but that is a testament to his skills and knowledge of the area and not to particularly favorable conditions. In addition to the climbs described in reports on the following pages, in mid-February he and Alex Honnold (USA) nearly completed a one-day Torre Traverse (Cerro Standhardt to Cerro Torre, crossing over Punta Herron and Torre Egger), retreating just two pitches below Cerro Torre's summit, after 20 hours of climbing.

On his second trip to Patagonia, young climber Marc-André Leclerc (Canada) brought down the house with a solo of the Corkscrew linkup on Cerro Torre. The Corkscrew climbs the lower half of the southeast ridge to the Via dei Ragni on the west face, covering over 3,000' with difficulties to 5.10 A1 WI6. He completed the ascent in 18 hours round-trip from the Col of Patience, an incredibly fast time. This is by far the hardest route ever soloed on Cerro Torre. Leclerc found fresh snow covering some of the rock and plentiful verglas. At one point he was forced to wait 40 minutes until the sun melted some ice and snow from the face. He only belayed by back-looping, doing so twice. He descended the southeast ridge.

Earlier in the season Markus Pucher (Austria) free-soloed the Via dei Ragni for a second time (he had already done so in 2013). His latest ascent was carried out in whiteout conditions. Later in the season, Caroline North and Christina Huber (both Germany) did the first female team ascent of the same route. Theirs was the second female team ascent of Cerro Torre and the first completely unsupported (the previous ascent relied on a rope fixed by another party on the crux pitch).

Approaching Col Trento from the east, Slovenes Luka Lindic, Luka Krajnc, and Tadej Kriselj traversed the three summits of Cerro Adela (Sur, Central, and Norte), descended to the Col de la Esperanza, and then climbed the Via dei Ragni on Cerro Torre. Earlier in the season, Krajnc and Kriselj climbed a new line on the west face of Mojón Rojo: Blockbuster (500m, 5.11).

Austrians Peter Ortner and Toni Ponholzer linked Tobogán and Spigolo dei Bimbi on Punta Herron with the Huber-Schnarf on Torre Egger to complete the first integral ascent of Tobogán (950m, 6b AI4 M6). On Cerro Domo Blanco's southwest face, Nicola Binelli and Tomas Franchini climbed a steep rock pillar on the left side, completing 12 pitches and retreating without continuing to the summit. They christened the pillar Pilastro Rampagaroi and their line Amico Vento, Amica Luna (400m, M6+ 6b+ A1).

The lower portion of the Pilar Este route on the east face of Cerro Fitz Roy has been littered with cable ladders and fixed ropes dating back to the first ascent in 1976. Matteo Della Bordella, Luca Schiera (both Italian), and Sylvan Schüpbach (Switzerland) made a commendable effort by cleaning off most of this trash, which was later brought to town by Iñaki Coussirat and Cristobal Señoret.

On Aguja Guillaumet, Ben Erdmann and Jonathan Schaffer (both USA) climbed Von Bürgermeister (400m, 5.11+), a new line on the right side of the west face. With Crystal Davis-Robbins, Schaffer went on to climb a partial new line on the north face of Aguja Poincenot, which they called John Henry (550m total with 300m new terrain, 5.11+) and also a new variation to the west ridge of Aguja Rafael Juárez (300m, 5.10+). In late February, Schaffer and Haley made the first ascent of Torrisimo by its northwest side (five pitches to 5.9 C1). This short but slender spire is located on the ridge between Torre de la Medialuna and Punta Pereyra.

Czech climbers Michal Brunner and Jindrich Hudecek climbed Invisible Line (400m, 5.11+ A1), a new route on the northeast face of Aguja Poincenot. It follows the massive crack and chimney system that runs parallel to and left of the Potter-Davis route.

Brette Harrington completed the first free-solo ascent of the mega-classic Chiaro di Luna (780m, 5.11-) on the west face of Aguja Saint-Exupery. Her inspirational ascent is the first female solo of any of the towers. Less than a week later, Leclerc also free-soloed the route.

– ROLANDO GARIBOTTI

CERRO TORRE GROUP, LA TRAVESÍA DEL OSO BUDA

FOR THIS PAST SEASON in Chaltén, my 12th trip to these mountains, Marc-André Leclerc and I blocked off January 15 to February 7 to climb together. Marc is quite young, but already a very accomplished technical climber. He arrived in Chaltén just before the longest weather window of the season, and we headed straight for the business: a "reverse traverse" of the Torres.

The original Torre Traverse, which Rolando Garibotti and I completed in January 2008 (AAJ 2008), linked Aguja Standhardt to Cerro Torre via Punta Herron and Torre Egger. In 2010 my longtime climbing partner Bjorn-Eivind Artun first illuminated the idea of a Torre Traverse in the opposite direction. At that time there were two missing segments: a direct ice route up the south face of Torre Egger (to avoid the time-consuming aid of the American route) and a route up the south

[Above] The reverse Torre Traverse: La Travesía del Oso Buda (1,200m, 6a+ 90° M6 C1), which climbs right to left, starting on Cerro Torre and ending on Aguja Standhardt. *Rolando Garibotti*

face of Aguja Standhardt. In the 2011-2012 Patagonia season, both missing segments came together. That December I teamed up with Argentine climber Jorge Ackermann to complete the often-tried south face of Aguja Standhardt, naming our route El Caracol (AAJ 2012). Three weeks later, Bjorn-Eivind and Ole Lied did the ice line up the south face of Torre Egger, creating one of the most amazing ice climbs on Earth: Venas Azules (AAJ 2012).

In late January 2011, Bjorn-Eivind teamed up with Chad Kellogg for the first real attempt on the reverse traverse. Their attempted ended before Torre Egger, but they did make the first complete descent of Cerro Torre's north face, which is daunting in and of itself. Unfortunately, Bjorn-Eivind died while climbing in Norway shortly after this attempt, and two years later Chad Kellogg was killed by rockfall while descending Fitz Roy. My first attempt was in late December 2012 with Canadian Jon Walsh. We started with the Ragni Route on Cerro Torre and descended the north face, but made it only halfway up Venas Azules. The reverse traverse not only was unfinished business for me, it also was tied to two good friends I had lost.

Marc and I approached the west side of Cerro Torre via Standhardt Col on January 18,

2015, and bivied just below the Col de Esperanza. We started up Cerro Torre's Ragni Route before first light, following two other parties. We soloed and simulclimbed low-angle ice to the base of the first technical pitch and then switched leads several times for the upper rime pitches. We reached the summit of Cerro Torre—my sixth time and Marc's first—at 11:50 a.m. We rappelled back down the top three mushroom pitches of the Ragni Route to reach the top of El Arca de los Vientos. Sleep is precious in Patagonia, so while we waited for the north face to go into shade, we pitched the tent and napped. Around 6 p.m. we buried a stuff sack full of snow in the mushroom and started rappelling down the north face. By 10 p.m. we settled into our tent on a chopped platform one pitch above the Col de la Mentira (a.k.a. Col of Conquest).

On January 20 we started up Venas Azules on Torre Egger at 8:15 a.m. I led the first three pitches; Marc led the fourth and fifth. On the sixth pitch he led blue ice into full-on vertical rime. Time slipped away as Marc hacked at the rime. Down at the belay, I suddenly realized we were making a big mistake. There was too much rime. For years I'd theorized about the possibility of climbing the first pitches of Venas Azules and then traversing on a ledge system to join the upper pitches of the American Route (Bragg-Donini-Wilson, *AAJ 1977*). I called up to Marc and he made a V-thread and lowered off. We then rappelled one pitch and I rushed off across a traverse into the American route, then led the upper half that route to the summit. We reached the top of Torre Egger at last light and bivouaced a few meters below the top.

On January 21 we had our fourth predawn wake-up in a row. We rappelled off Torre Egger's summit mushroom and quickly

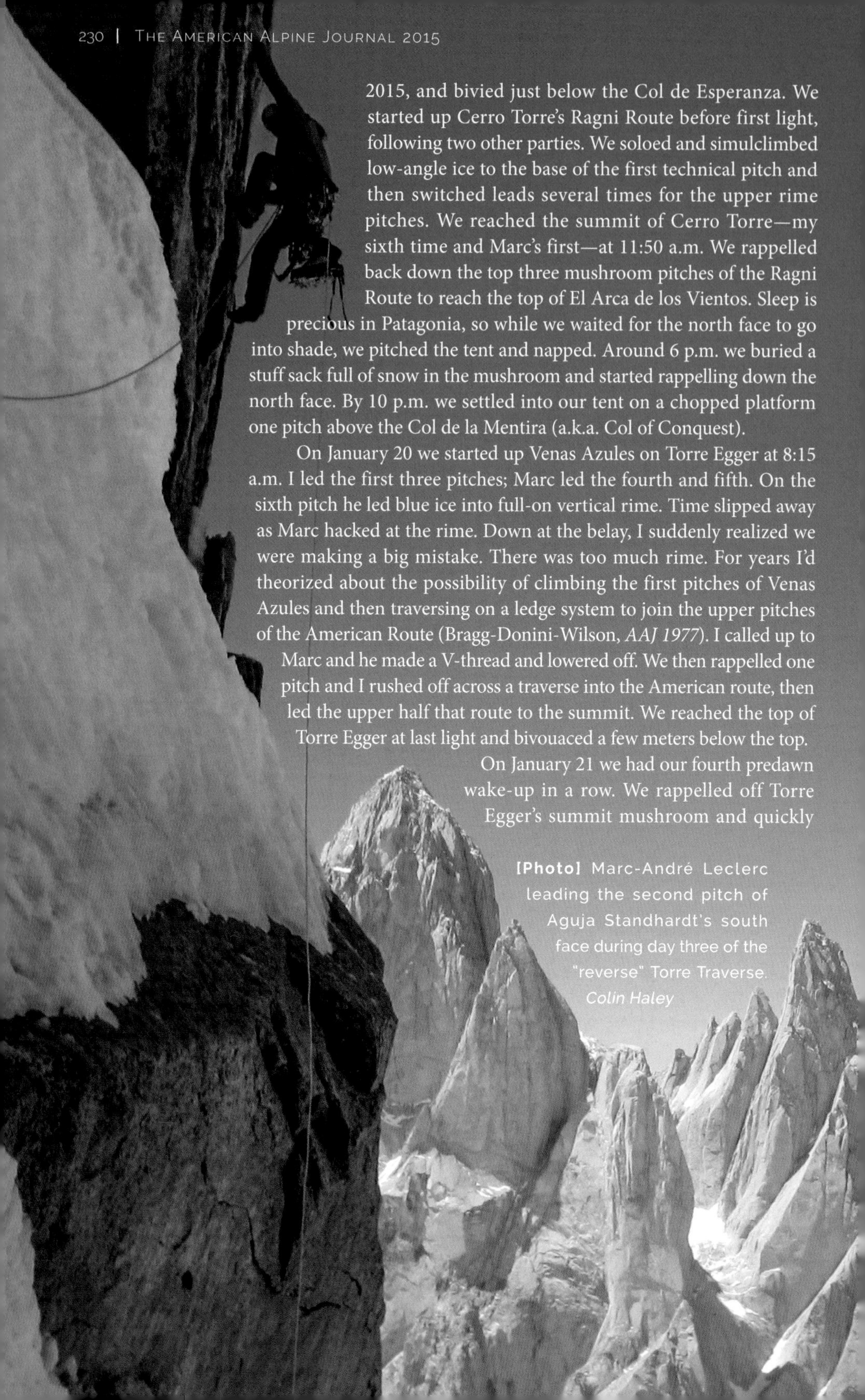

[Photo] Marc-André Leclerc leading the second pitch of Aguja Standhardt's south face during day three of the "reverse" Torre Traverse. *Colin Haley*

made our way down the Huber-Schnarf Route. Aside from a couple moves of M5 climbing, the south side of Punta Herron was short, quick, and easy. As we rappelled down Spigolo dei Bimbi, on the north ridge of Punta Herron, the wind began blowing our ropes around and we finally got one stuck—Marc did a great job climbing up to free it. It was noon and we were excited to be at the base of our last mountain, Aguja Standhardt, but uncertainty remained. The stretch above the col had never been climbed. To save weight we'd brought only Marc's rock shoes, and so he led four pitches to join El Caracol. This turned out to be more benign than I'd feared, but was certainly not cruiser. Marc seemed to have become faster each day of our climb. I took us up the last block, with one last fight. The final pitch of El Caracol is perhaps the most involved pitch on the entire traverse, with tricky mixed climbing followed by slightly overhanging thin aid, all plastered in thick rime ice. For the first time in a few days, though, I finally relaxed and took my time, as we were so close to our goal that I knew we could stick it out. At 11:10 p.m. we were both on top of Aguja Standhardt. We spent the night rappelling Exocet and Desarmada.

To some degree, the reverse traverse must have been for me what the Torre Traverse was to Rolo Garibotti in 2008—the culmination of years of planning and development as a climber. I finally got to play the same role, doing most of the leading and masterminding the strategy. Marc was a superb partner, and aside from a small route on El Mocho, the reverse traverse was his first climb in Patagonia. We named it La Travesía del Oso Buda (1,200m, 6a+ 90° M6 C1) in remembrance of Bjorn-Eivind and Chad. In Norwegian "bjørn" means bear, and bear in Spanish is "oso." Chad was Buddhist and his demeanor reminded me of a Buddha. I wish I could share our success with them. ▣

– COLIN HALEY, *USA*

CERRO TORRE, NORTH FACE, DIRECTA DE LA MENTIRA

DURING TWO DESCENTS of Cerro Torre's north face, I had been amazed by the crack systems rising straight out of the Col de la Mentira (the col between Cerro Torre and Torre Egger, a.k.a. Col of Conquest). The only established route on this side of Cerro Torre, El Arca de los Vientos (Beltrami-Garibotti-Salvaterra, *AAJ 2006*), traverses onto the northwest face from the col and then cuts back onto the north face halfway up.

On Febuary 2, Marc-André Leclerc and I climbed the lower east face to the Col de la Mentira in three blocks. We camped one pitch above the col and Marc started climbing just before 6 a.m., mostly aiding and chipping ice and rime out of the cracks. By the third pitch the sun hit us and climbing barehanded became possible. At the end of our fourth pitch we reached a glorious 100m finger-to-hand crack. Above the crack, El Arca traverses in from the right and we followed this to the top. Marc led the upper Ragni Route and we arrived on the summit at 9:30 p.m. We were back down at the glacier by 6:30 a.m., having made the first complete ascent of Cerro Torre's north face. Our "variation" Directa de la Mentira (1,200m, 6b+ C1) climbs 250m of new terrain. ▤ ▣

– COLIN HALEY, *USA*

CORDÓN RISO PATRÓN, CERRO BURACCHIO AND OTHER ASCENTS

THE CORDÓN RISO PATRÓN is a mountain range on the western edge of the Southern Patagonian Ice Field and one of the most remote areas of Chile. In the austral winter of 2014 our team of Franz Goerlich, Paul Sass, Uwe Seifert, and I (all Germany) reached the area by traversing the ice cap from east to west via skis over 20 days. In addition to several first ascents of slightly lower peaks, we climbed the highest and virgin summit of Cerro Buracchio (2,767m) by an alpine-style route up its south face: Ruido Blanco (650m, TD- 70–80°).

The Cordón Riso Patrón is dominated by two mythical and rarely seen mountains. The first, Cerro Riso Patrón (2,550m, estimated), has had only ascent, in August 1988, when a strong Italian team approached the peak from Fiordo Falcón. Casimiro Ferrari, Bruno Lombardini, and Egidio Spreafico reached the summit by the south-southeast face. The second mountain, Cerro Buracchio, remained unclimbed until now, but not un-attempted. Camilo Rada and partners made three ambitious attempts but failed due to bad weather.

[*Editor's note: Cerro Buracchio has been previously listed on several Chilean maps as "3,018." Additionally, the mountain was originally christened "Zenʾei-hou," which means "Peak Vanguard" (locally referred to as "Vanguardia"), by a Japanese expedition led by Hidetaro Sakagami in 1969. Because the Japanese name never became properly publicized, Rada and his team suggested the name Cerro Buracchio in 2002, in honor of the Chilean alpinist Christián Buracchio, who died in a plane crash in 2001. See www.pataclimb.com for further climbing history and geographical information about Cerro Buracchio and Cerro Riso Patrón.*]

Starting in mid-August from El Chaltén, several days of gear shuttles brought us to the Southern Ice Field via Paso del Viento. From there we traversed the glacier by skiing around Nunatak Viedma, heading west to Paso Rokko. The northern route to the peaks crosses Paso Rokko, heading due west toward the eastern summit of Cerro Burrachio. At the southern end of this route is a lower elevation pass, which we called Paso Buracchio. The pass slopes steeply

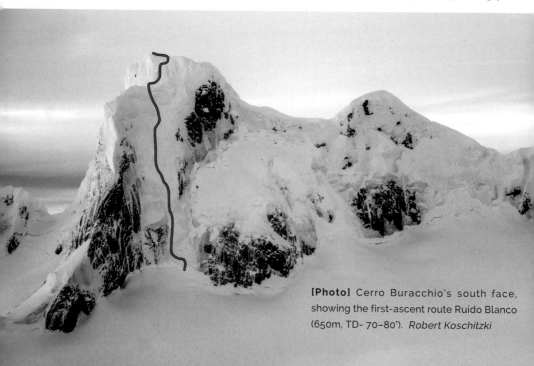

[Photo] Cerro Buracchio's south face, showing the first-ascent route Ruido Blanco (650m, TD- 70-80°). *Robert Koschitzki*

[Above] Cerro Riso Patrón from the east; main summit (right) and south summit (left). The 1998 Ferrari-Lombardini-Spreafico route climbs a ramp out of view on the main peak's shaded south side. The south summit has been attempted but is unclimbed. *Robert Koschitzki*

to the west and leads to the huge plateau below the south face of Cerro Buracchio. A corniced ridge descends due west, which likely provides access to the north face of Cerro Riso Patrón. We reached Cerro Buracchio on August 24. Next day we explored the plateau, with breathtaking views to the west of Cerro Riso Patrón.

After fixing a rope over the difficult bergschrund below Cerro Buracchio's south face the day before, Paul Sass, Uwe Seifert, and I began our ascent the morning of August 26. Leaving skis at the bottom of the wall, we started climbing the steep south face (70–80°) around 8:30 a.m. The excellent weather changed just before noon, and it snowed the rest of the day. After 12 pitches we reached the wind-exposed southwest corner in whiteout conditions. We fortunately found a system of ice gullies leading through the headwall. Two pitches later, at 6:30 p.m., we reached the top of Cerro Buracchio. Our route involved 650m of sustained ice climbing. Descending our route, we reached the bergschrund around 2:30 a.m. Due to the heavy snowfall during the day our ski cache was covered with snow from a slab avalanche that had released on the lower slopes. Exhausted and in darkness, we quit the search for our skis after one hour. At 3:30 a.m. we arrived at base camp, where Franz welcomed us with a hot meal.

August 27 was dedicated to ski rescue. We finally found them buried under two and a half meters of fresh snow. Without skis it would have been an interesting walk back across the ice cap.

Once we had recovered our strength, our food ration had shrunk to three days. We had to give up on Cerro Riso Patrón and head back to a food cache we had left east of Paso Buracchio. With some buffer, we then decided to explore south of Cerro Buracchio, the eastern side of the Cordón Riso Patrón, and in the Cordón Mariano Moreno, climbing several more summits before returning to El Chaltén via Paso Marconi. [*See the online version of this report for details on the numerous other peaks climbed and an overview map*]. 📄 📷 🔍

— ROBERT KOSCHITZKI, *GERMANY*

[Photo] Myles Moser stares up Una Fina Linea de Locura on the Central Tower of Paine. He and Amy Ness free climbed much of the route, up to 5.12, during their 19 days on the wall. *Amy Ness*

CENTRAL TOWER, UNA FINA LINEA DE LOCURA, FIRST CAPSULE-STYLE ASCENT

From December 30, 2014–January 17, 2015, Myles Moser and I made the first capsule-style ascent of the route Una Fina Linea de Locura (31 pitches, VII 5.12 A3) on the Central Tower in Torres del Paine. Our goal was to free every pitch of the 4,000' mostly aid line in a continuous ascent, and we did a lot of free climbing (up to 5.12), however weather, time, and extreme difficulty eventually thwarted our free climbing goal. [*Editor's note: Una Fina Linea de Locura (Calvo-Luro-Plaza, followed by Benedetti-Lloyd-Luro one week later, AAJ 1994) was originally graded 5.10 A3. It starts to the left of the 1974 South African route, which it crosses 250m up, and then climbs to the right of the South African route until joining the 1963 Bonington Route 200m from the top.*]

Much of our 19 days on the wall was spent pinned down with snow barreling onto our portaledge. Of the three total days without precipitation, we spent one day hauling, one day descending, and one beautiful day on our summit push. The initial 14 pitches went free, including two pitches up to the monstrous dihedral that defines the route. However, the majority of the dihedral contained back-to-back A3/A4 pitches which took us six days. By day 16 we were finally able to turn an ominous roof capping the top of the corner. From there we climbed two pitches (5.11 A2) and fixed our ropes 500' down to our portaledge. On the 17th day we set our alarm for 2:30 a.m., hoping to complete a summit push the next day. We went to bed hungry and anxious. Departing camp around 4 a.m., we saw stars for the first time in 18 days. The summit lay 1,500' above. The climbing was superb, with golden granite and soaring cracks. The original description suggested the terrain would ease off, but there was pitch after pitch of 5.11. We finally intersected the Bonington-Whillans route on the west-side shoulder and knew we were in the clear. We reached the *cumbre* late in the day.

From the summit, we made 13 rappels back to our high camp, updating anchors as we went. We shut our eyes and zipped our bags at 2 a.m., after a nearly 24-hour summit push and cleanup job. The next day, we forced downward. After rappelling several pitches with our two 300' ropes, chills went down our spines: An entire pitch of the route had fallen off the wall while we were above it—which now explained a roar, a rumble, and a giant scar on the glacier. This rockfall took out several anchors, slicing bolts off the wall and obliterating pitons. It left powdered, loose granite behind. We made it to the bottom that night. Shovels and hands were required to dig out our ice axes, crampons, and baggage from the massive rockfall.

We are happy to report that we removed over 1,500' of fixed line that has hung on the wall for many years, abandoned after the second ascent by a Chilean party. 🗎 📷

– AMY NESS, *USA*

CERRO COTA 2000, OSA MA NON TROPPO, FREE ATTEMPT

ORLANDO LOPEZ, FABIAN LONDONO, AND I hoped to free climb the complete route Osa Ma Non Troppo (700m, 7b A2/A3, *AAJ 2007*), established by Italians Michell Cagol, Rolando Larcher, Fabio Leoni, and Elio Orlandi. The route is just left of Cota 2000's central pillar, on the east face. We began climbing capsule style on January 29, 2015. Our main camp was atop the seventh pitch, where we spent six nights in all. Because there are no ledges, and therefore no snow to melt, we got a really good workout hauling almost 30L of water!

We did not succeed in our original free climbing plan due to a couple of minor injuries. However, we did free climb up to 5.12 and complete the second ascent of the route, reaching the summit on February 4. The rock was nearly always fantastic, allowing for unreal and sustained free climbing. We believe all but the third pitch could go free.

– JUAN SEBASTIAN MUÑOZ JARAMILLO, *COLOMBIA*

PAINE TOWER TRAVERSES

FROM JANUARY 15–18, 2015, two rope teams completed the third and fourth enchainments of the three Towers of Paine.

Oriol Baró (Spain), Paula Alegre, and Esteban Degregori (both Argentina) climbed and descended Torre Norte via the Monzino (400m, 5.10+), climbed Torre Central via the Bonington-Whillans (700m, 5.11) and descended the Kearney-Knight, and then climbed and descended Torre Sur via the Aste (1,100m, 5.11). This north-to-south enchainment was established by Steve Schneider solo (*AAJ 2002*). It does not follow the complete skyline but instead climbs a "W," first accessing the skyline via the col between Torre Norte and Central and then, after climbing Torre Sur, rappelling back down the line of ascent.

Iñaki Coussirat (Argentina) with Cristóbal Señoret and Juan Señoret (both Chile) started via the full skyline, climbing Torre Norte from the north, via Espiritu Libero (500m, 5.11 A1) and descending the Monzino. They then climbed Torre Central via the Bonington-Whillans (800m, 5.11) and descended the Kearney-Knight. Finally, they ascended and descended the Aste (1,100m, 5.11) on Torre Sur. Although they completed a traverse of the towers, they did not descend Torre Sur to the south (by the route Hoth). Pedro Cifuentes (Spain) established the "complete skyline traverse" in 2013, solo, over 29 days (*AAJ 2013*). Missing, however, in the initial report about his ascent was the fact that his endeavor was supported—he received equipment and supplies at his last camp. An alpine-style "complete skyline traverse" is still pending.

[*Editor's note: Both 2015 teams took four full days to complete their climbs. Though all the individual routes described above have been free climbed, neither team climbed completely free.*]

– ROLANDO GARIBOTTI

ANTARCTICA

SENTINEL RANGE AND HERITAGE RANGE UPDATES

THERE WAS A considerable increase in climbers in the Vinson Massif this season, with 207 people attempting Mt. Vinson (4,892m), and 187 of them reaching the summit.

In the Heritage Range, staff and visitors at the Adventure Network International (ANI) / Antarctic Logistics & Expeditions (ALE) camp on the Union Glacier continue to make numerous minor first ascents and new routes on the surrounding peaks. Many climbs can be done in a day from the camp and involve moderate climbing for several hundred meters on a variety of terrain. ANI keeps an updated book of routes at camp for prospective climbers to study.

– DAMIEN GILDEA, *AUSTRALIA*

LAHILLE ISLAND, GOLDEN FLEECE PEAK

JEAN BOUCHET (expedition leader and Chamonix guide), Marlène Cugnet, Bernard Frésier, Emilie Guilleman, Alexis Maget, Arnaud Pasquer, and I left the Falkland Islands on December 21, 2013, aboard Jérôme Poncet's robust motor-sailor Golden Fleece. As we sailed along the coast of Graham Land in late December we climbed several summits, including a nice snowy outcrop on the mainland opposite Appendice Island. A possible first ascent, this 800m summit (64.227°S, 60.902°W) is worth a visit.

On January 4 we made our first attempt on the northeast summit of Lahille Island. [*Lahille has four tops. The "central" was first climbed in January 2013, from the north, and named*

[Photo] Starting the first ascent of Lahille Island's northeast peak (a.k.a. Golden Fleece Peak), with the Golden Fleece moored in brash ice below. *Jean Bouchet*

[Photo] Exposed ridge climbing on the Seven Sisters traverse. Collection ExpeAntarctica2014

Mt. Louis (545m GPS, AAJ 2014)]. A threatening serac stopped us, so the next day we landed on the mainland directly opposite the island and climbed a possible new route along a ridge oriented east-northeast to west-southwest on Takaki Promontory (slopes to 50°). We didn't reach a particular high point, as toward the end of the ascent dangerous cornices forced us down a steep, snowy couloir. However, it proved to be an interesting route, with breathtaking views, even by local standards. On the 6th we climbed the highest point of Edwards Island (ca 400m) from the northwest, with a steep final slope. [*This was probably the second ascent, the first having been made on February 14, 2006, by Guy Cotter's 12-member expedition.*]

On January 7 we made a second, and this time successful, attempt on Lahille Island. We climbed the crevassed northeast slopes, then crossed a large bergschrund, where two axes and ice screws were needed, then followed a steep face to the east ridge. From there we reached the summit easily (650m, 65.544°S, 64.343°W). There was no known prior ascent, and we propose to call it Golden Fleece Peak. 🔲

– FRANCK MAZAS, *FRANCE*

WIENCKE ISLAND, SEVEN SISTERS TRAVERSE; CAPE RENARD, SOUTHEAST TOWER

LAURENT BIBOLLET, Emmanuel Chance, Yann Delevaux, Paul Dudas, David Lacoste, and I, operating from the yacht Podorange, made the first traverse of the Seven Sisters of Fief, above Port Lockroy on Wiencke Island. Starting on November 21, we climbed the most southwesterly sister from the south: Janssen Peak (1,085m, a.k.a. the Seventh Sister, first climbed in 2000). This gave ca 500m of snow and ice at 50–55°, with a 3m step of vertical snow right before the first top. We followed a fine snow ridge to the second top of Janssen and then made 10 rappels down the south side to the bergschrund, where we camped for the night. We had been unable to continue directly to the next peak because of ice mushrooms.

On November 22 we walked around Janssen Peak on the southeast side and climbed ca 300m of steep snow and ice to regain the ridge crest before the Sixth Sister. We followed the ridge to an overhanging snow mushroom at the base of the summit, then made a 30m rappel on the east flank. From that point, two pitches (80° ice; 60° snow) led to the top. We continued

[Above] Cape Renard Towers from Lemaire Channel to the southwest, with the line of Podronard (700m from the sea) on the southeast tower. Hart am Wind (900m, 1999), the route of the first ascent of the main tower, climbs directly up the rock face visible. *Collection ExpeAntarctica2014*

along the sharp ridge over each successive summit, with steep snow climbing (60–70°) on the ascents and several rappels usually required to descend from each top. The descent to the gap after the Third Sister was a trial of route-finding, as we were in complete whiteout. During the ascent of the First Sister (first climbed in 2001) a cornice broke and I fell 20m. We reached this final peak at 7 a.m. on the 23rd.

We descended to the south, then moved northeast before making eight rappels from Abalakovs and pitons down a wide couloir on the Port Lockroy (north) side, and finally reached our yacht at 3 p.m, after being on the go for 30 hours. It had been an exposed and committing route, more than 11km in length and graded TD+. Wings on ice axes were essential.

We traveled to Cape Renard and on December 1 made the first ascent of the Southeast Tower (700m). Starting from the ocean, an exposed approach under a serac was followed by slopes of 40° to reach easy glaciated terrain leading to the base of the southwest face. Once across the bergschrund, Laurent, Emmanuel, Yann, Paul, David, and I climbed 100m of 60° snow to arrive at a dome. A second bergschrund guarded three pitches of 55° snow, above which 200m of mixed rock and ice, where we got good belays from pitons and cams, was followed by another 100m of snow slanting to the left. The crux came right below the summit: 15m of M5, followed by a thin ice gully (70°), leading to 80m of atrocious snow. We slanted right, bypassing the final snow mushroom, to the flat, uncorniced summit. We descended our route in 10 rappels from deadmen and pitons. We named the 500m route Podronard (TD/ TD+), after our boat, and completed it in a 13-hour round trip. 📷 📄

— ANTOINE CAYROL, *FRANCE*

ANVERS ISLAND, VARIOUS ASCENTS

IN JANUARY 2015 a Chinese group led by Daliu (the first private Chinese mountaineering expedition to the Peninsula) and a British group led by me together climbed 10 summits, including two first ascents on Anvers Island. We climbed Peak 1,217m (nicknamed Little Dog), which lies between the Minaret and Shewry Peak, from the east side. We also climbed Peak 1,155m, which lies between Mt. Rennie and Mt. Moberly, from the west. We made second ascents of Shewry Peak (1,065m) and Mt. Rennie (1,535m).

Earlier, in October, I led a group of ski mountaineers that completed a new high-level traverse of South Georgia, from King Haakon Bay to Stromness. We crossed the Esmark Glacier, Zig-Zag Pass, and Kohl-Larsen Plateau before cutting through a narrow, nameless pass to reach the southwest tributary of the Konig Glacier. 📷

– PHIL WICKENS, *U.K.*

WRIGHT ICE PIEDMONT, FIRST ASCENTS

OUR MOUNTAINEERING TEAM of Ueli Gnädinger, Leif Langenskiold, Conrad Weiss, and me (all Swiss) left Puerto Williams on the catamaran Libellule on December 29. Out of our 22 days on the Peninsula only four had good weather: a three-day fine spell and two half days. We found much sea ice along the coastline south from Vernadsky to Adelaide. In the end we climbed 12 peaks, three of which were possibly first ascents. These three were all climbed from January 7–9 on the Wright Ice Piedmont.

On the first day we landed between growlers on a spot just south of Cape Andreas in Curtiss Bay, then used skis to ascend the glacier with pulks. After 7km we established camp at 600m. The weather wasn't particularly favorable during the first two days—practically a whiteout—so whenever there were temporary clearings, we immediately grasped the opportunity to try nearby peaks.

The first was unnamed Peak 824m (64°03.9'S, 60°40.5'W). After one failed attempt we reached the summit at around midnight on the 7th, following the southeast ridge over the steep, crevassed southeast shoulder at PD-. At 2:30 a.m. on the 9th we summited Langley Peak (977m, F, 64°03.4'S, 60°36.4'W). We skied over the south saddle, up to the south-southeast ridge, and used crampons for the last 50m to the easy southwest ridge leading to the top. Our third ascent, made during the morning of the 9th in improving weather, was unnamed Peak 982m (PD+, 64°03.7'S, 60°37.9'W). We approached from the southeast and climbed the steep northeast ridge. Ueli had to use the shovel to break through the capping cornice. We then continued along the east ridge to the summit, where the view onto the Wright Ice Piedmont and the Detroit Plateau was incredible. We would like to name this summit Mt. Libellule. 📷

– PHILIPP COTTIER, *SWITZERLAND*

SOUTH SHETLAND ISLANDS

LIVINGSTON ISLAND, TANGRA RANGE, FALSA AGUJA

ON JANUARY 8, 2015, Doychin Boyanov, Nikolay Petkov, and Aleksander Shopov (Bulgaria) made the first ascent of Falsa Aguja (1,680m) via the north ridge. They climbed from a camp on the vast plateau north of the main Tangra Range. The team measured the summit at 1,679.5m (compared with 1,690m in the 2004–'05 Bulgarian survey), confirming the peak is the second highest on the island, after Mt. Friesland (1,700m). The Bulgarian personnel have been referring to this mountain as "Great Needle Peak" rather than the translation of the official name, "False Needle," as they feel it is more appropriate and accurate. 📷

– DAMIEN GILDEA, *AUSTRALIA*

SOUTH GEORGIA

NORTH, MIDDLE, AND SOUTH TRIDENT PEAKS

THE 2014 Salvesen Range Expedition was an interesting winter experiment that completely failed to achieve any of its stated objectives. However, it remained hugely enjoyable, and we managed to snatch victory from the jaws of defeat by transferring successfully to the more amenable Allardyce Range, where we made first ascents of all three Trident peaks.

Our optimistic mountaineering team was Mark Dravers, David McMeeking, Nick Putnam, and me (all U.K.), Rodrigo Jordan (Chile), and Skip Novak (USA). After sailing from the Falkland Islands aboard the yacht Pelagic Australis, our first two attempts to access the Salvesen Range proved impracticable as a result of weather conditions. Plan C saw us motoring to Larsen Harbor, but in the face of violent winds we soon decided to abandon the Salvesen Range and turn to Plan X. Perhaps needless to say, having now abandoned a project two years in the planning, we soon were blessed with immaculate weather.

After climbing a few small peaks, we sailed to Possession Bay, hoping to ski from there to Fortuna Bay via the Kohl Plateau. After two days we had skied up the Briggs Glacier to a camp at ca 850m below Middle Trident. After a day of poor weather, September 5 dawned perfect and we skied to the col between Middle and South Trident. Middle proved a classic alpine climb. An elegant, curling snow ridge led to a vertical step, which we bypassed by a 60m gully. A second, briefly vertical step of fine South Georgian choss, plastered in rime meringue, gave good sport. The ridge now eased and a final snowfield led to the spacious summit, marked 1,337m on the current map. There was a perfect cloud inversion and not a breath of wind.

The following day the campaign continued with the first ascent of South Trident. An easy snow shoulder, followed by 60m of rime over choss, led to a sporting summit nipple, where there was just room for each person to take a turn standing atop.

Next day we made a predawn start, regained the col between the middle and north peak, and from there Rodrigo led us through a whiteout to the northern summit. We have suggested naming the three previously unclimbed Trident peaks after Greek goddesses of the sea: Thetis, Thalassa, and Tethys. A full report is available at the AAJ website, or visit www. stephenvenables.com.

— STEPHEN VENABLES, *U.K.*

THREE POSSIBLE FIRST ASCENTS

ON SEPTEMBER 15, eight ski mountaineers departed Stanley in the Falklands, aboard *Podorange*, for a 35-day trip. During our time on South Georgia we saw nobody on land other than at Grytviken, and there were no other yachts or cruise ships. We had hoped to enjoy camping and skiable objectives distant from the coast, but on all but five days it was windy, very windy, or extremely windy, invariably from the southwest to northwest. As there was snow down to the shore, we preferred to make the best of each day by skiing from *Podorange*, rather than spend time holed up in tents. We made numerous ski ascents and descents. The following summits may be new.

On September 23 we climbed a small summit above Blue Whale Harbor that we called Petrol Pique (456m, 54°04'49.5"S, 37°02'21.4"W). This was an impressive, steep little peak requiring a range of ski mountaineering techniques.

On October 2 we reached an unnamed summit of 836m at 54.434176°S, 36.278504°W. After a couple of hours' skinning up the Heaney Glacier, a bowl opening to our right was perfect for skiing. At the head were two summits. We chose the left and higher of the two, which gave an enjoyable alpine ascent. There was a tricky step low on the ridge. This peak would appear to be the highest in the small group of mountains between the Heaney and east branch of the Nordenskjold Glacier. If it doesn't have a name, we would like to call it Mt. Emma.

On the 9th we summited an unnamed peak of 494m at 54°02.284'S, 37°29.495'W. The peak lies between Rosita Harbor, our starting point, and the Brunonia Glacier. After descending a short way from the top on foot, we skied a great, steep line down to the Brunonia and the shore at Sunset Fjord. Our name for this peak is Mt. Armistice.

— JIM BLYTH, *FRANCE*

[Below] Skinning above Right Whale Bay, en route to Mt. Regulator (off picture right). The attractive summit in center is Peak 787m, by Ernesto Pass, possibly unclimbed. *Jim Blyth*

EUROPE

The following climbs appeared on the "Big List" of ascents prepared for the 2015 Piolets d'Or by Claude Gardien (Vertical) and Lindsay Griffin (AAJ/MountainINFO).

MONT BLANC MASSIF

GRANDES JORASSES (4,208m). Luka Krajnc and Luka Lindic (Slovenia) completed the first free ascent of Rolling Stones (1,100m, Prochaska-Rutil-Schlechta-Svejda, 1979) in March. The ascent took four days, and they graded the climb M8. 🔍

LES DROITES (4,000m). In March, Jan Straka and Pavel Vrtik (Czech) put up Le Vol du Dragon (1,200m, M7+ A2) on the northeast face, between the Czech Gully (1977) and Tournier Spur (1937), over four days.

MASSIF DES ÉCRINS

MEIJE (3,984m), NORTH FACE. Max Bonniot and Mathieu Maynadier climbed Eté Blizzard, with 470m of new terrain on the left side of the face (ED- 4 M6+ A1 70°) at the start of a seven-day enchainment through the Écrins in August.

AILEFROIDE OCCIDENTALE (3,954m), NORTHWEST FACE. Antoine Avenas, Jonathan Isorad, and Hélias Millerioux climbed Le Reactor (1,000m, 26 roped pitches, ED+ 6b M7 WI5+ R) over two days in June. 🔍

PENNINE ALPS

MATTERHORN (4,478m). Hervé Barmasse (Italy) enchained the four major ridges of the Matterhorn, solo, in 17 hours, climbing up the Furggen Direct, down the Hornli, up the Zmutt, and down the Lion. The March enchainment included the first winter solo of Furggen Direct.

TROMSO, BLAMANNEN, IKAROS, FIRST FREE ASCENT

IN EARLY JUNE 2013 I was lucky to complete a long-term project, a free ascent of Ikaros on the north face of Store Blamannen (a.k.a. Blamann), our local big wall. I say lucky because the ascent came unexpectedly early in the season, with snow at the foot of the wall and cold banks of fog building under our feet as we climbed.

The north face of Blamannen is one of Norway's three main walls (Troll Wall and Kjerag being the two largest). Located on the island of Kvaloya, it is no more than 400m high, barely deserving the moniker "big wall." But any lack in height is made up in steepness and severity. Robert Caspersen opened Ikaros in the summer of 1994, climbing solo over three days up a soaring line of cracks and dihedrals. Since the modern era of free climbing on Blamannen began with Erik Massih's attempts on Arctandria in 2005, seven long, difficult routes have been freed, from 7b to 8a+. Almost 20 years after Caspersen's first ascent, Ikaros seemed the most obvious place to look for a new free route.

I fixed rope from the summit, and for the next few weeks I hiked up after work, usually by myself, to clean the cracks and work the moves on a Micro-traxion. My friends Daniel Hallgren and Espen Jensen joined me for the free attempt, following or jumaring as I led the pitches. Surprising myself by succeeding on the crux first pitch (7c), I gritted my teeth for the next pitches while Daniel, belaying, disappeared in the rising fog. Eight hours after setting off, we summited in a complete whiteout, elated. Were it not for the fixed lines tying us to the ground we surely would have kept going, ever higher, like Icarus. 📷 🔍

– THOMAS MELING, *NORWAY*

LOFOTEN, VAGAKALLEN, CORNER KICK

OVER TWO DAYS IN AUGUST, Andreas Klarstrom (Norway) and Adam Pustelnik (Poland) climbed a very difficult variation to Freya (Jasper-Jasper, 1998, 800m 7c A3+) on the Storpillaren, the central pillar on the north face of Vagakallen (942m). After 13 pitches on Freya, the two broke left to a shallow corner system and climbed five new traditionally protected pitches (all 7c to 8a, one fixed beak) before rejoining Freya and following this and other routes to the top. The new line is called Corner Kick (900m, 9-/F8a). 🔍

– *INFORMATION FROM* ADAM PUSTELNIK, *POLAND*

TROLL WALL, KATHARSIS

ON FEBRUARY 9, 2015, we completed a new route on the north face of Trollveggen (Troll Wall) in the Romsdal area. Katharsis (1,100m, 27 pitches, VI A4 M7) was climbed over 18 days (January 23–February 9), including two rest days during Hurricane Ole. We did not fix any rope. Katharsis starts with the first two pitches of the French Route then ascends directly between the Russian Route and Arch Wall to a big ledge. From here we climbed a crack (A4) leading to overhangs. We continued straight through the roofs and then rejoined the French Route to the summit ridge.

Climbing Troll Wall in a team of two was a big challenge, and we are happy the conditions allowed us to do such a beautiful, natural, and logical line with no excessive drilling. Winter conditions made this climb very hard, with much ice in the cracks. 📷 🔍

– MAREK RAGANOWICZ *AND* MARCIN TOMASZEWSKI, *POLAND*

[Right] Marcin Tomaszewski starts pitch 23 of Katharsis on the Troll Wall. *Marek Raganowicz*

MIDDLE EAST

JORDAN / WADI RUM

NORTHEAST DOMES, FATAL ATTRACTION

Two SLOVAK CLIMBERS, Martin Krasnansky and Jozef Kristoffy, spent a month in the big-wall area of Wadi Rum in November and December. The goal was to establish a hard new route, and they found a line on Northeast Domes in the Jebel Rum massif. They climbed Fatal Attraction (420m, 8a+) in ground-up style, with six new pitches, including three of 7a or harder. Above the Champs-Élysées ledge, they joined Ramedame (Remy-Remy, 1986) and followed this route for another six pitches (up to 6b) to the top. They placed 11 protection bolts on the new pitches and outfitted the belays with anchor bolts.

The two Slovaks also repeated two of Jordan's hardest long routes: Glory (5 pitches, 8a+ sport, Blutrich, 2013) and Rock Empire (15 pitches, 8a, Benes-Rosecky-Sobotka, 2005). 📷

— *INFORMATION FROM* **JOZEF KRISTOFFY** *AND* **VLADO LINEK**

[Above] The crux first pitch of Fatal Attraction (8a+). *Martin Krasnansky*

OMAN / WESTERN HAJAR

JABAL MISHT AND OTHER AREAS

BRITISH CLIMBERS David Barlow, Aqil Chaudhry, Geoff Hornby, Jonathan Preston, and Susie Sammut climbed various new routes in the Western Hajar in the winter of 2013–'14. The Sidaq slabs at the northern end of the range had been visited once by Paul Knott and Dave Wynne-Jones. This climbing team added five routes of 200m to the Giant Slab, some longer, easier pillars of 450m in the Sidaq Gorge, and five routes up to 200m on slabby walls above the village.

Preston, Chaudhry and Hornby added a 475m new route to the southeast wall of Jabal Misht (a.k.a.

[Left] Straight Up (VI+) in Snake Gorge. *Lisi Steurer*

Jebel Misht): Grades of Shade (5+). Preston and Chaudhry then added two further routes to the southwest face of Misht: a direct line up the middle of the face (Jabal Rebel, 600m, 5+) and a route on the smaller face to the west (Comb Gully, 270m, 5-).

Elsewhere, Preston and Chaudhry slipped in a new line on the Karnrabab buttress, in between Downhill and Taubennest: Goats Aloud (335m, 6-). 🄾

— GEOFF HORNBY, *U.K.*

JABAL ASALA, SNAKE GORGE, WADI TANUF

WHEN WE PLANNED our trip to Oman in November 2014, terror attacks—according to several media reports—were on the daily plan on the Arabian peninsula. Because we wanted to get our own picture of the situation, we decided to go there and have a look. I don't want to oversimplify, but from what we saw, I guess the chances of being affected by radical activists in Oman are maybe as high as the chances of being struck by lightning.

When we arrived at the sultanate in mid-November it was still very hot. We decided not to try to identify specific routes and just climb the most beautiful lines that appeared in front of our eyes. In the end we did a few new lines on various formations and had one of the best rock trips ever: El Schuppo on the north face of Jabal Asala (500m, V+); Fantastica 2.0 (250m, VI) and Straight Up (200m, VI+) in Snake Gorge; and Crux Line (370m, VII) in Wadi Tanuf.

The routes are not super-hard, but we climbed in a clean style without leaving a single piece behind. The grading of the routes is similar to that in the Dolomites. 🄾 🔍

— LISI STEURER, *AUSTRIA, AND* FELIX
TSCHURTSCHENTHALER, *ITALY*

MAJILIS AL JINN, INTO THE LIGHT

IN FEBRUARY, Stefan Glowacz (Germany) and Chris Sharma (USA) climbed a 13-pitch route, Into the Light (8b+), out the ceiling of Majilis al Jinn. This gigantic limestone cavern is 100km southeast of Muscat and was accessed by a 160m free rappel.

Over 14 days, Glowacz and Sharma established their 300m line using mostly bolt protection. Sharma redpointed the route, with pitches ranging from 7c+ to 8b+. The pair had to wear headlamps to climb some of the pitches due to little natural light inside the cave. This climbing project, sponsored by the Red Bull beverage company, was undertaken with special permission of the Sultanate of Oman, and the completed route is not currently open to the public.

— *INFORMATION FROM* STEFAN GLOWACZ,
GERMANY

[Photo] Chris Sharma in Majilis al Jinn. *Klaus Fengler/Red Bull Content Pool*

AFRICA

OLOLOKWE, SOUTH FACE, MIRAGE

FROM THE TOP of Mt. Kenya, one can see a silhouette 70 miles north, rising nearly 1,500' above the desert of the northern frontier: Ololokwe (a.k.a. Sapache, "the overhanging head"). This impressive block of gneiss has been in the crosshairs of climbers' ambitions since the 1960s. Early attempts resulted in failure, mostly from heat and dehydration. Then, in 1965, Robert Chambers and Henry Mwongela established a route to the top along a rising, grassy ramp. A nearby, palm-filled chimney was climbed three years later by Ian Howell and Roger Higgins. However, this pristine mountain has long awaited a more fitting line. In 1971 Howell and Iain Allan tried the vertical, eastern wall. In true Kenyan fashion, their approach was blocked by an angry rhino who gave chase, and fortunately, for them, failed. They named the face the Oasis Wall, and their brave attempt ended about four pitches up.

There are not many unclimbed faces of Ololokwe's magnitude in the world, so about 10 years ago I started paying more attention. Looking at it from the air, checking it out on foot, photographing and studying enlarged images—I guess mine was becoming a typical climber's obsession. But self-doubt is a strong force, and I could always find excuses not climb it. Finally, in April 2013, Fish Shah, Tom Gilbreath, and I went in search of the Oasis. But we returned to Nairobi a few days later with our tails between our legs.

When a few climbers organized a trip to the northern frontier in April 2014, I had no reservations. Not much had changed. These are impenetrable looking walls, most capped by overhangs. I spent an entire day scouting Ololokwe—*do obsessions ever fade?* Around the campfire I asked if anyone would join me. Johannes Oos took no time to commit. I knew him as someone who liked his beer and smokes, and who throws as much climbing into the mix as possible. It couldn't hurt for one addict to have another for company.

The following morning, April 19, a two-hour walk got us to the base by 9:30 a.m. A fine groove revealed itself on the southern (left) side. Above us, about two-thirds of the way up the face, a giant nose hung down, forming a huge roof. We set off with a couple liters of water,

[Photo] The massive, tepui-like girth of Ololokwe. Mirage (1,400', 5.10+ A2) is the route marked on the southern end. The Oasis Wall (unclimbed) is the prominent steep wall on the (right) eastern side. *Google Earth*

food, and a pack of cigarettes and quickly climbed four pitches. The fifth pitch was the first to give us pause. After climbing 40m I found a stance below the steep headwall above. Above was a crack that might hold the key to the climb. The crack was thin, forcing the occasional piton, but a few aid moves brought me to a pigeonhole where I was able to fit myself and establish a belay. "Why don't we sleep up here and carry on the following day?" I asked Johannes. At first he rejected the idea. But after a short discussion all logic was off.

We slept just below the headwall on a grassy, sloping ledge behind a giant flake. Nights

[Above] Johannes Oos leads a steep pitch on Mirage below the looming headwall. *Alex Fiksman*

in the desert are surprisingly cold: The wind blows from all sides, unleashing a piercing chill on the sun-baked and weary. Hyenas whooped on the plains below as we slept. Morning brought a feeling of optimism and warmth, but not more water. We made the most of very little as Johannes grabbed the bottle and gulped with great exuberance. I wanted to slap him.

The route continued beautifully to a giant roof above a ledge full of old vulture nests. We could now see these massive birds gliding within arm's reach, carrying twigs or just soaring to and fro. Their beaks and talons met us at eye level, and their beauty and power were impressive. We climbed through the easiest break in the roof (5.10+). There was not much left in us, just the desire to be on top and off the face.

By early afternoon we reached a terrace 1,000' from the ground. It was richly overgrown: a lush garden of vines and cycads, acacias and aloes. After climbing five more pitches, with increasing vegetation, we reached the top, 32 hours after beginning this journey: Mirage (1,400', 5.10+ A2). Most of the climbing is sustained in the 5.9 to 5.10 range. Barely able to sit upright, we shook hands and shared a cigarette, hoping the sensation of smoke would in some way mimic the feeling of moisture. It was now 5 p.m. and two hours of daylight remained. We had no clear idea of how to get down.

We knew that Samburu cattle herders had taken their livestock to the top of the Ololokwe, so there must be a walk-off. We stumbled in the direction of camp. A five-hour ordeal ensued, barely illuminated by our depleted torches. Through the darkness we'd see the occasional light or a line of lights indicating a road in the distance. *A mirage perhaps?* Every now and then we'd sit without warning and take a miserable break. Demoralized, we kept on toward the lights. Suddenly there was shouting in the distance. It was our camp. The shouting was from our friends and they were coming to bring us water—*water!*

[*Editor's note: Ololokwe is a cliff approximately 2,000m long and averaging 400m of relief. See Alex Fiksman's feature article, "Kenya's Rocks," in AAJ 2005 for more information about Ololokwe and climbing in Kenya.*]

— ALEX FIKSMAN, *USA*

[Above] Majka Burhardt leads the single crack found on Majka and Kate's Science Project (600m, IV 5.10-). *James Q Martin*

MT. NAMULI, SOUTHEAST FACE

MT. NAMULI is located in the northeast of Mozambique, in the Zambezia province, and is a striking granite inselberg with twin summits topping out at 2,418m. In May, Kate Rutherford and I completed the first technical route up the mountain. Our 12-pitch route, Majka and Kate's Science Project (600m, IV 5.10-), was established both in the name of research and the intention to create a compelling climbing line. We completed the route while on the "Lost Mountain" expedition, combining rock climbing, cliff-side scientific research, and integrated conservation planning.

I first traveled to this part of Mozambique in 2011, with climber Sarah Garlick (USA), filmmaker Paul Yoo (USA), and herpetologist Werner Condradie (South Africa). Our goal was to determine if there was viable climbing on the 600m wall, if that climbing would allow access to relevant new terrain for science, and if the local community would welcome a project combining science and conservation.

During that first trip Garlick and I reconned the face via a vegetation-choked crack system. Given that we were there for science, we welcomed the vegetation right up until we had to figure out a way to dig through it to place protection. The crack was the only continuous line we could find on the southeast face—a wide expanse of undulating granite waves with open slabs broken up by grass and hedge tufts. Time constraints, coupled with the knowledge that we'd have to come back and re-lead everything on a full expedition in the future, halted our progress after three pitches. Each pitch took one and a half to two hours to lead, but we rappelled to the ground in one double-rope rappel. I vowed I'd return with ice axes and garden rakes…as well as entomologists.

Our primary 2014 expedition team consisted of climbers Kate Rutherford (USA) and I, along with scientists Flavia Esteves (entomologist, Brazil), Harith Farooq (herpetologist, Mozambique), and Caswell Munyai (entomologist, South Africa). LUPA, the Lost Mountain's Mozambican conservation partner, and a robust group of volunteers joined us. The expedition started at Malawi's Mulanje Massif (9,850'), where Rutherford and I warmed up our grass-climbing skills on Gordon's Gully on Chambe Peak (this route is detailed in Frank Easwood's *Guide to the Mulanje Massif*, which is out of print).

After traveling overland to Namuli and transporting our team to the base, we met with scientists to determine the best line to accommodate their research needs. The climbing route was established to connect scientifically interesting zones on Mt. Namuli. The science team prioritized a hanging pocket forest at ca 1,600m, a vegetated chimney above, and the higher altitude sedge communities near the summit. Rutherford and I climbed the route, slinging over three dozen grass clumps—known as sedges, some the size of an adult torso, other's the size of a child's ankle—for protection. Only 40' of the route took any natural protection. We placed a dozen bolts and bolted belays, all on lead. The ice axes stayed in camp, as the route took a natural slab and sedge line up the face. It's worth noting that it's been scientifically confirmed (by our entomologists as they peeled back the sedges to collect ants) that the sedges are simply adhered to the blank slabs, with no root systems penetrating the rock. A strategy of all points on and levitation was useful. The final two crux pitches were nearly perfect 5.10 slabs.

After our ascent we brought Farooq and Munyai partway up the face for their research, while Esteves completed a full ascent, with Rutherford and I collecting specimens along the way. Expedition members Peter Doucette and Charlie Harrison made the second ascent of the route before the expedition's end. More information on the route and research project, as well as a forthcoming film, can be found at www.thelostmountainproject.com. 🄾

– **MAJKA BURHARDT,** *USA*

[Photo] Majka and Kate's Science Project (600m, IV 5.10-), on Mt. Namuli's southeast face. The green sedges simply grow on the rock and are not attached by root systems. *Peter Doucette*

RUSSIA

Moscow

RUSSIA

Novosibirsk

2,900km
northeast

BILIBINO

IKATSKY RID

KAZAKHSTAN

TUVA

ALTAI

MONGOLIA

CHINA

CAUCASUS

TIEN SHAN

RUSSIA

CAUCASUS

CHANCHAKHI, NORTH FACE

AT THE END of January 2014 we realized our aim of making a new route and the first winter ascent of the north face of Chanchakhi (4,462m). Our team included four Ukrainian climbers: Mikhaylo Mironchak, Volodymyr Roshko, Dmytro Venslavovsky, and me. We had a lot of problems with the political situation in Ukraine, the Olympic Games, the high police and military presence, and some violent snowfall, which paralyzed certain cities in southern Russia. Despite all of this we were able to reach the climbing base of Cey in North Ossetia.

[Above] Difficult winter climbing on the north face of Chanchakhi. The first winter ascent took six climbing days. *Mykola Shymko*

To reach the mountain we spent two days walking through deep snow, which took a lot of power. On the day we arrived our thermometer showed –25°C and then died. We planned to climb the route in capsule style, using a portaledge camp. During the first two days we climbed approximately 200m on difficult ground with poor protection (A2 M4/5). The spindrift and low temperature (–30° to 35°C) turned this into a real fight. To climb 50m we spent three to five hours. Then came strong wind. After two difficult nights we decided to go down for a night's rest in the Nikolaevskaya hut. Dropping 700m made a big difference, and some sunny hours recovered our powers and increased our enthusiasm.

We returned to the mountain, and during the third day there was a lot of good mixed climbing as well as vertical, thin, porous ice that made protection impossible (A2 M5 WI5). The fourth day had enjoyable ice climbing and a vertical chimney with interesting mixed (up to M6). At 10 p.m. we set up our portaledge under an overhanging. The fifth day we climbed 35m of overhanging rock and three more pitches, and on the sixth day easy climbing led to the summit and we descended to ABC. Our route ascended 730m (16 pitches) on the main wall, plus another four pitches to the summit. 📷

— MYKOLA SHYMKO, *UKRAINE*

TUVA

TSAGAN-SHIBETU RANGE, VOSTOCHNY NORTH FACE

THE TSAGAN-SHIBETU RANGE is located in the western part of Tuva, the small Russian republic bordering Mongolia, west of Lake Baikal. The climate of Tuva is equivalent to the far north of Sibera, with treeline at 1,900–2,000m.

Mountaineers started developing the region in 1978, and since the early 1990s Krasnoyarsk Mountaineering Federation competitions (*alpiniads*) have been held here in late April. Climbs in the region are considered to be winter ascents if they are done before May 15. The highest point is Mt. Munkhulik (3,577 m), and at first climbers focused here, but they gradually moved east. Eventually they saw a mountain to the east that had a big, steep wall that was much more difficult than all other climbing routes of the region. This mountain was called Vostochny ("East") Peak (3,361m).

Reaching the peak requires ca 600km of driving from Abakan, followed by a trek along river ice to treeline. Mountaineers first attempted to climb the north wall in 1989, but

[Above] Alexander Zhigalov leading the lower rock buttress of the new route up Vostochny Peak's north face. *Stanislav Katanaev*

the climbing was too difficult and the weather too bad. The next attempt occurred 10 years later, in the beginning of May 1998. A Krasnoyarsk team led by Valery Balezin made the first ascent of a pillar on the left side of the north wall (given 6A but later "stripped" to 5B). This route was champion of the CIS in the rock climbing class that year. Today, Vostochny Peak boasts 12 graded routes, ranging from 1B to 6A, including four new lines this past season.

On May 1, Stanislav Katanaev and I, having repeated the 1999 Balezin Route (6A) on the left side of a pillar leading straight to the summit, decided to attempt a more direct route just to the right. Since we'd completed the Balezin Route in under 11 hours, without fixing rope, we planned to climb our new route in the same style: in a single push, with minimal equipment, and climbing mostly simultaneously.

We woke at 3 a.m. on May 3 and started climbing at 4:30 a.m. To save time I led the whole route. There were two cruxes. The first, on the ninth pitch, should be climbed early in the morning, because the overhanging crack is filled with rocks and frozen dirt, and when the sun comes out the protection points become very unreliable. The second crux is on the upper pillar: a series of thin, flaring cracks that required tension traverses to switch cracks.

We summited Vostochny at 5:35 p.m., climbing the entire route in a little under 13 hours. The route was 580m and graded 6A, but was much more difficult than the neighboring 6A route first ascended by Balezin. [*During the 2014 season, two other routes, both graded 5B, were completed on either side of the 1999 Balezin Route and the new Katanaev-Zhigalov Route.*]

[Above] The ca 600m north face of Vostochny Peak. (1) Ivanov-Zhigalov (5B, 2014). (2) Balezin Route (5B, 1998, first route up the face). (3) Katanaev-Zhigalov (6A, 2014). In all the face has 12 different routes. *Alexander Zhigalov*

On May 6, Timofei Ivanov and I climbed a new route on the rib to the left of Balezin's 1998 pillar route (the first route on the wall). We started at 8:15 a.m., following steep snow to the crux rock buttress below a big ledge halfway up, and summited at 4:50 p.m. The route was 630m (ca 20 pitches) and graded 5B. 📷 ▤ 🔍

– **ALEXANDER ZHIGALOV**, *RUSSIA, TRANSLATED BY EKATERINA VOROTNIKOVA*

IKATSKY RIDGE

THE BAYONET, NORTH BUTTRESS AND EAST RIDGE

IN FEBRUARY 2011, I came across a panoramic photo of a mountain wall, visible in the distance, that immediately captivated me. Then followed weeks of searching for options for getting there, multiple calls and meetings, and finally we were ready to go. We were four: Andrey Afanasiev, Svyatoslav Emanov, Ilya Ogleznev, and me. It took us one day in a cross-country vehicle, three days of snowmobiling, and three days of cross-country skiing to reach the area of the Ikatsky Ridge. We saw in front of us numerous walls that nobody had ever climbed.

This massif in Buryatia Republic, east of giant Lake Baikal, consists of five peaks of around 2,500m. The Bayonet stands in the center and has steep northern and southern walls. To the west is Yakov Pokhabov's Peak (named for the founder of Irkutsk), the highest point of the region (2,574m), also with two walls: northeast and northwest. To the east of Bayonet is Ostrog (ca 2550m), which has three walls: north, west, and south. To the northeast one can find Fighter Peak, with its own north wall. These walls all are 500m or higher. [*The Ikatsky Ridge lies to the east of the Barguzin Range, between the Barguzin and Upper Tsypa valleys. At its north end, the Ikatsky mountains meet the North and South Muiski ranges. These mountains can be reached from Kurumkan via the upper Barguzin Valley, but the road along the Barguzin River can only be used in winter.*]

That February, we carried loads to the base of the Ostrog wall, then went down to rest in base camp, and then nature let us understand we were in Siberia. The temperature dropped from a rather comfortable -20°C to below -40°. Having climbed three pitches on the wall, we retreated to save our lives. After spending some time in the safety of base camp, we made the first ascent of the Yakov Pokhabov's Peak by an easy 2B route.

Three years passed, and my current climbing partner, Vasily Ilyinsky, and I served in the army and summited many mountains. But the desire to really unlock this area never left. We found a third team member for support—Ilya Resnyansky—and left for a 20-day trip at the end of March.

Twenty-four hours after leaving Irkutsk we arrived at Dzherzhinsky Reserve. A car came for us, and we traveled 150km, 90 of which were on the frozen winter road. By 6 p.m. we reached the winter hut on the banks of the Barguzin River, and from there we went on foot. After a three-day approach we found ourselves under the wall. As soon as we got there we did the first ascent of a new peak, subsequently named Fighter. The views were incredible—the sheer 600m wall of Ostrog Peak particularly impressed us, reminding us of the Karavshin.

Our next goal was the north face of untouched Bayonet peak, the first technically difficult route in the area. Initially we planned to climb this mountain nonstop in a day as a warm-up before climbing Ostrog. However, on the first day we ascended only five pitches, climbing smooth slabs and cracks filled with ice. We sometimes climbed 15–20m without placing protection. We descended to the camp for the night and started again the next day. We managed to free the sixth pitch, thanks to the light boots we took with us, but the seventh pitch took many hours. It was a flaring, periodically disappearing crack that we could not hook, nor did we want to drills holes in the rock and turn it into Swiss

[Above] Approaching the Ikatsky Ridge along the frozen Barguzin River. *Vasily Ilyinsky*
[Below] Vasily Ilyinksy leading on the lower north face of the Bayonet. *Alexander Klepikov*

[Photo] The 500m-plus north walls of Ikatsky Ridge. (A) Ostrog. (B) Bayonet, with the line of the 2014 first ascent. (C) Yakov Pokhabov. Only one wall route had been completed in this area by the end of 2014. *Alexander Klepikov*

cheese, as long as there was a possibility to climb it in a different way.

By sunset we climbed to the ninth pitch and decided to keep climbing through the night. To tell the truth, night climbing was much easier psychologically—you could not see how many hundreds of meters were beneath your feet. I met the dawn standing on a skyhook and cautiously looking to the left, where my last protection was 10m away on the wall of a corner. The sun had risen, but did not warm us. The hook placement was crumbling, so I hammered a hole—the only skyhook hole on the route. When we reached the top of the lower buttress we saw there were several more pitches along the knife-edge to reach the summit tower.

On the summit ridge every crack and cavity was packed with snow and frost, there were many snow mushrooms, and the wind blew constantly. After working out five challenging pitches, we got to the final ridge. The sun was setting, so we took only bare necessities and ran to the top with the last rays. We summited at 9 p.m. on April 14. To descend, we rappelled our route on the summit tower, then followed a snow ledge and couloir to the west of the north pillar.

Bayonet was planned as a warm-up, so the next morning we packed up and moved under Ostrog. But when we put up the tent, the wind and snow swooped in and the temperature dropped to -25°C. We had only enough food left for three days, and when the storm did not abate next day, we realized that we would not be able to climb Ostrog during this expedition. 📷

— ALEXANDER KLEPIKOV, *RUSSIA, TRANSLATED BY EKATERINA VOROTNIKOVA*

CHUKOTKA REGION

BILIBINO TOWERS

IN AUGUST, Chris Fitzgerald and I traveled to the Chukotka region in far northeastern Russia to climb granite towers near the small town of Bilibino. To our knowledge, no routes had ever been climbed on these walls, which are north of the Arctic Circle (68°18'23.32"N, 165°50'5.75"E). We traveled about 60 km northwest from Bilibino by quad bikes and were dropped off 4.5km walk from our base camp (980m). We shuttled four loads and then camped at the base of a peak named Komandnaya (Commander) for 23 days.

We climbed or attempted six new routes on four different walls, generally north-facing with gentle slopes on the south side. The first two were on the General. The Turilov Route

(375m, 20/6a+) was climbed in a single push following the same crack system the whole way and all on natural protection. The second route, Basil Brush (465m, 23/7a), followed the central nose and was climbed over several days. It is a stunning, proud line with excellent crack and corner climbing, along with some bolted face sections; most belays are bolted.

We then did a route on the shoulder of Peak Komandnaya named Epaulette (280m, 17/5c), with pleasant climbing all on natural protection. In the next valley over to the east we climbed a route named Gardening Australia (305m, 18/5c) on Launch Peak, again all on natural protection.

Next we started a direct line on Komandnaya. We climbed up the center of the wall, establishing five pitches up to 20/6b. We got rained off about halfway, and after sitting

[Below] Peak Komandnaya (left) with (1) the attempted direct line. In center is the General, showing (2) Basil Brush (465m, 23/7a) and (3) the Turilov Route (375m, 20/6a+). *Chris Warner*

through four days of rain in base camp we were unable to complete the route by the time our pickup party was to arrive. The headwall we were about to start looked amazing. We walked back out in more rain and were driven to Bilibino. Then the sun came out and we managed a quick trip back to the mountains with our local friend Evgeny Turilov, a nuclear engineer who had helped us make local arrangements. Together we climbed a granite dome to the northwest of Komandnaya with a single pitch of 12/4a.

During our time in the area we also did some paragliding and walked through many of the surrounding valleys, where we saw many other towers and walls that looked great to climb. The quality of rock in general is excellent, though often wet or mossy. The Bilibino region is extremely isolated and was closed to foreigners and even non-local Russians 20 years ago. But once in Bilibino (the town serves mines and the northernmost nuclear power plant in the world), getting to the climbs is fairly simple, with a road that gets you close and relatively short walk-ins, with no glaciers or massive scree slopes. The people of Bilibino were very helpful and truly made this trip possible though their kindness and hospitality. 📷 🔍

— CHRIS WARNER, *AUSTRALIA*

[Above] Nearing the top of the Split Pillar, pitch four of Basil Brush on the General. [Below] Chris Fitzgerald in the valley to the east of Komandnaya, where the pair did one new route up the center of the peak at far right, dubbed Launch Peak. All the other walls are unclimbed. *Chris Warner*

KYRGYZSTAN

SVAROG, NORTH FACE

THE RUSSIAN TEAM of Vladislav Dubrovin, Vadim Kalinkin, Konstantin Markevich, and Dmitry Skotnikov completed the first ascent of Svarog (4,960m), the central peak of the north-facing wall at the head of the Ashat Gorge. The team spent 10 days ascending the wall, climbing capsule-style and using extensive aid, including dozens of bolts for protection, belays, and rappels. A blank wall and the nearly horizontal 15-meter roof above it (pitches 18 and 19) were climbed almost entirely with bolts. The climbers reported the route as 1,250m, with 700m on the big-wall portion, and graded the ascent 6B A3+. 📷 🔍

— INFORMATION PROVIDED BY **ANNA PIUNOVA**, *MOUNTAIN.RU*

AK-SU, ORTOTYUBEK, SOUTH FACE, ATLANTIDE

MATTEO DE ZAIACOMO AND I flew to Batken in southern Kyrgyzstan in mid-June and trekked two days to our base camp in the Ak-su Valley. The next day we checked out the south face of Ortotyubek (a.k.a. Ortotubek or Central Pyramid, 3,850m), and on June 24 we did the first ascent of Atlantide (700m, 6c+/7a) toward the right side of the face. We climbed onsight and left only one peg. During the last part we endured a thunderstorm, but we made it to the southeast ridge and descended at night from there, without going to the summit, returning to base camp after 22 hours.

We then attempted a previously climbed route, following the buttress on the left side of the same wall, but we didn't finish because of another thunderstorm. We climbed 500m, up to 7b, over two days, using a variation to avoid a blank

[Above] Line of the first ascent of the 1,250m north face of Svarog (4,960m), the last big face at the head of the Ashat Gorge. *Yury Koshelenko*

[Above] West side of (A) Central Pyramid and (C) Peak Slesov, showing (1) Atlantide (700m, 6c+/7a) and (2) La Bolla (230m, 6b), both climbed in 2014. Many other routes are not shown, including the southwest arête of Central Pyramid (arrow marks start), the famed Perestroika Crack (near right skyline of Slesov), and three routes on the west face of (B) Petit Tour Rousse. *Luca Schiera*

wall. This route had many holes where bolts had been removed. [*Editor's note: This is likely the southwest arête, established by a French team in the mid-1990s and free climbed at 5.12a, with variations, by Steph Davis and Kennan Harvey in 1997.*]

After repeating a route on the Petit Tour Rousse and the Perestroika Crack on Peak Slesov (a.k.a. Russian Tower, 4,240m), I soloed a new route on July 15, the day before leaving base camp, on the lower part of Ortotyubek. I called it La Bolla (230m, 6b) and climbed it in three hours, self-belayed with a Megajul. Nice slabs and flakes. 📷 🔍

– LUCA SCHIERA, *ITALY*

ZHIOLTAYA STENA, SOURIRE KYRGYZ; PIK PIRAMIDALNY, NORTH FACE

IN 1991, I was part of a French team visiting the Ak-su and Karavshin valleys. We established a number of routes, the most popular today being Perestroika Crack on Russian Tower (a.k.a. Peak Slesov, 4,240m). In September and October, Christophe Moulin and I returned with a young French team, and we climbed several rock routes and one mixed line. Two of these, we believe, might be new.

From September 20–23, Sylvain di Giacomo and I put up a new route on the east face of Zhioltaya Stena (a.k.a. Yellow Wall, 3,800m), a beautiful route with many nice cracks. We put bolts on the belays and slab sections, and climbed 13 long pitches (60m ropes necessary) up to 7b. There is an easy walk-off down the south face, so no rappel anchors were established. We named the route Sourire Kyrgyz (600m, ED). [*This line begins at the base of the classic Diagonal (500m, 5.10) and then climbs between Everything is Normal (ca 350m, 5.10b A2, Harkness-Matthiesen-Zemach, 2004) and Meresjev (500m, 14 pitches, IX-/IX A3, Zakora, solo, 2002)*].

Robin Coullet, Tiphaine Duperier, Jonathan Isoard, and Moulin climbed a line on the north face of Pik Piramidalny (5,509m), starting 500m right of Russian Roulette (*AAJ 2003*). They are unsure whether it is new because they found fixed nuts in the middle of the route, but this point easily could have been reached via the pillar to the left. The group climbed in two teams and made different starts. They reached the east ridge at 5,000m and continued toward the top until they were stopped by bad weather. They sat this out for one day, and on the next day, their fourth on the mountain, they decided to escape down the east ridge, a complex process, to a col at 4,000m, from which they descended to the glacier and their high camp. If the 1,300m route is new, they would like to call it La Banane (ED- M5 WI5). 📷 🔍

— FRÉDÉRIC GENTET, *FRANCE*

SILVER WALL, SOUTH SUMMIT; ZHIOLTAYA STENA, EAST FACE

IN 2014 the Russian Championships were held in the Karavshin. Afterward several teams stayed on to complete more climbs. On August 11, Anastasia Ermishina and Alexander Zhigalov made the first ascent of the 3,850m south summit of Silver Wall via the east ridge. Silver Wall is situated 1.5 hours' walk past Zhioltaya Stena (Yellow Wall). Just before 11 a.m. the pair reached the foot of the deep couloir between the main and south summits, where the 2011 Ternerev Route (5A) on the Silver Wall's southeast face begins. A conspicuous buttress rises from this point directly to the south summit. There was a fair amount of vegetation, but the 600m route (25 pitches) was generally straightforward (grade 4A), with good belay ledges. They reached the top at 5:20 p.m. and were surprised to find the south top a completely independent summit. They descended the couloir (about 2B) and were back at camp by 9:30 p.m., having simul-climbed up and down the peak.

The next day, in 9.5 hours, the same pair climbed a new route on the far left side of the east face of Zhioltaya Stena. They had anticipated a line at around 5A, but strenuous aid climbing and other difficulties produced a 600m route of 5B. Old bolts were discovered at the top of pitches five and seven, but subsequent information suggests they were left during a rappel descent by a Krasnoyarsk team after completing a different line. 📷 🔍

— LINDSAY GRIFFIN, *WITH INFORMATION FROM* ALEXANDER ZHIGALOV, *RUSSIA,*
TRANSLATED BY EKATERINA VOROTNIKOVA

PAMIR ALAI / KICHI ALAI

KOSH MOYNOK VALLEY, FIRST ASCENTS

OUR GROUP of six Czech and Slovak climbers visited the Kosh Moynok valey of the Kichi Alai mountains (a.k.a. Kichik Alai) in September. Approaching from the Kichi Alai valley, we reached base camp at ca 3,400m in two days. From here we climbed three peaks with no sign or record of previous ascents. Stanislav Ceip and Ondrej Uher climbed the northeast face and north ridge of the northern of two peaks southwest of base camp, which they called Palestra Peak (4,750m). Tibor Majer, Stefan Matuska, and I climbed 70th Anniversary of SNU Peak (4,880m), winding up a glacier from the north, with steep ice and powder snow near the top. Vladimir Bures and Matuska climbed Bars Peak (4,880m) via 400m of ice up to 50° on the west side, then followed the north ridge to the top. 📷 🔍

— MICHAL KLESLO, *CZECH REPUBLIC*

TRANS ALAI / ZAALAISKY RIDGE

KICHKESUU VALLEY, VERONIQUE AND ANNA, THE SIX BROTHERS

IN AUGUST AND SEPTEMBER 2014, I visited Kyrgyzstan with the Russian climber and guide Nikolay Totmyanin. Our destination was the east part of the Trans Alai chain and a little-explored north-south valley, the Kichkesuu (also spelled Kichkesu), that ends along the Tajikistan border. I found information about only two previous expeditions to the Kichkesuu Valley—a British team in 2004 (*AAJ 2005*) and a Swedish trip in 2012—though evidence of prior ascents was found during the 2004 trip. [*AAJ 2014 reports Russian climbs in 2010.*]

We met at Osh on August 26 and in a 4WD drove to a base camp just before the Kichkesuu River, a few kilometers from the entrance of the valley (3,550m). On August 30 we attempted an unclimbed summit (approximate location: 39°28'53.04"N, 73°26'27.07"E Google Earth), estimated at 5,300m to 5,400m, by a long ridge in two sections. Starting from a high camp at 4,330m, northwest of the peak, we climbed slowly with Nikolay breaking trail through deep snow. Nine hours after our departure from high camp, we arrived at a col at about 5,000m, and given the snow conditions and the hour we decided to not continue. Moreover, I was really tired—maybe I was not acclimatized enough, and I had lost 25 percent of a lung to cancer just two years earlier.

On the 3rd of September we returned to the valley and hiked toward its end with heavy bags. It took over six hours on the moraine to reach the site of a high camp at 4,350m, from which we would attempt an unclimbed summit to the southwest. The next day we approached the base of our mountain, climbed a 300m face, and reached a ridge that we followed west with mixed sections. The last part was delicate. The summit was a little rock platform (39°27'853"N, 73°23.544"E, 5,200m). In the absence of a known ascent, I proposed to Nikolay to name the summit Veronique and Anna, after my wife and Nikolay's wife, and to dedicate the route to my six boys by naming it the Six Brothers, with a grade of D-. As a storm arrived, we descended along our ascent route for two-thirds of the way, and then finished the descent along an east-facing snow couloir amid wind gusts and snowfall. 📷

– HENRY BIZOT, *FRANCE*

[Photo] Peak 5,395m (center), on the east side of the Kichkesuu River valley, attempted via the north side (facing camera) in 2014. The peaks at left are Chorku (6,283m, far left) and Turkvo (6,243m), both climbed during the Soviet era. *Henry Bizot*

[Above] The 3km ridge of Dragons Back (4,580m), traversed from right to left (TD- 6a) in 2014. *Supplied by Dennis Straathof*

OIBALA MOUNTAINS, VARIOUS ASCENTS

Joep Bovens, Jacos van Zelst, and I visited Kyrgyzstan in July and August of 2013. This was the second Dutch expedition to the Oibala region, where the people are very hospitable and welcoming. After driving from Osh, we established base camp in the grassy valley of the Kok Suu (Suu River). Most of the mountain routes are mixed, with snow on the lower slopes and rock or mixed terrain on the upper parts. Pure rock climbing is possible in the upper valley, with rock formations up to 150m. The rock is either very compact, and thus difficult or impossible to protect, or else very loose.

We did several first ascents, including Peak Irroli (4,613m) by the west ridge to the northwest ridge (AD); a traverse of Peak M (4,472m) by the main ridgeline from west to northeast (D); and a 3km traverse of the north-to-south ridgeline of Dragon's Back (4,580m), completed in a 17-hour round trip from base camp (TD- 6a). We also climbed a couple of good rock routes on Mel's Peak (4,194m), a small limestone summit rising out of the valley west of Peak BasBas (4,785m), and we repeated the 2011 route on Peak Marian (4,562m, *AAJ 2012*). [*Editor's note: This mountain was called Peak Bröö by the 2013 team, unaware of its earlier name. A PDF available at the AAJ website provides photos and details of all routes climbed by the 2013 expedition.*] 📷 📄

— **DENNIS STRAATHOF**, *NETHERLANDS*

KORONA FIFTH TOWER, ARIRANG

Instructors of the Extreme Rider Climbing School of Korea made plans to climb Korona Peak's Fifth Tower in July. Since the purpose was in part to make new lecture material with the help of the Seoul Broadcasting System (SBS), the expedition divided into a climbing Team A and a shooting Team B. Team A comprised Kim Se-joon, Byun Sung-ho, and Kwon Oh-young, and Team B comprised Park Myung-won, Kim Sung-doo, Jung Weon-jo, and Wang Jun-ho.

After two pitches were fixed, the bulk of the climbing began on July 16 but moved slowly because of the filming. We spent four days climbing the first eight pitches, climbing parallel

lines to improve the angles for filming, and sleeping in portaledges. The crux came on pitch seven. On the overhanging wall I took a lead fall, popping out an Alien cam and finally being caught 10m lower. When I started up again, my loosely laced shoe fell off. My belayer managed to retrieve my shoe after some rappelling.

After the eighth pitch the angle lessened and we followed the same line, with Team B in the lead. During the nights of July 19 and 20, we could not sleep much due to the flapping of our portaledge in high wind. July 21 was supposed to be summit day, but heavy snow and strong winds forced us to wait until early that afternoon, and after one moderate pitch and a 10m whipper off a slippery slab on pitch 12, we retreated to the portaledge atop pitch eight, where Team A also had sought shelter. We all stayed put there until the next morning.

On July 22, at roughly 11 a.m., all the climbers reached the top of the tower (4,850m). The route was named Arirang (13 pitches, VI 5.9 A3). [*Editor's note: The Korean route starts in the middle of a triangular buttress to the right of the Sadowski Route (5B, 1968) and stays largely independent of that route until reaching easier terrain in the upper third of the face.*] 📷

— **PARK MYUNG-WON**, *KOREA, TRANSLATED BY PETER JENSEN-CHOI*

PILLAR PEAK

From June 5-6, Vitaly Akimov, Dmitry Grekov, Stepan Maltsev, and Sergey Selivyorstov made the first ascent of Pillar Peak (4,050m). This splendid, 900m east-facing buttress is northwest of Peak Boks (a.k.a. Box), above the lower moraines of the Ak-Sai Glacier. The climb involved 18 pitches (Russian 5B, or TD 6c A1).

— *INFORMATION FROM* **AK-SAI TRAVEL**, *KYRGYZSTAN*

KASHKARATASH VALLEY, VARIOUS ASCENTS

IN 2013 AND 2014, the International School of Mountaineering (ISM) made its fifth and sixth visits to the delightful At Bashi Range, this time exploring the area around Peak 4,788.9m in the center of the range, reached via the long Kashkaratash Valley. [*Editor's note: This system of valleys and glaciers lies immediately to the west of the Mustabbes area, where an ISM team made numerous first ascents in 2010 (AAJ 2011). A British team returned to this area in 2013 and did many other ascents (AAJ 2014).*]

We approached by driving around the east and south sides of the range, but ran into difficulty at the main Aksai River, where a temporary crossing had been built after a bridge partially collapsed in floods. Unfortunately, the temporary structure collapsed under the weight of the Kamaz (six-wheel-drive truck) and the vehicle overturned, injuring three people, one of whom had to be airlifted to hospital. The team was able to continue in a second vehicle, and finally base camp was established south of Peak 4,788.9m, where the valley divides. The following week was spent climbing 10 peaks, from 4,365m to 4,600m, in generally good weather, with grades ranging from F to AD+, all to the west of Peak 4,788.9m and the Kashkaratash Central Glacier.

The team then moved to the Son Kul canyonlands and established five new routes in the superb Kokgrim Canyon, south of the main Son Kul canyon. These ranged from HVD to E3 and up to 250m in length.

In late August 2014, an ISM team returned to the Kashkaratash area to explore the mountains farther to the east. Advanced base was established at 4,000m beside a large glacial lake on Kashkaratash East Glacier. Conditions were exceptionally dry, Kyrgyzstan having had a long, hot summer with no significant precipitation since early June. This meant that virtually every snow and ice slope was bare water ice, making it arduous and time consuming to climb even relatively low-angle slopes, as everything had to be pitched (and usually abseiled in descent).

Two attempts were made on the jagged chain of peaks running up the west side of the glacier (a succession of rocky spires approached by various couloirs). These resulted in AD routes to Point Tanoguch (4,750m) and Point Penitent (4,700m). The most northerly peak of the chain was climbed by its northeast ridge at PD+ (Peak Tunduk Gildys, 4,730m). The summits on the east side of this glacier are generally lower and easier (although some would give fine technical routes).

[Right] Climbing Point Penitent (4,700m) on the west side of Kashkaratash East Glacier. *Pat Littlejohn*

The obvious snow dome at the north end was climbed via its west ridge at F+ (Peak Arie Gabai, 4,530m), while the next rocky summit southward, Peak James Bruton (4,727m), was climbed by its south flank, also at F+. Beside this the rocky ridge of Point 4,690m gave a nice AD climb.

A foray up Kashkaratash Central glacier led to Peak Dianne (4,439m) and Peak Dostuk (4,590m), which had been climbed the previous year from the west. Finally, starting from base camp, two scree peaks with craggy tops were climbed and traversed: Peak Kara (4,534m, F) and Peak Taaji (4,200m, PD). With better snow conditions, possibly in early summer, a future team could have a very productive trip to this area.

The team then climbed in a previously unvisited limestone canyon in the Son Kul region called Katchik-Kindyk, which gave three routes in the V/V+ grades, each over 200m long. Huge scope for adventurous rock climbing remains throughout this area. 📷 🔍

– PAT LITTLEJOHN, *U.K.*

TIEN SHAN / DJETIM BEL RANGE

ASCENTS NEAR ARABEL PASS

OUR FOUR-STRONG EXPEDITION spent August 5–21 climbing in the Djetim Bel Range, south of Lake Issyk Kul. Our base camp was west of the main road through Arabel Pass at 3,844m (N41.81562, E077.67891). With the exception of snowy and windy period from August 16 to 18, expedition members ventured out most days to explore the mountains to the south and north of base camp. Moving north meant crossing a range of hills just north of camp, an ascent of ca 150m, which we usually did via Cwm Da Loch, the lowest saddle between the two valleys. Ventures south were usually done via a dirt track down into the next valley. From there we climbed into smaller valleys, all of which are dominated by glaciers.

In all we did 13 day trips into these mountains and reached numerous summits, at least one of which had been previously climbed but many others were first ascents. Most routes were in the PD to AD range. [*Editor's note: Given the easy access to these mountains, as well as mining and surveying activity, it's likely that a number of peaks in this area have been climbed over the years. The team of Laurent Baraquin, Radim Blazicek, and Henrik Olsen climbed four routes in 2011, and other teams en route to the Khan Tengri area are known to have climbed in these mountains.*] 📷 📄 🔍

– EDITH KREUTNER, *AUSTRIA*

[Photo] Peaks of the Djetim Bel ascended in 2014. At left: Hoch Misha (4,627m, also climbed in 2011). Farther right: ca 4,500m peaks climbed and later traversed. *Stefan Schmid*

KOTUR GLACIER, VARIOUS ASCENTS

A GROUP OF NINE young British alpinists, led by Emily Ward, intended to operate from the Navlikin Glacier, at the southern end of which lie several unclimbed 5,000m peaks, including Peak 5,411m (incorrectly marked on the AAC map as 5,611m, north of Byeliy). Upon their arrival the glacier looked very crevassed, so they decided to reach its head by first going up the Kotur Glacier and then crossing a col to the west. Unfortunately, very unsettled weather and waist-deep snow on the Kotur during September meant that only four made it over the col. They were then pinned down by a storm and failed to summit anything.

Meanwhile, however, members of the expedition managed to climb every peak around the lower 8km of the Kotur Glacier, including two peaks north of Peak Jjin that don't appear on the map. Upon returning home, research confirmed every peak they climbed had been summited at least once before. However, their routes on Metel (4,850m), Greta (4,725m), and Lvitsa (4,631m) are likely new, and some others are partially new routes or variants. 📷 🗎

– LINDSAY GRIFFIN, *WITH INFORMATION FROM* EMILY WARD, *U.K.*

FERSMANA VALLEY, FIRST ASCENTS

THANKS TO AN Alpine Club symposium in 2012 and information from past expeditions, identifying objectives in the Western Kokshaal-too proved to be straightforward. The main goal for our six-member British team (Scott Gillespie, Huw Goodall, Robert Middleton, Hannah Moulton, Ian Peachey, and me) was the first ascent of Little Poobah (5,481m, 41°01'00"N, 77°29'20"E), a summit to the east of Grand Poobah (more properly Peak Byeliy, 5,697m).

Our driver got us to 4,100m on August 8, leaving us with relatively pain-free, mostly downhill carries to a 3,400m base camp at the start of the Fersmana Valley.

After the first ascent of Peak 4,645m via the west ridge (F), we made the first ascent of Peak Donstanski (4,780m) via its west couloir (600m, D 70°). From the top we headed north along a 5km PD+ ridge, crossing two more unclimbed summits, before darkness and blizzards forced us to descend to a camp at the terminus of the Sarychat Glacier. Once the snow had retreated sufficiently from the limestone faces above base camp, two of the team climbed a 350m HVS. One team then established a high camp below Little Poobah, but poor snow conditions prevented an attempt. The other group was more successful, summiting unclimbed Peak 4,789m (north ridge, PD) and Peak 4,849m (west face, 350m, AD). All the summits we climbed lie on the watershed between the Fersmana and the Palgov Glacier to its east. With little time left, we concentrated on the limestone faces above base camp, where we put up three new rock routes, up to 460m and HVS 5a. 📷 🗎

– ADRIAN DYE, *U.K.*

PIK KOSMOS, ATTEMPT

A POLISH EXPEDITION comprising Wojciech Anzel, Jakub Galka, Katarzyna Kowalska, Piotr Picheta, and Radoslaw Robak spent July 27–September 2 in Kyrgyzstan, with the aim of climbing Peak Kosmos (5,940m). From their drop-off point below the Kotur Glacier it was 36km to the base of the mountain. It took 11 days of ferrying loads to get a high camp established below the peak, and bad weather meant they were unable to climb any warm-up peaks. After hasty acclimatization toward the Grigorev–Palgov watershed, the team attempted a large snow couloir toward the right side of the north-northeast face of Kosmos, leading to the northwest ridge, west of unclimbed Peak 5,681m. They reached the crest (ca 5,300m) before retreating.

Kosmos is frequently, but erroneously, reported to be unclimbed. The mountain was climbed in the 1980s during the Soviet competition era, when it was referred to as Pik Schmidta. The Soviet team climbed the north-northeast face at 5B and then descended the northeast ridge.

– LINDSAY GRIFFIN, WITH INFORMATION FROM EMILY WARD, U.K.

GRIGORIEV VALLEY, FIRST ASCENTS AND PEAK DANKOVA VARIATION

ON AUGUST 30, thanks to the logistics of our excellent agency ITMC, Maarten Altena and I were dropped off just 10km from base camp. Over two days we ferried loads to a site at 3,500m at the confluence of the Grigoriev and Palgov rivers. We made an advanced camp on the Grigoriev at 4,100m and on September 5 set off for Peak 5,081m, a border peak at the southern head of the glacier. We climbed 300m of ice on the northwest face to a shoulder at 4,850m. The ice kept shattering, and what was supposed to be a warm-up route became a terrible struggle. We plowed across a gentle hanging glacier covered in deep snow and up the last section of the west ridge to the summit, our first over 5,000m. Ten rappels from Abalakovs got us down through the heat of the sun, with meltwater gushing over our clothes. The route was AD, and we named the peak Moker, Dutch for sledgehammer.

From the same high camp we climbed Peak 5,161m, another border peak farther east, hoping it would provide more suitable warming up than Moker. On September 7 we reached

[Above] Looking down the west ridge from the summit of Dankova. The original route followed the sharp crest from near its base. In 2014 the Dutch climbers came up from the left and joined the original line high on the mountain. *Arjan de Leeuw*

a 4,800m col on the frontier, west-southwest of the mountain, where we met strong southerly winds from China. Good névé on a 300m, 40° face led to the top. We descended the same way (PD+) and named the summit Peak September.

Back in base camp we rested and prepared for our main objective, the west ridge of Dankova (5,982m), the highest peak in the Western Kokshaal-too. On the 14th we reached the foot of the south face, avoided two overhanging steps via a gorge to the right, and arrived at a 70m wall. This was UIAA III but dreadfully friable; it led to a precarious leftward traverse on snow, thinly covering loose gravel. A second rock barrier was climbed via snow-filled cracks (II) to the west ridge. We then climbed an ice bulge that strongly reminded us of the Nollen on the Monch in Switzerland (four pitches of 60–70° with one

[Photo] Dankova from the Grigoriev Glacier to the southwest. (1) Dutch west ridge route (2014). The original route up this ridge gained the lower rock arête from the south and followed the full crest. (2) Approximate line of the 1998 Boiko Route on the southwest face. *Arjan de Leeuw*

vertical section), reached a hanging glacier at 5,200m, and camped for the night.

Next morning, as we worked our way up 40–50° névé leading to the upper rock band at 5,800m, we repeatedly debated turning around because of the intense cold. The couloir we intended to climb turned out to be hideously brittle rock covered in verglas, so we moved north in search of easier passage. To our great surprise we found a piton at the top of the northwest face, possibly dating back as far as the 1972 ascent (*see note below*). We went back to the couloir and entered into a dose of Scottish winter climbing, albeit with far less oxygen. After 30m things improved and we waded 70m through hip-deep snow to the summit. We rappelled and downclimbed the route, leaving no equipment in place, and graded the route D+.

Winter was kicking in, and our good weather vanished as we carried gear out to the dirt road. All that now separated us from an immense heap of mouthwatering shashliks was a bumpy two-day truck ride. 📷

— **ARJAN DE LEEUW**, *THE NETHERLANDS*

Editor's note: The first ascent of Dankova probably took place in 1969, when N. Strikitsa's party is reported to have climbed a 5B route up the huge southwest face. In 1972 a hard mixed route was completed on the northwest face, which rises almost 2,000m above the glacier. In 1998 a team led by Valeri Boiko added another 5B route to the southwest face. The west ridge of Dankova was climbed integrally, over the lower rock crest, during the Soviet era (party unknown). However, the upper ridge is a tapering triangular slope, and it is possible the Dutch climbed new terrain until close to the upper rock band.

TIEN SHAN / DJANGART RANGE

VARIOUS FIRST ASCENTS

ON AUGUST 4 a helicopter dropped Liz Holley, Stuart Lade, Paul Padman, Jill Plummer, Alex Reid, Max Stretton, Zoe Strong, Stuart Worsfold, and me in an ideal location to tackle climbs in the last few valleys of unclimbed peaks in the Djangart. These lie in the far east of the range. Base camp was in a beautiful valley by a river (41°45'36.57"N, 79°0'43.51"E). The next day we split into two groups and went exploring. Both groups headed east up the main Debnoy Valley: my group with a 4,837m peak in mind, the others going farther to look at a mountain on the Chinese border marked as 5,112m on the old Russian maps. The latter we thought might be the highest unclimbed peak in the range.

On August 6, Jill, Liz, Stuart Lade, and I headed up the unnamed glacier branch west of the Debnoy. It was dry and posed no problems. We climbed a boulderfield to a shoulder, then a 300m snow slope, and finally a very loose rock ridge to the top of 4,837m, which we named Peak Jis. In the meantime, Paul, Alex, Max, Zoe, and Stuart Worsfold established a high camp on the Debnoy and next day climbed Peaks 4,575m, 4,586m, and 4,612m on the border with China before returning to base. These five returned to their high camp a few days later and climbed four more peaks: two just east of the Debnoy, and two on the border at the western head of the glacier. The two at the western head were 5,052m and 5,112m on the map; the latter measured at 5,123m GPS and was provisionally named Peak Pinney.

On the 12th, Liz and I traversed Peaks 4,542m, 4,597m, and 4,639m on a ridge leading toward the summit of Peak 5,032m, now the only remaining unclimbed 5,000er in the range. These lay closer to base camp, on the western rim of the next main glacier west of the Debnoy. Jill and Stuart Lade put up a 500m rock route (D+) above base camp.

In total we made 11 first ascents and found no evidence of any previous climbing in this area, despite two teams having passed through. However, as always in this part of the world, Soviet records remain a mystery. We used Tien Shan Travel and would highly recommend them. 📷 🗎 🔍

— JAMIE GOODHART, *U.K.*

[Below] Peak Temple (left, 5,052m) and Peak Pinney (5,123m GPS). The first ascensionists climbed the rightward ramp up the hanging glacier to reach the broad saddle between the two summits, from which each was easily reached (AD). *Supplied by Jamie Goodhart*

TAJIKISTAN

ACADEMY OF SCIENCES RANGE, FIRST ASCENTS AND SKI DESCENTS

ORIGINALLY, Tom Coney, Rich Jones, Mark Thomas, and I had hoped to explore the Rushan Range, but as we neared our departure in late April we learned the snow level was higher than expected, and we decided to shift our focus to the Academy of Sciences Range (Akademii Nauk), farther to the north. This massif is best known for the mountain once known as Peak Communism (7,495m), now called Ismail Somoni, the highest mountain in the former Soviet Union. We planned to climb in the southern part of the range, west of the head of the huge Fedchenko Glacier. The area accessed by the Vanj (Vanch) Valley offers many unclimbed 5,000m peaks and great potential for first ski descents. This area was explored by Soviet teams, but other than their ascents of the largest peaks, including Peak Revolution (6,940m), little is known of their activities.

[Above] Heading up the Vanj Valley toward the Bear Glacier. *Ski Tajikistan Expedition*

Poi Mazor was the ideal starting point, as it has a serviceable ex-Soviet truck that can reach the Academy of Sciences Range in spring. Our home-stay family in this welcoming subsistence-farming village was unsettled about us heading into the mountains for 25 days—and we soon found out why. Heavy late spring snowfall, affected by the Central Asian sun, meant that enormous wet-slab avalanches dominated. At our advanced base camp, at 2,800m, we saw heavy rain and 20cm of snow but predominantly fierce daytime heat—we had been expecting it to be much colder. We started all of our climbs at 2 a.m. to escape the thick, sucking slush that developed below 4,000m after midday.

We first explored up Bear Glacier, but this route to the Fedchenko Plateau (5,000m) was deemed impassable, as the final section was a sheer wall of hanging seracs. On the descent I fell and cracked my fibula, ending any climbing hopes I had. The boys then took a two-day reconnaissance up the Abdulkahor (Abdukagor) Glacier and set Camp 1 at 3,800m. This glacier was just as crevassed as the Bear but offered a safer route to the upper Fedchenko, reached by Abdulkahor Pass at ca 5,050m. [*Editor's note: This was the route followed by two British expeditions in 1992 and 2005 (AAJ 1994 and 2006). These teams did several probable first ascents of peaks up to 5,900m.*] A wealth of unexplored peaks can be reached from the Abdulkahor, including one 6,300m summit, which had been our team's target. Due to oncoming bad weather and an injured team member sitting at ABC, however, they instead chose "Abdulkahor 1"

(5,350m), on the north side of the Abdulkahor Glacier. This they reached via technical climbing on a snow/ice arête. They then skied down the Abdulkahor Glacier.

Fresh bear tracks worryingly followed the skin track to over 4,400m, making us realize just how many Tien Shan brown bears were about near ABC. We decided to relocate to the RGS Glacier (Royal Geographic Society Glacier), about 5km from our pickup point, and try for another peak there. However, the RGS was far less welcoming, with 10km of 30° moraine and hollow snow before skins could even be put on. I heard the words "hideous" and "epic" used a few times after the first gear drop. Despite this Mark and Tom completed a two-day, alpine-style, likely first ascent of a 5,105m peak, with a short M6 crux at 4,800m. They skied an 800m, 45° couloir back down after dawn.

The Pamir houses hundreds of virgin peaks and boasts the longest glacier outside the Polar regions, which has never been fully traversed. We saw scintillating ridgelines, an imposing 1,000m north face off the Bear Glacier, more rock climbing firsts than you could shake a nut at, and a 6,000m peak that looked so much like K2 we dubbed it K2 Junior. We are already planning a midwinter trip for 2015. 📷 🗒

– SUSANNA WALKER, U.K.

[Above] Unclimbed Peak 6,123m from the northeast, en route to high camp. The west ridge, attempted in 2014, is on the far side. *Simon Verspeak*

MUZKOL RANGE, PEAK BUFFY, PEAK 6,123M

OUR FOUR-PERSON TEAM—Rebecca Coles, Rhys Huws, Simon Verspeak, and John Vincent (all U.K.)—traveled to the Muzkol area in early August with our primary objective being the unnamed and unclimbed ca 6,123m peak to the west of Dvuglavy (6,148m). Coles had attempted this peak in 2011.

We approached up the Muzkol River, placing base camp at 4,300m. To acclimatize, we slowly moved up a side valley to the southwest to establish a high camp at 5,200m below a col. With an early start, we crossed the ca 5,500m col and traversed below Peak 6,123m to reach the west ridge. We split into two teams and followed different lines to the ridge, but all of us retreated from about 5,900m because of very poor rock and lack of snow. (The snow line in this area was 5,300m on the north faces, while the south faces barely had any snow.) Coles and Verspeak then spent several days exploring another valley but found that glacial retreat had made their objectives unfeasible. Meanwhile, Huws and Vincent made two attempts, succeeding on the second, on a ca 5,500m peak opposite base camp. After hours of scree trudging, the two climbed snow up to 50° on the northwest face to reach the summit, which they have named Peak Buffy, in memory of a friend.

[Editor's note: The high, arid Muzkol Range saw exploration in the Soviet era, and again during the late 1990s by Andrew Wielochowski's commercial EWP expeditions. These teams picked off the major summits, including Dvuglavy. Peak 6,123m is perhaps the last unclimbed 6,000er in the group.]

— INFORMATION FROM REBECCA COLES *AND* SIMON VERSPEAK

MUZKOL RANGE, HIGH TRAVERSE AND FIRST ASCENTS

DURING LATE JULY AND AUGUST, a Latvian team did a two-week east-to-west traverse of the Muzkol Range, starting in the Ak Baital Valley and exiting the Zortash Valley. They completed several possible first ascents along the way, including Peak 5,580m, Peak 5,560m, and Peak 5,582m (Russian 4A, 38°27'24.8"N, 73°31'05.1"E). The latter was one of "six great peaks at the end of the valley," possibly all previously unclimbed. Traveling light for the long traverse, the team did not have enough technical equipment to attempt the others. Farther west, they did the third ascents of White Pyramid (6,038m) and Zortash (6,121m).

[Editor's note: In August 2013, Oleg Silin and partners reported the first ascents of Khafraz Peak (6,128m) and Riga Peak (5,608m) in the Yazgulem Range of the Western Pamir. For more information search www.traverss.lv.]

— INFORMATION PROVIDED BY OLEG SILIN, *LATVIA*

CLIMBING POTENTIAL IN THE ALICHURSKY MOUNTAINS

IN SEPTEMBER 2013, Matthew Traver traveled to eastern Tajikistan to produce a film about a Kyrgyz-Tajik hunter and herder named Orozbek, who lives in a small settlement overlooking the verdant Alichur Plains. During the month he spent with Orozbek, Traver and his companions explored the unclimbed North and South Alichursky Mountains, which overlook the Wakhan Corridor from the north. His full report and photos of these 4,900m to 5,400m mountains are at the *AAJ* website.

— INFORMATION PROVIDED BY MATTHEW TRAVER, *U.K.*

[Photo] Peak 5,384m and the rock ridge leading to Peak 5,361m (both unclimbed) within the Koluchkol Valley. *Matthew Traver*

PAKISTAN

LANGUTA-E-BARFI, SOUTH FACE, ATTEMPT

GETTING TO LANGUTA-E-BARFI (Langua-tai Barfi, 6,827m) was an organic process. Originally, Chris Todd and I intended to approach the mountain from the north via the Wakhan Corridor in Afghanistan. But by chance we discovered Languta-e-Barfi hadn't been climbed from Pakistan, so we decided to try it from the Rosh Gol Glacier. Few expeditions have visited the Rosh Gol, and none had previously reached the head of the glacier. [*The team exploring farthest up the glacier, a 1967 German expedition, made the first ascent of a peak of nearly 6,500m, off the ridge connecting Languta-e-Barfi with Koh-e-Langar, which they named Languta-e-Barfi South*].

For at least half of the 14-hour drive from Islamabad to Chitral, we had an armed police escort, which changed like clockwork every 20 to 30km. Two armed policemen accompanied us all the way to the start of the walk-in, and again on the return journey, proof that the Pakistani government is taking foreigners' welfare seriously. We reached the tiny village of Zondangram on June 25. Two long days' walk got us to Kotgaz (4,250m), the site of our base camp for the next month. It was a stunning place, with views up the glacier to Languta-e-Barfi and Koh-e-Langar (7,070m). To the west was Udren Zom (7,131m) and Shakhawr (7,116m), and to the east Saraghrar (7,349m).

A couple of days later Chris and I started our acclimatization in earnest, climbing a rocky ridge on Saraghrar to 5,000m. This gave a fantastic view into the upper Rosh Gol Glacier and south face of Languta-e-Barfi. After a rest day we tackled the 15km moraine bash to the base of

[Below] On the Rosh Gol Glacier with Koh-e-Langar to the east and part of the Saraghrar massif behind. *Pat Deavoll*

[Above] South face of Languta-e-Barfi and the New Zealand attempt. *Pat Deavoll*

the mountain, spending two nights at our 4,750m advanced base. We also climbed the initial broad gully of our chosen route to ca 5,200m, only to be chased down by afternoon avalanches and rockfall. To avoid this threat, we determined to get most of our climbing done by lunchtime.

On July 8 we trekked to advanced base for the second time, and the following morning were up at 3 a.m., intent on reaching Camp 1 at about 5,500m, where there appeared to be a flat spot on a small subsidiary ridge to the right of a big gully. It took a couple of hours to reach the base of the gully. We moved up the right-hand side and, when the snow softened, took to the ridge itself, climbing loose rock to a point just below 5,500m. In early afternoon we dug a tent platform and settled in. Next day we climbed the gully to where it narrowed and steepened, and made camp, again in early afternoon, on a perfect site at the top of the ridge we had been following the day before.

We made a 1 a.m. start on the morning of July 13, intent on reaching the crest of the southwest ridge. We climbed to the head of the gully (now narrow and steep) in the dark, then took a leftward-trending lead up some ice, which put us at the bottom of snow slopes leading up to the ridge. At 3 p.m. we found a great campsite on the ridge—the Afghanistan-Pakistan border—in a small alcove at 6,130m, with views across to Koh-e-Langar and Saraghrar to the east, and to Shakhawr just to the south of us. Because we had climbed over 700m that day, we decided to take an acclimatization day before trying for the summit.

After a day of rest, we were away by 1 a.m. in a temperature of -25°C. Straight away we found deep snow. At daybreak (5 a.m.) we reached a flat spot on the ridge where we had fantastic views down onto the Shakhawr Glacier in Afghanistan and the Wakhan Corridor.

The terrain steepened and we were climbing in deep snow laid over black ice. At around 4 p.m. we reached a spot high in a gully between a rock spur and a small ice cliff. At this point we were really struggling to move forward—we figured we were only a couple of hundred meters from the summit, but it would probably take us another four to five hours. The weather was deteriorating, and we could only see a few meters ahead. Going on meant a night out in bad weather. We made the decision to turn around, arriving back at camp sometime in the evening, assisted by our GPS.

[Above] The southwest face of Shakhawr (7,116m). *Pat Deavoll*

On the 15th we down-climbed over 1,000m to the base of the initial gully. It was very arduous, and we were so tired we could easily have made a silly mistake. We arrived on the glacier sometime around 9 p.m. and immediately made camp, ate the last dregs of our food, and crashed for the night. Next morning we headed off for base camp, 20km away. At one point Chris said, "I hear voices!" I said, "You are imagining things," but next moment our staff, Hayat, Naseerudin, and Irshadul, appeared over a mound of moraine, very glad to see us.

Ours was one of the few expeditions to the Hindu Kush since 9/11, and the only expedition in 2014. The people we dealt with (Tirich Mir Travel and the police who traveled with us) had nothing but our best interests at heart, but sadly we saw no other tourists or climbers. We can only encourage others to take advantage of the hospitality we encountered, and the fantastic mountains of the Hindu Kush. We would like to thank the New Zealand Alpine Club, the Shipton-Tilman Grant, and the Mount Everest Foundation for aiding our trip.

[*Editor's note: Languta-e-Barfi was first climbed by Poles in 1963 via the west spur to northwest ridge, and twice in 1973 via a different approach to the northwest ridge. There has been no known ascent since. For a photo from the Afghan side, see AAJ 2012.*] 📷

– PAT DEAVOLL, *NEW ZEALAND*

KARAKORAM / BATURA MUZTAGH

MUCHU CHHISH, ATTEMPT

IN AUGUST, Phil De-Beger, Tim Oates, and Peter Thompson (U.K.) attempted unclimbed Muchu Chhish (7,453m, among the highest unclimbed summits in the world for which it is possible to obtain a permit). The plan was to climb alpine-style along the south and west ridges, with a high traverse below the summit of Batura VI (7,400m). However, after finding hard ice on the lower section of the south ridge, and realizing they had no chance of climbing quickly enough if they pitched this section, they retreated from 6,000m.

The team then moved base camp to the Morkun Valley. From a bivouac at 4,900m, De-Beger and Oates attempted the south face of unclimbed Pregar (variously reported from 6,083m to 6,300m), retreating from 5,600m due to dangerous snow conditions. 📷

– LINDSAY GRIFFIN

IGLS PEAK

BEFORE MAKING A RARE south-to-north crossing of Chapchingol Pass, a team of mountaineers from Austria and Pakistan visited the Ghidims Valley to attempt an unclimbed summit clearly visible from the upper valley and Yahya Camp (4,400m). Starting from Shimshal at the end of an extraordinary Jeep road, we took three days to reach base camp in the Ghidims Valley via a crossing of Boesam Pass. After exploring possible routes we decided to climb up into the high, glaciated valley to the west of Dosti Sar (6,063m, see AAJ 2014), leading to North Ghidims Pass (a.k.a. Akalik Pass). On the way we passed four cairns marking an ancient trekking route. We made our high camp at 5,250m. Early on August 23 we set out for the summit. Due to heavy snowfall a few days earlier it was difficult finding our way through the steep labyrinth of snow and ice. Close to the top we needed to place several screws to cross a large ridge of ice. Christian Müller (Austria), Rahim Hayat and Naseer Uddin (both Pakistan), and I soon reached the summit, where we witnessed an incredible panorama.

[Above] Igls Peak (far right) from the Ghidims Valley. *Stephan Tischler*

We called the mountain Igls Peak (6,014m GPS, 36°41'26.64"N, 75°31'58.26"E). Igls is the hometown of the two Austrians, and in German is pronounced very similar to eagle. [*This peak is marked 5,932m on Jerzy Wala's 2011 sketch map and lies across the glacier northwest from Dosti Sar.*]

– STEPHAN TISCHLER, *AUSTRIA*

KUZ SAR I, NORTH TO SOUTH TRAVERSE, FIRST WINTER ASCENT

IN FEBRUARY, Sikandar Ali Khan, two Shimshali porters (Hajjat Kareem and Wazir Beg), and I climbed the northeast face of Kuz Sar I (ca 5,460m) from a camp at 4,700m and then descended the southwest face, returning to Shuijerab that same day. Despite lying close to Shimshal Pass, twin-summited Kuz Sar has not been climbed often because it lies directly opposite the higher and far more frequented Minglik Sar. Both peaks offer nontechnical ascents. 📷 📄

– SA'AD MOHAMED, *PAKISTAN*

TAHU RUTUM, WEST FACE ATTEMPT AND RESCUE

DURING THE SUMMER OF 2013 an attempt on Tahu Rutum resulted in a serious injury and rescue, followed by unusual difficulties between the Korean expedition, their logistical agencies, and Askari Aviation, the company responsible for rescue services for mountaineers in Pakistan.

Chang Kwi-yong had led of team of seven to attempt the west face of Tahu Rutum (6,651m). The climbing leader, Sim Kwon-sik, was hit by rockfall high on the face on July 26. Descending through the night and well into the next day, Sim's partners managed to get him to Camp 1, at 5,100m on the glacier, from which he was rescued by an Askari Aviation helicopter the next day.

However, the climbers had been issued their peak permit without depositing a rescue bond, resulting in their agencies in Pakistan and Korea being forced to borrow the balance owed for two helicopter flights from the unused rescue deposits of Czech and Italian expeditions that were returning from the Trango area—about $40,000 in all. Initially, the agencies were able to pay back only half of the money, leading Askari to announce several months later that the company would no longer rescue Korean mountaineers, and would request the Pakistan Ministry of Tourism not to issue any climbing permits to Korean expeditions. Fortunately, the problem was resolved in February 2014, when the expedition leader, climbing leader, agency manager, and related personnel agreed on a plan for repaying the funds.

— FROM INFORMATION PROVIDED BY OH YOUNG-HOON, *KOREA*

KARAKORAM / BALTORO MUZTAGH

PAIJU PEAK, SOUTH PILLAR, VIA 2T

ON JUNE 30 Spanish-Basque mountaineers Alberto Iñurrategi, Juan Vallejo and Mikel Zabalza arrived at their 3,400m base camp below Paiju Peak (6,610m) for a second attempt at the south pillar. In the summer of 2013 they had climbed the first 500m of the pillar, but bad weather and poor conditions prevented further progress.

The south pillar rises steeply from 5,000m to the top of a distinct granite tower at ca 6,100m. Above, snow slopes and steeper mixed terrain lead to the main summit. Paiju has only been climbed once: In 1976 an Alpine Club of Pakistan expedition placed Raja Bashir Ahmad, Manzoor Hussain, and Nazir Sabir on the summit via a route from the north, approaching up the Uli Biaho Glacier. Allen Steck joined the expedition to advise on technical climbing and reached a point 60m below the summit. In 1981 Italians climbed a difficult partial line on the left edge of the south face.

The three Basques established Camp 1 below the face at ca 5,000m and eventually climbed the pillar, capsule

[Left] Paiju Peak from the southeast. The line (approximate) shows roughly the upper half of the Basque route on the south tower. *Sebastian Alvaro*

[Above] The north face of Shipton Spire, with Bismillah marked. Gabo Cmarik and Dodo Kopold from Slovakia are the only other climbers known to have attempted this section of the face. *Dodo Kopold*

style, in a 10-day round trip from base camp. The route was difficult and sustained in the upper section, with climbing of 6b A3 M5. It was also threatened by stone and ice fall. Two camps were made on the wall, at 5,500m and ca 5,750m. The team climbed for 10 to 12 hours each day, and Zabalza felt the route to be the most demanding alpine climb of his career.

On July 26, as the climbers were approaching the top of the tower, a rock the size of a "medium microwave oven" hit Vallejo on the shoulder. The other two continued to the top of the tower, where they saw that the way ahead looked "suicidal." A difficult snow slope and ridge led toward a large serac barrier that was continuously disgorging chunks of ice. Two days later, all three exhausted climbers were safely back at base camp. The 1,100m route to the top of the south tower has been named 2T.

— *FROM INFORMATION SUPPLIED BY* ANA LARIZGOITIA, *SPAIN*

SHIPTON SPIRE, BISMILLAH (NOT TO SUMMIT)

Patrice Bret, David Girard, and I (France) spent mid-July to mid-August in Pakistan with the main goal of repeating one of the routes on Trango Tower. We spent around a week climbing the Slovenian Route, though the top pitches were in poor condition, and so we finished via Run For Cover.

The extraordinary weather allowed us an additional window of opportunity, and after two exhausting days of walking up the broken Trango Glacier, we set camp at 4,700m on the North Hainabrakk Glacier, below the serac-torn north face of Shipton Spire (5,885m). An obvious rock and ice spur, protected from icefall, rises directly to a point on the ridge west of the summit.

At 5 a.m. on August 5 we left camp and climbed a 100m goulotte to reach the crest of the spur. The rock above went free up to 6a/b and was followed by steep mixed terrain. We were forced to use aid from pegs and jammed axe blades to bypass the last crux. From there 150m of ice flutes took us to the crest of the west ridge, where we terminated the route after 16 hours of climbing. We made a bivouac on the crest at 5,500m and spent all next day rappelling from pegs and Abalakovs. We named the route to the ridge Bismillah (800m, TD+ 6a/b A2 WI4+ M4), which locally means "enjoy your meal." [*Editor's note: The north face of Shipton was attempted in 2006 by Slovakians Gabo Cmarik and Dodo Kopold, possibly using the same start to get to the plateau above the initial seracs. They bailed after 500m when Cmarik got sunstroke.*]

– PASCAL TRIVIDIC, *FRANCE*

ULI BIAHO GALLERY: FREETANGA ECUATORIANA

Felipe Guarderas and I climbed three established routes in the Trango Group in June and July. We summited Trango Tower via Eternal Flame, Little Trango via the original American Route, and Great Trango via the normal route. Prior to this we had attempted the 2011 Chibitok-Kopteva-Yasinskaya route Parallelniy Mir (A3 6a) on the north face of Great Trango. After around 35 pitches we gave up on this route, which was very disappointing. The first 1,000m are poor rock with many ledges. On the incredible pillar the first ascensionists drilled hundreds of holes so they could hook up blank walls for ca 200m. After that, who knows? It was heartbreaking for us, so we decided to bail and climb something better.

Our main objective was to establish our own route in this iconic area. We decided on a 700m wall directly above the west side of the Trango Glacier, named Uli Biaho Gallery by the Austrians that probably climbed it first via the line Nilam Nijang on the southeast pillar (*AAJ 2013*). Our route follows a perfect crack system, with very varied climbing, from flaring fingers to awkward offwidths. It took three days to complete, aiding (A2) most of the way due to vegetation and tricky protection.

After a couple of rest days, and with a good weather forecast, we came back to prepare the route for a free ascent. We placed a bolt and piton at each belay, and around eight more bolts to protect blank sections. Bad weather, gastrointestinal distress, and fatigue prevented us from completing a full free ascent, but we tried hard and enjoyed every pitch, which were as good as the ones on Eternal Flame. A completely free ascent would be about 7b+; however, it also can be climbed at around 6c A1+. We named the route FreeTanga Ecuatoriana (700m of climbing), a reference to a traditional dish of our country and also a naughty play on words.

– ROBERTO MORALES, *ECUADOR*

[Above] Uli Biaho Gallery showing FreeTanga Ecuatoriana. Nilam Nijang (2012) is mostly hidden around the left arête. *Roberto Morales* [Next page] Roberto Morales leading pitch one (7a) on FreeTanga Ecuatoriana. Trango Glacier below. *Felipe Guarderas*

LITTLE TRANGO, EID MUBARAK

"ARE YOU GOING TO CLIMB on the Trango Towers under the supervision of some Western climber?" This was the usual opening question. This would be followed by a barrage of inquiries about our skills, gear, past accidents, and everything that pointed toward the Towers not being made for Pakistani rock climbers.

Owais Khattak, Usman Tariq, and I spent three days transporting gear from a high camp at 4,800m to the base of Little Trango (ca 5,445m). Over the festival of Eid, July 29–30, Usman and I started up a prominent corner system on the southwest side of the formation until reaching the top of a pedestal, where we traversed down and right to join the American route (PM Wall, McMahon-Wharton, 2000) on the south face, then followed this to the summit. On the first day we climbed 190m before bivouacking. In total we climbed 250m at 5.10d A0. I led all nine pitches, and we named our line Eid Mubarak (Merry Eid). 📷

– IMRAN JUNAIDI, PAKISTAN

MASHERBRUM RANGE / CHARAKUSA VALLEY

K7 SOUTHWEST SUMMIT (BADAL PEAK)

RYO MASUMOTO, TAKAKI NAGATO, and I visited the Charakusa Valley for one month, and after acclimatizing on Sulu Peak we made our goal the southeast ridge of a previously unclimbed sub-peak that lies on the ridge extending southwest from K7 West (6,615m). This peak has a huge rock buttress on its southwest side, first climbed in 2007 by a Belgian-Polish team. Other expeditions completed new lines on the same wall, but nobody had reached the highest point. Some climbers began to call this untouched point Badal Peak (variously reported between ca 6,100m and 6,300m), after the name given to the 2007 route. To us it looked attractive: a chance to reach an unclimbed sub-peak via a new line. Even so, it was obvious that Badal was only part of a bigger massif. We hoped to climb Badal Peak and then continue along the ridge to K7 West.

As we scoped the southeast ridge, we realized it was extremely long, and so decided to fix all six of our ropes on the first section to save the time. On July 25, with light packs, we climbed eight pitches up to 5.11c. We descended, leaving all six ropes fixed. After regaining our high point, we set off on the 30th for a continuous ascent with two ropes and five days of food. Climbing on the ridge was generally fairly moderate, though there were several steep sections and awkward offwidths—complex route-finding was the true difficulty. There were even some pitches we thought would be five-star if they were in Yosemite. On day two we were forced to climb much trickier and looser terrain, and in the late afternoon had to climb a steep, sandy rock slope in rock shoes, as if we were scrambling up an avalanche slope.

When we woke on day three, it was cloudy with wind. Our progress slowed as the ridge became more complicated. Pitch 42 was excellent C1 following a perfect splitter on a very clean face. It led to the top of the most obvious rock pinnacle on the ridge. We then had to rappel the far side and continue on mixed terrain. Even if we reached the summit of Badal that day, we still would be only two-thirds of the way toward our goal, so we decided to stop and camp again on a ledge dug out of snow.

Next morning, after negotiating a couple of pitches of complex, technical mixed climbing, we reached a gentle ice slope leading to the top. After six pitches of simul-climbing, and two rappels, we finally reached the summit area of Badal. It was difficult to determine the true highest point, so we took a quick photo on one of the snowy bumps. To this point we had climbed 58 pitches, but were still a long way from our goal of K7 West. We quickly resumed climbing. However, poor weather, lack of food, unstable conditions on the ridge, and an injury to Masumoto's knee made us reconsider our options, and after seven pitches we decided to retreat. On day five we began the first of 20 rappels down the northwest flank of the ridge. We reached the glacier by nightfall.

We didn't name our climb, or the summit, but we totally agree with others that it should be called Badal Peak. Our route up the southeast ridge was over 1,600m, VI 5.11c C1 M5 70°, with lots of alpine trickery.

[*Editor's note: The first attempt to top the southwest buttress of K7 West was made in 2007 by Nico and Olivier Favresse, Adam Pustelnik, and Sean Villanueva, who climbed the west-southwest face for 1,200m at 5.12+ and five meters of A1 to low-angled rock and snow 300m below the top. They christened their line Badal. In 2009 Italians Cagol, Larcher, Leoni, and Orlandi made a new line to the right, Children of Hushe (7b A2), finishing at a lower point. In 2008 Slovenians Cesen, Hrastelj, and Sisernik climbed the south face to ca 5,700m, dubbing their line Luna (6c A2), a climb more or less repeated by Spanish climbers in 2010. Several of the lower pillars on the buttress have been climbed over the years. The completion of the full southwest ridge to the summit of K7 West remains one of the prizes of the Charakusa.*] 📷*

— **KATSUTAKA YOKOYAMA**, *JAPAN*

[Below] Looking northeast across the Charakusa Glacier. (A) Badal Peak. (B) K7 Middle (6,858m, unclimbed). (C) K7 (6934m). The summit of K7 West is hidden. (1) Very approximate line of Children of Hushe (2009). Badal (2007) is hidden but close to the left skyline. (2) Variante de Sol (2010). (3) Luna (2008). (4) Prezelj-Turgeon (finishes on top a distinct tower). (5) Southeast ridge with bivouacs (2014). The Anderson-House-Prezelj route (2007) up the southeast face to the summit of K7 West begins around the corner to the right. (6) Southwest ridge of K7, which still awaits an integral ascent. *Katsutaka Yokoyama*

NEPAL

NEW PEAKS AND OPPORTUNITIES

Nepal is a young republic, struggling to write its constitution. As new elections of the parliamentary assembly approached in the fall of 2013, the minister of tourism asked the ministry's mountaineering section to propose a list of new peaks to open to foreigners. Much later, in the fall of 2014, 104 new peaks were officially opened, 31 of these in West Nepal. The ministry also announced that no permit will be required for peaks under 5,800m.

Chosen quickly and without much thought to the development of mountaineering and tourism in the Himalaya, a significant number of the 104 new peaks will disappoint climbers. A number of these newly opened peaks, both in West Nepal and elsewhere, were probably chosen for their political significance. Lying on the border with Tibet, they clearly mark Nepal's territory with its powerful northern neighbor.

All that said, West Nepal is a huge area of unspoiled nature, with a mosaic of fascinating culture. A few peaks rise over 7,000m, and there are numerous peaks over 6,000m that are still virgin. From west to east, from the district of Darchula to Dolpo, the ranges along the Chinese border are: Guras, Nalakankar, Chandi, Changla, Gorakh, Kanti, Gautam, and Palchung. In the interior they run from Api through Saipal, Limi, Kanjiroba, Putha, and Churen.

It is a long, complicated, and expensive journey to reach the mountains of West Nepal. (There are four airstrips: Jumla, Gamgadhi, Simikot, and Juphal.) Everything is more difficult to acquire, including information, which makes success less certain. On the other hand, an expedition here will be a great adventure. There will be exploration and the pleasure of making

[Photo] In the valley of the Takchhe Khola (the upper Limi Valley), looking southwest at (left to right) the snowy shoulder of Point 5,490m, Ardang (6,034m), and Peak 5,519m. *Paulo Grobel*

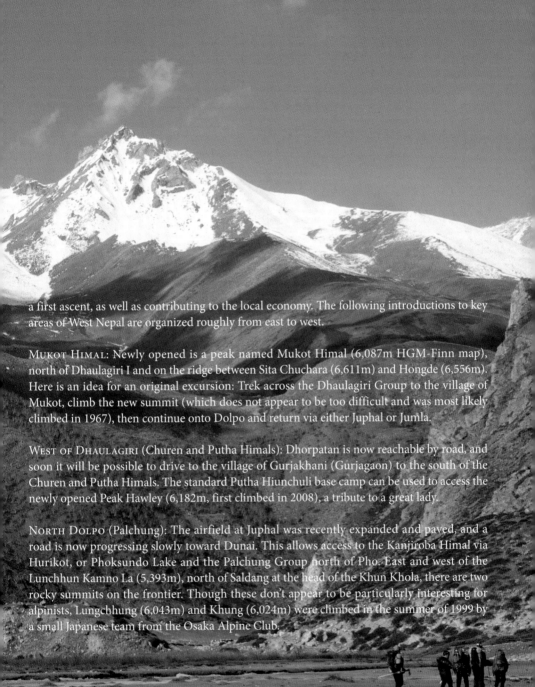

a first ascent, as well as contributing to the local economy. The following introductions to key areas of West Nepal are organized roughly from east to west.

MUKOT HIMAL: Newly opened is a peak named Mukot Himal (6,087m HGM-Finn map), north of Dhaulagiri I and on the ridge between Sita Chuchara (6,611m) and Hongde (6,556m). Here is an idea for an original excursion: Trek across the Dhaulagiri Group to the village of Mukot, climb the new summit (which does not appear to be too difficult and was most likely climbed in 1967), then continue onto Dolpo and return via either Juphal or Jumla.

WEST OF DHAULAGIRI (Churen and Putha Himals): Dhorpatan is now reachable by road, and soon it will be possible to drive to the village of Gurjakhani (Gurjagaon) to the south of the Churen and Putha Himals. The standard Putha Hiunchuli base camp can be used to access the newly opened Peak Hawley (6,182m, first climbed in 2008), a tribute to a great lady.

NORTH DOLPO (Palchung): The airfield at Juphal was recently expanded and paved, and a road is now progressing slowly toward Dunai. This allows access to the Kanjiroba Himal via Hurikot, or Phoksundo Lake and the Palchung Group north of Pho. East and west of the Lunchhun Kamno La (5,393m), north of Saldang at the head of the Khun Khola, there are two rocky summits on the frontier. Though these don't appear to be particularly interesting for alpinists, Lungchhung (6,043m) and Khung (6,024m) were climbed in the summer of 1999 by a small Japanese team from the Osaka Alpine Club.

KANJIROBA: Jumla has become the most reliable airport in West Nepal, and allows quick access to the south side of the Kanjiroba Himal. This area was explored a long time ago by Herbert Tichy and John Tyson. Dhud Kundali (6,045m), climbed by Tichy from the west in 1953, is now on the permitted list. The east ridge, climbed in 2008 and called A Torch for Tibet (III/AD+), is a classic alpine snow route. The main peaks of the Kanjiroba Himal have much character; most access routes are now known and were documented in a *Trek* magazine article ("The Kanjiroba Sanctuary"). In 1999, a British team, including two members on their honeymoon, discovered an adventurous route toward Kanjiroba base camp over the "English Col". Later we completed the "Honeymoon Trail" and found this base camp to be an ideal location for attempts on Kanjiroba North (6,858m) and Sanctuary Peak (6,207m).

[Above] Unclimbed summits of the Kanjiroba Sanctuary: Peak 6,313m (left of twin tops) and Kanjiroba Northwest (6,289m, right top). [Below] North-northwest face of unclimbed Peak 5,905m on the long northwest ridge of Kasi Dalpha. *Paulo Grobel*

Let's not forget the peaks in this area that were opened many years ago, like Kande Hiunchuli (6,627m), Patrasi (6,450m), or Kanjiroba South (6,883m), the highest peak in the range. On the northern fringes of the range, Lhasa Bhulu (6,102m) was climbed by Tyson at the end of an extraordinary journey. Lha Shamma (6,412m), north of Kagmara La in the southeast sector of the range, was first climbed in 1962 by an all-women British team, during an era when this region was little known.

On the western side, Bijora Hiunchuli (6,111m), visible from Jumla, is a small, snowy pyramid that captures the eye on landing at the airstrip. We have so far failed to climb the west ridge, but it is a great project for a team wanting to discover the joys of the "wild, wild west" for the first time. This is now a permitted peak, as is its larger neighbor, Kasi Dalpha (6,386m).

GAMGADHI AND MUGU (Kanti and Gorakh Himals): There is now road access to Gamgadhi and the Rara Lake area. While the airstrip at Gamgadhi is far less well served than Jumla, it gives more rapid access to the mountains on the Chinese border, between Dolpo and the Limi Range. In the east, four newly opened peaks close to Mugu now make the Koji Valley one of the most attractive in the region. Though ministry officials chose these peaks from

[Above] Eastern Limi summits, looking just south of east over the Nyalu La (4,988m) from the Ardang Glacier/Phupharka Plateau to the unexplored mountains due north of Simikot. In the center of the picture, the steep rocky face in shadow is most likely Peak 5,975m, while the higher snowy summit behind and left is Peak 6,265m, the highest in this group. Over to the right are Peaks 6,248m and 6,028m. *Paulo Grobel*

the map because of their strategic position on the border, not for their interest to alpinists, they allow climbers official access to the valley systems and the discovery of more exciting mountains. Kaipuchonam (6,329m), Kojichwa Chuli South (6,264m), Chandi (6,623m), Kanti Himal East (6,516m), Kogi Khang North (6,275m), and Takla Khang (6,276m) lie in the Mugu and Koji valleys. Some have already been climbed, occasionally under a different name (Tibetan or Chinese). They are generally much easier from the Tibetan side. British teams led by Julian Freeman-Attwood and Mick Fowler, as well as Japanese and Spanish, have climbed or attempted technical lines on the Nepalese side.

To the east are other new peaks: Mayung Thang Khang (6,449m), Tankya I (6,305m), Mariyang West (6,455m), and Yara Chuli (6,236m), as well as the previously permitted border summits of Danphe Sail (6,103m) and Mariyang (6,528m). There is still much exploration needed here to ascertain the best base camps and interesting routes to the summits

Gamgadhi airfield also provides access to the Gorakh Himal via the Tanke Khola. This long valley leads to the Kang La (5,358m), an old pass used for trading with Tibet. To the northeast work is in progress on a drivable track connecting the Mugu Valley with Tibet over Namje La. Farther west, accessed via Piplan and the Bolbihan Khola, lies the Gorakh, with peaks such as Assajyatuppa (6,265m) and Absi (6,254m). A British team has plans to climb in this area in the spring of 2015.

LIMI AND NALAKANKAR: Imagine the Écrins Massif in the French Alps before the arrival of English alpinists. All the summits in the Limi Himal are unclimbed—and there are 15 over 6,000m. Simikot is the closest airstrip. Obtaining a permit for Achvin (6,055m) would allow a base camp in the heart of the massif, but climbing any other summit in the range would require a certain bending of the rules. For a first visit to Limi the unclimbed Ardang (6,034m, *AAJ 2014*) would present an excellent choice, perhaps from the north via Toling, a somewhat technical ascent. Then there is the large glacier leading west to the virigin top of Tirawa Himal (5,876m). Some distance to the northwest, in the Nalakankar Group, above the village of Haiji, is the newly opened Takphu North (6,142m).

THE FAR WEST (Guras Himal): The district of Darchula, north of the Api Himal, is one of the poorest in Nepal and is little frequented by climbers or trekkers despite elegant mountains above 7,000m. In 1953 Tyson and Da Norbu climbed a border peak from the Yokanadi Khola (now the Yarwa Khola on the HGM-Finn map), the southerly branch of the Tinkar Khola. This peak was designated as part of the Yokopahar Himal, northeast of Nampa, but today is referred to as the Guras Himal. Although the location of this summit is unclear, Tyson looked down the far side into the Seti Valley. A difficult peak named Yokopahar (Nampa VII, 6,466m HGM-Finn) was brought onto the permitted list in 2002. There are now four more new peaks close by: Guras Himal (6,744m), Yarwa (6,644m), Jyachhun (6,388m), and Lasa (6,189m), all on the border and all looking rather technical, with complex, unknown access. Tyson's mountain bears some resemblance to Peak 6,330m (sometimes called Nampa V) on the rim southwest of Yarwa. Not far west lies the Indian border. *Many photos and more information about these areas can be found at the author's website: www.paulo-grobel.com.* 📷

– PAULO GROBEL, *FRANCE*

KANJIROBA HIMAL

PATRASI, WEST-NORTHWEST FACE, ATTEMPT

ALEK ZHOLOBENKO (U.K./Russian) and Bradley Morrell (U.K.) attempted Patrasi (6,450m), a sub-peak northeast of Kande Hiunchuli (6,627m), in October. The two made a difficult approach up the Chaudhabise Valley and over a 4,942m col to base camp in the Chyandayng Valley. It then took them four days to climb through very deep snow to the foot of the 1,000m face on Patrasi, during which time they traveled light and bivouacked. Upon reaching the face they realized Zholobenko had frostbite on his toes. They abandoned the climb and evacuated by an arduous trek through the previously unexplored valley below base camp, eventually reaching Dolphu in Mugu district and flying out from Rara Lake. [*The AAJ website has a fuller account of this exploratory adventure, along with a brief history of Patrasi and its neighbors.*] 📷 ▤

– *INFORMATION FROM* BRADLEY MORRELL, *U.K.*

MUSTANG HIMAL

VARIOUS ASCENTS AND EXPLORATION

NORTHWEST OF LO MANTHANG, the Mustang Himal previously was forbidden to both climbers and trekkers. The opening of new peaks in 2014 by the Ministry of Tourism radically changed this situation, and there are now beautiful climbs to be done in a spectacular environment of ice and desert. The track connecting Jomson with Lo Manthang greatly facilitates access to these peaks, close to the border with Tibet.

There are four authorized summits, and being below 6,500m they do not require a liaison officer: Mansail (a.k.a. Manshail, 6,242m, according to Official Border Map; 6,235m on the HGM-Finn map); Mansail South (6,251m; 6,248m); Mustang Himal (6,195m, both maps); and Ghyun Himal (6,099m; 6,110m). The finest summit in the group, well visible from Lo Manthang, is Dong Mar (6,337m, climbed in 1953 by Herbert Tichy). It's very likely that many of the small summits close to Lo have already been climbed.

In the spring we crossed the Mustang Himal by a fine route, partially trekking and partially mountaineering, with a few easy peaks thrown in. It deserves to become classic. The most northerly of three main valleys flowing east, then southeast, to Lo Manthang leads to the Mansail peaks on the Tibetan border. We trekked to this valley, and from a camp at 5,600m that we dubbed Mansail Base Camp, climbed a peak to the north and on the ridge east-southeast of Mansail, which we named Pema Himal (6,168m, HGM-Finn). We stopped 10m below its highest point, a collection of large granite blocks.

[Above] Seen from the north, Ame Pal Chuli East (6,176m) is on the left, separated from the higher Ame Pal Chuli West by Col du Replat. The east summit was climbed, and the col crossed, in spring 2014. [Below] Mansail from the east with the approximate line of the Japanese first ascent marked. *Photos: Paulo Grobel*

We then traveled east to the frontier and over the Nyamdo La, close to Windmilles Peak (6,250m), then turned south, crossing icefields east of the border, to reach the Col du Replat, which lies between the Ame Pal Chuli East (6,176m) and the higher Ame Pal Chuli West (6,229m). (Ame Pal is the name of the first great king of Lo.) We climbed the easy eastern peak. Descending south, we reached the head of the southern main valley and from there climbed another border peak: Dhane Himal (6,125m). While most of the group descended the main valley, Sonia Baillif, Jean-Paul Charpentier, Jangbu Sherpa, and I made a detour,

climbing over a nice peak that we named Jangbu Himal (6,167m), on the south side of the valley, before rejoining the group at Samdrub Ling.

This area is still little known to climbers and there are many goals, but a visit requires patience, much diplomacy, and an understanding of local life. The villagers of Nyamdo and Thingar are quite reluctant to see foreigners in their mountains, and will prohibit access until harvest time. It is necessary to include them in your organization as much as possible, and for the time being not plan to visit the area until the beginning of October. *For more information go to www.paulogrobel.com/mustang-himal-2014-cr.* 📷

– PAULO GROBEL, *FRANCE*

MANSAIL, NORTH FACE

THE TIMING WAS PERFECT. A team of female students from the Japanese Alpine Club was planning an expedition to the Himalaya, just as Nepal opened more than 100 new peaks, including Mansail (a.k.a. Manshail, 6,235m HGM-Finn map). The students were Eri Hasegawa, Yukiko Inoue, Kaho Mishima, and Mariko Nakamura. I was asked to accompany them as technical adviser. There is little information about this area on the border with Tibet, and we had to imagine what our peaks would look like by using maps and Google Earth.

From Lo Manthang we traveled through wilderness, crossing several streams and rivers, and, higher, passed through a gorge with boulders that may never have been touched. We constructed many cairns so we could find our way home. On September 20 we established base camp at 4,900m, and on the 25th, 20 days after leaving Japan, made Camp 2 at 5,685m by the stream flowing from the Nyamdo Glacier snout.

The south face of Mansail was a steep slab of rock, so we crossed a col on the east ridge to reach a glacier that rose to a point relatively high on the north face. There was a crack system and the angle was easier than on the south flank. Unusually for Mustang, it began snowing heavily and turned the upper climb into a mixed route. At 1 p.m. on the 29th we reached the top. It was snowing heavily, and once back on the glacier we were faced with white-out conditions. Continued snowfall stopped any further activity in these mountains. 📷 📄

– KEI TANIGUCHI, *JAPAN*

MUSTANG HIMAL, NORTH FACE TO WEST RIDGE

ON OCTOBER 17, Benjamin Jones, Jonathan Mancuso, and I left Kathmandu to explore four unclimbed and newly opened peaks in the Upper Mustang region. From Jomsom it took five days to reach a ca 4,875m base camp, and two days later we set a high camp at ca 5,670m on the glacier below three peaks: Mansail (a.k.a. Manshail, 6,235m), Mansail South (6,248m), and Mustang Himal (6,195m). We were unable to locate the fourth peak, Gyhun Himal (6,110m), due to lack of time. [*Elevations from HGM-Finn map.*]

First we attempted Mansail by the east ridge to north face but turned around on the granite mass below the summit because of inadequate rock gear. Our high point was ca 6,135m. Mansail South would pose a similar challenge, the entire climb to the summit lying over broken granite. We descended for a few days' rest and then returned to climb Mustang Himal on November 2. From high camp we crossed a low-angle glacier to reach the 40–60° north face, which we climbed on perfect névé and ice for ca 250m to the west ridge. Snow and broken granite led to the summit pinnacle, which we estimated at around 6,280m.

– MELISSA ARNOT, *USA*

DAMODAR HIMAL

NAR PHU, WEST FACE

IN NOVEMBER I led a six-member team to attempt the first known ascent of Nar Phu (5,921m HGM-Finn). This peak lies on the ridge east of the Chulu Group, north of the Kang La. It was brought onto the permitted list in 2012. We trekked for seven days to base camp, approaching Kang La from the southwest via a 1,000m scree slope, then moving north through knee-deep snow to a small glacier lake at 5,230m. From here we had a clear view of the southwest flank of Nar Phu, a large glacier leading to a steep icefall.

On November 22, Heather Bentley, Catherine Husted, Dawn Richardson, James Salt, Rhiannon Thomson, and I, with Dorje Sherpa, Shika Pandey, and Pasang Sherpa, set out at 3 a.m. We crossed a rock gorge and reached the glacier, where one and a half hours of plodding took us to the 100m icefall. A snow ramp on the right (45–70°) brought us to the upper glacier, from which we climbed the west face directly. We used running belays up 45–60° slopes covered in deep, sugary snow. About 180m from the summit we reached a very steep ice wall with a large crevasse at its foot. Fortunately, there was a well-positioned snow bridge that opened the way to the summit (PD+, 5,930m GPS, 28°43'00.71"N, 84°07'20.19"E).

– **BRIAN JACKSON**, *U.K.*

LUGULA, FIRST OFFICIAL ASCENT, SOUTH COULOIR AND WEST RIDGE

LUGULA (6,899M) is the highest point of the Lugula Himal in the most northerly section of the Annapurna Conservation Area. Seen from base camp on the Bharchapk Glacier to the south, it stands between Bhrikuti Sail (6,361m) on the left and Chako (6,704m). The east-west ridge connecting Bhrikuti Sail to Chako forms the Nepal-Tibet border.

In mid-April an eight-member expedition from the Hankuk University of Foreign Studies Alpine Club, led by Lim Il-jin, set advanced base at 5,450m, below the left side of Lugula's south face, and set about climbing the couloir falling from the col between Bhrikuti Sail and

[Above] Climbing the Biscuit Ridge. The col at the start of Lugula's west ridge is the notch visible above and right of the climbers. The ridge on the left leads to the summit of Bhrikuti Sail. *Provided by Peter Jensen-Choi*

Lugula. They placed Camp 1 on the ridge leading into the couloir. (The friable rock on this crest led them to dub it Biscuit Ridge.) Fixing ropes, they moved upward until the 18th, when they were forced down to base camp to collect the equipment needed to break through the final 80°, 60m ice face leading to the col.

On the 22nd climbing leader Hong Seung-gi forced the route to the col, and the team established Camp 2 on the crest of Lugula's west ridge. At 2:30 a.m. on the 23rd, five members, including Lim Il-jin and two Sherpas, set out for the summit. As the wind increased, Lim and two other members decided to retreat from 6,550m. The remaining climbers reached the top a little after 9 a.m.

Editor's note: An unauthorized ascent of Lugula was made in 2010. In early November a French party climbed Bhrikuti Sail by the south face and upper southwest ridge. The three French went to the summit from a bivouac halfway up the face at 6,070m, and returned to this bivouac the same night. On the 2nd one of the French reports moving east from the bivouac, gaining the west ridge of Lugula, and following it to the summit.

– *PROVIDED AND TRANSLATED BY* **LIM SUNG-MUK**, *KOREA*

PERI HIMAL

HIMLUNG HIMAL, SOUTH FLANK AND UPPER WEST RIDGE, NEW NORMAL ROUTE

IN OCTOBER I completed the new "normal route" on Himlung Himal (7,126m). This is one of the most frequented 7,000m peaks in Nepal, but the standard route via the west ridge has become increasingly exposed to avalanche danger. Three Nepalese died there in 2013. The new normal route, pioneered by a Swiss team around 2011, is interesting, relatively short, without particular difficulty (PD+), and with no objective danger. It shortcuts the previous route by ascending the south flank of the west ridge to reach its upper crest.

We began from what we are now calling the French Base Camp, which is considerably safer than the Swiss camp. In October 2014 that entire site was buried under an avalanche; on the same date in 2013 more than 50 people were camped there.

– PAULO GROBEL, *FRANCE*

LANGTANG HIMAL

NAYA KANGA, DIRECT NORTHEAST FACE; YUBRA, SOUTHWEST FACE, ATTEMPT

KIM JIN-SEOK AND OH YOUNG-HOON climbed in the Langtang Valley during February. The pair warmed up with an ascent of the easy east ridge of Gangja La Peak (5,652m), the first peak east of Gangja La. They then climbed Naya Kanga (5,863m) by the central couloir of the

[Below] Looking north onto the Kimshung Glacier. (A) Peak 6,781m (a.k.a Tsangbu Ri). (B) Langtang Yubra (6,048m). (C) Yubra (6,264m). (D) Dagpache (6,567m). Base Camp (4,200m) and Camp 1 (5,420m) are shown. *Oh Young-hoon*

[Left] The west face of Peak 6,192m showing the route Burning Kharkas, which stopped on the south-southwest ridge. [Right] In the dihedral approximately halfway up the west face of Peak 6,192m. *Photos: Evan Miles*

northeast face. The normal route on this trekking peak traverses across a large snow terrace below the northeast face to climb a little gully onto the crest of the northeast ridge, which is then followed to the summit (PD+/AD-). However, the two Koreans approached the northeast face directly, climbing around the right side of a large serac barrier to reach the western end of the snow terrace. After completing the central couloir to the summit (D for the entire ascent), the pair descended the normal route and continued down the ridge to reach their approach below the serac barrier.

After this they attempted the southwest face of Yubra (6,264m) at the head of the Yubra Glacier, but failed 200m below the summit. The pair got a permit for this peak from the Nepal Mountaineering Association, which has Yubra Himal (6,035m) to the northwest on its list of permitted peaks. Yubra probably has not had more than half a dozen ascents, by the northwest ridge or possibly the southwest face. The Koreans report a Japanese ascent on January 4.

— *INFORMATION PROVIDED BY* OH YOUNG-HOON, *KOREA*

PEAK 6,192M, WEST FACE (BURNING KHARKAS), NOT TO SUMMIT

FOLLOWING OUR AUTUMN fieldwork studying nearby glaciers, Ibai Rico (Spain) and I (USA but based in U.K.) climbed from the Langtang Valley. After acclimatizing with an ascent of Ganchempo (6,387m), we moved to the base of the Kimshung Glacier, north of Kyanjin village and elected to attempt an unnamed peak that lies to the east of the icefall outlet (28°15'10.51"N, 85°35'22.71"E, Peak 6,192m HGM-Finn map, forming the end of the west ridge of 6,567m Dragpoche/Dagpache). From the southeast corner of the Kimshung Glacier, an obvious and elegant central dihedral on the west face rises toward the summit.

After a day at base camp we ascended the steep ramp that gives access to the glacier and camped. At 1 a.m. on November 16 we started a cautious traverse of the heavily crevassed glacier, post-holing through snow in bitter cold (-25°C) and strong wind. There was a challenging lead through the bergschrund's overhanging lip, after which we simul-climbed 250m (AI2) to the base of the large dihedral. We then belayed six pitches, which varied from cruiser 65° cork ice to dead-vertical, thin, poorly protected WI5+. The terrain did not break naturally into pitches, and we needed to simul-climb 20m sections before finding a suitable belay. This resulted in mammoth 80m pitches. The dihedral came to a natural finish at a notch on the south-southwest ridge. Above, 80–100m of loose rock led toward the summit. We reached this point late in the afternoon and left the summit for a future party. Our descent involved numerous rappels from Abalakovs and the occasional piton backup, and then a downclimb of the AI2 section to the bergschrund. We regained camp at midnight. We named the route Burning Kharkas (650m, TD+ M4 WI5+ 90°). 📷 📄

– EVAN MILES, *U.K.*

DRAGMORPA RI, SOUTHEAST FACE, SECOND OFFICIAL ASCENT

ON APRIL 21 members of a 13-member Korean team—the Vision Expedition, led by Kim Tae-Hoon—summited Dragmorpa Ri (6,185m) on the Tibetan border, west of the upper reaches of the main Langtang Glacier. They ascended the southeast face. Although Dragmorpa Ri almost certainly was climbed in the past, the only previous official ascent took place on May 30, 2013, when the Russian Roman Gretzky also climbed the southeast face, starting farther left than the Koreans but sharing the same line higher up. 📷

– PETER JENSEN-CHOI, *KOREA*, ROMAN GRETZKY, *RUSSIA, AND* RODOLPHE POPIER, *FRANCE*

JUGAL HIMAL

LANGSHISA RI, NORTHWEST FACE, SNOW QUEEN

NIKITA BALABANOV, Viacheslav Polezhaiko, and I, all from the Ukraine, established base camp on the Morimoto meadow at 4,600m, opposite the northwest face of Langshisa Ri (6,412m), in October. From here we crossed the glacier and ascended 200m on moraine to an advanced base, just to the right of an icefall and below the central spur on the northwest face. During acclimatization, this approach took one and a half to two hours. At the end of our acclimatization phase we were hit by a huge snowfall at base camp—the same storm that produced tragic consequences in the Annapurna region. One meter of snow fell in two days.

One day after the storm ended, we set off for advanced base. Due to large amounts of fresh snow, from knee to waist deep, this took 12 hours. We considered taking a rest day, but decided not to waste the good weather and started climbing early next morning, October 17. Our equipment included two climbing ropes, one static rope, four ice tools (the second and third climber used one tool each), five days of food, and a satellite phone. We packed a bolt kit and aiders but used neither.

On the first day we reached the bergschrund at 4,900m, then moved into the couloir between the two main rocky ribs. We climbed together up this (fresh snow over rock slabs; 30° at start, rising to 60°), as there was almost no possibility of placing protection. Toward the top we slanted up to the left-hand rib, and at 3 p.m. reached the snowy crest, where, at 5,500m, we were able to shovel a tent platform for the night.

Day two marked the start of the technical climbing: snow-plastered rock slabs and poor ice. The leader spent much time removing fresh snow to find cracks for ice tools and crampons, and protection amounted to no more than four pieces in a 60m pitch. That day we climbed five pitches at M4/5 and 60–70°, and camped beneath a big rock buttress at 5,700m.

Next day we climbed six pitches, the leader often using the shovel and two tools for progress. Sometimes there was a meter of snow over rock, and the leader was not able to move until he'd thrown all this down on the head of his belayer. There was one particularly scary pitch on thin, hollow crust over slabs. Difficulties were again M4/M5 60–70°. At ca 5,900m we reached the start of the upper spur, where we bivouacked. On day four we climbed two pitches of M4, then four pitches of waist-deep snow, with sections of ice (WI 3/4 60–70°). On our fifth day we climbed snow and ice slopes of 50–70° with no protection. The main belay was mostly the leader sitting in a large hole he had dug. There was one pitch of perfect ice (WI 3/4), but it finished with no belay. That night we reached the large snowfield 200m below the top. The following day we slanted right to the shoulder on the southwest ridge, the leader having to shovel through chest-deep snow. Fortunately, from the shoulder, good névé led to the summit, which we reached at 11 a.m. on October 22.

The same day we returned to the shoulder and then descended the standard route on the south face to 5,700m, at first downclimbing and then rappelling ice sections from Abalakovs. Next day we continued down the face, then trekked around the mountain and back up to base camp, which we reached at nightfall. We'd had to stretch five days of food to eight and were therefore rather hungry. We named the route Snow Queen (1,500m, ED M5 WI4) after the Hans Christian Anderson tale, the large amount of snow on the approach and route, and the constant cold on the northwest face. 🖻

– **MIKHAIL FORMIN**, *UKRAINE, SUPPLIED BY* **ANNA PIUNOVA**, *MOUNTAIN.RU*

[Below] Langshisa Ri from the northwest. (1) Snow Queen (2014). (2) West-northwest face (For Kanga Chu, Two Friends, Van Morrison and a Goat, ED1 80˚, Vanja Furlan, solo, 1994); this was the first time this side of the mountain had been attempted, the first time the peak was traversed, and the first known alpine-style ascent of the mountain. *Evan Miles*

CHUGIMAGO NORTH, WEST FACE; CHEKIGO, SOUTH FACE (NO SUMMIT)

PAULA ALEGRE (Argentina) and Oriol Baro (Spain) went to the Rowaling in October with a raft of photos but no clear plans. They left with two new lines, one of them to a previously virgin summit. Alegre and Baro first cast their eyes over the south side of the Rowaling, where they spotted an unclimbed sub-summit of Chugimago, a peak of 5,945m that is best described as Chugimago North. Starting more or less in the middle of the west face, the couple slanted left through the initial rock barrier before ascending steep but relatively straightforward snow to reach the north ridge via a short section of mixed. An airy but easy crest led to the summit.

They descended most of the north ridge before downclimbing and making five rappels along the northern edge of the west face. The round trip from the base of the wall took 12 hours. Baro suffered from slight edema during the outing, with a swollen face, so the pair named their 700m line Infleti (TD).

Now acclimatized, Alegre and Baro moved to the north side of the valley for a crack at the previously unclimbed south face of Chekigo (6,257m). From the lowest point in the center of the face, they slanted left up a snow ramp to reach a depression between two vague spurs. Gaining the depression via an icefall, they climbed a dozen long pitches, steep with some mixed, to reach the west ridge. Unconsolidated snow on the ridge prompted them to stop at ca 6,150m, a few hundred meters from the top. They made a rappel descent into the wide snow couloir between Chekigo and its smaller western sub-summit Chekigo Sano, and then followed this down to the glacier and their high camp. The round trip had taken 15 hours, and the incomplete 1,050m route was named Sopeti (TD+/ED1).

– LINDSAY GRIFFIN

CHEKIGO, SOUTH FACE, SHIVA–STRAIGHT TO THE TOP

OUR FRIENDS Paula Alegre and Oriol Baro were already in the Rowaling when Jordi Corominas, Jonatan Larranaga, and I arrived. In a week or so we were at the base of Chugimago North (5,945m HGM-Finn map), planning to make the second ascent of Infleti, climbed by Oriol and Paula some days earlier. (*See previous report.*) There was a rock entry, then some mixed, and a finish over straightforward snow. It proved quite tough for us, as we were still trying to come to terms with the altitude, but the panorama, including Everest, Tengkangpoche, Tengi Ragi Tau, Menlungtse, and Gaurishankar, was unbeatable.

After two days' rest we decided to head for Chekigo (6,257m), where we had spotted a direct line up the south face to the summit. Although the line took a central spur, the initial section of the route was serious threatened by a large serac barrier to the right. We had to move fast through this section, and decided to travel light, hoping to climb and descend the face in a day. We began at midnight with a mixed section (M5) that was difficult to protect. Above were four pitches up to M4 and AI5, but as we were still "running" we had no time to enjoy them. Snowfields allowed us to move up and left, away from the serac. Next came three steps that we had observed from below the face. The first proved straightforward, but the second and third were AI5 or 5+. We were now at ca 6,000m. The climbing became a little run-out, and we were only able to place reasonable protection of a section of sustained M6. Above that, 300m of unconsolidated snow, where we had to be careful, and a little mixed climbing, led to the top.

Our idea was to descend the line taken by Oriol and Paula after their ascent of Via Sopeti.

[Photo] The south face of Chekigo. (1) South face of Chekigo Sano. (2) Descent from Via Sopeti. (3) Via Sopeti (not to summit). (4) Shiva–Straight to the Top. *Manu Cordova*

It took a long time to descend the west ridge to their exit point, but after that it was simply a question of rappelling to the bottom, which we reached 20 hours after starting the route. We named our line Shiva–Straight to the Top (1,200m, AI5/5+ M6), and felt fortunate to be able to climb a peak of which previous ascents can probably be counted on the fingers of one hand. 📷

— MANU CORDOVA, *SPAIN*

CHUGIMAGO, FIRST KNOWN ASCENT, WEST FACE

AFTER VISITED ROLWALING in 2013 (*AAJ 2014*), I headed back with new objectives. This time my partner was Sam Hennessey (U.S.), with whom I'd climbed in Yosemite. Despite the rapid growth of tourism in Rolwaling, with numerous trekking parties, the number is small relative to the Khumbu. The result is an authentic cultural experience in this traditional Sherpa land. There are also many interesting peaks and virgin faces. Our goal was Chugimago (Chukyima Go, 6,258m), and to acclimatize we went to the Ripimo Shar Glacier and its eponymous ridge, from which we could see various mountains and observe climbing conditions. We then spent three days below Chugimago, to examine the west face, and we also climbed Yalung Ri (5,647m), which gave an excellent view of the face.

Once we got a forecast for a three-day weather window, we set off and pitched our tent below the face. We were then surprised by light snowfall, so rather than soak our tent before beginning the climb, we moved beneath an overhanging boulder. Early next morning we started up the face in the dark. On the first part we met deep snow; the middle section provided excellent alpine ice and mixed, while fine fresh snow on the upper wall slowed us down. We eventually reached the north ridge and pitched our tent before sunset.

Next morning 150m separated us from the summit, but because of the sharpness of the ridge, drifted snow, and a few rocky sections, it took three hours. From the top we could see other aspects of the mountain, and it was clear Chugimago is technically demanding on all sides. We returned to our tent, descended our route, and made it back to base camp that night. We completed the ascent and descent of the 900m route over Oct 11–12, and graded it 90° M4. 📷 📄

— DOMEN KASTELIC, *SLOVENIA*

[Above] The west face of Chugimago, with the American-Slovenian route. In the foreground is Peak 5,794m. *Domen Kastelic*

[*Editor's note: Chugimago was first brought onto the permitted list in 2002. When sorting out formalities with the ministry in Kathmandu, Kastelic and Hennessey were informed that the mountain was unclimbed. Until recently, the first ascent had been credited to a Scottish party in 1952 led by Tom Mackinnon, which also claimed first ascents of the now popular trekking peaks Yalung Ri (5,647m) and Ramdung (ca 5,925m). Study of the vague reports and sketch maps—but useful photos—in their journals reveal that their third summit was not, in fact, Chugimago but instead Peak 5,794m (see also AAJ 2013). Chugimago was reportedly attempted in the 1970s—on one occasion a German team retreated 200m below the top of the north ridge. While Chugimago's location makes it likely it would have received unauthorized ascents, these would have been relatively technical and none have been reported.*

In addition, although it is clear the Scots made the first ascent of Ramdung, they did not ascend Yalung Ri, but rather the rocky summit Yalung Ri North (5,634m). The second ascents of Peak 5,794m and Ramdung were made by Alf Gregory's 1955 expedition. To avoid further confusion, heights quoted here have been taken from the HGM-Finn map.]

DRANGNAG RI, SOUTHWEST FACE AND SOUTH RIDGE, ATTEMPT

AFTER ACCLIMATIZING on Chekigo Sano, a two-person team made a spirited attempt on the magnificent southwest face of Drangnag Ri (6,757m). Starting slightly right of center from the glacier basin at 5,400m, they climbed rock to French 5, vertical ice (WI5 or 5+), and mixed terrain to reach the south ridge, where they stopped for their third bivouac (6,500m). Bad weather forced them to retreat the following day. To that point they had climbed 1,100m at TD+/ED1.

This difficult peak is awaiting a third ascent. The first, in 1995 via the east ridge, was made by Chris Bonington, Ralph Hoibakk, Bjorn Meyer-Lund, and Sherpas Lhakpa Gyalu and Pema Dorje. Bruce Normand reached the summit alone in 2005 via the west face and southwest ridge.

– LINDSAY GRIFFIN

PARCHAMO, WEST FACE; TENGI RAGI TAU, WEST FACE ATTEMPT

AFTER A SEVEN-DAY TREK with porters, Tino Villanueva and I arrived at our 5,300m base camp below the west face of Parchamo (6,279m). We had planned on objectives a little further up glacier, but the new snow that fell in mid-October and caused deaths in the Annapurna region still had not settled.

After scoping the west face of Parchamo for a couple of days, we made a recon mission to the start of the technical difficulties, giving our bodies a chance to acclimatize. On our fourth day after arriving at base camp we set off to attempt the previously unclimbed face. We felt confident the line would go and decided to travel light, taking only one 60m rope. The route involved 1,200m of technical climbing with difficulties to AI4 M5. It started with firm névé, water ice runnels, and solid granite. However, as is often the case in the Greater Ranges, the real difficulties began high on the route, with deep trail-breaking through faceted snow over steep ground. We topped out after 12 hours of mostly simul-climbing and summited in the dark.

With building winds we descended the standard route on the north ridge, as planned. Gusts of more than 40 mph and ambient air temperatures nearing 0°F made the descent rather more full value than we had hoped. On the rounded portion of the ridge we dropped a little onto the east flank in hopes of escaping frostbite-inducing gales coming from the west. This was counter-productive, as the east side cliffed out and we had to regain the crest to continue our descent. We wandered back into base camp around midnight on Halloween, but still had enough energy for a little celebration the next day.

After a much-needed break, during which we crossed Tesi Lapcha Pass to recuperate at Thame in the Khumbu, we walked to the foot of Tengi Ragi Tau's west face. We battled a steady

[Below] Alan Rousseau above 5,000m on one of the hardest pitches encountered during the attempt on the west face of Tengi Ragi Tau. *Tino Villanueva*

stream of face-numbing spindrift on the lower face, but by midday the winds had dropped and our progress was steady. Calf-burning front pointing characterized the start of the route, while a few pitches offered exciting mixed steps and thin water-ice slabs. The most engaging pitch involved feet cutting out with only a knifeblade for pro.

As the sun was setting, Tino popped onto a snow ledge just wide enough for our tent. We had arrived at our first planned bivouac, beneath a slightly overhanging wall at 6,200m. All night we could hear objects whiz past; fortunately, only small ones bounced off our ultra-thin tent.

Our second day started with a series of traverse pitches across a ribbon of alpine ice, and progress was again quick until we came to an unconsolidated convex roll. We tiptoed below and climbed a couple of loose rock pitches to bypass it. We reached our second planned bivouac site—the highest spot we felt we could sleep—with a little light left. Above was a rock band and the final exposed summit snow slopes; we had climbed more than 1,500m and were 400m below the summit. However, the spot felt too exposed to objective danger for us. We debated and then agreed to go down. In a little over eight hours, about 25 60m rappels brought us down to the base of the wall.

Once again the Rolwaling had served up exciting objectives, valuable learning experiences, as well as a big old slice of humble pie. We would like to thank the AAC for supporting us with a Lyman Spitzer Award. 📷 ▤

– ALAN ROUSSEAU, *USA*

MAHALANGUR HIMAL / KHUMBU SECTION

KANGCHO NUP, NORTH FACE, ATTEMPT

IN THE AUTUMN SEASON, David Kovarik, Tomas Svoboda, and I, from the Czech Republic, attempted the impressive north face of Kangcho Nup (a.k.a. Kangchung Nup or West, Cholo, or Abi; 6,043m HGM-Finn map). The twin Kangchung peaks (west and east) lie south of the Gyubanare Glacier, and according to all information available had seen no attempts on their steep, mixed north faces.

We approached via Gokyo, and on October 11, after acclimatization, established advanced base below the north face. During the next few days Typhoon Hudhud deposited ca 50cm of new snow. It wasn't until October 18, when conditions had stabilized, that we were able to make our attempt. The face had changed radically—slopes up to 65° were now covered in heavy snow. We climbed gullies on the right side of the face, making two bivouacs. The first, at 5,500m, was uncomfortable, with only sitting room; the second, at 5,800m was beneath a small rock tower on the west ridge. Due to the poor rock quality, protection was sometimes purely psychological and at other times impossible. Difficulties on steep sections reached WI4 M6. Just beneath the second bivouac we had a lucky break, when we released a large avalanche that completely cleaned the couloir we had just climbed. Above this bivouac, conditions got significantly worse and at around 5,900m we decided to retreat, after 1,200m of height gain.

[*Editor's note: Kangcho Nup was first climbed in early April 1953, as part of acclimatization and oxygen testing during John Hunt's Everest expedition, via the ca 50° east ridge from the col between Nup and Shar. This route was repeated the following autumn by Charles Evans and three Sherpas, who also made the first ascent of the lower Kangcho Shar (marked 6,083m on the HGM-Finn map).*] 📷

– MARTIN KLESTINEC, *CZECH REPUBLIC*

[Above] Approching the Kangcho peaks up the Gyubanare Glacier. Kangcho Shar on left. The attempted route on the north face of Kangcho Nup is marked. *Martin Klestinec*

TAWOCHE NORTHWEST, NORTHEAST FACE, ATTEMPT

ON OCTOBER 31, João Garcia (Portugal) and Angel Salamanca (Spain) made the best attempt to date to reach the virgin summit of Tawoche Northwest (6,335m), a marked top on the unclimbed northwest ridge of Tawoche (6,495m). This summit had previously been attempted in 2012 from the Cholatse-Tawoche col (*AAJ 2014*).

The pair made the first known attempt on the northeast face, hoping to make a nonstop ascent. They had difficulty accessing the bottom of this face at 4,800m, as deep autumn powder snow over hellish moraine forced them to make two gear carries. Then, starting at 4 a.m., they made a rightward-slanting ascent of the face to reach the northwest ridge of Tawoche, at ca 6,100m, left of the summit of Tawoche Northwest. They moved fast, but breakable crust or powder snow on the less steep sections proved tiring. They were continually bombarded by spindrift, and found it impossible to protect the upper 55° snow section. This steepened to a 70° exit onto the ridge via a difficult cornice, also climbed without meaningful protection. They were close to the virgin summit, but the ridge to the top looked extremely dangerous, so the two decided to retreat, using Abalakovs, snow mushrooms, and snow stakes as rappel anchors. They arrived back at their camp at 10 p.m.

The 1,300m ascent was graded TD+ V/5 M5 R, and although the team did not summit or join an existing route, they have named the line Jaime, after a mutual friend who died in a climbing accident. 📷

– *INFORMATION PROVIDED BY* **ANGEL SALAMANCA**, *SPAIN*

[Above] The east face of Lobuche East. (1) East Face Couloir. (2) Korean Route. (3) Ave Maria. (4) Two Arrows Flight. (5) East ridge. *Yuri Kilichenko, provided by Rodolphe Popier*

LOBUCHE EAST, EAST FACE, TWO ARROWS FLIGHT

ON APRIL 27, Yuri Kilichenko, Makcym Perevalov, Petro Pobebeghnyi, and Yuri Vasenkov from Ukraine completed a new route on the ca 900m east face of Lobuche (Lobuje) East. Incorrectly marked as Abi on the official HGM-Finn map of the Khumbu, Lobuche East is considered one of the more difficult trekking peaks and relatively few climbers have reached the true summit.

A Japanese team likely made the first ascent of the 6,090m-peak, via the southeast ridge, in 1979. Over four days in late October 1984 Todd Bibler and Catherine Freer climbed the east ridge, which rises above the screes northwest of Lobuche village. They reported difficulties up to 5.8, though an American repeat in 1990 took five days and found difficulties of 5.9 and A1. The first ascent of the east face took place in spring 1986, when Henry Kendall and Jeff Lowe climbed a snow/ice couloir well left of the main rock wall. Alison Hargreaves and Mark Twight repeated this line a few days later. The East Face Couloir (TD, Scottish 5) exits onto the southeast ridge, and some subsequent ascensionists have found it can be very thin.

In September 1990 the Czech brothers Michal and Miroslav Coubal forced a route directly up the center of the steep, slabby rock wall of the face, creating Ave Maria (UIAA VIII-) in a five-day, alpine-style ascent. Two years later, in September 1992, and on their third attempt, Koreans Kim Jae-soo, Lee Sung-chun, and Park Young-sik started left of Ave Maria, slanted up to join it after a few pitches, then moved left, climbing 20–50m left of the Coubal route before crossing it again near the top. They completed their route over 15 days, using fixed rope. After climbing the first 13 difficult pitches (some sections overhanging) they were caught by bad weather but continued up the remaining six and a half pitches to the top of the face without incident.

The new Ukrainian route lies roughly midway between Ave Maria and the east ridge. The four men first climbed an ice couloir (up to 70°) behind a buttress separated from the face, then followed this with four 60m pitches up the steep lower rock wall. Difficulties here were A2/A3 and 6b, with around 40 percent of the climbing on aid. The angle now eased, and the team set up a bivouac (ca 5,570m) and the same day fixed their ropes up to the base of the second steep section. They spent two nights at the bivouac site to recover from the exertions of the first day. Up to this point they found traces of a previous attempt: three or four old bolts with carabiners on the lower wall, and slings, bolts, and carabiners at the first bivouac site. They estimated these to be around 10 years old.

The four Ukrainians climbed the second wall in four 60m pitches, up to 6b, before making a second bivouac at ca 5,950m, just below the east ridge. Here they were forced to break into their emergency provisions: a can of morale-boosting red caviar. Next day they finished up the top section of the east ridge (straightforward climbing over rock, ice, and snow), reaching the summit at 1:30 p.m. They descended the normal route (southeast ridge) in bad weather and reached the village of Lobuche the same day. About 40 percent of the route was climbed in rock shoes, the rest in more conventional boots. The rock was generally compact, but with many detached blocks, which the climbers had to negotiate carefully. They placed a few bolts at belays. They named the route Two Arrows Flight (Russian 6A), because, looking up at the two steep sections from below, they realized they would have to climb both in a direct line.

– *INFORMATION PROVIDED BY* **YURI KILICHENKO**, *UKRAINE,* **RODOLPHE POPIER**, *THE HIMALAYAN DATABASE, FRANCE, AND* **LIM SUNG-MUK**, *MAN AND MOUNTAIN, KOREA*

LHOTSE, SOUTH FACE, ATTEMPT

FROM EARLY SEPTEMBER to early November, Hong Sung-taek (leader), Choi Jin-cheol, Choi Hyung-woo, Jun Jae-min, Lim Jun-ho, and several climbing Sherpas attempted the south face of Lhotse. This was Hong's third expedition to the south face. In difficult conditions, with nearly continuous snowfall, the team followed parts of several routes or previous attempts to 7,700m before retreating. 📷 📄

– *INFORMATION PROVIDED BY* **PETER JENSEN-CHOI**, *KOREA*

THAMSERKU, SOUTHWEST FACE, SHY GIRL

FROM APRIL 27 TO MAY 3, Alexander Gukov and Alexey Lonchinskiy from St. Petersburg, Russia, made the coveted first ascent of the southwest face of Thamserku (6,618m). Despite being an obvious target, within easy distance of Monjo (much of the southwest face is seen by Everest trekkers during their ascent to Namche Bazaar), there had been only one known previous attempt. In October 1986 the four-man Spanish team of Jose Manuel Gonzales, Jose Luis Fernandez, Azucana Lopez, and Miguel Rodriguez first climbed to a bivouac at 5,700m in the prominent central couloir. The next day they continued through a difficult rock barrier (65°–90°) to a second bivouac in an ice cave at 5,900m. On the third day they reached 6,300m, where they used hammocks to bivouac. By now they were experiencing significant problems with their stoves, and next morning they found the gas had leaked and there was no way they could melt snow. Reluctantly, they abandoned the climb a little over 300m below the top.

Before their attempt, the two Russians ascended the Kyashar Khola from Monjo toward base camp for the normal route on Kusum Kanguru. Camping in the main valley at ca 4,100m, they made an acclimatization attempt on Point 5,572m, which lies on the northwest ridge of Kusum Kanguru. They failed, descended to Monjo, and then traveled to Island Peak, which they summited, camping for the night at 6,000m.

Returning to Monjo, they headed once more along the Kyashar Khola before striking up the hillside to the left, toward the southwest face of Thamserku. There were no paths; they kept right of a long spur, wading through dense bush and over grassy talus. With heavy packs it took them two full days to reach a pleasant base camp at 4,850m.

From there they set off in alpine style, carrying a small tent without poles that they could

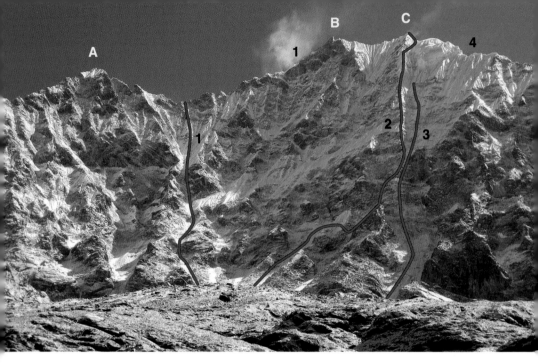

[Above] Southwest face of Thamserku. (A) Pt. 6,341m. (B) Rocky foresummit (ca 6,600m). (C) Main top (6,618m). (1) Japanese Route (1979, approximate line). The Japanese continued up the west ridge to the summit. (2) Shy Girl (2014). (3) Spanish attempt (1986). (4) Upper south ridge (1964, New Zealand). (5) Russian descent in 2014. [Below left] The Russians carried a tent with no poles for their seven bivouacs on Thamserku. [Below right] Pitch two on the southwest face of Thamserku. *Photos provided by Anna Piunova, Mountain.ru*

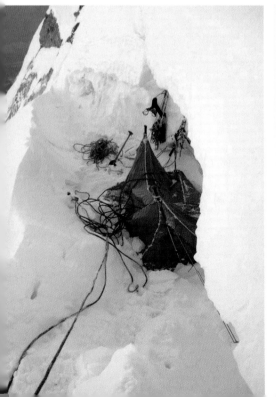

use as a sort of hammock where there was nowhere big enough to cut a tent platform. The pair took the objectively safer central spur, immediately left of the couloir attempted by the Spanish. Gukov and Lonchinskiy made six bivouacs before reaching the summit, finding the climbing to be mainly snow, ice, and mixed, with an average steepness of around 70°. There were many sections of M4–M5, and four pitches of A2: two right at the start, and two in the steep, rocky middle part of the spur, immediately above the second bivouac. The second pitch after this bivy was probably the crux (and was exposed to spindrift), and the following pitch also was difficult, stretching to 80m because of the impossibility of arranging a belay earlier.

From the top they descended the south ridge for seven rope lengths, bivouacking for a seventh time at 6,300m, before making 22 rappels down the southwest face to the glacier. They measured the height of the face as 1,623m, and estimate a total climbing distance of 1,900m to the summit. They named the route Shy Girl, and consider the overall grade to be Russian 6A/6B.

To date there have only been six confirmed ascents of Thamserku, four of these from the south. The peak was first climbed in 1964 by members of Edmund Hillary's Himalayan Schoolhouse expedition. Lynn Crawford, Pete Farrell, John McKinnon, and Richard Stewart approached the south ridge from the basin below the southwest face, climbed a difficult couloir onto the crest, and then followed it a long distance to the summit. They found the climbing to be exceptionally difficult—much like a technical ascent in the Andes, with steep flutings, mushrooms, and cornices. Four camps, 1,200m of fixed rope, and 30m of rope ladder were used. The route has never been repeated in its entirety, though the Korean team that made the fourth ascent of the peak in 1984 reached the south ridge from the east.

In 1979 a Japanese team climbed a spur left of the main southwest face to reach the crest of the west ridge at a col right of the prominent 6,341m top on the crest. Just below this point they made their last camp, at 6,300m. From there Sakai Hosogai and Satoshi Kimura set out for the summit and found difficult climbing to get to the rocky foresummit at ca 6,600m. Here they were forced to bivouac before continuing to the main top next day.

– **LINDSAY GRIFFIN**, *FROM INFORMATION PROVIDED BY* **ANNA PIUNOVA**, *MOUNTAIN.RU*

SAKATON, SOUTHWEST FACE

AFTER PASSING INITIATION TESTS in Benasque during a cold weekend in February 2012, the new Spanish team for alpinism (Equipo Español de Alpinismo) began its training and improvement program in the Pyrenees and Alps. For two years, led by Mikel Zabalza, director of training, the group climbed great routes—even new ones on some of Spain's famous walls. And so we came to the final expedition. Mikeltxo Ajuria, Roger Cararach, Alberto Fernandez, Faust Punsola, Mikel Zabalza, and I found ourselves in the Kyashar Valley. The month we had available did not seem long enough for all the potential objectives.

Our first acclimatization peak was Kusum Kanguru Northwest (5,572m), which gave us a beautiful climb up the southeast ridge (300m, V M). We then split the team to climb the east ridge of Kusum Kanguru East as far as a small summit of ca 5,900m (600m, 70° V+ M), and the northeast ridge of Kusum Kanguru Northwest (500m, IV+). Then it was time for the main objectives: Mikel, Mikeltxo, and I would go for the west ridge of Kyashar, while the other three would try a new line on a peak that we would subsequently call Sakaton. [*This is Peak 6,325m on the long south ridge of Kangtega. On the opposite side this top rises only a little way above the glacier.*]

Snow conditions were bad, and we were forced down from both peaks. Bad weather kept us pinned at base, where there was 30cm of fresh snow. With one week left in the expedition, we all set off for Sakaton, hoping a sunnier aspect would provide more consolidated snow.

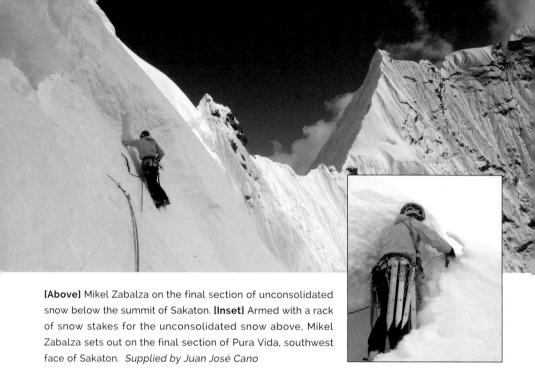

[Above] Mikel Zabalza on the final section of unconsolidated snow below the summit of Sakaton. [Inset] Armed with a rack of snow stakes for the unconsolidated snow above, Mikel Zabalza sets out on the final section of Pura Vida, southwest face of Sakaton. *Supplied by Juan José Cano*

Mikel, Alberto, and I went first; Roger, Fausto, and Mikeltxo would follow a day later.

We slept the first night at the foot of the southwest face, then followed a wide couloir of 50° threatened by a serac. We climbed unroped for speed, finally slanting left with some relief to the ridge and a rocky area. We climbed 100m up the crest and made our second bivouac. While Mikel excavated the tent platform, Alberto and I climbed two mixed pitches of M5. That night our friends slept at the foot of the face.

Next day we climbed rapidly, simul-climbing slopes of 50–70°, always on the south flank, where we felt the snow would be more stable. We passed the high point of our group's previous attempt, and then climbed big slopes of snow and ice (sections of 70–80°) to reach a shoulder

[Below] Looking northeast over the Kyashar Glacier toward: (A) Thamserku (6,618m), (B) Kangtega North (6,685m), (C) Kangtega (6,783m), (D) Sakaton, with Pura Vida marked. Part of Kyashar (6,770m) is seen on the right. *Supplied by Juan José Cano*

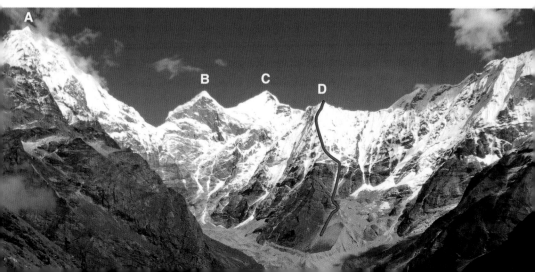

at 6,200m, breathless. At this point poor snow made upward progress difficult, but watching Mikel gave us a lesson in negotiating adverse snow conditions, and when all three of us reached the summit it was a marvelous moment.

Twenty rappels saw us back at our top bivouac during the night. There we found our colleagues resting in preparation for their summit attempt. When we awoke they were already high on the mountain—they climbed through most of the night and reached the top while we were still descending. We named the route Pura Vida (1,300m, TD+ M5 80°) as a tribute to the late Iñaki Ochoa, who had been a friend of Mikel since childhood.

With this journey we reached the end of an important part of our training to be alpinists. There have been many different experiences over the last few years, which without doubt will help us understand better this strange game, our passions, and the mountains.

– *INFORMATION FROM* JUAN JOSÉ CANO, *TRANSLATED BY* CORAL ESTEVEZ, *SPAIN*

LUMBA SUMBA HIMAL

LUMBA SUMBA PEAK, NORTH RIDGE

ON APRIL 22, Dave Barker, Phil Booth, Ken Hopper, Rory Sellar, and Paul Vardy (U.K.) made the first known ascent of Lumba Sumba Peak (5,740m), the most easterly and lowest of a collection of three summits sometimes called the Three Sisters. The remote Lumba Sumba Himal lies between the massifs of Makalu and Kangchenjunga, with Lumba Sumba Peak situated just south of a recently developed trekking route connecting the Tamur River Valley in the east to the Arun Valley in the west. The high point of this trek is Lumba Sumba Pass at 5,155m.

Approaching Lumba Sumba Peak from the north through deep sugar snow, the climbers crossed the long north ridge, making an advanced camp at 5,160m. Next day they followed a wide hidden couloir leading to steep ground at the right edge of the northeast glacier. Above this steep terrain, they were able to follow the glacier and climb steep snow slopes to the crest of the north ridge, which they followed for 250–300m to the summit. Given conditions on the day, the overall grade was considered to be TD-, with sections of Scottish III.

Lumba Sumba and Lumba Sumba Peak appeared on an earlier list of permitted mountains, with heights of 5,670m and 5,672m, respectively, but with no coordinates. By cross-referencing information and photos from trip reports detailing the traverse of Lumba Sumba Pass, using up-to-date maps and Google Earth, the team was able to determine that Peak 5,740m on the HGM-Finn map was Lumba Sumba Peak. 🖸

– LINDSAY GRIFFIN, *WITH INFORMATION FROM* PAUL VARDY

OHMI KANGRI HIMAL

PABUK KANG, CORRECTION

THE NAME OF THE PEAK climbed by Tim-Macartney Snapes' team in 2010 is not Pabuk Kang, as stated in *AAJ 2011*, but Nangamari I, labeled as Peak 6,547m on the HGM-Finn map. Pabuk Kang (6,244m) lies on the frontier ridge approximately two kilometers to the east. The origin of the name Nangamari is uncertain, but older Swiss maps designate the peak Nangayama.

– RODOLPHE POPIER, *THE HIMALAYAN DATABASE, FRANCE*

NUPCHU, CLARIFICATION

AAJ 2014 PUBLISHED a panorama looking from Syao Kang toward the Kangchenjunga massif, on which was marked the peak Nupchu (6,044m). While this correctly identifies the peak marked as "Nupchu" on the HGM-Finn map, it is not the peak climbed in 1962 by Sasuke Nakao's Japanese expedition and named Nupchu. The Japanese climbed a separate peak about 2km west along the watershed ridge, marked on HGM-Finn with a spot height of 6,172m. To avoid confusion, it is proposed that this be referred to as Nupchu I, and the unclimbed lower peak as Nupchu II (6,044m).

Nupchu I has two tops, and the east top is the one marked on the map at 6,172m. However, Google Earth implies the west is perhaps slightly higher. It is not completely clear whether the Japanese, who made their final ascent from the east, continued the short distance to the west top. The Japanese also named "Sato Peak," which is Point 5,788m on the HGM-Finn map, south of Nupchu I.

– LINDSAY GRIFFIN *AND* RODOLPHE POPIER, *FROM INFORMATION PROVIDED BY*
RICHARD SALISBURY, *THE HIMALAYAN DATABASE*

KANGCHENJUNGA HIMAL

BOKTOH CENTRAL, NEW ROUTE AND TRAVERSE

NOT FAR FROM the famous peaks of Kangchenjunga and Jannu, the Dudh Pokhari (or Yamatari) Glacier basin offers beautiful peaks for lovers of unspoiled corners of the Himalaya. Boktoh, east of the Lapsang La, has a steep and impressive north face. The main summit (6,114m) was climbed in 1991 during the Slovenian Kangchenjunga expedition, when Marko Prezelj, Uros Rupar, and Andrej Stremfelj ascended the east ridge from the south, while acclimatizing for greater things. The central summit (6,037m HGM-Finn) was believed to be unclimbed.

Hélias Millerioux, Rémi Sfilio, and I arrived in Kathmandu in early October, and on the 11th set off for Taplejung. Boktoh is in the Kangchenjunga Conservation Area, a protected region where trekking permits and a Nepalese guide are required. After 16 hours on a bus and 10 hours on a jeep (where there were 19 people crowded into nine places) we reached Taplejung, and on the 13th, with five porters, set out on foot. Happy, finally, to stretch our legs, we took four days to reach Ghunsa, where we took a day's rest. On the 18th we set off to acclimatize, eventually reaching a 5,400m col opposite the mountain, where we spent the next two days reading books and studying the north face of Boktoh.

There were three lines on the north face. We dismissed one as being too threatened by serac fall; the other two were both attractive, and we opted for a couloir on the right, leading to the west-northwest ridge of the central summit.

We then made two attempts on the line. On the first, we gave up quickly in heavy snowfall. We decided to hide our supplies before returning to Ghunsa, as Nyunchutui (snow leopard) are known to frequent this area.

We returned to advanced base on October 29 and set sail at midnight, reaching the bergschrund (4,600m) in two hours, and climbing the first 300m snow/ice slope by daybreak. Technical alpinism in the Himalaya normally follows a pattern of climbing economically during the initial days, then giving it all on summit day. We did exactly the opposite, prompted by the configuration of the face and the reasonable altitude.

Rémi opened play with a steep pitch of WI5. The route continued over ice and mixed toward a very steep corner we had scoped from below. This was the crux: Iced chimneys, delicate mixed, very steep ice steps, and poor protection kept our nerves on edge. Night caught up with us after these three difficult pitches, and we began to feel the altitude. The last 30m to the ridge should have been easy, along a straightforward snow slope. However, with totally unconsolidated snow it took almost as much time as the technical pitches. Finally, 23 hours after leaving the tent, we arrived on the ridge at 5,600m, where we made our first bivouac. The 950m couloir below had contained passages flirting with WI6 and sections of M5. We chopped out a tent platform and finally got to sleep at 2 a.m.

We woke at 6 a.m., were slow to get started, and left at 8:30, deciding to avoid

[Right] Jonathan Crison in the narrow corner that forms the central and crux section of the French route on the north face of Boktoh Central. [Below] North face of Boktoh with Nyunchutui and the Snow Cougar. (A) Boktoh La. (B) Boktoh Main (east). (C) Boktoh Central. (D) Boktoh Southwest. *Photos: Hélias Millerioux*

[Above] The Boktoh Glacier rises to Tso Kang South (6,000m), with Boktoh La hidden on the right. There are no recorded ascents of this fine peak, though the higher Central Summit (6,111m) was climbed in 1959 by René Desmaison and Lionel Terray. *Rémi Sfilio*

a rock buttress on the arête by dropping 100m down the south flank to a hanging glacier, then ascending this and rejoining the ridge via a couloir. After 400m of mixed climbing we were back on the crest at 2 p.m. Progress along the ridge was now painfully snow, due to unconsolidated snow and exposure. At 5 p.m. we stopped for our second bivouac at 6,000m, where the ridge terminated on a small glacier plateau.

Less than 1km now separated us from the main (east) summit of Boktoh, but due to snow conditions we abandoned the idea of traversing to this summit and descending the original route, and settled for the central top. (This had no recorded ascent, but one can't rule out the possibility of an unauthorized climb.) We measured the height as 6,074m. We reached the top at 9 a.m., happy-ish but feeling a bit like a cat that has climbed a tree and now wonders how to get down. Our meows, however loud, would have no effect. Toward the southwest we saw a glacial plateau leading to the top of a spur (designated Boktoh Southwest) that appeared to drop directly to Lapsang Pass (5,100m). We decided to chance our luck.

Descending 300m of ice flutes to reach the plateau, we crossed it slowly to find there was a series of arêtes descending west-southwest toward the valley. There were several possibilities but only one solution, starting to the south of Boktoh Southwest. Finally, after much downclimbing, several rappels, and a fine snow couloir, we reached the pass. It was 4 p.m. and we were amazed, as we thought a bivouac was inevitable during the descent.

Ghunsa and dahl bat were only six hours away, and the prospect of more synthetic food at advanced base had no appeal. We rang our Nepalese friends in Ghunsa to order the meal, then set off. This should have been straightforward, but we lost the trail in the night, ended up playing bushmen in the forest, and waded rivers up to our waist. We reached the village at 11 p.m. Our summit success was not good news for everyone in town: Next day we celebrated by eating a number of chickens. We named our route Nyunchutui and the Snow Cougar (1,400m, WI 5+/6 M5 90°). 📷

— JONATHAN CRISON, *FRANCE*

KANGCHENJUNGA, NORTHWEST FACE AND NORTH RIDGE, VARIANTS

In the pre-monsoon season the international team of Adam Bielecki, Artem Braun, Dimtry Sinev, Alex Txikon, and Denis Urubko planned a new direct route up the northwest face of Kangchenjunga (8,586m). After arrival at base camp on April 20, however, a few days of observation showed regular serac fall on the proposed line. They switched their main objective to the north ridge, the original 1979 British-French line on this side of the mountain.

They established Camp 1 at 6,000m, and on the 29th Bielecki found a difficult but safe line to reach their proposed site for Camp 2 at 6,600m on the northwest flank. At that time the team was unaware that this line, to the right of the original route to the north col, had been climbed in 1983 by a Bavarian group. Above Camp 2, where the Bavarian route heads off right up the northwest face, this year's team opened a new 450m variant, following a leftward slanting route on steep snow and ice slopes.

The team established Camp 3 on the crest of the ridge on May 8. To reach this point they had climbed 20 pitches, fixing the entire wall with 1,000m of rope. On May 9 they fixed their last 250m of rope to 7,300m and sent a message to Kathmandu to request more. This duly arrived, and on the 17th Bielecki and Txikon climbed through the Castle, a 150m rock step giving access to the upper snowfields. They avoided the normal couloir by three long new pitches on rock to the right (up to M5). This section was fixed and Camp 4 placed at ca 7,650m.

Bielecki, Sinev, and Txikon set off next day with bivouac gear, planning to traverse the mountain. Braun and Urubko left later but decided the slope was too dangerous and went back to Camp 4. The first three broke trail to 8,350m, where they decided it was too late in the day to continue. They regained camp after 22 hours of hard effort, with Txikon suffering from frostbite in his thumb. At first they decided they all would go down the next day, but during the night Urubko had a change of heart. Leaving at 5:10 a.m. on the 19th, he followed the track past the high point and reached the summit at 9:40 a.m.

While some of Urubko's new routes on 8,000m peaks, such as Cho Oyu and Broad Peak, have been more difficult, he felt the north ridge of Kangchenjunga to be the hardest existing route he'd climbed. Lamentably, the team left all their fixed rope on the mountain. 📷 🗐

— LINDSAY GRIFFIN, *WITH INFORMATION FROM* DENIS URUBKO, *RUSSIA, AND* RODOLPHE POPIER, *THE HIMALAYAN DATABASE, FRANCE*

[Below] Alex Txikon on the northwest face of Kangchenjunga at 6,200m. *Denis Urubko*

LADAKH

KISHTWAR / ZANSKAR

HIMACHAL PRADESH   CHINA

GAHRWAL / KUMAUN

PAKISTAN

•Dehli

NEPAL

INDIA   SIKKIM

INDIA

EAST KARAKORAM

[Above] Looking west from the summit of Tusuhm Kangri. (A) Peak 6,222m. (B) Nya Kangri (6,520m; Divyesh Muni's expedition attempted this in 2008 but was unsuccessful on the south ridge). (C) Main Rassa Glacer. (D) Glacier 2. *Rajesh Gadgil*

RASSA GLACIER, TUSUHM KANGRI, RASSA KANGRI, GENERAL EXPLORATION

IN 2001 A GLIMPSE of the Rassa Glacier during our expedition to the Arganglas Valley (*AAJ 2002*) indicated great potential for climbs and exploration. Due to security restrictions and a remote location, many mountains and valleys of the East Karakoram have been left untouched. In mid-July, Rajesh Gadgil, Vineeta Muni, Atin Sathe, and I, along with several Sherpa climbers, trekked three days up the Arganglas Valley until stopped by a raging river originating from the Phunangma Glacier. We were forced to trek to the glacier and cross the icy snout in order to continue to our base camp at 4,820m below the Rassa Glacier.

On August 2 we established an advanced base at 5,220m and began to explore one of the many subsidiary branches of the Rassa, dubbing it simply Glacier 1. From a camp at 5,780m we attempted Peak 6,219m and succeeded on our second attempt, after fixing 300m of rope on the southwest face. We named the peak Tusuhm Kangri (34°39' N, 77°51' E), which in Ladakhi means triangular peak in the corner. (All coordinates and altitudes are from our own GPS readings.)

On August 18 we reached a new camp at 5,635m at the northwest corner of Glacier 2, but a quick reconnaissance convinced us that we would have better climbing options on

Glacier 3 to the north. By the 20th we were at a high camp (5,810m) on this glacier, below Peak 6,250m, one of the most prominent summits in the area.

Next day we climbed a southeast-facing, 200m ice face (50-60°) to gain the summit ridge, which we followed to the west along a knife-edge. Given the prominence of this peak, we christened it Rassa Kangri (34°40 N, 77°49' E). Next day we reached the head of the glacier and Shukpa Pass (6,110m), which we saw gave gentle access to the South Shukpa Kunchang Glacier, and onward to the Shyok River. This could provide a possible alternative to the well-known Saser La for linking the Nubra and Shyok valleys.

Our thoughts were now on exploring an alternative route back to the Nubra, and we had been eyeing a high col that would lead us to the Sumur Nala further north. On August 25, after ascending Glacier 5 and then failing to cross the West Rassa La (5,930m), Rajesh, Atin, Vineeta, Pasang, and I ascended Glacier 4 and reached the East Rassa La (6,000m) by 11 a.m. We were relieved to find a feasible route down the far side. That night we camped at a beautiful spot by Sumur Lake (5,230m), and the next day walked down the remaining 18km of Sumur Valley to the Nubra at Samsthaling Monastery.

— DIVYESH MUNI, *HIMALAYAN CLUB, INDIA*

RONGDO VALLEY, MARIUSHRI, SOUTH FACE AND SOUTHWEST RIDGE; TARA, NORTH RIDGE; AMITABHA, NORTHWEST FACE AND RIDGE

RONGDO IS A REMOTE VALLEY in the eastern part of the Nubra. Historians of South Asia are familiar with this area, as it holds an ancient trade route between Yarkand and northern India (part of the Silk Road). Rongdo Valley is located south of the original trade route, on the east side of the Shyok River. The area has seen virtually no tourists, save for a very small number of climbers and researchers.

Having met our congenial liaison officer, Tongpangkokba Jamir, in Leh, on July 28, Graham Rowbotham and I traveled the intermittently disappearing sand road to Rongdo

[Below] The summit ridge of Amitabha (6,335m). *Graham Rowbotham*

village (3,270m), where it was wonderful to meet locals who remembered me from 2012 (*AAJ 2013*). Over the next three days, we walked northeast for ca 21km to our 2012 base camp at 4,802m. We placed two advanced base camps up a south arm of the southeast Shukpa Kunchang Glacier, the higher at 5,880m.

On August 13 Graham climbed the wedge-shaped peak north of ABC 2. He followed the south face and southwest ridge to the 6,167m summit, which he named Mariushri (male Bodhisattva of wisdom; PD). On the 15th, fairly clear skies in the morning prompted us to depart early for the peak just above camp. We followed the broken north ridge and mixed snow and ice slopes to a section of delightful ice climbing at ca 45°. The rocky summit was cold and windy; the GPS read 6,248m. We named the peak Tara (female Bodhisattva of compassion; AD).

We returned to base camp and on the 20th moved down to the last camp we had made before reaching base, at a ca 4,600m shepherds' encampment. From there we moved up a valley to the southeast, where we established a new advanced base at 4,952m. Graham left at 3 the following morning and soloed a 500m rock gully to a wet, slabby ramp and ice slope leading to the northwest face of a high peak. The face led to the northwest ridge, which he followed over a foresummit and several rock towers to the main summit at 6,335m. Graham named the peak Amitabha (Buddha of infinite light; AD+). 📷 🗎

– JOIE SEAGRAM, *CANADA*

LADAKH

LUNGMOCHEY KANGRI, NORTHEAST RIDGE

IN LATE AUGUST, Chuck Boyd, liaison officer Suman ("Hapi") Kant, Ladakhi sirdar/guide Stanzin Desal, and I climbed the northern and most accessible summit in a cirque south of Hundar and Wachan. The peaks of this cirque, rising to 6,000–6,070m, form part of the east rim of the Thanglasgo Valley. We climbed along the snow-stone boundary forming the crest of the northeast ridge and never felt the need to break out a rope. At the summit our altimeters read 6,070m. We noticed that the west slope was easier and fairly snow free, so we descended that way. With Stanzin's help we named the peak Lungmochey Kangri, after the local name for the cirque. 📷 🗎

– ANDY SELTERS, *USA*

TELTHOP, NORTHWEST FACE AND SOUTHWEST RIDGE

TELTHOP (6,185M) is situated north of Leh and is accessed via the Kardung La (at 5,350m the highest motorable road in the world) and Nubra Valley. This is an area of considerable political and military sensitivity, and the majority of peaks above 6,000m require an X visa from the Indian government, plus an Indian Army liaison officer.

Starting from Hundar village, we followed a steep valley rising southeast. Three days of trekking, with an ascent of 1,500m, took us to base camp in a wide, green valley at 4,800m. From here a line of five peaks extends to the south: Telthop is the highest and most southerly peak in this range (older maps confusingly mark this peak farther northeast).

We placed an advanced base at 5,100m, below the glaciated northwest face of Telthop, bounded by the north and southwest ridges. We left camp at 1 a.m. and climbed 250m up steep moraine and then 130m of 70° hard ice on the left side of the snout to reach a level section of

[Above] The northwest face of Telthop. *Chris Horobin*

glacier at ca 5,500m. We climbed the northwest face direct and then accessed the north ridge higher up, just below some rocky steps. After a final climb on steep and loose rock, the summit was reached at around 10:30 a.m. by Matt Barnsley, Roland Chuter, Bob Shiels, and me (all U.K.), Chuck Boyd (USA), Dawa Narbu Sherpa, Tashi Phunchok Zangola, and Liaison Officer Virender Singh (all Indian), and Phujung Bhote (Nepal). In descent we reversed the route to the point where we had accessed the ridge, then dropped down steep and extremely loose rock/scree slopes to the glacier under the southwest face. We gave the route an overall grade of D. 📷 🗎

— CHRIS HOROBIN, *U.K.*

RUPSHU, VARIOUS FIRST KNOWN ASCENTS

IN JUNE AND JULY, Karl Herberger made a number of solo ascents of high peaks in this area. On June 27 he traversed Peak 6,100m from east to west and then climbed the southeast ridge of Spangnak Ri (6,390m). Peak 6,100m (a.k.a. Kiager Ri) is a largely dry peak that was climbed via the west ridge by Indians in 2012. Spangnak Ri's southeast ridge was climbed twice in 2012, the year the peak was officially opened to climbing, and had been climbed prior to this by the southwest face.

On July 1 Herberger climbed the northwest ridge of Chalung North (a.k.a. Kula North, 6,405m, 33.1526°N, 78.4209°E).

On July 13 he climbed Shuchule (6,535m, 32.9926°N, 78.5102°E). He first climbed Shuchule West (ca 6,470m) from the west, but then found the connecting ridge to the main summit unsafe, so he descended southeast until picking up the southwest ridge of Shuchule, which he followed to the top.

Herberger's last mountain was Peak ca 6,295m (33.8201°N, 78.2325°E) in the Eastern Ladakh Range, an easily accessible top on a long ridge rising south from the Leh road, south of Pangong Lake. He climbed the south ridge (UIAA III) and descended the south face. 📷

— EBERHARD JURGALSKI, *GERMANY*

ZANSKAR

CHOMOTANG GROUP, MACHU KANGRI, EAST RIDGE AND TRAVERSE

MACHU KANGRI (6,086m), west of Leh, is located 8km south of the Sisir La and 12km southeast of Chomotang. In mid-June, Karl Herberger (Germany), well acclimatized and approaching over the Sisir La, made a bivouac at ca 4,700m, north of the peak. Next day, June 20, he climbed to the east ridge and continued over several tops and a foresummit to the main peak (34.0295°N, 76.7941°E GPS), which he reached at 4 p.m. He descended to the west and returned to his bivouac that night. 📷

— EBERHARD JURGALSKI, *GERMANY*

GOLDEN SENTINEL, NORTHWEST FACE

GALINA CHIBITOK (Russia) and Marina Kopteva (Ukraine) spent seven days in September making the first ascent of the 900m northwest face of Golden Sentinel (ca 5,200m). They graded the route 6B (VI A2/A3). Golden Sentinel is the second major rock tower north of Shafat Fortress (ca 5,900m), first climbed by Jonny Copp and Micah Dash in 2007. An Italian expedition, the CAI Curbattt Group, made the first ascent of Golden Sentinel, also in 2007, approaching from the Suru Valley. The Italians climbed two routes: the north ridge and the east face, both at UIAA VI. 📷

— LINDSAY GRIFFIN, *FROM INFORMATION SUPPLIED BY* ANNA PIUNOVA

KANGE VALLEY, VARIOUS FIRST ASCENTS

PROMPTED BY SERGI RICART, a guide, photographer, and great friend since adolescence, Sidarta Gallego and I decided to forgo our main mountain guiding season and head for Zanskar. Our objective was a peak we knew only as "Tapion," a photo of which had been my computer wallpaper for some time. We arrived in Leh in late June.

Our goal lay at the head of a side valley immediately before reaching the Pensi La, but the river that guards the entrance was so high, even early in the morning, that we were unable to gain access. We were forced to turn to Plan B. This was the Kange Valley, situated farther east toward Padam. Here we had no problem entering the valley, thanks to a footbridge seen previously on Google Earth. We established base camp near the foot of the glacier at a place known as Rapsail Demo.

Close by, a 5,400m rocky summit, Yun Ri, provided our first route, Tempesta Nocturna (700m, 6b). The summit, situated on the west side of the valley and with no known ascents, was a splendid vantage point on our next objectives. After one day's rest, we loaded big packs and headed to the top of the valley and a peak we called Kange Ri (6,020m). We reached the top by the 1,200m north face. It was classical snow/ice climbing at TD+, and we named the route Via Grifone after our sponsor. We descended south, which proved harder and longer than expected.

After another rest day, we felt ready to explore one of the biggest faces around, on an unclimbed summit, which we named Piri Ri (5,850m), on the east side of the valley. On the first day we climbed five pitches and went back to camp. On the second day we reached the top of pitch 20. Up to this point we had climbed good granite, although many rope lengths were very wet; we used rock shoes but no chalk! Here we made a bivouac without sleeping bags. The following day we continued over snow, ice, and rock, and then the mixed west ridge, the last

[Photo] The 1,200m Via Grifone on the north face of Kange Ri. *Oriol Baro*

200m testing our weakened state. We reached the summit by noon, and named the route Es Falles (1,550m, VI/4 M4 6b A1).

To the right of this route is a steep rock buttress with a conspicuous pinnacle at around half height. We next climbed this lower buttress to the summit of the pinnacle, finding signs of previous passage along the way (1,080m, 6c A2+). After fixing our climbing ropes, we climbed this route with one bivouac.

With the weather still holding, there was no question of wasting time, and we headed off to Rapsail Ri, a small rock peak (5,000m maximum) on the east side of the valley, only 20

[Photo] Piri Ri from the west. (1) Es Falles. (2) Previously climbed route to pinnacle. *Oriol Baro*

[Above] Kang Yatze from the north showing the Spanish line (possibly new) to the northwest ridge. *Sidarta Gallego*

minutes' walk from our base camp. Here, on the west face, we opened Via del Luichy (300m, 7a), dedicated to Luis Alfonso, a friend and prolific author of climbing guidebooks. The route terminated before the summit. This completed 21 days at or above base camp, in an area where there are still many possibilities.

After time off in Padam, we decided to attempt our original goal in alpine style from Pensi La. Crossing the river was exciting, but this time we got to the mountain. We spent two days walking to its base, took a day off in bad weather, and then made our attempt. Unfortunately, we were forced to retreat in a storm. We later found that this elegant peak was the twin-summited Z2 (6,175m), first climbed in 1977 by Italians via the south ridge. Our route, the south ridge of the lower (6,080m) of the two summits, had been attempted by Italians in 1982. We climbed past the smooth granite slab that had stopped the Italians, and the way ahead looked easier, but….

Back in Leh we still had a week before our return flight and decided to climb the popular trekking peak Kang Yatze (6,400m) in the Markha Valley. We tried what may have been a new line on the north-northeast face, more dangerous than difficult, taking 12 hours to reach the crest of the northwest ridge at ca 6,200m, the last three pitches over tricky mixed ground. The rock was very poor at this point, so we did not continue to the summit but instead descended the normal route over the lower northwest top (Kang Yatze II, ca 6,200m). We called our line to the northwest ridge Palestinian Iliure (800m, VI/4+ M5). 📷

– ORIOL BARO, *SPAIN*

RARU VALLEY, SONAM RI, WEST FACE

In 2011, when I traveled to the Raru Valley with a group of young climbers, members of the expedition made the first ascent of GoCook Peak (6,050m, *AAJ 2012*) and noticed an unclimbed 6,060m mountain to the northeast. In June 2014, hoping to find the best snow conditions for making ski descents, Laura Bohleber, Eric Gachet, Christelle Marceau, Pierre Morand du Paquier, Jérémy Pernet, and I installed base camp on the Katkar Glacier below Katkar Kangri

(R35, 6,148m, *AAJ 2013*). At 7 a.m. on June 27 we left our high camp, just below the snout of the small glacier east of Katkar Kangri, and reached the west face of Peak 6,060m. The skiers climbed 50° slopes to the virgin summit and then, just as the sun hit the face, they started on their 1,000m descent, which they completed safely, carving excellent turns. We named the peak Sonam Ri, which in Tibetan means the "summit that brings good luck." 📷

– STÉPHANE SCHAFFTER, *SWITZERLAND*

LENAK VALLEY, L15, EAST FACE

I LED A FOUR-MAN TEAM from the Gakushuin University Alpine Club to the Lenak Valley, having seen a picture of L15 (6,070m) in Kimikazu Sakamoto's *AAJ 2012* report. We were fascinated by its elegant shape, and by a snow ridge on the left side of the image that we felt would provide a good route. [*In 2012 a four-member Japanese team planned to attempt this peak, but once at its base they decided it was too dangerous due to steep unstable scree and potential avalanches, and instead made an ascent of L13 (AAJ 2013)*].

On August 12, Kazu Ghalamkari, Masayuki Harada, Mizuho Kajita, and I established base camp at 4,830m. After reconnaissance of the east and west faces, we pushed a route up the east face as high as 5,600m by August 20. Since we all felt good, we decided to return to base camp and make a one-day summit ascent on August 22. We left camp at 5 a.m., and by 11 a.m. we had reached steep névé, where we had to climb one at a time. After six pitches on the final sharp ridge we reached the loose, rocky summit. During the descent we belayed down eight pitches. We left no equipment on the mountain. We named this peak Gyalmo Kangri after consultation with our Zanskari guide; Gyalmo means "queen" in Ladakhi.

– SHUHEI YOSHIDA, *JAPAN*

[Below] L15 (left) and L14 (6,180m, no known ascent) from the Lenak Glacier, as seen in 2011. The route of ascent on L15 faces the camera, climbing the large snow slope of the east face and final sharp ridge. *Kimikazu Sakamoto*

KISHTWAR HIMALAYA

BARNAJ I, NORTH BUTTRESS, ATTEMPT; BARNAJ II, SOUTHEAST FACE (NO SUMMIT)

FUNDED IN PART by the Lyman Spitzer Award, Tim Dittmann, Jared Vilhauer, and I reached the Kishtwar Himalaya from the north in mid-September. We shared our base camp (4,400m) on the east side of the Hagshu Glacier with Slovenian and British teams. Our goals were the unclimbed Barnaj peaks.

For the first 10 days we acclimatized on a couple of previously unclimbed 6,000ers close to base camp. These gave straightforward snow climbing. We then set off for our primary objective, the north buttress of Barnaj I (ca 6,300m). There were a number of elegant weaknesses on this 1,500m face, and we opted to skirt the left side of the lower face before entering a deep chimney system that appeared to cut into the center of the mountain. The chimney posed the biggest question, as there was no spot on the glacier from where we could see clearly into it.

Starting with four days of food and fuel, we climbed 600m of beautiful ice, the upper half a brilliant gully system with several sections of AI4 and one long section of vertical ice (AI5). We bivouacked on a sloping snow slope, and the next day continued a few pitches to the base of the chimney at ca 5,730m. The climbing above looked incredible, with much steep ice, but the chimney was subject to constant rockfall, and after waiting most of the day for direct sunlight

[Below] On the north buttress of Barnaj I. *Jared Vilhauer*

to leave, we decided we simply couldn't justify the risk. We started a series of 20 rappels down the route.

With only a few days left we made an attempt on the southeast face of Barnaj II (ca 6,400m). This line was not as technical and we made a single push, climbing 1,500m of snow, easy mixed, and relentless 60° ice, until after 14 hours Jared clawed his way through the cornice and the three of us reached the summit ridge at ca 6,250m, with an hour of daylight remaining. The terrain above appeared to be an unaesthetic pile of vertical choss, and without bivouac gear we decided to go down. Before starting the descent, we climbed to an arbitrary high point on the ridge at ca 6,275m, from which we enjoyed stellar views of the entire Kishtwar Range just as the sun was setting. Twenty-eight rappels got us to the glacier. We reached camp at sunrise, 26 hours after setting out.

This region holds beautiful, steep mountains, with essentially no non-technical peaks. Although the logistics are expensive, we would highly recommend this area for "Alaska-like" climbing at moderately high altitudes. 📷

– SETH TIMPANO, *USA*

HAGSHU, NORTH FACE, AND OTHER FIRST ASCENTS

ALES CESEN, MARKO PREZELJ, AND I had hoped to try Rimo III in India. We learned that a British team was also planning to attempt the mountain, and in May we found the British had been refused a permit—our agents and the IMF advised us to find another goal.

We were disappointed, but after a few days of brainstorming we applied for Mukut Parbat; obtaining a permit for a mountain near Kamet was supposed to be simple. We kept in close contact with our agent, knowing that it was typical for the permit to be issued only a few weeks prior to arrival. To proceed with a permit requires an Indian visa, for which it is necessary to have airline tickets, so we bought tickets and freighted food and equipment to India. We were therefore shocked to learn, two weeks before departure from Slovenia, that we had to find another objective. We asked the IMF for clarification, but none was forthcoming. Ten days before our flights our agent told us the IMF was suggesting we climb an "open peak," for which a regular tourist visa would suffice. He added, "Hagshu peak in Kishtwar, with approach from Zanskar, is a good option, and there are other peaks in that region too…. Please let me know if this is agreeable to you."

We found limited information on this peak [*see AAJ 2014 for the history of climbing on Hagshu*], but with little alternative decided to confirm the permit with our agent, and at least explore the area. A few days before departure learned that the legendary British climbers Mick Fowler and Paul Ramsden were planning to attempt the unclimbed north face. After the bureaucratic chaos on the part of the IMF, and our continuous goal-changing to accommodate their demands, we were not too upset by this news and felt there would be enough room for everyone. [*See Paul Ramsden's report, below, for the British viewpoint on these events.*]

In Delhi the IMF gave us a permit for September 7–October 14. When in Leh with our agent, however, we received a message from the IMF that we would need to leave base camp by September 26. This would give us 10 days at or above base camp. The request was, of course, unacceptable and we refused. On the first of our two days' trek to base camp we met two Americans, and were surprised to hear that they too had a permit for Hagshu, even though they had no intention of climbing it.

As we approached base camp at 4,400m on the west moraine of the Hagshu Glacier, we were surprised by how attractive Hagshu appeared compared to the few photos we'd seen.

There was an obvious line on the north face and we decided to go for it. First we needed to acclimatize, and an extremely sharp, elegant peak above the base appeared to be of an appropriate height and difficulty for our first climb. On the 16th we bivouacked at a saddle below the east ridge, and the following day climbed the ridge to the summit in eight hours. It was longer and more difficult than expected, challenging us right to the top. We named the peak Lagan (5,750m), and our 700m route was TD- M5.

After a rest Ales and Marko went to establish advanced base (4,660m) under Hagshu and inspect the west wall, which also appeared interesting. The next day, the British arrived at base camp and Ales and Marko climbed Peak 5,680m in front of Hagshu, from which they had good views of both west and north walls. All three of us then went to climb Hana's Men (ca 6,300m), which lay to the east of Hagshu and would give good views of our descent along the 1989 Polish Route. [*Hana's Men was first climbed in 2013 by the south face (AAJ 2014).*] We climbed a steep couloir on the west face, with good conditions making for rapid progress. The line was logical and led to the west rib at 6,000m. We climbed compact rock on the crest to a bivouac at 6,200m. In the cold morning we reached the north summit, rappelled and downclimbed the northeast face, and returned to base camp the same day. The 1,100m climb was TD.

After a three-day rest we moved to advanced base, and at 3 a.m. set off for Hagshu's north face with a small tent, two sleeping bags, and food for two bivouacs. Deep powder gave way to more rapid travel up the snow cone leading to the central part of the wall. We climbed unroped for ca 300m to the steepest part of the face, where we found very steep ice that was mirror-polished by spindrift and brittle as glass due to the cold. The upper face was surprisingly difficult, and there was nowhere suitable to bivouac. Finally, at 2 a.m., having been on the go for 23 hours, we found a good spot on a narrow rib at 6,320m.

We started late next day and, helped by the warmth of midday sun, continued with pleasant rock climbing to the north peak. From there we climbed and waded along the undulating ridge to the main (south) top, which we reached at 5 p.m. on the 30th. Nice weather persuaded us to stop and bivouac a few meters below the top. Next morning we descended the Polish route; during the steep rappels we all agreed that in 1989 the Poles had done an excellent job. We finally reached the glacier, and the last two hours to advanced base were spent meandering between moonlit crevasses. The 1,350m north face was ED 70–90°. We thank the Alpine Association of Slovenia for their support. 📷

– LUKA LINDIC, *SLOVENIA*

HAGSHU, NORTHEAST FACE AND TRAVERSE

THE NORTH FACE of Hagshu (6,657m) looks an immaculate climb, and our expedition to its north face started much like any other expedition. Lots of research and Mick Fowler's prodigious organizational skill meant that permits were in place nine months before we were due to depart. With flights booked there was nothing to do but sit back and anticipate another Himalayan adventure.

A week before we were due to depart, our agent informed

[Photo] Ales Cesen starting his first lead on the north face of Hagshu. *Marko Prezelj*

[Above] Hagshu (6,657m) from the northeast and Peak 5,680m (right), showing the 2014 climbs. (1) Fowler-Ramsden. (2) Slovenian Route. (3) Cesen-Prezelj ascent on Peak 5,680m. The two descended Peak 5,680m near the left skyline, heading toward Hagshu. *Marko Prezelj*

us that another expedition had left the Indian Mountaineering Foundation the day before with a permit for the north face of Hagshu. Much emailing ensued to little effect, and none the wiser we set off for India. In Delhi the IMF apologetically confirmed they had accidentally given the Slovenian team of Ales Cesen, Luka Lindic, and Marko Prezelj a permit, but had since notified them that they must leave the mountain before we arrived. Feeling confused but hopeful that the matter would be resolved when we reached base camp, we made the journey to Hagshu via Leh and Kargil.

On arrival at base camp, we met Luka Lindic, who had been expecting us and knew of our intentions on Hagshu. With his partners out of camp on a reconnaissance, he admitted they had received the instruction from the IMF to leave the mountain before our arrival at base camp, but had chosen to ignore it. Following the withdrawal of their permit to Mukut Parbat, several weeks before they departed for India, they were in need of a last-minute alternative, and an online search had highlighted our planned expedition to Hagshu. Although they knew nothing about the mountain, they clearly presumed that it must be worth climbing if we were planning to go there. [*See Luka Lindic's report, above, for the Slovenian account of the permit acquisition and decision to climb Hagshu.*]

Not sure how to proceed, and with the rest of his team out of camp, we decided to press ahead and acclimatize on a nearby peak. Hopefully we could discuss the matter with the entire team on our return. Unfortunately, on getting back from our acclimatization trip, we had the dubious pleasure of watching the trio climb the north face.

Nevertheless, determined to make the best of the situation, we turned our attention to the northeast face of the mountain. The route was good and quite hard through the central rock band, but lower down was subject to more objective danger than we would normally accept. Clearly our judgment had been clouded by a determination not to follow others. Footsteps on the summit were a new experience for us.

We returned from India determined to put the whole matter behind us. However, the subsequent award of a Piolet d'Or to the team for climbing the north face again raised the issue of ethics in alpinism. Ethics are not just about the physical issues of bolting and fixing ropes, but also about behavior toward one's fellow alpinists and the so-called fellowship of the mountains.

We wasted an entire year's planning and were extremely disappointed by the frank admission of what we consider a breach of ethics from our fellow alpinists. Expeditions have reported their objectives before departure for many years, in order to raise support, highlight sponsors, and make other climbers aware of their intentions. Typically, it's been part of expedition mountaineering to respect this, and we had not had one of our routes so blatantly poached before. We feel that the behavior of the other team lacked respect and integrity, and should not be held up as an example of what alpinism is about. No matter whether it is a good climb or not.

— PAUL RAMSDEN, *U.K.*

[*Editor's note: Subsequently, the IMF held an official enquiry into the Hagshu incident and quoted from their rules that it "reserves the right to allot a particular peak to more than one expedition in the same season, and that the route/face allowed may be same or different for each expedition." However, the IMF agreed that until its rules were suitably revised, it would be instructing its staff as follows: (a) If more than one permit is issued in the same season to a particular route on a peak, each expedition would have a clear separation of seven days at base camp. I.e., it is expected that one team will have left base camp seven days before the next arrives. (b) Special requests for reservation of "first ascent routes" would be entertained on a first-come, first-served basis, provided a special application is made to the IMF. If the request were accepted, confirmation would be given, in which case there would be a "validity" date by which the peak fee must be deposited. The IMF is currently redoing all of its forms and guidelines, and it is unclear how long it will take before the above guidelines are made public. In addition, the government of India is proposing to lift the ban on satellite phones, as confirmed by the president of the Adventure Travel Operators Association of India, which was responsible for pushing this policy change. However, it may take some time before these new regulations pass through all the government bureaucracy.*]

SHIEPRA, SOUTH FACE; KHARAGOSA, EAST FACE AND SOUTHEAST FACE; KISHTWAR SHIVILING EAST SUMMIT, EAST PILLAR

AT THE START of September, Andreas "Dres" Abegglen, Thomas Senf, and I left Switzerland for Kishtwar, a magical and remote region I first visited in 2011. We were greeted in Kashmir by a late and heavy monsoon, but despite mass flooding and terrible road conditions we made it to our first base camp on the 13th.

Eager to make up for lost time, we set out for a peak that we believe to be previously unclimbed, immediately north of the Muni La. [*This peak lies immediately south of the old trekking route over the Umasi La, and a little west of the pass.*] We climbed the south face with a bivouac at 5,100m and reached the 5,885m summit on the 16th. Difficulties were WI3 UIAA IV 75°. We descended the exposed west ridge, making a series of rappels before going down a 50° ice slope. We named the peak Shiepra, and the route Maaji (Hindi for mother). More correctly,

[Above] Looking west down the Haptal Valley. (A) Agyasol (6,200m). (B) Kharagosa (5,840m) and the line of Pinky. (C) Cerro Kishtwar and the line of Challo. *Visualimpact.ch/Robert Frost*

it was our liaison officer, Ran Jan, who named the peak, after the wife of the Hindu god Shiva.

The weather at this point was perfect and conditions seemed promising, so we set off for another virgin peak, the sharp, high summit on the long ridge that runs east-southeast from Kishtwar Shivling. Below the mountain is a prominent rock formation that looks like a playboy bunny, so naming this peak was easy: We called it Kharagosa, Hindi for rabbit. Approaching from the northeast, we bivouacked at 4,800m and then crossed the glacier to the foot of the east face. There we slanted right, across the lower face, before climbing back left toward the ridge. Three demanding pitches of UIAA V led to the crest, which was in fact the right edge of the much easier southeast face. We followed this to the 5,840m summit. The date was September 21, and we named our route Pinky (1,000m, M4 6a) after the most beautiful woman in the nearby village of Sumcham.

We still had time left and so decided to move our base camp beneath Kishtwar Shivling, arriving there on the 29th. The first and only ascent of this impressive ca 6,040m mountain was made in 1983 by Dick Renshaw and Stephen Venables, via the north face. We opted for the east pillar, the target of several previous expeditions. We made our first bivouac at 4,700m and then followed a 50° snow/ice ramp to a saddle at 5,400m, where we bivouacked again. Above, we moved right before climbing 10 demanding pitches in a hidden couloir (WI5 90°), reminiscent of the Supercanaleta on Fitz Roy. Tricky mixed terrain led to the foot of enormous capping cornices. It was October 1, and the gods were smiling on us: We chanced upon a tunnel big enough to climb through, and arrived on the east summit at 5,895m. We regained the saddle after 14 rappels, spent another night in the tents, and the following morning descended to base camp. We named the route Challo (WI5 M6), which means "let's go" in Hindi.

We arrived home with rucksacks full of great memories of unforgettable climbs, and having had a lot of laughs together. This has only strengthened my bond with this breathtaking area. 📷

— STEPHAN SIEGRIST, *SWITZERLAND*

NEW ROUTES AND VARIATIONS

IN AUGUST and September, Arunas Kamandulis and I (Lithuania), and Cyrill Boesch and Elias Gmuender (Switzerland), spent just over 20 days in the Miyar Valley. We were surprised to find ourselves the only team at base camp, and to see only a single party of trekkers during our stay.

To acclimatize we climbed a new variation on Toro Peak (ca 4,900m). We then set our sights on the upper Takdung Glacier, hoping to climb the southeast faces of Lotus Peak (sometimes spelled Lotos) and Neverseen Tower. Both peaks have been climbed from the neighboring Chhudong Valley, and the latter has a handful of established routes, yet the faces above the Takdung had not been attempted.

We hiked up the Takdung in deteriorating weather. After a few days of waiting we set out during a clear night for Lotus Peak (ca 5,670m). After some initial easy pitches, beautiful granite unfolded with splitter cracks linked by fine face climbing. By the time we reached the summit clouds were closing in again. Rappelling in a heavy downpour of rain, snow, and all the water phases in between, we were happy to have squeezed this route into a short window of opportunity. We called it Splitter and Storm (500m, 6a).

On our last day at base camp, we got a half-day of good weather, and this allowed us to make a dash up a new variation on Iris Peak (ca 5,200m). We started up the first few pitches of the 2009 route D'yer Mak'er (*AAJ 2013*) to reach a big ledge, which we followed up right to the main part of the south face of Iris Peak. There we climbed a slanting system of chimneys and cracks to reach lower-angle terrain, where for about one pitch on the west ridge our climb shared the Peschel-Schaar line (*AAJ 2012*). With snow beginning to fall, we traversed back to the headwall on the south face and finished via beautiful cracks leading straight to the summit. We called this variation Bollywood Drama (550m, 6b), since we were not sure until the very last day whether we would be able to give this route a shot. 📷 📄

— GEDIMINAS SIMUTIS, *LITHUANIA*

[Below] The east sides of (A) Lotus Peak, with the 2014 route Splitter and Storm, (B) Neverseen Tower and (C) Enzo Peak, seen across the Takdung Glacier. *Gediminas Simutis*

[Above] Looking southeast into the attractive peaks of the Mulkila Range from the summit of Yunam. Search the AAJ website for reports on ascents in the area. *Indian Lahaul Expedition 2014*

HAATHI, SOUTHEAST FACE; TIKONA, NORTHEAST RIDGE

A SIX-MEMBER Indian expedition led by Rajan Rikame climbed two new peaks just west of the Manali-Leh Highway at Kilingsarai (ca 260km drive from Manali), north of the Baralacha La. Peak 5,980m (32.87°N, 77.39°E) was climbed on July 31 by Rohan Rao, Prashant Sawant, and support staff by the east-southeast ridge and face. The team proposed the name Haathi. The second summit, Peak 5,920m (32.81°N, 77.38°E), was climbed on August 3 by Rajan Rikame, Bholaram Thakur, Kaivalya Varma, and the same three support staff, via the northeast ridge and descent of the northwest ridge. The proposed name is Tikona. This peak lies southwest along the ridge from the previously climbed Yunam (6,130m), which the Indians also ascended, from the southeast. All three peaks are non-technical, but despite extensive research the expedition found no recorded ascent of the first two.

– LINDSAY GRIFFIN

MT. SUTD, NORTHWEST RIDGE

ON AUGUST 31 a team of young climbers from Singapore University of Technology and Design, led by Edwin Siew, reached an unnamed summit (6,010m on the Leomann map) in the Karcha Valley. The team approached from Batal along the Karcha Nala, and then south up its right branch to an advanced base camp at 4,936m, below the largest of the four main glaciers that rise south from the Karcha River. From a high camp at 5,490m, below a col marking the base of the northwest ridge, the team followed the ridge nearly 2km to the summit (6,056m GPS, 32°15.39'N, 77°42.23'E, AD). They propose naming the peak after the university: Mt. SUTD. 📷 📄

– *INFORMATION FROM* EDWIN SIEW, *SINGAPORE*

LINGTI VALLEY, FIRST ASCENTS

UNTIL RECENTLY the areas northeast of the Spiti Valley were closed to non-Indians. Encouraged by Harish Kapadia, who led the only two teams known to have explored east of the Lingti Nala (valley), Dave Broadhead, Mike Cocker, Geoff Cohen, and I received permission to enter this region in September. Hamish Irvine failed to receive his permit before leaving the U.K. and was not allowed to go above base camp.

From the road head at Lalung, we trekked for five days northeast of the Lingti Nala, over arduous and complex terrain, to reach base camp (5,130m, 32°12.841'N, 78°20.803'E). From here we explored and mapped the extensive Langma Plateau, and on September 9 climbed a subsidiary top, Peak 5,782m, via a short steep couloir (WI2) on its northwest face. We named the climb Fossil Gully on account of the numerous fossils around base camp and the combined age of 189 for the three first ascensionists.

After establishing a high camp to the south at 5,807m, we first climbed Tangmor (5,920m, 32°11.030'N, 78°21.775'E) via its north-northwest ridge. On the 13th we reclimbed Tangmor and continued on to summit Taklu (5,927m) by its north ridge.

After making two more intermediate camps on the ridge to the east, we made the first ascent of a peak we named Chota Sgurr (5,924m, 32°11.329'N, 78°23.576'E) on September 19. This summit lies at the western extremity of a high cirque at the head of the Talung Nala, and was climbed by the sharp north ridge. The very long continuation ridge to the east would eventually lead to unclimbed Peak 6,531m (Survey of India map). On separate days, team members also did the second and third ascents of Langma (5,796m), a peak first ascended by the 1983 Kapadia expedition. 📷 ▤ 🔍

– DEREK BUCKLE, *U.K.*

BHAGIRATHI I, SOUTHWEST FACE VARIANT TO WEST RIDGE (ATTEMPT)

CHRISTINA POGACEAN and I had planned to attempt Chaukhamba II during our honeymoon. However, for reasons beyond our control, we could not get porters and staff anywhere near our proposed base camp. With Bhagirathi I (6,856m) as the nearest feasible option, we decided to attempt its southwest face. Unfortunately, we had little idea of existing routes on Bhagirathi I. We opted for the far left side of the face, leading to the foot of the obvious tower on the west ridge (first climbed by British in 1983). In late September, over two and a half days, we climbed the southwest face to the big tower (UIAA VI+) before retreating in poor weather. 📷 ▤

– COSMIN ANDRON, *ROMANIA*

SHIVLING, NORTHWEST RIDGE AND WEST FACE

IN MAY our five-member expedition planned to attempt two routes on Shivling (6,543m). Rainer Treppte and I (German) wanted to try a new route on the left side of the northeast face, while Niels Delenk, Henning Stoll (both German), and Heiner Heim (Switzerland) would climb the normal route up the west ridge and prepare the descent for Treppte and me.

[Above] Shivling from the northwest. (1) Top section of north pillar (German-Swiss, 2000). (2) Czechoslovak Route (1987). (3) Japanese Route (2005). (4) Portuguese attempt (2014). (5) German Route (1996 and again in 2014). (6) West face, normal route (Indo-Tibetan Border Police, 1974). (C1) Portuguese camp 1 (5,550m). (C2) Camp 2 (5,800m). (H) High point of second 2014 Portuguese attempt (left variation). *Daniela Teixeira*

We stayed at base camp for three weeks, during which we had a constant fight with snowfall—a meter of fresh snow fell. As India strictly prohibits the use of satellite phones, we had no contact with the outside world and therefore no forecasts. We made a few unsuccessful attempts on the northeast face, always thwarted due to storm and avalanche danger. Just before our departure, I decided to try a speed ascent of the mountain with Delenk, and opted to repeat my 1996 route up the west face—a line I had vowed never to do again.

Compared with Shivling's other flanks, the west face is relatively low angle, but, unfortunately, it is overhung by a huge, broad serac barrier. A low-relief, mixed ridge—the west face normal route—rises to the middle of the serac barrier, and was followed in 1974 to make the first ascent of the mountain. In September 1996 I had arrived with three other climbers, planning to make the second ascent of the east ridge (Bettembourg-Child-White-Scott, 1983). However, the team dynamics were not right, and we gave up the idea [*later in that same month John Bouchard and Mark Richey made the second ascent, in alpine style*].

In the last week of the expedition I studied a route on the west face that would give a rapid ascent to the summit. Rainer Picher and I left base camp and made a bivouac under the northwest ridge. After four hours' rest we set off on our new line, which climbs part of the northwest ridge, then the west face to the serac, before making a rising traverse left to the upper northwest ridge and main summit. It took eight hours. We rested 30 minutes on top and descended to base camp the same day. Due to the lengthy exposure to the serac, I swore I would never repeat this route.

Nonetheless, I started toward the west face with Niels Delenk in the afternoon of May

27. Hampered by fresh snow, we had reached only 5,200m on the approach to the northwest ridge crest before we stopped to bivouac. The weather began to clear and the temperature fell to -25°C. After a few hours' rest we began to climb, finding it tricky to negotiate snow-covered slabs in the dark. However, we were in good shape and changed lead often. It was possible to follow my 1996 line, and we moved fast from rock pillar to rock pillar to minimize the objective danger. At 10 a.m. we reached the summit and then reversed our route all the way to our bivouac site. That same evening the other three members arrived, and we slept there together. The following day they followed our track and also reached the summit.

The steepest ice on this route is 60-70°, with some mixed ground at M4/5. However, while the technical difficulties are not high, the route is exposed to the giant serac for a significant distance, and is only suitable for a speed ascent. It's a mental challenge for fast climbers. 🔘

– WALTER HOELZLER, GERMANY

SHIVLING, NORTHWEST RIDGE AND WEST FACE, ATTEMPT

AFTER ABANDONING AN ATTEMPT on the unclimbed east ridge of Meru, due to "abominable" snow conditions, Daniela Teixeira and Paulo Roxo switched to the direct northwest ridge of Shivling. Starting on the right side of the north face, beginning at ca 5,000m, they climbed to 5,650m with one bivouac, heading for the northwest ridge, before finding unconsolidated snow over steep granite slabs and retreating.

On October 11 they tried again, this time aiming to reach the northwest ridge at a lower point, following a German route first climbed in 1996 and repeated in the spring of 2014. [*See report above.*] They bivouacked twice, at 5,500m and 5,800m, and on the third day climbed through a rocky barrier well to the left of the German line. Steep, technical climbing and traversing over hard, black 55° ice, directly under the huge serac that crosses the west face, prompted them to escape the firing zone and retreat. Up to their high point at ca 6,000m, they reported difficulties of WI4 M5 55°. 🔘

– INFORMATION FROM PAULO ROXO, PORTUGAL

JANAHUT (6,805M) SOUTHWEST BUTTRESS AND SOUTHWEST RIDGE (ATTEMPT)

JANAHUT HAD BEEN ATTEMPTED by five previous teams. In June we became the sixth—and the sixth team to fail. This mountain was first attempted in 2002 by an Austrian team. In 2004 Pat Deavoll and Marty Beare (New Zealand) made a strong attempt up the big couloir on the west face, reaching 6,400m. During the same expedition, Malcolm Bass, Andy Brown, and Paul Figg (U.K.) reached ca 6,000m on the southwest buttress. In 2010 and 2011, Bryan Hylenski's team made attempts from the glacier to the southeast, using fixed ropes and reaching around 6,500m on the southwest ridge.

On June 9, at 11 p.m., we left our tent at 5,050m at the foot of the southwest buttress and crossed the bergschrund at 1 a.m. We climbed unroped up snowfields and short gullies, and by 10 a.m. had reached a well-protected bivouac site beneath an overhang at 5,900m.

At 2:30 a.m., with the face safely frozen, we were off again. Among pockets of wind slab, we stayed roped and moving together, weaving through white granite towers. It was a ferociously cold morning, with temperatures around –30°C, so it was a relief to emerge into the sunshine. We had climbed the southwest buttress but were still a long way from the summit. A loose, scratchy rock pitch and a few rope lengths on a steep ridge of hard ice brought us to a

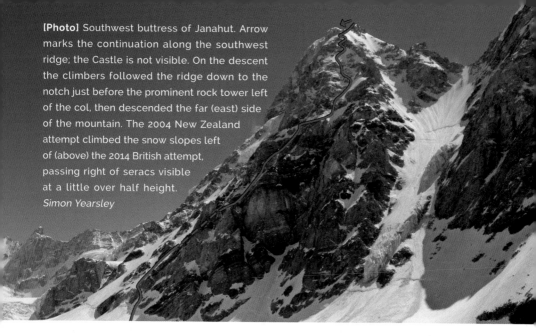

[Photo] Southwest buttress of Janahut. Arrow marks the continuation along the southwest ridge; the Castle is not visible. On the descent the climbers followed the ridge down to the notch just before the prominent rock tower left of the col, then descended the far (east) side of the mountain. The 2004 New Zealand attempt climbed the snow slopes left of (above) the 2014 British attempt, passing right of seracs visible at a little over half height. *Simon Yearsley*

large rock gendarme at 6,300m, where we chopped a tent platform (the Eyrie).

We set off at 4 a.m., leaving the tent pitched. After another couple of pitches up the hard ice ridge, the angle eased to a long horizontal section, with occasional technical sections through short rock steps. Ahead lay a formidable 80m rock barrier, which we had named the Castle. Malcolm led the first of the technical cruxes, with steep mixed climbing. However, the sting in the tail was an awkward, holdless chimney, which Simon led, ending at a short wall on top of the Castle.

We had reached 6,660m. It would be dark in less than two hours, and the summit was 140m above, while our tent, stove, and food were 360m below. The freezing wind continued to strengthen. We decided to descend. By the time we regained the Eyrie, we had been on the go for 21 hours. We spent the few hours left of the night making endless brews and bowls of noodles, and the following day we slept, ate what remained of our food, and planned our descent to the glacier 1,300m below.

At 9 a.m. on the 14th we left the Eyrie to descend the shorter east side of the mountain to a high glacial basin. By 8 p.m. we were relieved to be on flat ground. It was the end of our fifth day, and the evening meal was two cups each of ginger and lemon tea, made from used teabags scavenged from the rubbish bag. The icefalls below proved surprisingly benign, and by midmorning we were walking the 5km down to our campsite at the foot of the buttress. We would like to thank the Mount Everest Foundation, the British Mountaineering Council, and the Alpine Club for their support. 📷 📄

– MALCOLM BASS *AND* SIMON YEARSLEY, *U.K.*

BRAHMASAR II; SICKLE SPIRE; BRAHMASAR DU TACUL

ON OCTOBER 1, Jim Elzinga, Steve House, Buster Jesik, Colin Simon, and Steven Van Sickle gathered in Delhi for the final expedition of the 2012–2014 Alpine Mentors program. [*This is a U.S.-based, volunteer-run program to train young alpinists. See feature article in this edition.*] The goal was the first ascent of Brahmasar I (5,850m), which rises between the Satling and Dudhganga glaciers, just south of Thalay Sagar. An easy four-day trek through a series of beautiful mountain villages led to a base camp at the mouth of the Bhilangna River.

Advanced base was established three hours' walk above base camp at the toe of the Dudhganga Glacier. During reconnaissance, Steve and Steven climbed a peak they named Sickle Spire (5,334m, M5), which is part of a feature dubbed Brahmasar du Tacul, a 5,415m sub-summit on the ridge south of Brahmasar.

After more reconnaissance Buster, Colin, and Steven decided to head for a prominent couloir on the southwest face of Brahmasar. Jim and Steve climbed a parallel mixed route to the right. The first half of both routes was 45° snow, leading to a rock headwall. From this point Jim and Steve climbed straight up their mixed line (M6) to bivouac at the prominent notch between Brahmasar I and II. The next morning they turned south and climbed two pitches to the top of Brahmasar II (ca 5,830m). This was the second ascent. [*In 2002 Keith Milne and Gordon Scott reached the southeast face of the peak via a long crossing from the Satling Glacier. They climbed a steep, narrow couloir (Scottish IV) to the notch between Brahmasar I and II, and then a UIAA IV chimney to the summit of Brahmasar II.*]

The team of Buster, Colin, and Steven headed up left from the top of the 45° snow and into fun WI3/4 pitches. Their couloir had very few ledges, and steeper climbing than they had assumed. At around 4 p.m. they found a ledge large enough to fit 90 percent of their two-man tent. They endured a cramped bivouac and the following day turned around in the face of serious choss 50–100m below a col on the west ridge. They rappelled the route from that point.

The team's final climb was to the highest point of Brahmasar du Tacul. After much post-holing Buster and Steven followed fun ice and firm névé to the summit boulder problem. 🔲

– *INFORMATION PROVIDED BY* STEVE HOUSE, *USA*

KUMAUN HIMALAYA

ADI KAILASH, CHEEPAYDANG, SOUTH FACE AND SOUTHWEST RIDGE

IN SEPTEMBER and October I led a multinational team to the Adi Kailash range of Eastern Kumaun. This massif is wedged between the Kali Ganga, Darma Ganga, and Kuthi Yankti valleys, and between the Nepalese and Tibetan borders. The range contains at least eight peaks exceeding 6,000m. The mountain called Adi Kailash (Little Kailash) is lower, at 5,945m. It is a peak of religious and mythological significance, with close topographic resemblance to holy Mt. Kailash, 110km to the north in Tibet.

The only approach currently permitted by the Indian Mountaineering Foundation and the Uttarakhand state government follows the Mansarovar-Kailash pilgrim trail from Darchula, up the Kali Ganga gorge, then northwest to Kuthi village, Jolingkong base camp, and Parvati Lake. Inner Line permits are required. Although a road is slowly being pushed up the gorge, the trek is still over 60km and takes three days.

Prior to 2002, the only known mountaineering in the region had been undertaken by members of the Indo-Tibetan Border Police. The 2014 expedition was the fourth I have organized to this area (see *AAJ 2003, 2005, 2007*). In 2004, we climbed to within 15m of the sacred summit of Adi Kailash, and in 2006 we climbed the higher parent peak of 6,120m, naming it Ishan Parbat. Several sub-6,000m peaks also were ascended during these expeditions, but by 2014 no other 6,000ers in the range were known to have been climbed.

We established base camp at 3,990m in the Nama Valley, 5km southwest of Kuthi village, and reconnoitered the extensive Nama Glacier cirque. The weather was fine, but conditions

[Above] Cheepaydang at dawn from Kuthi village to the northeast. The 2014 team ascended the south side of the mountain. *Martin Moran*

on the south faces were abnormally dry. Fierce seracs and icefalls deterred many approaches, and we focused our interest on the mountain known to local Kuthi people as Cheepaydang (Peacock Peak). Cheepydang has three summits, the central being the highest, with a knife-edge ridge linking them and a tremendous 1,000m north wall. Above the Nama Glacier on the south side, a slanting snow-ice couloir offered the safest line of weakness.

On October 2-3, Michael Page, Gordon Scott, and I ascended the gully system, finding snow and ice to 60° and mixed climbing to Scottish IV. We made a high camp at 6,160m on the crest of the southwest ridge. On the 4th we made a short ridge traverse (AD) to the summit, which we measured at 6,220m. We descended the gully system the following night, making eight 60m rappels from ice threads to gain easier ground, and returned to base camp on the 6th. The overall difficulty was D.

Cheepaydang is estimated to be the second-highest summit in the range. The highest is known as Brammah Parbat (ca 6,321m), 2km north of Cheepaydang. To the south of the Nama Glacier lie beautiful and difficult Rajay Jue (6,178m) and the snow massif of Peak 6,196m. South again are the Sela peaks (named Yirjenagung on early maps). These form an impressive wall of 6,000m-plus summits with an isolated pyramidal peak to their southwest. The Sela peaks would be best approached from the Darma Valley to the west, but at present Indian authorities do not permit access via this route.

Apart from administrative complexity, the main deterrent to further development is the bad quality of the underlying rock, a bewildering layering of compressed mudstones tilted to a near-vertical stratification. Nonetheless, this is a beautiful and remote area for exploratory climbing. 📷 🔍

– MARTIN MORAN, *U.K.*

ADI KAILASH RANGE, CONCORDIA PARBAT

STEVE KENNEDY, ANDY NISBET, AND I traveled as far as the Nama Glacier as part of a larger group led by Martin Moran. While he, Michael Page, and Gordon Scott were ascending screes below Cheepaydang, prior to making its first ascent, we left camp on the Nama Glacier and began an ascent of a major northern tributary. We moved slowly to assist our acclimatization, placing two camps a few hours apart. Above our top camp (ca 5,300m) any further sites appeared to be potentially threatened by objective danger.

On October 4 we set out at first light for the col at the head of the glacier, hoping to climb a peak directly above it. We found a reasonably safe route to the col, and then Steve and I followed a fine, steep, and exposed snow arête to the southwest, crossing moderate rock to the summit of our peak. We had no altimeter, but estimated the height to be 5,850m; our route was AD in difficulty. The next peak along the ridge looked to be the same altitude, but we did not go any farther as the rock was extremely loose. We named our peak Concordia Parbat, as the many-tongued Nama cirque resembles the Concordias of the Alps and Karakoram. The northern tributary of the Nama we named Jasuli Glacier after a local woman who was famous for her charitable activities in the 18th or 19th century.

The Nama Glacier area is impressive, but future pioneers would benefit from careful study of our photos: Despite a large number of mountains, moderate or safe lines appeared quite limited. 📷

— DES RUBENS, *U.K.*

[Below] On the north branch of the Nama Glacier (a.k.a. Jasuli Glacier). Concordia Parbat is the pointed peak immediately left of the col at the head. The climbers ascended to the col and then followed the ridge to the top. *Des Rubens*

[Above] Rinpoche's Temple Peak and route of ascent. [Below] Exploring the Zemu Ridge. *Photos: Alberto Peruffo*

TONGSHYONG AND SOUTH SIMVU GLACIERS, EXPLORATION, FIRST ASCENTS

FROM APRIL 12 TO MAY 31, Francesco Canale, Enrico Ferri, Davide Ferro, and Andrea Tonin (Italy), Cesar Rosales Chinchay (Peru), Anindya Mukherjee (India), and I as leader operated on the Zemu side of Kangchenjunga, one of the most fascinating and little explored areas of the Himalaya. Political and administrative difficulties, together with an impracticable forest, have thwarted exploratory ambitions for more than a century. Our main purpose was to study access routes to the Zemu Ridge and Zemu Peak (7,780m, one of the highest unclimbed summits in the Himalaya) from the Tongshyong Glacier, close to Zemu Gap (5,861m).

Our first challenge was finding a route through the labyrinthine Talung Gorge. Our porters gradually gave up and went home. On the third day they were frightened by the discovery of the body of a clergyman, seated on a bed of voluntary death, and on the fifth day, shocked and tired, they abandoned us. After six days in the forest we established base camp at 3,700m.

Mukerjee's team left to explore the South Simvu Glacier, as described below. The rest of us made an advanced base at 5,050m, then tried to approach the Zemu Ridge and were the first to cross an amazing snow/ice plateau leading to the immense south face of Kangchenjunga. We reached a col we named Colle Sella (5,440m) and from there climbed two summits, Alpine Guides Peak (5,550m) and Sella Col Peak (5,470m).

We then extended our exploration to the entire Tongshyong Glacier, ca 12km in length. We reached three cols, one of which gave direct access to the Talung Glacier to the west. We named it Porta Maraini (5,220m), after the great Italian mountaineer Fosco Maraini. From here we climbed three peaks: both summits of Cime della Fratellanza (5,360m and 5,380m,

PD) and Rinpoche's Temple Peak (5,684 m, 700m, TD 65°).

On May 10 we embarked on the second phase of the expedition in the 8km-long South Simvu Glacier, where Mukherjee's team had just been (*see following report*). This glacier rises in three levels. After reaching the col giving access to the first level, we negotiated 1,000m of complex route-finding through crevasses and ice walls to reach a gap at the head of the glacier that we named Porta della Rivelazione Perenne (6,036m). We were just above the Zemu Gap, and the whole Zemu Ridge lay in front of us. After descending to Advanced Simvu Camp at 5,100m, we spent the final days climbing the most attractive mountain of this glacier, the north summit (5,750m) of what we called the Three Peaks of South Simvu. This required a high level of technical climbing (650m, TD+ 75°) on a sharp, exposed ridge. *Much more information on this expedition is available at www.k2014.it.* 📷

– ALBERTO PERUFFO, *ITALY*

SOUTH SIMVU GLACIER EXPLORATION

IN MAY I took part in an expedition organized by Alberto Peruffo to explore the Talung and Tongshyong glacier basins, southeast of Kangchenjunga. While the rest of the members busied themselves investigating the countless possibilities for new routes, I set off for the last unexplored glacier from the Talung Valley: the South Simvu.

Why a complete glacier basin so close to Kangchenjunga remained unvisited for so long is fascinating. Early maps had little detail of this region, and it wasn't until Douglas Freshfield's historic "circumnavigation" in 1899, complete with cartographer Professor Garwood, that we had a good map as close to perfect with reference to the other glaciers flowing into the Talung Valley. But there was no sign of South Simvu. It did not appear until the production of the Swiss map in 1951. It is also visible on Tadashi Toyoshima's 1977 sketch map, which in all my

[Below] The previously unseen south face of the Simvu twins, across the South Simvu Glacier from 6,000m on Peak 6,130m. *Anindya Mukherjee*

expeditions to Sikkim I have found to be most accurate.

My observations from three previous trips here had given me a fair idea of how to access the South Simvu. (Like the Tongshyong immediately to its west, this glacier is invisible from the Talung gorge.) On May 3, Lakpa Sherpa, Thendup Sherpa, and I left base camp at the confluence of the Talung and Tongshyong glaciers and climbed lateral moraine for five hours toward what we felt was the entrance to the South Simvu. For the next couple of days we reconnoitered up the valley in poor visibility, until a clear morning saw us climbing the true right side of the icefall giving access to the upper glacier plateau. It took as seven hours to reach a camp on the névé at 5,300m.

Next day we awoke with excitement to clear skies and saw the Simvu twins (6,812m, 6,811m) to our north. To the north-northeast, beyond the 5,215m col leading to the Passanram Glacier to the east, lay Siniolchu (6,887m), while Narsang (5,825m), Jopuno (5,936m), and Pandim (6,691m) were visible to the south. To the northwest, on the watershed ridge dividing the Tongshyong and South Simvu glaciers, stood two unnamed peaks of 6,350m and 6,130m. Thendup and I roped up and started for the nearest objective to camp: Peak 6,130m.

In the next four hours we climbed through a narrow gully east of Peak 6,130m and reached the base of its summit rock pyramid. However, not having come prepared for any real climbing, we could not continue. Our high point of 6,000m provided a perfect vantage for photo-documentation of surrounding peaks, and after doing so we descended. Next morning we set off for base camp.

– ANINDYA MUKHERJEE, *INDIA*

ZUMTHUL PHUK GLACIER, EXPLORATION

In November the predominately Irish expedition of Jack Bergin, Martin Boner, Kevin Higgins, Ursula McPherson, Keith Monaghan, Alan Tees (leader), Jimmy Tees, Thendup Sherpa, and I became the first group to complete the traverse of the Zumthul Phuk Chu gorge, reach the

[Below] Siniolchu Rock Needles (5,712m, left) and Siniolchu (6,887m), seen over the Zumthul Phuk Glacier lake. *Anindya Mukerjee*

Zumthul Phuk Glacier, and carry out exploration.

Our team arrived in Beh at the end of October. A walk of three short days took us to Talung. With the help of porters who blazed a trail through the rhododendron forest with machetes, we reached a base camp at 3,800m, above the worst of the vegetation. Half an hour above camp lay a beautiful lake, and to the left the Siniolchu Rock Needles. From an advanced base, the group reconnoitered a route to a shoulder on the Siniolchu Rock Needles. The following details are taken from Martin Boner's diary.

The eventual route led up a gully (Scottish 3/4), on thin ice and névé, giving access to easier angled slopes. A high camp was established at 4,740m. The following day, three hours of hard labor led to the col above, from which there were magnificent views of Kanchenjunga, Talung, Kabru, and Pandim. It was decided to name this Brothers Tees Col (5,250m). Snow leopard tracks were visible.

The following day advanced base was moved to the other side of the moraine to give better access to the northern side of the Zumthul valley. A second high camp was placed farther up, at 4,768m, and it was noted the upper valley was much wider than depicted on the map. On November 13 the party climbed to a narrow opening on a sharp ridge, which they named Mari Col (5,046m). From there they discovered a massive intact glacier rising to Siniolchu's east ridge, with a series of unclimbed peaks at its head. They ascended a small rock summit of 5,100m that they named One Hand Peak. Next day they descended to base camp, and on the following day made a tough seven-hour walk through mist and rhododendron down to Talung. [*The full version of this report at the AAJ website describes the earlier exploration of the area around the Siniolchu Rock Needles.*] 🔲 📄

– ANINDYA MUKHERJEE, *INDIA*

LAMA ANDEN, SOUTH-SOUTHEAST RIDGE

IN THE WINTER OF 2014, Tyler Adams, Bryan Hylenski, and I organized a trip to Sikkim with the help of Anindya Mukherjee. After a five-day approach via Talung Gompa and the Ringi Ghu Valley, we decided to attempt Lama Anden (5,868m, a.k.a. Lama Wangden, Lama Ongden, or Lamo Angden).

We began the climb from the foot of the southwest glacier. On February 2, Tyler and I climbed ca 300m of moderate ice (50°) up the glacier, above which easy walking led to the base of a headwall near a subsidiary pinnacle. A single pitch of moderate climbing (5.6) through a few horizontal bands of rotten rock led to a belay under a large chockstone in a chimney. Fifteen meters above lay the crest of the south-southeast ridge.

Once on the crest we followed it north along broken and, in places, very loose rock. Several gendarmes had to be negotiated via the east flank. At the largest, just south of the main summit, we made a short rappel from a piton onto some steep snow on the east side of the ridge. A traverse of two rope lengths across this snow brought us to a ledge, where we unroped and scrambled up loose rock, scree, and snow to a false summit and then finally the true summit. During the descent, we headed down the west flank from the big gendarme where we'd made the short rappel during the ascent. Downclimbing and rappels put us on the glacier. At 10 p.m., 20 hours after setting out, we reached our tent at the bottom of the glacier. [*Editor's note: There has been some confusion in the climbing history of Lama Anden. The main summit likely was climbed by the mid-1940s, but the exact route is unclear. Search the AAJ website for this report to read the full history of attempts and more details on the 2014 ascent.*] 🔲 📄

– JOHN MILLER, *USA*

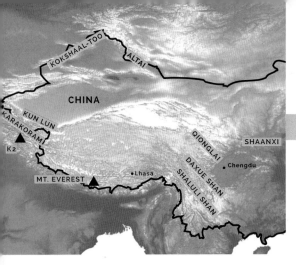

On the map: KOKSHAAL-TOO, ALTAI, CHINA, KUN LUN, KARAKORAM, K2, QIONGLAI, SHAANXI, Chengdu, DAXUE SHAN, SHALULI SHAN, Lhasa, MT. EVEREST

CHINA

WESTERN KOKSHAAL-TOO

KYZYL ASKER, SOUTHEAST FACE, WAR AND PEACE

IN 2009, Sergey Nilov, Sergey Mikhailov, and I tried a new line on the ca 1,150m face to the right of the Russian route on Kyzyl Asker's southeast face (Mikhailov-Odintsov-Ruchkin 2007). The weather was very bad and we eventually ran out of time, 300m from the 5,842m summit. In the intervening years we dreamed about returning to finish this climb.

In July, Dmitry Grigoriev, Sergey Nilov, and I were back in Kyrgyzstan. As an acclimatization climb we traversed four summits on the ridge east of the Kyzyl Asker Glacier. Our aim was to spend three nights above 4,500m. Starting to the north, we climbed over Pik Beggar (4,640m), Pik Ecstasy (4,720m), and Pik Yurnos (4,720m) to the summit of Pik Gronky (5,080m). From there we retraced our steps to the col before Yurnos and descended to the Komorova Glacier, where we cached gear that we would take to Kyzyl Asker. Later, it took us two days to ascend the Komorova Glacier and cross Window Col to establish camp below the east-southeast face.

Compared to 2009 there was much less snow on the glacier and the bergschrund was far bigger. We started up our five-year-old line on August 1 and climbed four and a half pitches in a steep, narrow icefall to reach a small, sloping ledge, where we hacked out a site for our tent. We were forced to remain here at Camp 1 an extra day due to bad weather. Above, the ice axes were not needed until we reached Camp 4, 60m above our high point in 2009. The granite was good, with many cracks for cams, nuts, pitons, and Russian hooks. Unfortunately, almost all the wide cracks were choked with ice, so screws also were useful. At the end of each pitch we found and used our old belay/rappel anchors (mostly single 8mm bolts, the only gear left in place after our previous attempt). Camps 2, 3, and 4 were similar to Camp 1—all required four or five hours of ice excavation before gaining just enough space to erect our single tent. The weather was unstable throughout, and at both Camps 2 and 3 we spent an extra day before moving on.

On August 10 we fixed our last rope beneath three big snow mushrooms on the crest of the northeast ridge. During the night the weather was awful, and I was annoyed with myself for not continuing the previous day. However, when we reached the top of the ropes the sun started to appear, warming us. We crossed the crest and, moving together, reached the snow-capped rock summit. The same day we managed to descend to Camp 1, and the following day were congratulating each other on the glacier. We named our route War and Peace. It gave 1,350m of climbing at an overall grade of 6B (or ED), 6b A2 M6. The rock is well featured with many cracks, and once started on the route you will never lose the line. We left only rappel anchors. Given the relatively small number of teams that have visited this area we were surprised and dismayed by the amount of garbage we saw.

– DMITRY GOLOVCHENKO, *RUSSIA*

[Above] Sergey Nilov tackles thin mixed climbing on the first pitch above Camp 4. *Dmitry Golovchenko* [Below] Kyzyl Asker from the southeast. (1) This unclimbed ice couloir has seen many attempts. (2) Southeast Pillar, Belgian Route (2013). (3) Southeast Pillar, Russian Route (2007). (4) War and Peace (2014). (5) Sal con Cebolla (2014). On the second known ascent of the mountain, in 2004, Pete Benson and Matt Halls climbed a couloir just off the right edge of the picture to the northeast ridge, then traversed the north face before climbing direct to the summit. *Esteban Mena*

[Below] On the second 5.12a crux of Sal con Cebolla. *Esteban Mena*

KYZYL ASKER, SAL CON CEBOLLA (TO NORTHEAST RIDGE)

IN LATE AUGUST, Rafael Caceres, Nicolas Navarette, Carla Perez, and I climbed a new route on a pillar to the right of the main east-southeast face of Kyzyl Asker (5,842m), reaching the upper northeast ridge. We spent several days in Urumchi dealing with logistical problems relating to Chinese customs, before finally leaving town on August 9. Three days by bus over very good roads brought us to a small Uygur house, where we were hosted for the night and supplied with motorbikes, camels, and donkeys to transport all our equipment to a base camp at 3,600m. We reached there on the 12th after five hours of easy trekking.

We first spent a couple of days making a cache at ca 4,100m before establishing a tent below the wall at ca 4,550m. Over the next week, due to unstable weather, we were only able to fix 11 pitches. This section is on great rock, mainly in cracks but also with some face climbing to connect crack systems. Pitches nine and 10, both involving overhanging climbing with good pro, are the technical rock cruxes at 5.12a.

On the 22nd we left the tent and moved up to Camp 1 in a portaledge on the wall. Over the next two days we climbed four more pitches to reach the base of the final corner system below the summit ridge.

Realizing that good weather doesn't last long in this range, we decided to make a summit bid on August 28. We started from Camp 1 at 3 a.m. and reached the ridge at 11 p.m. We decided to treat this high point (ca 5,700m) as our "summit": A storm had already started, and snow conditions on the final ridge did not appear favorable. The last pitches on ice and mixed had been amazing, though threatened by icefall—one of the team was knocked out during the ascent. We spent the next eight hours descending to Camp 1, and from there we continued to the glacier the same day, knowing that the weather would not improve, and that our "hiking permits" were just about to expire.

While we never experienced any horrible wind, the temperatures varied wildly, from scorching hot days on the lower wall to -30°C during our summit bid. We named the route Sal con Cebolla (Salt with Onions) after our diet on the glacier: We ate mainly onions and noodles during the expedition because Chinese customs officials had confiscated all the food brought from Ecuador. The 1,100m route had difficulties of 5.12a C1 WI5+ M6+. 🖻

– ESTEBAN MENA, *ECUADOR*

KUN LUN

KOKODAK DOME, SOUTH RIDGE

AN UNCLIMBED 7,000M PEAK? Yes, but then maybe no. Yes, because until July 24 no climber had set foot on the ca 7,129m summit of Kokodak (a.k.a Kokodag) Dome. No, because the prominence of Kokodak Dome with respect to neighboring Kokodak Peak (7,210m) is not exactly known, and may not match the requirement for a high mountain range such as the Kun Lun. The Dome is situated in the Kongur group, northwest of Kokodak Peak (Kokodak I), climbed in 2006 by an American-Russian expedition (*AAJ 2007*). Our trip was organized by German tour operator AMICAL, led by German climber Luis Stitzinger, and began on July 6. We were 14 climbers from Austria and Germany, along with two Nepalese Sherpas.

On July 12 we established base camp at 4,300m, and during the next 10 days made several approaches to higher elevations, setting up camps at 4,850m, 5,525m, and 6,300m. Chhongba Sherpa and Singi Lama fixed ropes on the riskiest sections. We followed more or less the same route as the 2006 expedition to about the same altitude as our Camp 2, where they traversed right. Above, we entered untrodden territory.

At 3 a.m. on the 24th we set off for the top from Camp 2. It was cloudy and windy, but despite an early temperature of -10°C, not too cold. At 8 a.m. Luis reported over the radio, "We can see the summit for the first time." This proved rather premature, because farther up he realized there were three peaks at approximately the same altitude. They had to use GPS to determine which was the highest: 38°38'04.3"N, 75°08'51.9"E, 7,137m GPS. 📷 📄

– STEFAN NESTLER, *GERMANY*

LIUSHEN TAG, SOUTH FACE, ATTEMPT

IN SEPTEMBER, Zaheer Durrani, Stefan Jachmich, Susan Jensen, Gus Morton, Alison Stockwell, and I attempted unclimbed Liushen Tag (6,595m, 35°59'38.07"N, 81°35'38.73"E), south of the town of Keriya (Yutian) in Hotan Prefecture. The northern slopes of the massif are heavily glaciated, and the topography makes access difficult. To its west lies the deep gorge of the Kurab (Ak Su) River, which cuts through the Kun Lun and gives access to the Tibetan Plateau. Since the 19th century, traveling this gorge has proved difficult and time-consuming, with numerous river crossings for pack animals. In the early 1960s a road was built by prison labor, but it disintegrated quickly. We expected a five-day walk up the gorge from the village of Pulu, but on arrival found that gold miners had recut the road. It is now possible to drive up to 5,000m.

The southern aspect of this range is dry and cold, with a very high snow line. Toward the end of the month water sources higher on the mountain disappeared entirely, limiting our choices of camps. We thoroughly explored possible approaches to the upper part of a prominent spur on Liushen Tag's south face, which leads to the southwest ridge at a height of ca 6,300m. Susan, Stefan, and (separately) Zaheer reached a high point of 5,900m on the left flank of the "Tower." Zaheer and Gus made the first ascent of the snow-covered peak south of base camp (6,004m GPS; 35°55'14.72"N, 81°34'33.22"E). This was repeated some days later by Susan and Stefan.

Access to this area is particularly difficult, with numerous permits required at a local and regional level, partly as a reaction to the death of three Russians a few years ago in an unofficial rafting expedition. Permits for the mountain totaled an exorbitant £9,500. 📷 📄

– JOHN TOWN, *U.K.*

AGHIL RANGE, EXPLORATION OF THE DURBIN KANGRI GROUP

IN JUNE AND JULY I led a group to explore the peaks north of the Shaksgam River. The aim was to establish the climbing potential of the 6,000m peaks on both sides of the Kizil Davan, the 5,700m pass connecting the Shaksgam (via the Kulchintubulak River) to the Zug-Shaksgam ("False Shaksgam") Valley, and also of the peaks on both sides of the upper Zug-Shaksgam. While a number of teams have visited the Shaksgam, primarily to climb 8,000m peaks and 7,000ers such as Chongtar and the Crown, the number to have visited the Zug-Shaksgam can still be counted on the fingers of one hand (Mason, 1926; Shipton, 1930; Lebedev, 2010). Although the last team provided photos and significant written information, and performed the first crossing of the Kizil Davan, the region had yet to be visited by climbers.

As befits such a remote and relatively expensive region, we formed a large expedition around three, mostly autonomous teams: Rob Duncan, Jesse Mease (both USA), Dmitry Shapovalov (Ukraine), and I (U.K.); Lukas Brexler, Harald Kirschenhofer, and Christof Nettekoven (Germany); and Ales Holc and Peter Meznar (Slovenia). From the Kyrgyz village of Ilik, with seven camels, we trekked up the Surukwat River for two days to the base of the Aghil Davan, crossed this pass (4,805m), and dropped into the Shaksgam on the third day, arriving at our base camp (36°02'43"N, 76°41'52"E) at 4,100m on the Kulchintubulak River, some 3km from the Shaksgam.

At this point we separated into our three exploration teams. The German party's activities may be found in the report below. The Slovenians began by exploring the slot canyon leading northeast from base camp, which curved around to a glacier beneath the north face of Durbin Kangri II (6,755m). We began by exploring and acclimatizing around Kizil Davan pass (5,710m), accessed by heading southeast up the boulder-strewn main valley of the Kulchintubulak and the glacier above. We climbed a peak north of the pass (6,184m, 36°00'25"N, 76°48'25"E) and tried another peak, but were turned back by soft snow over slabby rock. Shapovalov and I also climbed the highest point south of the Kizil Davan (Point 5,858m).

Shapolvalov then joined the German team, while Duncan, Mease, and I prepared to attempt an ice line on the north face of Durbin Kangri I (6,824m). However, our hopes were dashed by impossible ice conditions and soft, friable, featureless rock, which forced a retreat from the first technical pitch at 5,200m. All nine members were back in base on July 2. The Slovenians had already climbed a 6,200m summit (36°04'22"N, 76°47'13"E), which they named Kamnik Peak after their home village, and they left for Durbin Kangri II on the July 3. This was the beginning of two days of rain and cold temperatures, which dropped considerable amounts of snow above 5,000m. On the 5th we returned to our advanced base up the Kulchintubulak, but decided on the morning of the 6th, after another snowy night, that the northeast ridge of Durbin Kangri I was much too objectively hazardous.

On the 7th the weather became very warm and remained that way for the rest of our stay. We crossed the Kizil Davan and descended to the Zug-Shaksgam, making camp in much the same place as Mason in 1926. On the 8th we followed the Zug-Shaksgam for 10km, frequently wading through slot canyons in knee-deep water, to the southern side of Kaimuk Kangri (6,952m), gaining excellent views of many 6,000m summits between the two rivers, as well as of the eastern ramparts of Durbin Kangri I. On the 9th we followed a tributary river southward from the Zug-Shaksgam intending to access the east face of Burnag Kangri (6,821m), the dominant peak between the rivers in this section. However, our hopes were dashed after around 1km of

[Photos] Peaks of the Zug-Shaksgam: (Above) The unclimbed Peak 6,490m and its neighbors. (Below) Unclimbed Burnag Kangri (6,821m) from the northwest. *Photos: Bruce Normand*

wading and scrambling in a seemingly endless, narrow slot canyon, from which we had to retreat before hypothermia and rising waters made our dangerous situation deadly. By the 12th we were back in base camp beside an almost unrecognizably swollen Kulchintubulak River.

On the 13th we learned from home that the Slovenians had not been heard from since the 5th. The next day we tried to follow their footsteps up the valley they had ascended, but it turned into another slot canyon, with icy, muddy, rushing water far above our knees, and we were forced to retreat. We invoked emergency procedures, which involved the Slovenian Embassy in Beijing requesting a Chinese military helicopter. On the 16th we tried to return to our advanced base, with a view to crossing the east ridge of Durbin Kangri II at 6,200m and looking down into the basin where Holc and Meznar were last heard from (they reported being

[**Left**] Unnamed and unclimbed Peak 6,622m in the Zug-Shaksgam. [**Right**] Dangerous wading on the approach to Burnag Kangri. *Bruce Normand*

at 5,600m waiting for better weather). However, our efforts were thwarted yet again by high water. On the 20th we used the effects of a brief cold spell to cross the main Shaksgam and begin the trek out, before the river could become impassable until late August.

On the 22nd a helicopter arrived at our camp at the foot of the Aghil Davan in the morning. Over the next three days, the pilot made several flights in search of the Slovenians, but no evidence of their presence could be found. Ales Holc and Peter Meznar are presumed to have died in a trekking or climbing accident on or around July 6. Both climbers had long track records of difficult ascents in the high mountains. Each was married with three children aged up to 12. Most of all, both were warm, witty, open, and lively characters whose friendship and love will be missed by many. [*Editor's note: A fuller account of the search for the Slovenian climbers, plus more photos of unclimbed peaks, are available at the AAJ website.*] 📷 📄

– **BRUCE NORMAND**, *CHINA*

AGHIL RANGE, DURBIN KANGRI GROUP, XIAO KANGRI

As PART of the Shaksgam Expedition led by Bruce Normand, Lukas Brexler, Harry Kirchenhofer, and I (all from Germany) visited the Durbin Kangri group in June. From the team base camp, we three followed the canyon leading toward Durbin Kangri I, which narrowed to just 2m and was prone to rockfall from both sides. Sometimes we had to climb over boulders bigger than a house, at other times traverse conglomerate cliffs. It took four hours to achieve just 300m of altitude on a 5km section. We followed the glacier below the mighty, 1,700m-high north face Durbin Kangri I to reach a basin, where we eventually established a high camp (5,409m). I'd had surgery just 12 days before departing for China and had to step back. Dmitry Shapovalov then joined Harry and Lukas for an ascent of a snow peak directly opposite the north face of Durbin Kangri I. Following a natural line up 50° névé slopes to the summit ridge, and avoiding intervening rock towers, the three reached the summit (6,102m, 36°01'07"N, 76°47'38"E) on June 30. Neighboring unclimbed peaks of ca 6,290m and 6,453m could be of interest to future expeditions. We named the summit Xiao Kangri (little snow/ice peak), as it is dwarfed by the massive Durbin Kangri peaks.

Later, Dmitry and Lukas summited a previously unclimbed rock tower directly north of base camp. The fragile rock and conglomerate was held together mostly by good luck. Kulchintubulak Tower (5,290m, 36°03'13"N, 76°42'27"E) is a prominent feature when viewed up the Shaksgam Valley from below Aghil Pass. We departed base camp on July 5.

Editor's note: Prior to 2014 the only summit to be reached north of the Shaksgam River was Peak 6,366m, located southeast of Durbin Kangri and west of Burnag Kangri. This was climbed in 1997 by a New Zealand team led by John Nankervis. 📷

— **CHRISTOF NETTEKOVEN**, GERMANY

SHALULI SHAN

JARJINJABO SPIRES, NEW ROUTE AND GUIDE

IN AUGUST 2014, Garrett Bradley, Christopher Miller, and I climbed a 10-pitch (ca 400m) route on the south face of Jabo Tower in the Garrapunsum Massif. The upper portion of the route joined lines established in 2002 and 2004. With little to no information on the climbing in this area, we found the lines confusing. For this reason, I have written a comprehensive guidebook for the entire Garrapunsum and Xiashe massifs. In addition to the rock climbs, I've added information about mountaineering routes on the major peaks in the area. The guide will be available in PDF format from www.junshanclimber.com. 📄

— **MIKE DOBIE**, CHINA

[Below] Jammo (a.k.a. Janmo, left) and Jabo in the Jarjinjabo Massif. Both are ca 5,370m, with Jabo the higher. (1) Athans-Ogden-Synnott (2002, 5.10d to the summit block). (2) Japanese Route (2001, 5.10a A1, climbed free in 2004, with a variation, at 5.10d). (3) Knight-Laforest (2004, 5.10c to summit block). This pair was the first to climb the 60m summit block (5.9 chimney pitch and face pitch of 5.11 R). (4) Athans-Ogden-Synnott (2002, 5.11a). (5) Knight-Laforest (2004, 5.11). (6) Chandler-Ditto-Knight-Laforest (2004, 5.10). (7) Bradley-Dobie-Miller (2014, 3 pitches, 5.10). Many variations to these routes are not shown. Well to the right is a 5.9 route (Athans-MacKinlay, 2002) that reaches the east ridge and continues along it to the summit. *Garrett Bradley*

JARJINJABO AREA, NEW ROUTES

OVER 14 DAYS in July and August, Marcos Costa, Liu Yunqing, Zhoulei, and, for part of the time, Dawei (a 5.14 climber from Yangshuo) climbed eight routes, opened seven new lines, and summited four different peaks. Routes included Jarjinjabo's fourth peak (5,087m) via Hail Party (a five-pitch approach of 5.10, followed by a hike up a gully and then eight pitches up to 5.11b). This route lies above Rim Route (*AAJ 2014*). They also climbed Zhoulei's Gift (ca 280m, 8 pitches, 5.12b) directly above the monastery, following a superb corner high on the route.

— *INFORMATION PROVIDED BY* MARCOS COSTA, *CHINA*

GONGKALA SHAN, KAWARANI I, NORTH FACE

WE WERE ATTRACTED to the Garze Tibetan Autonomous Region by Tom Nakamura's map depicting "Sichuan's most outstanding unclimbed peaks." One of these was Kawarani I (5,992m). From the road head near Garze town, to the northern side, we walked for two days through occasional deep snow to gain a camp below the north face. On February 20 we climbed the face, up and down in a single day, moving unroped on 45–50° snow the entire way.

Editor's note: In 2005 British mountaineers attempted to gain access to the southern side of the Kawarani peaks, but after establishing an advanced camp at 4,800m, they were told to leave by a group of monks from the lower village. In 2007 a second British party failed to gain permission due to religious celebrations. In 2011 Japanese were granted a permit, but on arrival in China discovered this had been rescinded. 📷

— MARCOS COSTA *AND* BRUCE NORMAND, *CHINA*

DAXUE SHAN

HAIZI SHAN, WEST FACE

IN LATE JANUARY, accompanied by Garrett Bradley, we traveled to Haizi Shan (a.k.a. Yala, 5,820m) to attempt a line on the west face. Base camp was at an excellent hot springs beneath the face. On the 29th we started climbing up the central snow couloir at 5 a.m. [*This couloir lies immediately left of the southwest ridge, attempted in 2005 by Jon Otto's team. After abandoning the climb ca 200m below the summit, they made a rappel descent of this central couloir.*] Garrett did not feel sufficiently acclimatized and bivouacked at the top of the couloir (ca 5,400m). We climbed snow and mixed terrain for a further 200m to reach the crest of the upper southwest ridge, which we followed to the snow/ice summit ridge at 5,700m. We reached the top of the mountain at 5 p.m. in excellent, if windy, weather. This is probably the third ascent of the peak, which received many attempts before it was finally climbed in 2006 by Malcolm Bass and Pat Deavoll, via the north face. It is more or less certain the mountain was climbed later the same year by Christine Boskoff and Charlie Fowler. 📷

— MARCOS COSTA *AND* BRUCE NORMAND, *CHINA*

XIAO GONGGA, NORTHWEST RIDGE;
TYROL SHAN, WEST FACE AND SOUTH RIDGE

WHEN SIMON GIETL was climbing with the DAV expedition squad in the Dolomites during the summer of 2013, he learned about their trip to the Minya Konka (Gongga Shan) range the

previous year, during which they did the first ascents of two peaks (*AAJ 2013*). Simon enlisted two other Tyrolean climbers, Daniel Tavernini and me, and one year later, on October 6, we flew from Munich. The journey to Chengdu, onward to Kangding, and then a final trek with 14 mules, a cook, and liaison officer to a base camp at 4,000m went without a hitch.

On October 17 we established advanced base at 4,600m below the north flank of Xiao Gongga (5,928m, a.k.a. Little Konka, Ruiche Gongga, or Tshiburongi). We set off early next morning for the northwest ridge, climbing unroped for the first one and half hours. Three short pitches then led to a little plateau, above which the snow was quite deep. The slope above eventually steepened to 60°. A final mixed section on the crest deposited us on the summit at 1 p.m. The 1,300m route was graded 60° M5, and on it we passed three belay stations. [*It is not clear from whom these might have originated—known ascents and attempts have chosen other lines. See AAJ 2012.*]

We now turned to our main target, the steep, west-facing rock buttress leading to the summit of Stifler's Mom, first attempted by French climbers in 2009 (*AAJ 2010*). The 2012 DAV team had also considered this buttress but instead climbed the peak (and later named it) via a broad snow gully to the left and then the crest of the rocky north ridge (1989 Steps Toward Heaven, *AAJ 2013*).

We shifted high camp to the head of the Tshiburongi Valley, at 4,950m, after which there was an overnight snowfall of 20cm. We climbed four pitches up a line to the right of the French attempt, but freezing conditions, which were far too cold for rock shoes, forced us to abandon the attempt.

Instead, we turned to the unclimbed summit between Stifler's Mom and Melcyr Shan. We started up the line You Happy, We Happy (Gottler-Hones, 2012, WI5), a variant start to Nubiline, the first route up Melcyr Shan. The crux of this section was thin, hollow, and only mitigated by a couple of cams in the side wall. Above, we moved up 50–60° snow to gain the col between the unnamed peak and Melcyr Shan. The 40m rock climb to the summit was in the sun, with no wind, and on beautiful granite. Daniel took the lead and climbed to the top at UIAA VI-. We named the summit Tyrol Shan (ca 5,860m). We rappelled the 700m route and returned to base camp, where later we established a few rock routes on an east-facing crag 30 minutes' walk from the tents. The majority of these were one pitch and some only top-roped; Mortadella, by Simon, went at 7c. 📷 🔍

— **VITTORIO MESSINI**, *ITALY*

UNNAMED PEAK CA 6,460M, SOUTH-SOUTHWEST RIDGE

AFTER CLIMBING HAIZI SHAN (*see report above*), we headed to the southwest side of the Minya Konka Range with Garrett Bradley. A number of southern outliers of Minya Konka (Gongga Shan, 7,556m) remain unclimbed. From the road end at 2,700m, the approach to these peaks is a steep and mostly trail-free hike up a riverbed and old moraines to the foot of a glacier beneath the south face of what we originally thought was the Tai Shan massif. After hiking for two days, February 2 and 3, we camped below a large boulder that protected us from the rockfall we witnessed during our approach.

On the 4th we aborted a summit attempt at 6,200m due to high winds. On the morning of the 6th, the winds had calmed substantially and we followed the south-southwest ridge on steep snow and 40°–50° blue ice all the way to the summit. The descent proved challenging as the winds picked up and we had to brace ourselves many times against gusts exceeding 50 mph.

The map in our possession showed this virgin summit to be Tai Shan (6,468m), although we were clearly on a west top, with the true summit being an east top 5–10m higher and 500–700m along the ridge. In later correspondence with Gregor Duerrenberger, a member of the 1981 Swiss expedition that climbed several peaks here, he confirmed that Tai Shan (6,410m) is a peak farther south along the ridge, which on later maps has mistakenly been designated Jinyin Shan. The Swiss climbed from the Hailougou/Hailoko Valley to the east, summiting the true Tai Shan by the northwest ridge. ▣

– MARCOS COSTA *AND* BRUCE NORMAND, *CHINA*

QIONGLAI SHAN / SIGUNIANG NATIONAL PARK

[Above] Abi from the southeast. (1) West face and southwest ridge: Shivering (5.7 M3 AI2, AAJ 2011; this route was repeated in February 2011). (2) Graduation Exam. On the original ascent of Abi the climbers followed this couloir all the way to the southeast ridge, then moved onto the east face. (3) Southeast ridge (700m, D+ M5, as graded by the 2012 climbers). *Liu ZhiXiong*

ABI, SOUTH FACE AND SOUTHEAST RIDGE

ON SEPTEMBER 20 I made a solo ascent of Abi (5,694m) at the top of the Shuangqiao Valley, climbing some new ground left of the southeast ridge before following a previously climbed route to the summit. From a camp at 4,600m, it took one hour to reach the glacier, which fortunately had only few, obvious crevasses.

The lower part of the rightward-slanting gully on the south face is split by a rock rib. I began on the left, eventually crossing the loose rib to the right side. The hardest part was about AI2+. My plan had been to follow this gully to the southeast ridge, as the original climbers of Abi did in 2004. However, as the mountain warmed in the sun, I began to experience serious rockfall. The rock buttress on the right side of the south face (left of the upper gully) looked safe, not vertical, and composed of relatively sound granite. I climbed this to the crest of the southeast ridge and then followed the ridge to the top, back-roping the steep mixed chimney above a big step. Above, I was able to take off rope and crampons and rock climb more easily to the summit, which I reached at 1 p.m. I descended the southeast ridge, making many 20m rappels, and reached my tent by 7 p.m.

I named my variation Graduation Exam (1,100m of climbing, 5.9 M4 AI2+ 50°), as I found I matured my mental processes by climbing solo. There are other possible routes on the main wall of the south face.

– LIU ZHIXIONG, *CHINA*

HUANG GUAN FENG, EAST FACE AND SOUTH RIDGE

HUANG GUAN FENG (5,515m) or Crown Peak, due to its three-pinnacle summit in the shape of a crown, is the first large peak immediately east of Yutu Feng/Jade Rabbit Peak (5,578m), on the north side of the upper Bipeng Valley (Peak 38 in Jon Sullivan's *AAJ 2009* map). In March, Bao Yifei, Tim Boelter, Marcos Costa, Huang Siyuan, Liu Yunqin, and Jon Otto reached the northeast ridge at 5,483m but were forced to retreat. Costa, Huang, Liu, and Otto returned in October for a second attempt, starting on the 21st from a high camp on the glacier east of the peak. Their previous line was too exposed to stonefall in this warmer season, so they chose a line much farther left on the east face. They followed a steep mixed couloir, with the third pitch—mainly vertical, with a small overhang—forming the crux. After eight pitches it was dark, and at 10 p.m. all except Costa, who remained outside in his sleeping bag, squeezed into a small tent for a bivouac. The following morning one pitch took them to the ridge between the south and main tops. At 2 p.m. they reached the main summit (GPS 5,518m or 5,525m, 31°14'42.1"N, 102°50'28.4"E) and then descended in bad weather and spindrift. The 500m route was graded TD AI4 M4/5.

– XIA ZHONGMING, *GERMANY*

SHUANGQIAO VALLEY, ICE AND MIXED; LIERENFENG, EAST FACE

I ARRIVED IN SIGUNIANG on Christmas Day 2013 with the goal of developing hard dry-tooling and mixed climbing. Ice climbing is a relatively new sport in China, and mixed climbing has only recently picked up traction. There were only three established mixed routes in the Shuangqiao valley, one by French climbers in 2010 and the other two by more French and me (a Brazilian living in China) during the winter of 2012-'13. By the end of the 2014 winter season the valley had 14 modern mixed climbs, nine of which I put up. Highlights include Lepton (M8+), Welcome to SQG (M8), Antimatter (M11), and Dark Matter (M11)—the last two were China's hardest mixed lines as of April 2014.

On January 6, 2014, I repeated Baijiu Hangover (M8 WI5+), a route put up by French climbers the previous winter. As I descended I drilled three bolts on a line a few meters to the left (one on the first pitch and two on the second). I returned on January 23 with Bruce Normand and redpointed it: How to Train Your Dragon (M7 WI5+).

I also joined four other climbers for an attempt on virgin Lierenfeng (5,362m) above the Shuangqiao Valley. We planned an ascent of the east face by two different routes that would intersect in the middle. We walked around three hours from the road, camped, and then at 5 a.m. on January 10 started climbing. Wu Kang (China) and I began in a moderate snow gully, with the occasional ice pitch (AI3) and short sections of mixed. After 350m we traversed left toward the central gully. Wu waited here with Ricky Cheng from the other party while I soloed the remaining 300m of gully and a nerve-wracking 80m of loose rock to the summit, where I met Yann Delavoux, France, and Xiao Liu, China. We all descended together to the rest of our party and then down to camp. 🖼

– MARCOS COSTA, CHINA

[Above] The south face of Daogou East showing the two established lines: (1) South Pillar (2014) and (2) South Face–Salvage Op (2005, 650m, 5.10d). The face has suffered earthquake damage since this photo was taken in 2005. *Joe Puryear*

SHUANGQIAO VALLEY, PEAK 5,467M, PEAK 5,184M, DAOGOU EAST

FROM SEPTEMBER 11–OCTOBER 5, I visited the Shuangqiao with 33-year-old Marcos Costa, a Brazilian living for the last seven years in China. Marcos is undoubtedly the driving force in the current explosion of new route development in the country, from the sport climbs at Getu to trad climbing at Liming and incredible ice and alpine climbing throughout Sichuan.

Our main objective was the still unclimbed "Great Wall of China," the 900m west face of Seerdengpu (5,592m). Within days of our arrival we were ca 300m up this wall, taking a solid beating from the constant rockfall that curses this beautiful peak. After some close calls we bailed—this was my sixth attempt, on as many different routes, over the course of three separate trips, to try to tame this beast.

We switched focus to unclimbed Peak 5,467m, directly to the south. After 10 hours of climbing we reached the summit by what we believe to be the first ascent of the long and complex southeast ridge: Moo Moo Ridge (1,000m, 5.10+ R).

We then hiked into the wonderful sub-valley named Dagou, home to an impressive collection of jagged peaks and walls, including the northwest faces of Daogou East and West, as well as recently climbed Dayantianwo (5,240m, *AAJ 2014*) and Peak 5,180m. We were interested in unclimbed stuff, and two substantial features stood out: Peaks 5,120m and 5,184m. In the valley we met four French climbers who were heading up to attempt the impressive east face of 5,120m, on which they subsequently succeeded (*see following report*). Marcos and I set out for the southwest face of Peak 5,184m.

A recent snowstorm had deposited an uncomfortable amount of white on the rock, but we persevered through hours of screaming barfies and established a "fun" 300m 5.11, the Scream, to the summit of this previously virgin peak. From here, Daogou East and West dominated the skyline, and we knew where we were going next. But before that we spent a few days cragging on an impressive 200m overhanging orange wall that stood just to the west. No doubt this would have routes all over it if it weren't so hard to get to.

With just under a week before my flight home, Marcos and I headed up the sub-valley of Xiaogou for a look at the south faces of both Daogous and Chibu. We were immediately drawn to a brilliant granite pillar on the south face of Daogou East (5,462m). We climbed through squalls of snow and sleet, shivering our way up incredible cracks and good granite. The best pitch was perhaps the last: a 40m 5.11 thin-hands splitter. So much fun! We found no anchors or signs of a previous ascent, and our subsequent research determined that the earthquake of 2008, which killed approximately 69,000 people and permanently scarred every peak in the park, had lowered the previously recorded 5,466m summit and almost completely erased the original route on the south face by Chad Kellogg, Joe Puryear, and Stoney Richards (2005). We dubbed our route South Pillar (700m, 5.11+); our ascent was only the second recorded of this peak. [*The 2012 ascent of the northwest face, reported in AAJ 2013, was actually on a completely different mountain: Peak 5,383m on the southern rim of the Xiaogou Valley, east of Tan Shan. This unnamed summit was likely unclimbed before the 2012 French ascent.*] 🔘

– PAT GOODMAN, *USA*

FOUR PIGS PEAK

Aurélie Didillon, Simon Duverney, Elodie Lecomte, and I arrived below the mountains of Siguniang on September 16 and spent a couple of days trekking above the Shuangqiao Valley to take stock. Conclusion: the mountains are very beautiful, but after the 2008 earthquake many are crumbling. In addition, the cracks seem very grassy. One formation, Peak 5,120m,

[Below] (A) Shizi Peak. (B) Four Pigs Peak (Peak 5,120m) from the northeast with the line of Le Réscapés de la Forêt Magique. *Sébastien Ratel*

high in the Dagou Valley, grabbed our attention. It looked steep and more compact than the other peaks, but unfortunately it is also one of the most remote. [*Peak 5,120m is situated on the western side of the upper Dagou cirque, south-southeast of 5,240m Dayantianwu. The lower south summit of Peak 5,120m was climbed via the east face in 2013, by Japanese climbers, who named it Shizi Peak (5,057m, AAJ 2014)*]. Even with two porters the bags we carried to the foot of the peak were heavy, and the forest, which we thought "magical" on first acquaintance, became a real trial. The porters left us halfway—the sight of the enormous scree slope that followed did little to motivate them.

[Above] On the final day of the ascent of Four Pigs Peak. *Sébastien Ratel*

We split the team; some ferried loads, while others started on the route. We managed to fix the first 100m, finding an ice axe essential to remove vegetation. The weather was poor, and we returned to the valley lodge to dry out. When we emerged, locals were predicting the arrival of winter, but the forecast promised a three-day window.

We returned to our high point and slept on the wall in our portaledges, but it snowed throughout the night and in the morning the face above was white. Fortunately, it stopped at 11 a.m. and we continued until midnight through grim conditions. When we woke next day it was snowing again, but once the sky appeared less "heavy" we set off aid climbing, leaving all of our bivy gear at the camp. The last pitches to the ridge were enjoyable, and the ridge itself very pleasant. We managed a smile on the summit. Life was beautiful, but the descent was long. The following day we were back at the lodge. We named the summit Four Pigs Peak, and the route of ascent up the east-northeast face and north-northwest ridge is called Le Réscapés de la Forêt Magique (600m, 7b A2). 📷

– SÉBASTIEN RATEL, *FRANCE*

SHARK'S FIN, SOUTHWEST FACE, NIGHT FOG, STAR SKY

I WAS ATTRACTED to Peak 5,086m, the Shark's Fin, but only knew of He Chuan's 2010 attempt. A lack of information brings uncertainty, more challenge, and extra fun. Above the Dagou Valley the Shark's Fin presents two faces: The northwest face is a compact slab leading to crack systems; the southwest face is concave with a nearly vertical headwall, and is rich in crack systems.

Approaching the face is easy thanks to a yak trail. On September 19, Wu Donghua and I climbed two pitches and fixed 120m of rope. After a day of rain, we jumared to our high point and soon were simul-climbing steep terrain. By noon we were halfway up the route. The crack system above was filled with mud. Digging it out to place protection slowed us down, and we resorted to aid. At 6 p.m. we reached a good ledge 60m below the summit and bivouacked

[Above] The southwest face of Shark's Fin. (1) Night Fog, Star Sky (2014). (2) The 2010 and 2011 Chinese attempts. *Gu Qizhi*

there. The final section, which we climbed in two pitches, was vertical and thin. Sometimes, pitons would only go in halfway. After a three-hour struggle we reached the top and found old rappel anchors. During the bivouac we had been able to see starlight through the night mist, so we named our route Night Fog, Star Sky (ca 650–700m, 5.11a A2). [*Editor's note: To about three-quarters height this route follows the line attempted in 2010 and 2011 by Gong Xiaorui, He Chuan, and Wu Peng, after which it moves left and climbs directly toward the summit. John Dickey, Dylan Johnson, and Chad Kellogg climbed the northwest ridge in 2010 but stopped below the 25m summit block due to steep, unprotectable granite.*]

– GU QIZHI, *CHINA*, *TRANSLATED BY* XIA ZHONGMING

POINT 5,182M, SOUTH FACE, LEGENDS

DURING A TRIP to the Changping Valley with Fred Beckey and friends in October 2013, I met Jim Donini. While other Beckey expedition members established a new route on Joey Shan (5,178m, *AAJ 2014*), Jim and I reached a 5,182m unclimbed top just down the east ridge from Peak 5,235m. This peak lies north of the entrance to the Chiwen Valley, north of Pomiu (Celestial Peak), and on the west side of the Changping Valley before it makes the big bend to the west. Our route was south-facing and warm.

On October 8 we climbed from a high camp at 4,572m, crossing several spicy snow and rock fields, to a final four pitches of good rock that finished on top of a large monolith. The route was generally easy, 5.5 or so, but there is one mandatory move of 5.10 near the top. We had hoped to reach the main peak but were short on time. I called the route Legends due to the strange occurrence of being on a trip with legend Fred Beckey and winding up climbing an unclimbed, unnamed top with legend Jim Donini. 📷

– CAMERON KERN, *USA*

SIGUNIANG, SOUTH FACE, TRAGEDY

HU JIAPING and Liu Zhixiong died November 29 while descending from Siguniang (6,250m). The two had just climbed a difficult route on the south face. (Their goal was a new line, but it is thought they may have repeated Free Spirits, the line climbed in 2009 by Yan Dongdong and Zhou Peng.) After summiting they failed to appear at base camp by the time their porters arrived. This triggered a search, and the bodies were discovered on the glacier below the face.

Hu Jiaping (b. 1983) prepared climbing courses, instructed beginners, and took part in indoor competitions in Shanghai. In 2011 he summited Gang Pushkar in the Qilian mountains via a new route, and in 2012 he made an attempt on Xiao Gongga. In 2013 he made a single-push attempt on Tianhaizi with Liu Zhixiong. Liu (b. 1988) started climbing at college in 2007, eventually redpointing 5.12d and onsighting 5.12a. In 2012, alpine terrain became his new playground, and he subsequently climbed Jianzi Shan, Lierenfeng, and Abi (the last two ascents are reported in this edition). 📷

– CHEN TING *AND* WU XIAOJIANG, *CHINA, TRANSLATED BY* XIA ZHONGMING

POMIU, ASCENT AND TRAGEDY

IN AUGUST a Chinese team including veteran climber Wu Peng made possibly the third ascent of the southeast ridge of Pomiu, first climbed by American Keith Brown in 1985 and repeated in 2010 by Russians, who found ca 1,500m of climbing up to 6c. They summited after four days of climbing through cold, wet weather, with little food and water. Rappelling the ridge from the summit, they reached a ledge at ca 5,200m, at midnight and during a storm. The ropes were frozen and could not be pulled, so they sat for the night. Wu Peng seemed hypothermic, shivering and mentally confused. Next day, as the other two members were pulling the ropes, he fell into a gully on the south face. A rescue team found his body six days later at 5,050m.

Wu Peng (b. 1972) is best known for developing the Baihe (White River) climbing area, two hours' drive from Beijing. Some of his alpine rock routes, such as Rising Wind Horse Flag and the Shark's Fin, both with He Chuan, have been reported in the *AAJ*. He opposed excessive bolting, especially bolting next to cracks, but he also put great effort into sourcing reliable bolts, and if you have clipped a bolt throughout most of China, you've probably benefited from his work. He also founded the Internet climbing forum Rock Beer (http://bbs.rockbeer.org), the oldest in China. 📷

– WEI YU, HE CHUAN, *AND* HUANG MAOHAI, *CHINA*

SHAANXI PROVINCE

QIN MOUNTAINS, ZHONG NAN SHAN, QIEZI FENG, FAIRY FINGERS

CYCAL-YANG FAN and Ye Yun climbed a new route on the granite formation called Qiezi ("Eggplant") Feng in July. After rappelling the line to clean it and place bolted anchors on all 18 pitches, they climbed the first seven pitches (up to 5.10b and heavily vegetated) on July 20. They spent the night in a portaledge and the next day climbed the remaining 11 pitches to the top. Pitches 8–12 formed the crux and involved a continuous vertical crack, from tiny fingers to offwidth. Pitches 13–15 had discontinuous cracks and run-out climbing up to 5.10b. The top pitches were easier and joined existing routes. They named the route Fairy Fingers (520m, 5.12b) after the thin finger cracks. 📷 🔍

– XIA ZHONGMING, *GERMANY, AND* CYCAL-YANG FAN, *CHINA*

[Right] Cycal-Yang Fan on pitch 10 (5.11a) of Fairy Fingers. See next page for route line. *@Rockqd*

[Left] Fairy Fingers on Qiezi Feng (see report on previous page). *Cycal-Yang Fan* [Right] Never Give Up on the 600m south face of Hua Shan's south tower. *Qing*

QIN MOUNTAINS, HUA SHAN, SOUTH FACE, NEVER GIVE UP

Hua Shan is the West Mountain (Xi Yue) of the Five Great Mountains in Chinese traditional and religious custom. Cable cars and impressive "via ferrata" pathways lead to the various tops. Hua Shan has five peaks, but the south and highest (2,154m) has the most climbing potential. It is a 600m granite cylinder that became better known to Western climbers after Leo Houlding (U.K.), Carlos Suarez (Spain), and Wang Zhi Ming (China) made the first ascent of the impressive west face via Northern Celestial Masters (600m, British E6 6b and a few points of aid) in 2009. Zhu Xiaofei and I took seven hours to get to the bottom of the south face from the town of Huayin, via a valley to the west.

We started up on July 8 with a portaledge and haulbag, and over the next week, with a couple of days of rain that prevented any climbing, we completed 20 pitches. Dealing with mud and grass in the cracks was very time-consuming. On the 13th we climbed four pitches, of which the second had the most awful climbing I've done. A steep crack gave access to a 20m, 40cm-wide chimney leading to 10m of overhanging offwidth. Running it out for 15m in the chimney made me feel quite ill. The fourth pitch that day featured a loose chimney, and Zhu was hit in the face. He was covered in blood and insisted on going to hospital, but eventually came around.

Near the top we encountered the second crux and also a human leg bone in a tree branch—a tourist had fallen from the top. We topped out after midnight. We named the route Never Give Up (600m, 5.10+ R C2+). One bolt was placed at each of the campsites, and we used a small piton twice on pitch two; the rest was clean aid. 📷 📄 🔍

— HE CHUAN, *CHINA*

TIBET

PHOTOGRAPHIC SURVEY OF PEAKS

BETWEEN OCTOBER 11 and October 25, Tsuyoshi Nagai (82), Tamotsu Nakamura (79), and Tadao Shintani (70) drove 4,500km across southern Tibet to photograph lesser-known mountains. The team first visited the Goikarla Ryugu range, which extends some 250km from near Lhasa to Bayizhen, of Nyinchi Prefecture, but complex valleys and ridges hindered their views of 6,000m peaks. Then they headed to the far south of Tibet and, despite frequent checkpoints limiting access to the frontier with Bhutan and India, they photographed the east face of Tarlha Ri (6,777m) and peaks ranging south to Bhutan, as well as every side of the holy mountain Yalaxianbo and its massif. They also reached the holy lake Puma Yumco (4,980m), now closed to foreigners, and photographed Kulha Kangri (7,538m, a.k.a. Kula Kangri) and other mountains near the Bhutan border. In addition, they made a two-day excursion north of Lhasa to the Nyainqentanglha West (Nyanchen Tanghla West), photographing Qungmo Kangri (7,048m) and peaks visible from the north bank of the holy lake Nam Tso. Photos and maps from this "Blue Sky Expedition" will be found at the *AAJ* website. 📷 🔍

— *INFORMATION FROM* **TAMOTSU NAKAMURA**, *JAPAN*

GYAO KANG, NORTH SPUR AND EAST RIDGE

GYAO KANG (6,735M), the most northerly of the bigger peaks in the Lapche Kang Range, is a fine snowy summit that can be climbed in a day from a base camp to the north at 5,890m. The slope angles are such that it would be an agreeable peak to climb and descend on skis. In the spring of 2012 I had climbed the west ridge; I returned in the autumn of 2014 for the unclimbed east ridge. After an attempt on the north ridge of Lapche Tsokchung (6,370m), east of the great turquoise lake of Lapche Tso, we crossed Colangma Pass (5,890m) and descended to the valley below Colangma Lake. From Gyao Kang base camp we reached the summit in seven hours via the north spur and east ridge. The grades of this route and the west ridge are both around PD+. A direct route up the north face is also possible. There are other interesting peaks accessible from the Colangma valley, but the problem is always the same: how to get a permit to climb them. 📷

— **PAULO GROBEL**, *FRANCE*

[Photo] (A) Colangma (6,952m). (B) Peak 6,860m. (C) Peak 6,745m. (D) Gyao Kang. The 2014 ascent of Gyao Kang followed the east ridge (near left skyline). *Paulo Grobel*

MYANMAR

HKAKABO RAZI, WEST RIDGE ATTEMPT

OUR TEAM OF SIX—Emily Harrington, Mark Jenkins, Renan Ozturk, Cory Richards, and I, along with base camp manager Taylor Rees, headed to the far northern reaches of Myanmar in the fall to attempt the west ridge of Hkakabo Razi, in the eastern tail of the Himalaya. We hoped to secure an accurate GPS reading from the summit to lay to rest the question of whether Hkakabo Razi is the highest mountain in Southeast Asia. Hkakabo Razi has only seen one ascent—a fact that can be attributed to both the politics of Myanmar and the utter remoteness of the mountain. The region was closed to foreigners until 1993. It wasn't until 1996 that Takashi Ozaki of Japan, with Burmese climber Nyima Gyaltsen (a.k.a. Namar Jonsain), made the summit via a climb of the north face and east ridge.

Ozaki reported the height of Hkakabo as 5,881m (19,295'), exactly matching that of a British Survey map from 1925. (He did not use GPS.) In 2013, a group of Americans led by Andy Tyson summited nearby Gamlang Razi (*AAJ 2014*) and ascertained its height to be 5,870m (19,259'). But Russian survey maps and Google Earth showed Gamlang slightly *higher* than Hkakabo Razi. Someone needed to stand atop Hkakabo with a GPS to solve the mystery.

We would head into the jungle from Putao, a beautiful, remote town. However, we could not leave for four days because the government of Kachin state placed us under town arrest. On August 31, just six weeks before our arrival in Putao, two Burmese climbers had disappeared during a summit bid on Hkakabo Razi. Because this was a national Myanmar team, a massive effort was launched by the government and a private citizen, billionaire and armchair mountaineer Tay Za, to search for the missing climbers. The search continued into

[Below] The summit of Hkakabo Razi as seen from the American team's high point on the west ridge. *Mark Jenkins*

[Above] High camp on Hkakabo Razi, with the west ridge continuing at left (the high point visible is a false summit). Twin-summited Gamlang Razi is in the distance at far right. *Hilaree O'Neill*

October, when one of the rescue helicopters crashed, killing the pilot, while bringing supplies to the Hkakabo base camp. Our arrival in Putao coincided with the subsequent search for the crashed helicopter. We theorized that our town arrest was an effort to limit bad publicity. In the end, the two Burmese climbers were not found and it was never established whether they reached the summit of Hkakabo Razi.

It took us 16 days to reach base camp from Putao: three days on motorcycles and 13 days of walking. We had numerous porter issues along the way, and the trail was incredibly rugged and dangerous. Two days before reaching base camp, we encountered a Japanese team of three climbers descending from a failed attempt on the same route we aimed to climb: the west ridge. They were very forthcoming with information but left no doubt that the climbing would be complicated.

On the 30th of October we established our base camp at 13,200'. After only one day of organizing, we made our way to Camp 1 at 15,700'. In two days we were established at Camp 2 at 17,300' after an arduous climb up the steep north side of the mountain on ice, loose rock, and rotten snow. In two more days we were set up at Camp 3 at 18,200' on the west ridge of Hkakabo Razi. We hadn't seen the summit since leaving base camp: Living up to its mystery, the peak kept itself hidden by rock gendarmes.

After a single rest day, Renan, Cory, and Mark headed for the top with supplies for one bivy. After eight hours of climbing, the three hunkered down for a windy, freezing, and mostly sleepless night. To give an idea of the complicated, circuitous nature of the route, they had gained only a few hundred feet in elevation from our high camp. After a few hours the next morning, a little beyond the Japanese high point, Mark arrived at a spot from which he could see the rest of the route to the summit, and he knew the climb was over. The terrain ahead would undoubtedly require a second bivy, this time without the tent and sleeping bags they had left behind.

The unfortunate consequence of climbing a serrated ridge of rock and ice meant the retreat took nearly as long as the ascent, and the three did not return to high camp until sunset. Their high point on the west ridge was 18,840'. Mark guessed there was another 500–700' of elevation gain to reach the summit.

Our trip was far from over. We still had nearly 150 miles of downclimbing and jungle walking to reach civilization. We spent the better part of two weeks, with no rest days and not nearly enough food, retracing our steps. Despite the hardships of the trip, it was a comfort to walk over familiar terrain. The summit elevation of Hkakabo Razi is still a mystery and its reputation as, in Ozaki's words, "one of the most difficult and dangerous mountains in the world," has been cemented in my mind.

— **HILAREE O'NEILL**, *USA*

BORNEO

MELINAU GORGE, JUNGLE FEVER

OVER TWO WEEKS in July, a British team of climbers and film crew journeyed into Sarawak to establish a new route in the Melinau Gorge and to document the wildlife we found there. Given the number of people involved and the associated noise level, the wildlife took note and quickly dispersed. However, Waldo Etherington, Leo Houlding, and I managed to climb a 350m route, given a tentative grade of E5 6a, on a big limestone cliff on the southwest face of Mt. Benarat in Gunung Mulu National Park. Each pitch was climbed onsight with no aid, other than the last pitch, which was bolted due to the lack of gear placements. This went free at around 7b.

Gunung Mulu is a UNESCO world heritage site that hosts some of the largest caves in the world, and due to the sensitive nature of the area, permits and guides were required. A team of local guides and porters assisted us in making the three-hour boat ride up the river and into the national park. Three hours of jungle walking brought us to a first glimpse of the wall we were about to climb.

We picked the line of least resistance, mainly due to time constraints and the soft, loose limestone. Reaching the top of the first pitch was amazing, giving bird's eye views over some of the tallest tropical trees in the world. After five days we reached the summit of the route we called Jungle Fever. Graded

[Above] Leo Houlding on the second pitch of Jungle Fever (350m, E5 6a) on the southwest face of Mt. Benarat in Gunung Mulu National Park. *Matt Pickles*

somewhere in the E5 region, there are many spots with poor protection, giving you a serious desire not to fall off. Given our need to film the route, all belays were fully bolted.

To our knowledge there are no other routes on this wall, and the only other people known to have gone to the summit are locals who descend into the small caves 50m from the cliff top to collect bird nests, a delicacy throughout the region. There is a large scope for new routes, but cutting tracks though the jungle can take as long as two or three hours per kilometer, so the cliffs even slightly farther up the valley will create a much bigger challenge. 📷 📄 🔍

— MATT PICKLES, *U.K.*

NEW ZEALAND

POPE'S NOSE, EAST FACE, SECOND WINTER ASCENT AND FIRST SOLO

ON JULY 18 I took advantage of excellent local conditions to make the second winter ascent of the east face of the Pope's Nose (2,700m) in Mt. Aspiring National Park, but failed to link it with the northeast face of Mt. Aspiring (3,033m). Had I been successful, this would have resulted in the super-route of the Southern Alps that has been the dream of a generation of New Zealand climbers.

A poor winter had dampened enthusiasm for climbing in the remoter areas of the Alps, but conditions were excellent at Aspiring, with lots of melt-freeze creating awesome ice conditions at mid-altitudes. Access was never going to be easy but finally was resolved with a long slog around the Maud Francis, Avalanche, and Hood glaciers. Conditions on the face were excellent—certainly far better than those experienced by the first ascensionists. In such conditions the climbing is classic rather than technical. A difficult passage on the northeast face of Aspiring forced my retreat on day five of the trip, but trained climbers with a rope would have succeeded.

– GUY MCKINNON, *NEW ZEALAND*

Editor's note: The first ascent of the east face of Pope's Nose, by Brian Alder, Lionel Clay, Nick Cradock, and Dave Fearnley, took place in the winter of 1996. The four men helicoptered to the foot of the face and spent two days climbing their route (VI 6). With helicopter access now illegal,

[Below] Mt. Aspiring and the Pope's Nose from the Matukituki Valley. (1) The 650m east face of Pope's Nose (lower face hidden). After soloing this face, Guy McKinnon attempted the northeast face of Aspiring (hidden on right side of the peak). (2) Shooting Star (Dare-Joll, 2014). *Guy McKinnon*

Guy McKinnon approached the face "on its own terms." McKinnon began the ca 14-mile approach on July 14, and after a hoped-for shortcut into the Kitchener Cirque did not pan out, he did not reach the foot of Pope's Nose until July 17. On July 18 he completed the first solo of the 650m face in five hours, roughly following the 1996 line (18 pitches during the first ascent). After a bad bivy in a crevasse on the Upper Volta Glacier, McKinnon climbed about 250m up the northeast face of Aspiring (Bell-Bogie, 1978) before poor ice on a bulge prompted his retreat. In a whiteout, he made his way across the Bonar Glacier on the southwest side of the peak and then down to the shelter of the French Ridge Hut.

In March 2014, McKinnon did the first solo ascent of the 750m east face of Fastness Peak, generally following the Sveticic-Dickson Route, an alpine rock climb (IV 5, 1990).

MT. ASPIRING, SOUTH FACE, SHOOTING STAR

DANIEL JOLL AND I CLIMBED a new route on the south face of Mt. Aspiring (3,033m) on September 6. The route climbs through the right side of the lower rock band before traversing left across the central ice fields and finishing directly up an ice gully to a top-out high on the Coxcomb Ridge. After delicately passing a two-tiered cornice above the bergschrund, we climbed 12 60m pitches on the face and a further four pitches along the upper Coxcomb to reach the summit, about 14 hours after starting. We climbed our new route Shooting Star (720m, IV 5+ or WI 3+ M4) as a tribute to a close friend, Ari Kingan, who died tragically in August in a fall near the base of the northwest ridge of Aspiring, during his descent from a climb of the south face. [*Eleven routes and variations ascend the ca 500m south face of Aspiring. Shooting Star is a completely independent line, starting between the Whiston-Hyslop (1976) and Leo Hugo (Bernard-Cayrol, 2002), and finishing right of 24 Hour Party People (Edwards-Metherell-Neal, 2005).*]

– BEN DARE, *WITH ADDITIONAL INFORMATION FROM* DANIEL JOLL *(ALPINETEAM.CO.NZ)*

DARRAN MOUNTAINS, MARIAN PEAK, MATER DEI

IN FEBRUARY, Ben Dare and Daniel Joll, who did the first ascent of the south face of Marian Peak (2,102m) in March 2013, added a second alpine-rock line on the left side of the 1,000m face. Mater Dei (20 pitches, New Zealand 20) shares the same start as the 2013 route, called Maid Marian, and then branches left to climb the upper face.

– *INFORMATION SUPPLIED BY* BEN DARE, *NEW ZEALAND*

EARL MOUNTAINS, MT. SUTER, SOUTH FACE

REARING ABRUPTLY OUT of a small glacial lake, an unbroken 800m to 1,000m cirque wall stands guard over the head of the Falls Creek drainage. Dominating the center of this wall is Mt. Suter (2,094m). The bulk of Suter's south face thrusts proud of the main wall to form a prominent buttress of compact granite. Dark and foreboding, it is streaked with a series of discontinuous ice smears that offer little in the way of an obvious line. On the left side of the buttress, however, is a deeply recessed corner with a continuous white ribbon of ice.

On July 19, in the inky blackness of a midwinter pre-dawn, Stephen Skelton and I stumbled through the broken moraine field that litters the valley floor. Twenty pitches and 18 hours later, again in darkness, we topped out. The climb offered some of the best alpine ice conditions I have ever encountered and kept us guessing until the very final pitch. Nine pitches of moderate terrain led to the prominent corner system. From here the angled increased as we climbed 11 pitches of sustained ice at WI3 to WI5 in the depths of the recess. These included a harrowing horizontal traverse on thin, vertical ice onto the main face when the corner blanked out after pitch 16, and a 30m runout on Patagonia-esque unconsolidated snow to reach the ridgeline. The Darrans winter grade in these conditions is VI, 6 (WI5).

We bivied in a shoulder-width niche in the rock just above the face. In the morning, after completing the final few pitches to the summit, we hurriedly started down. This proved to be an adventure itself, taking a further 15 hours to complete the 6km traverse of the east ridge and the 1,700m descent into the Hollyford Valley. 📷

— BEN DARE, *NEW ZEALAND*

[Right] Starting the second pitch of the upper corner on Mt. Suter. *Stephen Skelton* [Bottom] The line of the first ascent on the south face of Mt. Suter. The route required 20 pitches and 18 hours of climbing. *Ben Dare*

MARQUESAS ISLANDS

[Above] The north side of Poumaka, showing (1) American route (2014) and (2) German route (1996). *Andy Mann*

POUMAKA, TE VA ANUI O KAU KAU

IN 2007 I CAME ACROSS folk tales about ancient glowing orbs on pointy rock summits in the South Pacific. Fascinated by these rumors, I soon discovered images of the Marquesas Islands, north of Tahiti, and the volcanic rock towers of the island of Ua Pou. It was one of those moments of pure clarity: I knew I would go there.

In the spring of 2013, alone, I visited Ua Pou. The towers played hide-and-seek behind clouds and constant rain for three days, teasing and tormenting me. Finally I met Kau Kau, who agreed to go into the jungle with me. We spent days trekking through thick forest with huge haulbags full of climbing and bivy gear, and made it to the base of a couple of towers. We camped in the rain, had a lot of laughs, and then retreated. I was not prepared for a solo ascent in the island's insane rain and jungle madness.

In February 2015 I returned to Ua Pou, this time with wonderful friends—Angie Payne, Keith Ladzinski, and Andy Mann—and fully prepared for any amount of rain. After three planes and a two-hour boat ride, we made it to Ua Pou, where my first visit now paid off. I had arranged all the logistics with my friend Kau Kau and others before we arrived. We quickly headed into the jungle, a dozen of us carrying waterproof loads of gear. Our goal was Poumaka, the legendary master of Ua Pou and the surrounding islands.

With Kau Kau leading the way, we started climbing through steep jungle toward the base of the master tower. Four pitches of jungle mayhem brought us to the top of a knoll beside the tower. We moved into a high camp there. The plan was that I would lead all the pitches and Angie would belay and clean, while Andy and Keith captured imagery. Angie, one of the world's best boulderers, had never done anything like this, but her energy is so positive, her focus so intense, her attitude so genuine that I knew she would crush this.

I started the first lead with crampons strapped to my free climbing shoes in order to get through the initial jungle stuck to vertical stone. I took them off after 20 feet, once I could touch rock. Wet rock. Muddy rock. The wall was soaked. I continued free climbing and tried to place a couple of cams—no way they were going to hold in the muddy, thin crack. But a couple of pins hammered in nicely. Then I had to do a little runout on vegetation and muddy stone. *WHIP!*

SLAM! A cam ripped out and I crunched onto the ground. Fortunately, the vegetation worked as a nice crash pad. I could tell Angie was a bit freaked out. "No worries, I'm OK," I reassured her. By the time I made my way up the first pitch, I could literally wring water out of the rope and webbing. It would be this way for eight days.

The next day we started up pitch two on overhanging, coral-like rock. My second piece of protection, a small nut, popped out. *WHIP! SLAM!* I fell hard beneath Angie, my knee smacking into the toothlike rock. I could feel blood running down my leg into my socks and into my shoes. I said to Angie, "Don't worry, I'm fine, really." I got back on lead and made my way through the delicate rock, digging into muddy cracks for every placement. Had I not brought a couple of dozen beaks, this route would not have been possible. One of the pitches got an A4 rating, though I later pulled it down to A3+. I think the rain, mud, and being constantly soaked added to the sense of difficulty.

[Above] Mike Libecki and his arsenal of muddy beaks after pitch two. *Keith Ladzinski*

On the day of our summit push we got an early start and jugged the fixed lines to a decent ledge at the end of the fifth pitch. From here I traversed around a corner and into vertical rock covered in vines and thick flora. I felt like a spider, hoping that equalizing my limbs on vines would somehow hold me. By the time I started the last pitch it was close to dark. Twenty minutes later I was on the summit, the wind and rain threatening to blow me off the top. I radioed down to the team, "Someone's gotta come up and clean. Then let's get outta here!" We rappelled the route and celebrated with Kau Kau back at our high camp. Our route had four jungle pitches and eight pitches on the main tower, and is called Te Va Anui O Kau Kau ("In Honor of Kau Kau," 1,500', V 5.11 A3+ JM (Jungle Mayhem).

[*Editor's note: Poumaka was first climbed in November 1996 by the German team of Hansjörg Schurz, Mario Weippert, and Siegfried Weippert, by a line on the north face (12 pitches plus scrambling, UIAA VII), to the right of the 2014 team's ascent. Siegfried Weippert had made two previous trips to Ua Pou (January 1988 and August 1995), during which he and various other climbers ascended most of the large towers on the island.*] ▶

– MIKE LIBECKI, *USA*

MOTUTAKAE, WEST FACE

IN APRIL 2013, Andrew Burr, Mason Earle, Bronson Hovnanian (all USA) and George Ullrich (U.K.) climbed an eight-pitch new route (5.10+) up the steep west face of this seaside spire. The tower was first climbed via the lower-angle north ridge by a German-Marquesan pair (1988).

– *INFORMATION FROM* CLIMBING 330 *AND* MASON EARLE

BOOK REVIEWS

EDITED BY DAVID STEVENSON

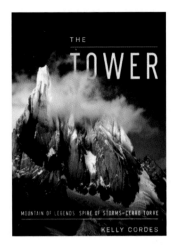

THE TOWER: A CHRONICLE OF CLIMBING AND CONTROVERSY ON CERRO TORRE

BY KELLY CORDES. PATAGONIA BOOKS, 2014. 400 PAGES. HARDCOVER, $27.95.

The Tower is not only the definitive book about Cerro Torre—it's also one of the finest examples of a subgenre of mountaineering writing that is surprisingly rare: the biography of a single peak. It calls to mind Heinrich Harrer's *The White Spider*, and Kelly Cordes' authoritative treatise deserves its place on the shelf next to that classic account of the Eiger Nordwand.

Rather than plod chronologically through the various ascents and new routes on the spire once declared "the hardest mountain in the world," as Walt Unsworth's comprehensive but often lugubrious doorstopper does for Everest, Cordes wisely frames his book around the central enigma of Cerro Torre. A brilliant soloist in his native Italy, Cesare Maestri claimed the first ascent by an incredibly difficult route in 1959, after his partner Toni Egger plunged to his death on the descent, leaving no witness to corroborate or contradict his claim. Stung by detractors who suspected a hoax, Maestri returned in 1970 with a 150-pound, gas-powered compressor to drill his infamous bolt ladder toward the summit on the opposite side of the mountain—a bizarre stunt that only reinforced the suspicions of those detractors.

Still alive at 85, Maestri has long since stopped talking to the press about what is probably the greatest controversy in climbing history. To examine the mystery from every possible angle, Cordes has ransacked obscure journals and newspaper clippings in four different languages and made numerous trips to Europe to interview everyone who might cast light on the story. He also covers in depth and judiciously the furor that erupted after Hayden Kennedy and Jason Kruk chopped some 150 of Maestri's bolts on the way down from their "fair means" ascent of the route in 2012.

Cordes is a Patagonia veteran with many fine routes in the Cerro Torre and Fitz Roy massifs to his credit. *The Tower* thus veers toward a personal memoir, especially in the last pages, when he discusses his near-fatal ice climbing accident on what should have been a warm-up route in Montana, which left him with the fear that he would never be able to climb well again. Yet the personal story is understated and modest, and Cordes goes out of his way to salute the deeds of such stellar Patagonia pioneers as Ermanno Salvaterra and Rolando Garibotti.

Just as *The Tower* stands as the definitive work about Cerro Torre, it also delivers the irrefutable verdict on Maestri, in the process co-indicting his 1959 teammate, Cesarino Fava, who was not on the summit push but went to his deathbed insisting on Maestri's truth. Cordes' sad but well-earned conclusion:

"That is where Cesarino Fava and Cesare Maestri failed. They failed themselves, they failed those who believed in them, and they betrayed the code of trust that is essential to climbing

mountains. I believe the ways we treat the things and people we profess to love are expressions of who we are."

The Tower is a major contribution to mountain literature worldwide. And as Kelly Cordes' first book, it represents an astounding achievement.

— DAVID ROBERTS

THE CALLING: A LIFE ROCKED BY MOUNTAINS

BY BARRY BLANCHARD. PATAGONIA BOOKS, 2014. 440 PAGES. HARDCOVER, $27.95.

The Calling: A Life Rocked by Mountains is Barry Blanchard's story of rising out of what would have been a soon-to-be-forgotten life to becoming one of North America's most cherished and respected alpinists. Raised by a single mother of mixed blood in tough Albertan neighborhoods, Blanchard's emotionally painful childhood lessons lead to his avowal to never abuse women. In turn, his conversion into "climber" follows a familiar theme: hero figures, men living to higher ideals, great literature (*The White Spider*), and the proximity of the vertical world (the Canadian Rockies). In short: born into a potentially crummy life, he found his way out. *The Calling* is that story.

Blanchard's vision for alpinism, the apex of his early career, and the most gripping tale of this book play out on the Rupal Face of Nanga Parbat, where he, Kevin Doyle, Ward Robertson, and Mark Twight launch up the tallest face on Earth and get totally hosed. Reminiscent of René Desmaison's *Total Alpinism*, Blanchard's account brings the reader into the suffocating force of the cold world eating its prey one cell at a time. In some ways "The Avalanche" chapter is an expression of the ideal depicted in Al Alvarez's *Feeding the Rat*, in which the idealized self finally matches the actual person. What makes the story of Nanga Parbat so remarkable is that it was a shared experience.

The body of the book is a stream of progressively more difficult routes with partners each stepping up to perform greater and greater acts of heroism and nerve. It's funny as well, really funny, no doubt because Blanchard is such a practiced storyteller. Listening to him describe George Lowe's nasally whine—"I KNOW!!"—was enough make this reviewer wet his britches.

As much of Blanchard's being is founded in merit, there must have been some disappointment that's left unspoken here. He was tuned and poised for Everest's West Ridge when political aspirations of others were placed ahead of merit, and Blanchard and Doyle were first displaced and then forbidden a summit bid. While a difficult pill to swallow, Blanchard sucks it up and moves on, setting in motion a vision for what would unfold on Nanga Parbat.

Reading *The Calling* left this reviewer longing to have moved to Canmore when the window opened and found a way into that special tribe. My hope for future generations of readers and alpinists is to find their inspiration in Blanchard's words. Why? Because Bubba is the real deal.

— CHARLIE SASSARA

ONE DAY AS A TIGER

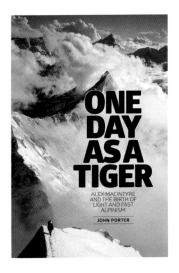

By JOHN PORTER. VERTEBRATE PUBLISHING (U.K.), 2014. 230 PAGES. HARDCOVER, £20.

Late at night on an expedition to Afghanistan in 1977, John Porter gazed through a hole in the wall of his tent, torn by the gales that swept the barley fields and arid hills. A multitude of stars blazed through the dark. "The sky is so incredibly clear above me now," he recalled. "I can see nebulae, and areas where opaque clouds of gas obscure what lies behind, like the impenetrable darkness that looms in the soul even when it is most content."

In many ways, the imagery of this scene lies at the heart of *One Day as a Tiger*, Porter's memoir of his friend, the great British climber Alex MacIntyre, who was killed by rockfall in 1982 on the south face of Annapurna. Long before the Swiss alpinist Ueli Steck completed his rapid solo on the same side of that 8,091-meter mountain, MacIntyre was part of a group of visionaries who brought fast and light styles to the world's high peaks. By the end of the 1980s, many of his peers had also died in the mountains. Awarded the Grand Prize at the Banff Mountain Book Festival, *One Day as a Tiger* documents an era marked by both intense wonder and grief.

Over the course of the book, Porter examines the unfolding of a systematic ambition from the Alps to the Himalaya: "[MacIntyre] believed in a methodology that if you did a, then b, then c, what would result was x, then y, then z. It was the sort of logic that only fate can undo." And as he explores the accumulation of individual decisions, chance events and personality traits that might have contributed to MacIntyre's achievements and (indirectly) to his death, Porter interweaves climbing scenes with leitmotifs of mathematics and chaos, reason and imagination. When a friend points out, "You say that climbing is mainly about having fun and having life-fulfilling adventures, but it seems to me that you leave on a trip with x members in your team and you come back with y. Assuming y is less than x, what have you gained?" Porter responds with one of the book's most compelling passages: "What we gain is a bit like dark matter. We know it has to be there because we know the universe has mass and energy we cannot see or measure, but we cannot say what it is. But the fact is, we keep on trying to describe it."

Paradoxically, it's in the impossible effort to communicate these unknowns that Porter's writing shines. Sarah Richard, MacIntyre's girlfriend, tells Porter, "I would love to have carried on that dialogue [MacIntyre and I] had. That is what death is, the end of dialogue." Nonetheless, as Porter muses, "The end of dialogue is not the end of the story." A sense of an imagined alternate history, in which MacIntyre survived, haunts the narrative: What might MacIntyre have thought, Porter repeatedly wonders, of our modern climbing world; what person might he have become? If MacIntyre's character remains partly enigmatic, that reticence is a testament to the author's own growing understanding of the limits of knowledge. For there are more elusive mysteries than that of alpinism amid the "dark matter" that so many of us seek, glassing the dazzling walls of great mountains, the distant galaxies of starlit skies, or the invisible depths of human souls.

— KATIE IVES

COLD FEET: STORIES OF A MIDDLING CLIMBER ON CLASSIC PEAKS AND AMONG LEGENDARY MOUNTAINEERS

BY DAVID PAGEL. SELF-PUBLISHED, 2014. 384 PAGES. PAPERBACK, $19.95.

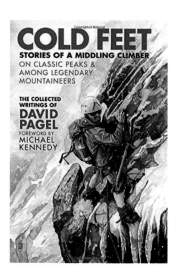

There are only a few climbing writers whose work I genuinely look forward to diving into an armchair with. Jim Perrin tops the list, and Chris Bonington's early work is up there. Then there's Pagel—Dave Pagel. An American. And now, thankfully, he's collected his published stories into a book, along with a lot of other wonderfully creative and thoughtful material.

I first met Pagel through the pages of *Climbing* magazine in 1983. "Mind Games," his essay about a climbing trip to Colorado and Wyoming, blew my mind. (I was 17.) It was as if he had stripped away everything he knew about climbing and was just observing. And he was. Much of the story centers on a psychological battle between Pagel and his partner to see who can get the other to lead a pitch of Tulgey Wood: "When God built Devils Tower, He smiled graciously upon rock climbers. When He chiseled out the third pitch of Tulgey Wood, He was either in a hurry, a particularly unpleasant mood, or making a very bad joke." The pair makes it up the climb, and it's both a touching story of friendship and a hilarious discussion of things we all try to avoid, namely death.

"Mind Games" is the smallest tip of the iceberg in *Cold Feet*, Pagel's new collection. Throughout he recounts both his extremely vast climbing experience (from Lotus Flower Tower to Mt. Kenya) and offers observations on just about everything related to climbing— from scary gear that "frays" his mind to the strangeness of topographic diagrams. Plus, he knows the H word—humility—although I'd argue that not all of the climbs and expeditions he describes are as "middling" as the title suggests. You have to be fairly experienced just to get up some of these things, and you have to have incredible patience. Your average climber would never get up the Eiger, nor be able to handle the intricacies of a trip to Kenya—the taxi system alone is like playing bumper cars.

The book is divided into seven sections, ranging from stories of Pagel's exploits to "Perspective," thoughts on the whole climbing world. For example, there's a chapter in here called "The Truth is Out There," in which Pagel coughs up his thoughts on everything from Mallory and Irvine to the YDS grading system.

And this is the coolest part, I think: "Verse." In this day and age, putting poetry out there is the biggest risk a writer can take, especially a writer delving into the tough-person world of climbing. Pagel does it with panache, class, and eloquence.

Pagel is what I like to describe to my daughters as a "big brain." He gets it. He gets the whole worldwide, intellectual, and cultural climbing scene. Not many climbing writers do. In fact, very few of us do. His experiences and thoughts are so fresh and raw and unmolested with BS that *Cold Feet* is one of the best reads on the climbing horizon.

We should all strive to do so well.

— CAMERON M. BURNS

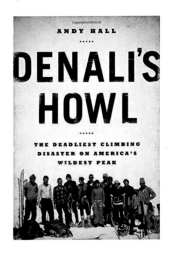

DENALI'S HOWL: THE DEADLIEST CLIMBING DISASTER ON AMERICA'S WILDEST PEAK

BY ANDY HALL. E.P DUTTON & CO. (PENGUIN GROUP), 2014. 272 PAGES. HARDCOVER, $27.95.

Blind dates don't often work out well, but they only last a night. Climbing with people you don't know—especially for a month on a mountain like Denali—has the potential for epic conflict. This was borne out in the 1967 expedition that encountered, in addition to conflict, the worst storm recorded on the mountain. In a review of James Tabor's book *Forever on the Mountain* (AAJ 2008), this summary I wrote serves as an introduction to the saga:

"...three Colorado climbers, led by Howard Snyder, joined forces with a team of nine Pacific Northwest climbers, led by Joe Wilcox, because the NPS required parties to be at least four in number. The fourth member of the Colorado team had to drop out at the last moment, so that thrust these two teams...together. It was not to be a happy marriage and would end in tragedy when seven of the Wilcox party died from exposure some days after they (six of them—one stayed in high camp) elected to climb to the summit from their 17,900-foot camp during a lull in a fierce storm.... Their desire to gain the summit and their relative inexperience were surely the key elements that clouded their judgment to do the prudent thing, which would have been to descend from high camp. This decision was theirs, not, as suggested years ago, that of their leader, Joe Wilcox."

Over the past 40 years, my assumption regarding the causes was similar to most of my peers: a mountaineering disaster that was the result of inadequate leadership (Joe Wilcox), expertise, and conditioning, exacerbated by a one-two punch of severe weather events. Many of us relied on our personal experiences on the mountain, mine being a 45-day first ascent of the East Buttress with five others in 1963. We also read the report and analysis written in the journal I edited, *Accidents in North American Mountaineering*. Shortly thereafter, Howard Snyder's book *The Hall of the Mountain King* laid the blame solely on Joe Wilcox' doorstep. Wilcox' book, *White Winds*, not published until 1983, did not change many opinions.

This new account by Andy Hall, former editor and publisher of *Alaska* magazine, is meticulous and thorough in its examination of the details before, during, and after the expedition. As the five-year-old son of then-Superintendent George Hall, he has early memories of the aftermath. He was prompted to write this book because author James Tabor tried to lay blame for the climbers not being rescued on his father, on the chief ranger, and on the Alaska Rescue Group (ARG). Those few of us who were there during that era know full well that potential for rescue was low, because communication devices were unreliable at best and park personnel had not been hired for an expectation of mountain expertise, even though the park and the ARG would assist if they could. We assumed we were on our own.

It is well worth the read for the deep insight regarding the climbers (especially Joe Wilcox and Howard Snyder, whom Hall interviewed recently), the members and efforts of the ARG, and the Mountaineering Club of Alaska. In 1967, the latter group, under the leadership of Frank Nosek, presented a Certificate of Honorary Membership to Superintendent George Hall in recognition of his efforts to keep Denali open to climbers despite incredible pressure to close it down.

— JED WILLIAMSON

THE CALL OF THE ICE: CLIMBING 8,000 METER PEAKS IN WINTER

By Simone Moro, Foreword by Ed Viesturs, translated by Monica Meneghetti. Mountaineers Books, 2014. 224 pages. Paperback, $19.95.

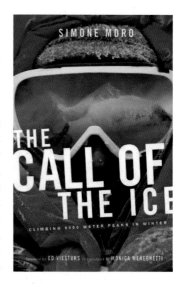

Simone Moro (Italy) is a remarkable high-altitude specialist, likely well known to Americans for the recent controversy with Ueli Steck and Jon Griffith on Everest, or perhaps for his first winter ascent of Gasherbrum II with Denis Urubko and Cory Richards, as chronicled in the short (excellent) film *Cold*. This is Moro's third book, but the first to be translated to English. His climbing CV (one of three appendices) lists 45 expeditions through 2012, including 12 attempts on Nanga Parbat, three of those in winter. As Moro points out in his preface, there are two subjects to this book: winter and the "nearly impossible."

The entire book was written in 20 days on his 2012 Nanga Parbat attempt, "with frozen and gloved fingers and a hot water bottle under the laptop to conserve the battery in the coldest hours." Each chapter begins with a note marking his progress on that climb. He starts with his first winter climb on Aconcagua and moves quickly to a summary of the avalanche on the south face of Annapurna in which Anatoli Boukreev and Dimitri Sobloev were lost and he miraculously survived. He has written elsewhere and at greater length of this, but it's a powerful and formative experience well worth repeating: "truly my lost extreme adventure." His later partnership with Urubko, a Kazakhstani like Boukreev, is central to many of the climbs recounted here.

All the climbing is intensely rendered. Despite Moro's claim that his memory "sucks," he provides many closely observed details suggesting the opposite. Throughout he is rational and opinionated, for example in his response to criticism over his satellite connection: "As if those chunks of battery-operated plastic rendered the cold less intense or the danger virtual." This book is among the very best reportage from the "nearly impossible" that we have.

– DAVID STEVENSON

LETTERS FROM CHAMONIX: STORIES AND A NOVELLA

By David Stevenson. Imaginary Mountain Surveyors (Canada), 2014. 230 pages. Paperback, $24.95.

Longtime AAJ books editor David Stevenson's collection of short fiction won the Banff Mountain Book Award for Fiction and Poetry in 2014. The following is quoted from remarks by Anik See, Banff juror, with permission.

In *Letters from Chamonix*, Stevenson captures the spirit and passion of climbing without the cliché, jargon and often predictable plots and characters. Each short story is as diverse in characters and challenges as each climb is from the next. Combining authentic scenes and plots with all of the elements that make good stories, the reader is treated to several points of view of what it's like to be a climber—and the never-ending array of psychological states climbers endure to do the thing they love—while also including the experience of non-climbers who are left behind by tragedy. With this collection, Stevenson has made it clear that he is a man as dedicated to the craft of writing as he is to climbing. A boon for mountain fiction.

IN BRIEF BY DAVID STEVENSON

HANGING ON: A LIFE INSIDE BRITISH CLIMBING'S GOLDEN AGE. BY MARTIN BOYSEN. VERTEBRATE PUBLISHING (U.K.), 2014. 288 PAGES. HARDCOVER, £20. According to the publisher: "wry, laconic, and self-deprecating." In other words: quintessentially British. Vertebrate has a great list of new titles and is keeping many classic books in print.

TRAINING FOR THE NEW ALPINISM: A MANUAL FOR THE CLIMBER AS ATHLETE. BY STEVE HOUSE AND SCOTT JOHNSTON. PATAGONIA BOOKS, 2014. 464 PAGES. PAPERBACK, $35. Not even House can do the Czech Direct on Denali in 60 hours right off the couch. Alpine success, he maintains, is 90 percent hard work, as specifically detailed in this book via training plans, photos, graphs, illustrations, and anecdotes. With cameo appearances from contemporary greats Ueli Steck, Mark Twight, and Voytek Kurtyka, among others.

CLIMBING STRONGER, FASTER, HEALTHIER: BEYOND THE BASICS (SECOND EDITION). BY MICHAEL A. LAYTON. SELF-PUBLISHED, 2014. 708 PAGES. PAPERBACK, $34.95. "This is not a 'training for climbing' or 'how to' book. This is a toolbox: a reference to add to your knowledge or springboard for further inquiry," Layton writes. A gigantic toolbox filled with training, health, and other stuff, from "Post Isometric Relaxation" to "Being a Jerk About Your First Ascent."

TEARS OF THE DAWN. BY JULES LINES. SHELTERSTONE (U.K.), 2013. 288 PAGES. HARDCOVER, £20. Memoir of Britain's "most accomplished free solo climber." The winner of the prestigious Boardman Tasker Prize for 2014, a reliable indicator of excellence.

REINHOLD MESSNER: MY LIFE AT THE LIMIT. INTERVIEWED BY THOMAS HÜETLIN; TRANSLATED BY TIM CARRUTHERS. MOUNTAINEERS BOOKS, 2014. 256 PAGES. PAPERBACK, $19.95. A book-length set of two interviews conducted in 2004 and 2014. At 70, with countless books behind him, Messner remains compelling. Bonus advice for writers: "You get more for chopping wood than you do for writing."

HIGH SUMMITS: 370 FAMOUS FIRST PEAK ASCENTS AND OTHER SIGNIFICANT EVENTS IN MOUNTAINEERING HISTORY. BY FREDERICK L. WOLFE. HUGO HOUSE PUBLISHERS, 2013. 703 PAGES. HARDCOVER, $49.95. This massive history is organized by continent and chronology. The 370 first ascents in the title barely scratch the book's surface: There are 2,000 climbing events chronicled here. A great reference, fascinating for its hundreds of miscellaneous facts.

IN MEMORIAM

EDITED BY JAMES BENOIT

Many of these articles have been edited for length. The full tributes may be read at the AAJ website: publications.americanalpineclub.org. Online readers also will find In Memoriam stories about Don Liska, Dave Pegg, and John Turner. A tribute to Bob Craig, who died in January 2015, is available at the website and will be published in AAJ 2016.

JOHN M. BOYLE, 1935–2014

A NATIVE OF SAN FRANCISCO, John Boyle was a global adventurer. After serving in the U.S. Army in Germany (1954-1956), he worked on a satellite program that took him to tracking stations in remote regions of the world, inspiring him to explore Africa, the Middle East, and Asia in challenging expeditions.

John was a member of the successful 1983 American expedition to the Kangshung Face on Everest, on which he served as base camp manager and expedition engineer. He designed and implemented a motorized rope system to transport 3,000 pounds of equipment and supplies up a rock headwall, saving significant time and reducing risk to climbers. The expedition completed the first ascent of the last unclimbed face of Everest, getting six climbers of the 14-member team to the summit.

In preparing for the expedition, John began collecting logs and photographic material of past Himalayan expeditions, searching for detailed geographic information. This collection grew over the years to 2,500 books in 28 languages, 400 expedition reports, and 100 videos and films, with about half of the books autographed by expedition participants. In 1997 he donated the collection to the AAC, which is now the home of the John M. Boyle Himalayan Library.

John was a passionate sailboat racer and longtime member of the St. Francis Yacht Club in San Francisco. He also loved trains. In the 1970s, when Charlie Crocker decided to rejuvenate the Sierra Railroad Company and restore the Jamestown roundhouse and steam operations, John bought shares in the effort to bring back to life this gem of California history. Railtown 1897 is now part of the California State Parks system.

Among other successful business engagements, John served as chief financial officer of Crocker Bank in San Francisco from 1974 until the its merger in 1981. He retired from a career in banking and finance to Santa Fe, New Mexico, where he was active in the "Car Table" group of car aficionados, and a supporter of the performance arts.

— MELISSA BOYLE MAHLE

ERIC BJORNSTAD, 1934–2014

ERIC BJORNSTAD, the greatest chronicler of climbing on the Colorado Plateau of the American Southwest and a pioneer of significant climbs from Mexico to Alaska, passed away on December 17 at age 80. Eric was born October 23, 1934, in Phoenix. He struggled academically and left school after graduating from junior high. In the 1950s he lived in the Bay Area and then moved to Seattle, arriving in the University District with 26 cents in his pocket. He soon met a student named David Hiser, and they began roped climbing together. Not long afterward, Eric met Don Claunch.

"From that point," Eric wrote in an unfinished autobiography, "I embarked upon a blitzkrieg of mountaineering. The days [when] I was grounded to work life, I jogged, traversed brick buildings, mantel-shelved window sills, stemmed doorways, ticked off dozens of one-legged squats, ascended and descended two- and three-at-a-time stairs, and practiced two-finger chin-ups on half-inch door jams, and as I read newspapers each page was crumpled up in the fist to increase finger strength."

One day in 1960, while hanging around the Seattle REI store, Eric found a note written by Ed Cooper, who was looking for someone to share expenses and driving to the Bugaboos. There, Eric soloed Eastpost Spire while Cooper dealt with a stomach bug, and then the two made the first ascent of Howser Peak's north face. Eric soon met Fred Beckey and teamed up with him on whatever Beckey thought they should climb. Eric would later say that 90 percent of his climbs were done with Beckey. The two forged a bond that would never be broken (even after some of their massive and colorful falling-outs). During the 1960s, with Seattle's best, Eric established dozens of new climbs of all grades and sizes, from the local crags to Alaskan peaks, his best known climbs including the first ascent of the northeast buttress on Mt. Slesse (1963) in British Columbia and the first ascent of Mt. Seattle (1966) in Alaska.

Eric's first trip to the desert Southwest was, not surprisingly, with Beckey. In 1965 they attempted the "South Buttress" on Shiprock (later completed by Beckey and often called the Beckey Buttress) and went on to do the first ascents of Echo Tower (1966), the third route climbed in the Fishers, as well as Middle Sister (1967) in Monument Valley.

In 1970, Moab rock-shop owner Lin Ottinger invited Eric and Beckey to fly over Canyonlands with a pilot friend to look at a tower he had found: Moses. During a subsequent visit to Taylor Canyon, Eric climbed Zeus, a neighbor to Moses (Beckey stayed on the ground). They returned in 1972 with Tom Nephew, Jim Galvin, and Gregory Markov. After five days and two bivouacs on the north face, on Eric's 36th birthday, they reached the summit. It was arguably the last major tower to be climbed in the Moab area.

After two decades of trips to the Moab area, Eric finally moved there full-time in 1985. Soon he began plowing away at the *Desert Rock* guidebook (1988). At one point he told this writer he'd put 10,000 hours into *Desert Rock*, and that figure was likely conservative. The result was what many regard as the finest guidebook produced in the United States up to that time.

I've read of people suggesting Eric Bjornstad was a "desert rat" and a "climbing bum," both of which are colorful descriptions, but Eric was much more. He had great knowledge and appreciation of the arts, literature, desert ecology and history, Native American beliefs and traditions, poetry, geology, philosophy, glassmaking, and woodworking. Despite great shyness, Eric also was a teacher of sorts. Any book you wanted to borrow, any part of the natural world you wanted explained, any information about poetry, literature, and music you needed, Eric would offer it up. Even better were his personalized tours of his favorite places in the desert.

Eric had knowledge, experience, and keen sensibilities beyond most climbers you will ever know. And thankfully, for all of us, he used them wisely.

– CAMERON M. BURNS

JOE FIREY, 1918–2013

JOE FIREY WAS ONE of the most endearing, enduring, and accomplished mountaineers in the Pacific Northwest. An active hiker, climber, and skier for nearly 70 years, he pioneered exploratory mountaineering and ski touring in the Northwest, especially in the Washington Cascades and Coast Mountains of British Columbia.

Joe began his mountaineering adventures as a teen living in Seattle during the Great Depression, when he had to fashion his own crampons and other gear. The tone for his future expeditions was set in 1936, when Joe and a friend completed a two-week ascent of Mt. Olympus starting from the Brinnon ferry dock on Hood Canal, a round trip "hike" of 120 miles.

In the 1940s Joe climbed with Joan Wilshire, who shared his passion for mountaineering. They married in 1950 and raised their children, Carla, Alan, and Nina, while still actively climbing. Joe was a well-known professor of mechanical engineering at the University of Washington from 1954 to 1981.

By the mid-1970s, the names of Joe and Joan Firey and their friends John and Irene Meulemans could be found in the summit registers of practically every big peak in the Cascades. Over the years Joe and Joan undertook 51 climbing trips and 37 ski tours lasting a week or more. Sadly, Joan died in 1980 (*AAJ 1981*). Joe's trips continued until 2000. In all, Joe made first ascents of at least 16 peaks plus 17 new routes in the North Cascades, and the first ascents of at least 27 peaks plus 19 new routes in the Coast Mountains.

Joe was brilliant at finding feasible routes over alpine terrain in remote places. His climbing successes depended also on his fortitude in climbing unstable rock, and his willingness to bivouac if necessary. Joe's cheerful equanimity never wavered, no matter how thick the mosquitos, how wild the weather, how daunting the objective, or how desperate the circumstances. He was an endless source of puns, both good and bad, but funny either way. He was exceptionally intelligent, with a marvelous memory, which he retained until the very end of his life. Joe died at age 95 at the end of December 2013.

Lowell Skoog has produced a beautiful and detailed account of the lives and mountaineering activities of Joe and his family entitled "The Indefatigable Fireys." As of 2015 it can be found at www.alpenglow.org/ski-history/notes/comm/firey-joe.html.

– PETER RENZ, JON WELLNER, *AND* MICKEY SCHURR

EITAN GREEN, 1985–2014

ON MAY 31, Eitan Green, 28, a fellow guide, and four other climbers were swept off Mt. Rainer's Liberty Ridge, apparently in an avalanche. Eitan died far too soon, but at least he lived having never lost the magic of climbing. Eitan first climbed at age eight, when he and his dad passed a rainy day rappelling with a guide at Otter Cliffs in Acadia. A dozen or so years later, Eitan was guiding on that same cliff.

In college Eitan excelled. Despite his rebellious independence, Eitan wasn't too iconoclastic to realize he had to pay his way. He held a job with campus security while working for his EMT license. Later, driving an ambulance around central Maine, Eitan found himself face to face with poverty and poor health that few of his peers were aware of. Eitan brought this dollars-and-cents reality with him as he pursued a career in guiding. One summer Eitan worked as a support cook on Mt. Rainier. When he wasn't at Camp Muir, Eitan lived in a tent on a lawn next to a house where guides slept inside. Back home in New England, he found work at guide services and mastered technical skills on the region's storied crags.

Eitan's passion for climbing dovetailed with his intense focus on academics. He learned Nepali and traveled to the Himalaya in order to research global climbing communities. He graduated magna cum laude from Colby College in Maine. The mountains ("an office with a great view but a leaky roof," he'd joke) were perhaps the only place large enough to contain Eitan's great talents.

One of his first jobs after college was maintaining the spigots that create the ice flows at the Ouray Ice Park in Colorado. It was a wet, bone-chilling affair, but Eitan kept at it, at times resorting to shoveling snow and living in his car to pay his way. Soon thereafter, Eitan found work at San Juan Mountain Guides in Ouray, teaching clinics on the very ice he'd created. He also gained a spot on the Alpine Ascents International roster. After five years on the job, Eitan seemed to have arrived. He started talking about buying a house, getting married, and starting a family. And he began drafting plans for a guiding service that would improve the security and livelihood of guides.

Eitan was loved because he cared about those around him. His smile was radiant—it seemed to wake people up from any dark day. One of his closest classmates at Colby remembered Eitan as someone "who made you feel like you mattered." It was no surprise to learn that guides, climbers, and non-climbers alike held memorial services for Eitan across the country.

– PATRICK BAGLEY

MARK HESSE, 1950–2014

MARK HESSE, climber, conservationist, and access activist, passed away in early 2014. A fit 63-year-old man, he was climbing alone in a Boulder, Colorado, climbing gym and no one saw him fall. The gym employees who rushed to his aid were unable to revive him.

Mark had a long and storied climbing career, including a solo ascent of the Scott-Haston

Route up the huge South Face of Denali in 1982. A few years later, in 1986, Mark partnered with Craig Reason, Jay Smith, and Paul Teare to make an alpine-style first ascent of the northeast buttress of 22,241-foot Kangtega in Nepal. He also did new routes in the Canadian Rockies.

Mark climbed extensively in Colorado, Utah, and other states, doing many first ascents. In 1973, Mark joined Dan McClure to climb a new route up the overhanging right side of the Diamond on Longs Peak, which they called Its Welx, as well as the Central Ramp up the remote east face of Mt. Alice in Rocky Mountain National Park.

These vertical adventures instilled in Mark not only a lifelong love for climbing but also an abiding passion for climbing environmentalism and the protection of sensitive climbing areas. In 1984, Mark took over the American Mountain Foundation (AMF), which morphed into the Rocky Mountain Field Institute (RMFI) in 1987. He served as the organization's executive director until 2008, and under his leadership it built sustainable climber-access trails and staging areas below cliff sectors throughout Colorado and Utah. These areas include Shelf Road, Indian Creek Canyon, Eldorado Canyon, the climber trail to Castleton Tower and Moses, as well as Colorado 14ers like Crestone Needle. For his conservation efforts and stewardship of climbing areas, Mark was awarded the David Brower Conservation Award by the American Alpine Club in 1995.

Mark also was program director for Southwest Outward Bound School and worked on projects with Colorado College, the Access Fund, and the Colorado Fourteeners Initiative (CFI), of which he was a cofounder. One of his greatest achievements was the founding of the Santa Fe Mountain Center in 1977. This nonprofit program used wilderness adventure as a therapeutic tool for at-risk populations, and it continues that work today.

Prior to his death, Mark Hesse had moved from Colorado Springs to Boulder, spending more time with his wife, Julie, and enjoying climbing, hiking, and mountain biking. During this time he began writing a trail-building manual for the Access Fund and worked to establish the Front Range Climbing Stewards, a hotshot trail crew.

Besides his many achievements, Mark had a wonderful sense of humor and a ready smile. He was a loyal husband and father and a friend to many. Mark is survived by Julie Asmuth, his wife of 30 years, and their two daughters, Hartley and Laurel. While he left this world of rock and ice far too young, he left behind a legacy that will continue to touch the lives of American climbers.

– STEWART M. GREEN *AND* DENNIS JACKSON

CHAD LEWIS KELLOGG, 1971–2014

ON THE 10TH OF FEBRUARY, as he was headed out the door with partner Jens Holsten to climb Fitz Roy, Chad emailed me with instructions to have a specific bouquet delivered to his

sweetheart, Mandy, back home in Seattle on Valentine's Day. Tragically, the delivery of that bouquet coincided with his death by rockfall during the Fitz Roy descent.

Born in Omak, Washington, and nurtured in the fertile environment of Cascadia and the Seattle climbing community, Chad's life was marked by a prodigious commitment to climbing. While he never achieved the elite technical ability to push the limits of the rock, ice, and mixed grading scales, he was a cardiovascular locomotive, and he had an unparalleled capability and desire to endure suffering in the mountains. This led him up mountains all over the world, including many new routes and several speed records. He rented out both his houses in Seattle in favor of living out of his truck and taking as many as three major expeditions each year, often two to the Nepalese Himalaya and another to China or South America, funded largely through his own labor doing residential remodeling and construction, plus a few reliable sponsors and grants.

His persistence at his chosen objectives was bewildering: three attempts at a speed record on Mt. Everest, two attempts on a new route on the most difficult face on the unclimbed Lunag Ri with plans for a third, the first American solo new route on the south face of Aconcagua, and the epic first ascent of the southwest ridge of Siguniang, just to name a few. A 50-hour single push, a midnight solo blizzard training session on Mt. Rainier ending in a self-rescue with a shattered arm—this type of thing was Chad's go-to entertainment. Failure, injury, and terrible personal loss, particularly the death of his wife, Lara, in a climbing accident in 2007, only added fuel to his persistence.

But there was much more to him than hard-edged perseverance. Wherever he was, he found opportunities to help people and keep things working right, sometimes even at the expense of his personal missions. In spite of his propensity to go solo, he really loved climbing with his friends, cracking bad puns and jokes with a toothy grin. Through his climbing pursuits, his devotion to his friends and his community, and his newfound Buddhist faith, he had overcome many of the demons that had haunted him and was finally at peace. Even so, he was not ready to leave us—he was only ready to begin teaching us the lessons of his life: that life is too short, it can end at any moment for any reason, and each day is a gift. Do not hesitate to grab your dreams, for tomorrow they may be out of reach.

– DAN AYLWARD

COLE KENNEDY, 1990–2014

COLE KENNEDY WAS KILLED in July when a collapsing cornice swept the northwest couloir of Piramide de Garcilaso in Peru, where we were climbing together. In those few brief seconds the climbing world lost an incredibly driven and strong climber, his family lost a hilarious and unbelievably smart son, and many others, including me, lost an incredible friend.

Cole and I met during our freshman year at Colorado College. Of all the new and exciting things we were exposed to, none captivated us quite like climbing. Within a year we were driving all over the Southwest—to the Black Canyon, to Castle Valley, to Nevada—in search of rock. We took some big falls, we got benighted, we got lost in the woods, we had run-ins with various deans around campus, and Cole started to climb hard—really hard. After school, climbing and skiing were his priorities—and rightly so, as he was a natural at both. He became a true all-arounder, soon boasting a resume replete ice and alpine routes up to WI5, V11 boulder problems, and redpoints up to 5.13b.

Being partners with Cole was simultaneously frustrating and inspiring. You would lead a pitch and feel like you were at your absolute limit, and he would follow so casually and smoothly that you immediately started racking your brain for excuses, even though he hadn't said anything. At first you would write it off: "That pitch was just his style." But later the style would change, and he'd be kicking your ass just as hard, and you'd run out of excuses.

Really what it came down to was that Cole knew how to really try hard, and because of that he could succeed at anything he chose to do. When he found something he loved, he drove himself to be the absolute best. He was never judgmental of others' abilities, and he was calm, encouraging, and matter-of-fact in a way that made you feel comfortable pushing yourself. Cole also believed there was always room for moments of complete and total nonsense in the mountains, no matter how serious the situation was supposed to be.

Cole was the one you could always count on when you weren't feeling up to a hard or scary lead, the one you were glad you were with when things didn't go according to plan, the standard to which every partner should both seek out and aspire to be.

– JOHN COLLIS

CHARLIE PORTER, 1950–2014

CHARLES TALBOT PORTER, who died so unexpectedly on January 23, grew up in Pepperell, Massachussetts, where his father was a doctor and his mother, Barbara Cooney, was a well-known author and illustrator of children's books. His formal education ended when he graduated from prep school in 1969, by which time he had already become a keen mountaineer, hitching west in the summers to climb in the Canadian Rockies and the Cascades.

In 1969 he visited Yosemite for the first time, jumping straight in at the deep end with an ascent of the Nose with Bugs McKeith. But it was his solo first ascent of the Dawn Wall route in 1972 that really sparked the Porter legend. After dropping one of his haulbags on the first day, he carried on for another nine days, sleeping each night in a hammock improvised from slings and his remaining haulbag.

A few weeks later he was back up on El Capitan, making the first ascent of the Shield, followed by Tangerine Trip and Mescalito (1973), Grape Race and Horse Chute in 1974, and Excalibur in 1975. But Porter was too energetic, too curious, too much of an explorer simply to remain year after year in Yosemite. In June 1974, with Gary Bocarde, Michael Clark, and John Svenson, he climbed the 800-meter southwest wall of the Moose's Tooth in Alaska, lugging a gigantic moose's antler all the way up the wall to leave enshrined on the summit, just for the hell of it. The following winter he drove the British Burgess twins up to Canada in his beat-up VW van to join his Nose companion, Bugs McKeith, on the first ascent of a world-classic ice climb, Polar Circus. Having improvised his own pitons in Yosemite, here in the Canadian Rockies he wielded his own homemade ice axe with radically angled pick.

In 1976 he upped the ante on his continent's highest peak: Denali. The Japanese team that was patiently sieging the Cassin Ridge, preparing daily fresh vegetables in their pressure

cooker, was astonished by the ruddy-faced young American who rushed past them, alone, carrying just a 20-pound pack. A violent headache forced him to bail on the first attempt, but after a day's rest he went back up. At around 19,000 feet, "I felt my lungs bubbling, so I took a bunch of diuretics, and when I got to the summit I peed all my body liquids out. I didn't feel too good, but I made it down okay."

That near miss from what was probably pulmonary edema may be the reason that Porter never went to the Himalaya. But even if he had put up big Himalayan climbs, he wouldn't have told the world much about them. He seems genuinely to have been uninterested in the trappings of fame. Hence we have only the sketchiest details of his Cassin climb and of what was probably his most ambitious achievement of all: the solo first ascent of the north wall of Mt. Asgard, on Baffin Island, in 1975, an ascent that has been called the world's first Grade VII.

His last big Alaskan climb was the first ascent of Middle Triple Peak in the Kichatna Spires, with Russell McLean, in 1976. Three years later the pair visited the Paine group in Chile. They didn't succeed on the climb, but for Porter that was just the beginning of a whole new life of exploration. He had taken with him a kayak converted for rowing, with sculling oars and a sliding seat. In this minimalist craft he set off alone on an odyssey lasting over a year, rowing hundreds of miles through the Patagonian channels, finishing off by rounding Cape Horn.

Porter was entranced by Patagonia and after that solo voyage he made Chile his home, settling eventually in the world's most southerly harbor, Puerto Williams. He acquired a 42-foot steel ketch, which he renamed Gondwana and used as a floating base for visiting scientists. For the next three decades he devoted his life to scientific research in Patagonia, with occasional forays to more distant outposts such as South Georgia. Over the years he became an inseparable, seemingly permanent part of the unique southern landscape of sea and mountains, and so it was a huge shock when he died from a heart attack, aged just 63.

– STEPHEN VENABLES

WILLIAM LOWELL PUTNAM III, 1924–2014

BILL PUTNAM'S LONG PROMINENCE in mountaineering organizations, national and international, tended to obscure his stature as one of the foremost mountaineers of his generation.

Brought up by his father to love the outdoors, he began his mountaineering career by joining the Harvard Mountaineering Club and the Appalachian Mountain Club. As soon as Bill turned 18, such learning as had been taking place at Harvard was interrupted by his acceptance into the recently organized mountain troops, with which he trained in Alaska and the West. When the troops were regrouped as the Tenth Mountain Division and sent to Italy, he saw combat as a lieutenant and platoon leader, emerging with two purple hearts along with bronze and silver stars for gallantry in action.

Resuming his geological studies at Harvard in 1946, he organized and led the first American ascent of Mt. St. Elias (18,008'). It was on this climb that Bill realized he was unable to function above 16,000 feet, owing to the extensive damage to his lung and the deeply embedded shrapnel remaining from the wounds received in Italy. Accordingly, while many of his friends won fame on the high peaks of other continents, Bill turned to the mountains of western Canada, absorbing their geography, history, and lore. Even Bill did not know the precise number of first ascents he had made in his lifetime, but he guessed around 200. Most of these were in the Selkirks, and only those who have tried it themselves can fully appreciate the difficulty of struggling through the thick and punishing underbrush of this range—until then the least explored in Canada—to gain some isolated and untrodden peak.

Bill's training as a geologist and his keen sense of history led him to issue in 1947 an enlargement and revision of J. Monroe Thorington's *Guide to the Interior Ranges of British Columbia* (1937), which he continued to revise over three subsequent editions, the last in 1971. He also built three huts in the Interior Ranges, the largest of which he deeded to the Alpine Club of Canada and which is now named the Bill Putnam Hut. For his many services to Canadian mountaineering he was made an honorary member of the ACC and the Association of Canadian Mountain Guides.

In 1969 Bill was elected to the Council (later Board of Directors) of the AAC, and he served this board in one capacity or another for the next 30 years, becoming president in 1974 and treasurer from 1977 to 1991. An old iconoclast and rebel himself, he always had a sympathetic ear for the outsider and did much to make the newer Western members of the club feel at home among the traditional Easterners.

Bill's was the era in which a quiet word to a high-ranking official could cut through bureaucratic procedure to keep mountains open for climbing, and in this regard the club often benefitted from his service on the National Advisory Board of the U.S. Forest Service. Always conscious, moreover, of the club's role in the scientific aspects of mountain exploration, he led his family in creating the Roger Putnam Fund for Alpine Research, in honor of their father.

Following his resignation as treasurer, Bill was elected an honorary member of the AAC and awarded the Angelo Heilprin Citation, an award for service to the club that he himself had devised during his presidency. Upon the death of Henry Hall Jr. in 1987, he was elected Honorary President, in which capacity he continued to act as the historian and conscience of the club during a period of rapid growth. For 30 years, either formally or informally, Bill also acted as the club's delegate to the International Union of Alpine Clubs (UIAA), and in 2002 was elected vice president as well as an honorary member.

Space prevents more than a mention of Bill's noteworthy career in television, beginning with the founding in 1952 of WWLP in Springfield, the first licensed UHF television station in the United States, or his role as chair of the NBC affiliates organization and his election to the Broadcasting Hall of Fame in 2001. He was sole trustee of the Lowell Observatory in Flagstaff, Arizona, from 1987 to 2013, during which time the observatory partnered with the Discovery Channel to build one of the world's most advanced telescopes. He also served on the board of the Mt. Washington Observatory, an important institution for the science of meteorology.

The subjects of his numerous books, all written with his usual immediacy and panache, range from freedom of the press to railway tunnels. At the time of his death he was working on a projected three-volume history of the passes of the Swiss-Italian Alps. The first of these volumes examined the much-debated question of which pass Hannibal had used to lead his army into Italy, approaching the issue from the point of view of the elephants.

Bill's nearly superhuman energy was matched by his imposing physical stature and the strength of his convictions. Coupled with the last was a frank outspokenness that sometimes gave offense. An irreverent sense of humor characterized him from boyhood to old age. As a young member of the AAC he tested the limits by successfully having his dog—baptized Henry Pinkham for the occasion—elected a member of the AAC. As Bill pointed out the dog had indeed made the climbs specified on his application.

Bill had a strong sense of justice and engaged in many battles on behalf of those wronged by life, both in politics and on a personal level. His long campaign to rehabilitate the reputation of the pioneer climber Fritz Wiessner, wrongly blamed in Bill's opinion for deaths on the ill-fated 1939 K2 expedition, ended with Fritz elected to Honorary Membership in the AAC and with publication of *K2: The 1939 Tragedy* (1992), written with Andy Kauffman.

Other than his parents, the one person to whom he consistently deferred was his beloved wife Kitty Broman, his longtime business partner, whom he married in 1999 after the death of his first wife, Joan Fitzgerald, in 1993. Kitty's loss in early January left Bill deeply bereft during the 10 months that remained to him before his own death at the venerable age of 90.

In conclusion, I can do no better than to cite the words of his friend John Radway: "Bill was life writ large—brilliant, vigorous, and creative—sometimes abrasive but full of love for his friends and for humanity. He will always be with us."

– T.C. PRICE ZIMMERMANN

GIBSON REYNOLDS, 1924–2014

GIBSON REYNOLDS, who took part in pioneering expeditions that helped open the Saint Elias Range to mountaineering in the 1950s and made first ascents of several of its peaks, passed away on April 20, 2014. Born and raised in the flatlands of Alabama, Reynolds served in the U.S. Army Signal Corps in Europe during WW II. In the final months of the war, he found himself stationed on the summit of Zugspitze, the highest peak in the German Alps, manning a communications relay station. As the war wound down, Reynolds taught himself to ski and rock climb using discarded Nazi equipment.

Returning to the Massachusetts Institute of Technology, Reynolds joined the Outing Club and eventually became friendly with a group of Seattle-based climbers that included legendary U.S. mountaineer Pete Schoening. With Schoening, Reynolds took part in an expedition that made the first ascent of Mt. Augusta (4,290 m), in 1952, followed by the second ascent of King Peak (5,173m) three weeks later. Schoening later wrote that of all his expeditions, including a famous attempt on K2 the following year, he considered the 1952 King Peak expedition the "most adventurous."

Reynolds returned to the northern end of the Saint Elias range in 1954 and 1955, aiming for the first ascent of University Peak (4,411m), at the time the highest unclimbed summit in North America. In 1954 the team was battered by avalanches and falling seracs that left Reynolds with a broken arm. He returned the following year on an expedition that survived ice falls, crevasses and bad weather to reach the summit via the north ridge. It was a feat not repeated until 1998. The expedition also made the third ascent of Mt. Bona (5,005m)

Reynolds was a life member of the AAC, joining in 1947 and serving as chairman of the New York section from 1960 to 1965. He continued to hike and climb throughout his life. After getting his degree from MIT, Reynolds became an aerospace engineer who helped pioneer the exploration of outer space. Working first for Bendix Corp. and later Allied-Signal Corp., Reynolds was part of the team that designed control systems for Apollo space missions, including the manual throttle used by U.S. astronaut Neil Armstrong to land the first lunar module on the moon.

In 1962, Reynolds married Monica M. Monahan of Dublin, Ireland, an early member of the Irish Mountaineering Club who served as secretary of the AAC; they settled in Tuxedo, N.Y. He is survived by his wife, five children, and five grandchildren.

– MAURA REYNOLDS KELLEY

BARBARA WASHBURN, 1914–2014

AT THE AGE OF 24, a Smith College graduate, Barbara Polk was happily employed as the secretary of the Harvard biology department. But in the spring of 1939, Clarkie, the mailman, convinced her to audition for a job at the New England Museum of Natural History, whose leadership had just been taken over by an ambitious young mountaineer named Bradford Washburn.

Her stint as Brad's secretary was short-lived. The two were married on April 27, 1940. Three months later, with a trio of male teammates, Barbara and Brad stood on the summit of Mt. Bertha, a 10,200-foot snow and ice peak near Alaska's Glacier Bay, having forged the mountain's first ascent—this despite the fact that Barbara's sole previous climb was a summer stroll up Mt. Chocorua in New Hampshire. She found out in a Juneau hospital after the expedition that she was pregnant.

On September 25, 2014, Barbara Washburn died in her home in Lexington, Massachusetts, less than two months short of her 100th birthday. With her passing, America

lost one of its truly great adventurers and pioneer climbers.

In 1941, Brad set his sights on an objective considerably tougher than Mt. Bertha—13,832-foot Mt. Hayes in the Alaska Range. The same drive and vision that led Brad to transform the moribund Museum of Natural History into the world-class Boston Museum of Science, and to revolutionize Alaskan mountaineering, made him a hard man to say no to. So when Brad insisted that Barbara come along on the Hayes expedition, she said yes, even though it meant leaving a newborn daughter behind.

The only previous attempt on Hayes had been led by Brad's close friend Charlie Houston in 1937. High on the north ridge, that strong team had been stopped cold by a serpentine, corniced knife-edge. In 1941, after weeks of effort interrupted by prolonged storms, Brad's team faced the same ridge, clearly the crux of the route. And at that moment the climbers put Barbara in the lead. Their rationale was that, as the lightest member of the team, if she slipped or broke off a cornice and took a horrendous fall, she would be the climber the others would have the best chance of safely belaying.

Brad led his second expedition to Mt. McKinley in 1947, and Barbara was along again, despite her misgivings about leaving behind a family that by then consisted of three young children. On June 6, outperforming most of her male teammates, she became the first woman to stand on the highest point in North America. (The second female ascent of McKinley would not come for another two decades.)

Beginning in 1964, and continuing for two decades, Barbara taught kids with dyslexia and other reading disorders at Shady Hill School in Cambridge. Some of the most gratifying rewards in her life came when those tutees returned as adults to thank her for steering them along paths of professional success.

Barbara and Brad were married for 67 years. They were ideal companions and partners in the field, not only in Alaska but also in such monumental projects as mapping the Grand Canyon (697 helicopter landings on obscure buttes and ledges in the 1970s). Her memoir, *The Accidental Adventurer* (Epicenter Press, 2001), is a classic and a delight. I knew Barbara for five decades. The behind-the-scenes stories she told me about her life with Brad, and the hijinks and foibles of their companions on various expeditions, easily could have filled another charming book.

— DAVID ROBERTS

NECROLOGY

In addition to those covered above, AAC members who passed away in 2014 included:

DONALD J. LISKA	DAVE PEGG	ROBERT L. SMITH
MARK MAHANEY	JACOB RENNEBERG	J.D. TALADAY
SYLVIA MONTAG	MELL SCHOENING	JAROD VONRUEDEN
ALEXANDER NEWPORT-BERRA	PHILIP M. SMITH	

CLUB ACTIVITIES

EDITED BY FREDERICK O. JOHNSON

CASCADE SECTION

THE CASCADE SECTION held numerous festivals, clinics, and social events throughout the year. Highlights included our Send & Social events at the Seattle Bouldering Project, where climbers could compete in events such as crash-pad stacking and a Nerf gun obstacle course. We ended the year there with our holiday party in December.

The Rockfest Climbing Festival, presented by the AAC, Northwest Mountain School, and Leavenworth Mountain Sports, featured Audrey Sniezek as guest instructor and presenter. This annual gathering in Leavenworth also hosted its first bouldering competition and rallied 150 Northwest climbers to celebrate the start of climbing season. Ueli Steck stopped by Seattle on his national tour and sold out the University of Washington's Kane Hall with over 700 people. AAC President Mark Kroese emceed and helped host a VIP event that included such noted climbers as the Freds (Beckey, Dunham, and Stanley), Melissa Arnot, Kate Rutherford, Audrey Sniezek, and Brent Bishop, among others.

Other events included the Reel Rock Film Tour at Vertical World, hosted by Second Ascent, which raised $2,000 for the AAC and brought in 52 new members. Steve House and Scott Johnston provided an advanced training clinic, based on their new book *Training for the New Alpinism*, at Seattle Bouldering Project. At the annual section dinner at Salty's in Alki, over 100 members enjoyed a Blake Herrington slideshow about rarely climbed routes in Washington. The Cascade Section also has partnered with local nonprofits in a regional Outdoor Alliance to help inform land managers about climber-related policy and planning decisions.

— EDDIE ESPINOSA, *NORTHWEST REGIONAL COORDINATOR*

OREGON SECTION

ONCE EVERY MONTH, AAC members in Portland gathered at a local brewery for Pub Club, an informal social gathering that provides members with access to an amazing network of local climbers and instant camaraderie, based on a shared passion for climbing and the AAC. In May we hosted our annual dinner at the historic Timberline Lodge. Scott Johnston, co-author of *Training for the New Alpinism*, was our keynote speaker and shared some very helpful training tips. The silent auction and raffle helped raise money for the local Live Your Dream grants.

At mid-year Jesse Bernier came on board as section co-chair, joining existing co-chair Heidi Medema. Jesse is based out of Bend, where we hope to grow the club's presence. Once the weather cooled, we headed to Smith Rock, where, with the support of our friends from CAMP, we hosted the third annual Craggin' Classic, with clinics, food, film, and more. We capped the weekend with a successful service project, helping to repair a washed-out section of trail in the popular state park. In December, AAC members and Live Your Dream grant winners Ally and Jon Skeen opened a special evening with Ueli Steck with a quick talk about their AAC-supported adventure. Then the Swiss Machine gave a very inspiring presentation of his mountaineering feats to a sold-out house.

— HEIDI MEDEMA, *CO-CHAIR*

SOUTHWEST SECTION

AS IN THE LAST SEVERAL YEARS, the Southwest Section had four principal events in 2014: a climbing/restoration weekend in Joshua Tree National Park in March; a stewardship day at Idyllwild in June as part of the fourth annual Idyllwild Climbers Festival; helping with the Fall Highball in Bishop; and the annual holiday dinner, at Taix French Restaurant, with a slide-show by Pete Takeda and a silent auction that raised $1,100 for the section.

— JIM PINTER-LUCKE, *CHAIR*

IDAHO SECTION

IN 2014 THE Idaho Section enjoyed consistent participation of its members and persistent engagement with non-members in the mountaineering and outdoor communities—a concrete step toward further strengthening ties with the community in 2015.

In April the section invited Mike Libecki for a dinner and meet-and-greet in Boise. In June we sponsored a clean-up day at Laclede Rocks, an Idaho gem with a wide variety of climbing, overlooking the Pend Oreille River. The event affirmed our local climbers' interest in resource preservation through volunteer work.

In September many of our members gathered at the Idaho Mountain Festival, the largest annual gathering of climbers and outdoors people in the state. The festival, in its third year, was sold out despite bad weather. The AAC made connections with key Idahoans, including a local state legislator. In October, Longleaf Wilderness Medicine, based in northern Idaho, partnered with the AAC to provide wilderness education for climbers. Climber education and safety were key agenda items for the section in 2014, and are expected to remain significant in 2015.

— KAMMIE CUNEO & JASON LUTHY, *CO-CHAIRS*

NEW MEXICO SECTION

IN SEPTEMBER, New Mexico State University teamed with our section, Climbers of Hueco Tanks Coalition, Organ Mountains Technical Rescue Squad, Mesilla Valley Bosque State Park, Southwest Environmental Center, Southern New Mexico Trail Alliance, and the New Mexico Wilderness Alliance to put on the first annual Las Cruces Climbing Festival. This ambitious event attracted about 800 people for three days, culminating with a climbing competition at NMSU.

In November, Aaron Miller organized a work day for Diablo Canyon outside Santa Fe. The AAC, NMCRAG, the Stone Age Climbing Gym, and Santa Fe Climbing Center all provided swag, food, and drinks.

In 2014 the Organ Mountains–Desert Peaks National Monument was created, and in September I attended an informational meeting with the BLM to represent climbers' interests in the new monument. The pre-existing status of the Organ Mountains as a BLM wilderness study area is still in effect, and as the rules for wilderness study areas are more restrictive than national monument rules, nothing significant has changed from a climbing perspective. This situation likely also pertains to the Rough and Ready Hills near Las Cruces, which are also in the new national monument.

— PAT GIOANNINI, *CHAIR*

NORTH CENTRAL SECTION

OUR SECTION CONTINUES TO GROW and build local support. This past year we teamed up with the Black Hills Climbers Coalition and the Access Fund to build and redevelop some major climbers' trails in Custer State Park. We also teamed up with the Black Hills Climbers Coalition to co-sponsor the Reel Rock Film Tour, which continues to be our largest event of the year, bringing 300 climbers to Rapid City for the night. In the coming year we look forward to developing an annual fall climbers' gathering in Custer State Park and working with the Black Hills Climbers Coalition to develop a climbers' campground.

— MARK JOBMAN, *CHAIR*

WESTERN SLOPE SECTION

THE YEAR STARTED with the 19th annual Ouray Ice Festival, which, as usual, was well attended. The evening programs were very popular, especially the Ueli Steck show on Thursday, where people had to be turned away. We also spent time at the festival with members of the Ridgway High School climbing club. We demonstrated key alpine knots and discussed their uses, as well as other climbing topics.

Our second major event was the annual Penitente Canyon anchor replacement weekend in June. We focused on a few routes in the main canyon and then started upgrading routes in the Rock Garden. Over 20 routes were modernized, with specifics posted to Mountain Project. Thanks are due to the Strands for providing the beer and BBQ. The AAC also provided some nice swag for the Western Colorado Climbers Coalition in support of its purchase of Mother's Buttress in Unaweep Canyon, south of Grand Junction. I am happy to announce that the purchase was completed in October! Lastly, in June I hosted the first Climbers Meetup at the Buena Vista Crags near my home. A few of us ventured out to repeat a new 12-pitch backcountry route on Davis Face, and various single-pitch routes also were climbed.

— LEE JENKINS, *CHAIR*

FRONT RANGE SECTION

IN FEBRUARY THE Front Range Section hosted a large Friday-night gathering at the new Earth Treks gym in Golden, before the AAC Annual Benefit Dinner. Five hundred AAC and Earth Treks members showed up for the event, which included free climbing, beer, and awards presented by Phil Powers. The highlight of the evening was the "Earth Treks vs. AAC" climbing comp. Lynn Hill wowed the crowd with her upside-down acrobatics and general mugging. The wild-card competitor was Chris Sharma, who at the final moment climbed for the AAC, clinching the win for the visiting team.

The AAC Colorado Climbing Posse, using the website Meetup.com, greatly increased the number of its outings, with membership growing to 125 climbers. There were after-work rock climbing meetups and weekend trips to farther destinations. The Posse is for AAC members only, thus providing another perk for Front Range members. The section teamed up with Action Committee for Eldorado to sponsor the Eldorado Canyon Climbers Picnic. There were demos from Sportiva, a BBQ on the back porch of the Eldorado visitor's center, and a slideshow on the history of climbing in Eldorado Canyon by guidebook writer Steve Levin.

— CAROL KOTCHEK, *CHAIR*

GREAT LAKES SECTION

Once again the Great Lakes Section hosted two major events in 2014. The section continues to grow, due in large part to these events. The 2014 Michigan Ice Fest brought 411 participants to Munising for another year of excellent ice conditions at Pictured Rocks National Lakeshore and Grand Island. The Ice Fest is the largest gathering of Midwest climbers and the section's biggest event, which results in new members for the AAC and the Access Fund.

In the fall we hosted Climb Up 2014! with Down Wind Sports, a four-day event on the south shore of Lake Superior. Climbing ethics, adventure stories, and much more were discussed around the campfire after long days of climbing at Silver Mountain near Baraga.

— BILL THOMPSON, *CHAIR*

MIDWEST SECTION

For the third straight year the AAC was proudly represented at the Reel Rock Film Tour at the University of Illinois' Chicago campus. A big thank you to Bob Swartz, who manned our information table as close to 200 climbers and outdoor enthusiasts gathered for the only screening in the Chicago area. The club-sponsored insignia giveaways and raffle prizes are always a crowd favorite.

— RAY KOPCINSKI, *CHAIR*

NEW ENGLAND SECTION

In February our section helped the International Mountain Climbing School sponsor the 21st annual Ice Fest in North Conway, New Hampshire. The Theatre in the Woods hosted Friday night's event, where the AAC had a membership table along with a silent auction to benefit the Live Your Dream grants.

In March we hosted our final annual dinner, an event originally started by prior chair Bill Atkinson almost 20 years ago. Bill's goal was the preservation of Ken Henderson's films of the first ascent of Pinnacle Gully on Mt. Washington and the Whitney-Gilman route on Cannon Mountain. William Clack, an audio designer and filmmaker, was the technical adviser and interviewed Ken in 2000. This was the inaugural showing of the digitized Henderson films and a fitting closure to our dinners.

We also hosted two BBQs at the base of Cathedral Ledge in North Conway, in July and October. Thanks to Rick Merritt, who does an awesome job as grill-master. Once again Chad Hussey hosted our annual It Ain't Over 'Til It's Over cragging day at Ragged Mountain, Connecticut, in early November. Sadly, this year we were rained out, but stay tuned for next November.

— NANCY SAVICKAS, *CO-CHAIR*

METRO NEW YORK SECTION

Despite the heavy involvement of the Metro NY Section in preparations for the AAC's Annual Benefit Dinner in Manhattan in January 2015, the section maintained an active series of outdoor and indoor events throughout the year. Once again we journeyed to the Adirondacks to ice climb and ski in January and to hike, rock climb, and canoe in May. These events, always sell-outs, have been a fixture on the section's calendar for a quarter century. In

June we hosted two memorable sit-down dinners and slideshows, one with Jimmy Chin, the famed adventure photographer, and the other with Wade Davis and Conrad Anker on the British expeditions to Everest in the 1920s. This theme was repeated in a special screening at the Rubin Museum of John Noel's historic film on the doomed Mallory-Irvine expedition of 1924. The section's traditional Annual Black Tie Dinner in December was postponed to the following year due to the proximity to the AAC's annual dinner. However, as a substitute we hosted Ueli Steck in a reception and slideshow attended by more than 500.

Since 1980, when I assumed the chairmanship of the New York Section, I have dutifully chronicled our local happenings on these pages. This is my last such submission, as I am retiring from that post, to be succeeded by Howard Sebold. Howard has been one of our most active and valuable volunteers, in a section that has many. My thanks go to all who have helped make the Metro NY Section such a vibrant climbing community.

– **PHILIP ERARD**, *CHAIR*

MID-ATLANTIC SECTION

THIS YEAR WE ORGANIZED regular social events, including the Reel Rock Film Tour, Banff Mountain Film Festival World Tour, and Send & Socials. Our joint section events—the Delaware Water Gap Multi-Pitch Summer Sufferfest, the New River Gorge Craggin' Classic, the Joint DC and Mid-Atlantic Ice Craggin' Day, and our unique Oktoberfest Top Rope Social and Dinner—are now regular annual gatherings.

We hosted two climbing competency clinics: Silas Rossi's "How to Train for Big Objectives" and Karsten Delap's session on rappelling. We also sponsored bouldering competitions in central Pennsylvania and New Jersey. These efforts at outreach and education have helped to build our community, recruit ambassadors and members, and increase climbing experience and competence.

Live Your Dream grantees Anthony Nguyen and Ben Beck-Coon were forced to postpone their aid ascent of Zion's Moonlight Buttress until the spring due to injury, but have communicated with us throughout the process, including this note from Ben: "We set out to do something that was truly a dream for us, but facing down challenges, dealing effectively with frustration, and adjusting course when necessary are, I think, what will ultimately become the strongest foundations for our progress as people and as climbers."

In 2015 the section embarks on a pilot program to reorganize into chapters, using 15 section ambassadors to organize and deliver local programming and events. Additionally, we are actively partnering with local climbing gyms as a means to build, maintain, and increase membership.

– **BARRY RUSNOCK**, *CHAIR*

INDEX

COMPILED BY RALPH FERRARA & EVE TALLMAN

Mountains are listed by their official names. Ranges and geographic locations are also indexed. Unnamed peaks (eg. Peak 2,340) are listed under P. Abbreviations are used for some states and countries and for the following: Article: art.; Cordillera: C.; Mountains: Mts.; National Park: Nat'l Park; Obituary: obit. Most personnel are listed for major articles. Expedition leaders and persons supplying information in Climbs and Expeditions are also cited here. Indexed photographs are listed in bold type. Reviewed books are listed alphabetically under Book Reviews.

A

Abi (Nepal) *See* Lobuche East
Abi (Sichuan, China) **348-9**
Academy of Sciences Range (Tajikistan) 269-70
Acevedo, Elvis 220-1
Achuma (Quimsa Cruz, Peru) 215
Acropole des Draveurs (Quebec) 178-9
Adela, Cerro (Patagonia) 228
Adi Kailash Rg. (Kamaun Himalaya, India) 333
Africa 246-9
Aghil Range (Karakoram, China) 342-5
Aguilera, Volcán (Chile) *art.* 70-7, **74**, *map*72
Agyasol (Kishtwar, India) **324**
Ailefroide Occidentale (France) 242
Akimov, Vitaly 262
Ak-su (Pamir Alai, Kyrgyzstan) 257-8
Ala Archa (Kyrgz Ala-too, Kyrgyzstan) 261-2
Alaska *art.* 22-32, 91-5; 148-67
Alaska Rg. (AK) *art.* 22-32; 155-62
Albardón del Potrero Escondido, Cerro (Central Andes) 217
Alichursky Mts. (Tajikistan) 271
Alldred, Cath 188
Allfrey, David *art.* 62-9
Alpine Guides Pk. (Kanchenjunga Himal, India) 334-5
Alpine Mentors *art.* 78-85
Alps (Europe) 242
Ame Pal Chuli East (Nepal) **287**
Ame Pal Chuli West (Nepal) **287**
Amitabha (Karakoram, India) **311**-2
Amuchástegui, Lucas 217
Anacoreta, Cerro (Chile) *art.* 70-7
Andes (Chile/Argentina) *art.* 70-7
Andes, Central (Argentina-Chile) 216-21
Andes, Northern (Argentina-Chile) 216
Andreas Klarstrom 243
Angel (Revelation Mts, AK) 148-51
Anglada, Oriol 191
Ansilta 7 (Argentina) 216
Antarctica 236-41

Antipasto, Aguja (Patagonia) 224-**6**
Anvers Island (Antarctic Peninsula) 238-9
Arabel Pass (Tien Shan, Kyrgyzstan) 264
Arganglas Valley (Karakoram, India) 310-1
Argentina-Chile 216-35
Arizona 131
Arnot, Melissa 288
Arosio, Tito 198-201
Ashat Gorge (Kyrgyzstan) 257
Asperity (Waddington Rg., CAN) 168
Aspiring, Mt. (Southern Alps, New Zealand) **361**-2
Augustin P. (Kichatna Mts, AK) **154**-5
Avellano Towers (Patagonia) 223-4
Avenas, Antoine 242
Aylward, Dan 377-8

B

Baby Molar (Greenland) *See* Milk Tooth
Badal P. (Masherbrum Rg., Pakistan) 280-**1**
Baffin Island (CAN) *art.* 46-56; 179
Bagley, Patrick 376
Baltoro Muztagh (Pakistan) 276-80
Barker, Dave 305
Barmasse, Hervé 242
Barnaj I (Kishtwar, India) 318-9
Barnaj II (Kishtwar, India) 318-9
Barnard, Mt. (Sierra Nevada, CA) 123
Barnes, Jim 120-1
Baro, Oriol 235, 314-6
Barronette Pk. (MT) 135
Bass, Malcolm 329-30
Bastille Buttress (Sierra Nevada, CA) 123-4
Batura Muztagh (Karakoram, Pakistan) 274
Bautismo, Cerro (C. Frontal, Argentina-Chile) 218-9
Bayonet (Russia) 252-**4**
Beartooth Mts. (MT) 135
Beisly, Gregg 212
Beluga Spire (Baffin, CAN) *art.* **57**-61
Benarat, Mt. (Borneo) 360

Benes, Ondrej 194
Berry, Nik *art.* 62-9
Bhagirathi I (Western Garhwal, India) 327
Bighorn Mts. (WY) *art.* 97-107, *map* 98
Bijora Hiunchuli (Nepal) 284
Bilibino Towers (Chukotka, Russia) 254-6
Binfa, Pedro 223
Bipeng Valley (Sichuan, China) 349
Bizot, Henry 260
Bjornstad, Eric *obit.* 374-5
Black Canyon Nat'l Park (CO) 141-2
Blanca de Ectelion, Torre (Central Andes) **221**
Blyth, Jim 241
Boktoh Central (Kangchenjunga Himal, Nepal)
    306-8, **307**
Bolivia 206-15
Bomber Mt. (Bighorn Mts., WY) 140
Bonniot, Max 242
Book Reviews 366-72
*The Call of the Ice: Climbing 8,000 Meter Peaks in
    Winter* by: Simone Moro 371
The Calling: A Life Rocked by Mountains by: Barry
    Blanchard 367
*Climbing Stronger, Faster, Healthier; Beyond the
    Basics (Second Edition)* by: Michael A. Layton
    372
*Cold Feet: Stories of a Middling Climber on Classic
    Peaks and Among Legendary Mountaineers* by:
    David Pagel 369
*Denali's Howl: The Deadliest Climbing Disaster on
    America's Wildest Peak* by: Andy Hall 370
*Hanging On: A Life Inside British Climbing's
    Golden Age* by: Martin Boysen 372
*High Summits: 370 Famous First Peak Ascents and
    Other Significant Events in Mountaineering
    History* by: Frederick L. Wolfe 372
Letters From Chamonix: Stories and a Novella by:
    David Stevenson 371-2
One Day as a Tiger by: John Porter 368
Reinhold Messner: My Life at the Limit Interviewed
    by: Thomas Hüetlin 372
Tears of the Dawn by: Jules Lines 372
*The Tower: A Chronicle of Climbing and
    Controversy on Cerro Torre* by: Kelly Cordes
    366-7
*Training for the New Alpinism: A Manual for the
    Climber as Athlete* by: Steve House and Scott
    Johnston 372
Borneo 360
Boucansaud, Mt. (Revelation Mts., AK) **151**-2
Bouchet, Jean 236-7
Boyle, John M. *obit.* 373
Brahmasar du Tacul (Western Garhwal, India)
    330-1

Brahmasar I (Western Garhwal, India) *art.* 78-85,
    84
Brahmasar II (Western Garhwal, India) 330-1
Brazeau, Chris 176-7
Brazil 194
British Columbia (CAN) 168-72
Brown, David 223-4
Brunner, Michael 229
Bubbs Creek Wall (Sierra Nevada, CA) 125-**6**
Buckle, Derek 327
Buffy, P. (Tajikistan) 270-1
Bugaboos (British Columbia, CAN) 172-3
Buil, Cecilia 191-2, 219-20
Buracchio, Cerro (Patagonia) **232**-3
Burkhardt, Majka 248-9
Burnag Kangri (Karakoram, China) **343**
Burns, Cameron M. 369, 374-5
Byeliy, Pik (Tien Shan, Kyrgyzstan) 265
Bylinski, Artem 207-8

C
C. Blanca (Peru) 195-
C. Central (Colombia) 193
C. Central (Peru) 201
C. de Ansilta (Andes, Argentina) 216
C. Frontal (Argentina) 217-9
C. Huayhuash (Peru) 196-201
C. Occidental (Peru) 215
C. Quimsa Cruz (Peru) 215
C. Real (Bolivia) 206-15
C. Urubamba (Peru) 202-4
C. Vilcabamba (Peru) 205
C. Vilcanota (Peru) 204-5
Cajon de Arenales 218
Cajón de Espinoza (Central Andes) 221
Caldwell, Tommy *art.* 12-21
California *art.* 12-21, 86-90; 115-29
Campanario, Torres del (Central Andes) 217-**8**
Campanillas Negro (Colombia) **193**
Canada 168-79
Cano, Juan José 303-5
Cape Farewell Region (Greenland) 188-9
Cape Renard (Antarctic Peninsula) 237-**8**
Capricorn Pk. (Rocky Mts., CAN) 175-6
Capulin Canyon (NM) 145-7
Carter, Seth *art.* 86-90
Cascade Mts. (US) 110-3
Castle Dome (Sierra Nevada, CA) 126-**7**
Caucasus 250
Cayrol, Antoine 237-8
Central Piramidalny (Pamir Alai, Kyrgyzstan)
    257-**8**
Cerro Torre (Patagonia) 227-31
Chainopuerto, Nevado (C. Urubamba, Peru) **203**

Chaltén Massif (Patagonia) 227-31
Chalung North "Kula North" (Ladakh, India) 313
Chamberlain, Mt. (Sierra Nevada, CA) 121-3
Chanchakhi (Caucasus, Russia) 250
Charakusa Valley (Masherbrum Rg., Pakistan) 280-1
Chearoco (C. Real, Peru) **206-7**
Cheepaydang (Kamaun Himalaya, India) 331-**2**
Chekigo (Rowaling Himal, Nepal) 294-**5**
Chibitok, Galina 314
Chicon, Nevado (C. Urubamba, Peru) 202, **203**
Child, Aaron 155-6
Chile *art.* 70-7
China 338-56
Chi-Young, Ahn *art.* 33-7
Chomotang Group (Zanskar, India) 314
Chota Sgurr (Himalchal Pradesh, India) 327
Chugach Mts. (AK) 162-4
Chugimago (Rowaling Himal, Nepal) 294-**6**
Chukotka Region (Russia) 254-6
Chumpe (C. Vilcanota, Peru) 204-5
Churen Himal (Nepal) 283
Cisne, Nevado (Chile) 220-1
Clanton, Zach 160
Clarke, Chris 210-3
Cloud Peak (Bighorn Mts., WY) *art.* 97-**107, 103,** *map* 98; 140
Coast Mts. (AK) 165-7
Colangma (Tibet) **357**
Coles, Rebecca 270-1
Collett, Benjamin 139
Collis, John 378-9
Colmillo, Cordón (Patagonia) 223
Colombia 193
Colorado 140-5
Colorado, Cerro Patagonia) *see* Pirámide
Colque Cruz, Nevado (C. Vilcanota, Peru) 204-**5**
Coltrane, Daniel 111-2
Concordia Parbet (Kamaun Himalaya, India) **333**
Condori, Juvenal 209
Cooper, Kevin *art.* 22-32
Cordova, Manu 294-5
Cordy, Paul 169
Corona del Diablo (Chile) 220-1
Cosi, Carlo 196-8
Costa, Marcos 346, 348, 349-50
Cota 2000, Cerro (Torres del Paine, Patagonia) 235
Cottier, Philipp 239
Coussirat, Iñaki 235
Crabtree Crags (Sierra Nevada, CA) 121-3, **122**
Cramer, Jack 140-1
Crison, Jonathan 306-8
Crown Tower (Patagonia) 223-4

Cycal-Yang Fan 354

D

Daderbrum (Greenland) 184-8
Dagpache (Langtang Himal, Nepal) **290**-1
Damodar Himal (Nepal) 288-9
Dan Beard, Mt. (Ruth Gorge, AK) 158-60
Dankova (Tien Shan, Kyrgyzstan) 266-**7**
Daogou East (Sichuan, China) **350**-51
Daogou Valley (Sichuan, China) 352-3
Dare, Ben 362-3
Darran Mts (Southern Alps, New Zealand) 362
Daxue Shan (China) 346-8
De Deeuw, Arjan 266-7
Deavoll, Pat 272-4
De-Berger, Phil 274
Delicias Cordón de las (C. Frontal, Argentina-Chile) 218-9
Della Bordella, Matteo 184-8, 228
Denali (Alaska Rg., AK) *art.* 91-5, **92-3**
Dentiform (Waddington Rg., CAN) 168
Despair, Mt. (WA) **110**-1
DeWeese, Kevin 117-9
Dhorpatan (Nepal) 283
Dike P. (Revelation Mts, AK) 148-51, **150**
Ditto, Ben *art.* 46-56; 180-2
Djangart Rg. (Tien Shan, Kyrgyzstan) 267-8
Djetim Bel Rg. (Tien Shan, Kyrgyzstan) 264
Dobie, Mike 345-6
Donini, Jim 353
Donstanski, Pik (Tien Shan, Kyrgyzstan) 265
Dragmorpa Ri (Langtang Himal, Nepal) 292
Dragon's Back (Alai, Kyrgyzstan) **261**
Dragon's Spine (Ruth Gorge, AK) 160
Drangnag Ri (Rowaling Himal, Nepal) 296
Droites, Les (France) 242
Drygalskis Galvo (Greenland) 182
Durbin Kangri (Karakoram, China) 342-5
Dye, Adrian 265

E

Earl Mts. (Southern Alps, New Zealand) 362-3
Earle, Mason *art.* 62-9; 365
Egger, Torre (Patagonia) **227**
Eggers Island (Greenland) 188-9
El Capitan (Yosemite, CA) *art.* 12-21
El Gigante (Mexico) 191
El Güpfi (Greenland) 184-8
Elder, Steve 113-5
Elephant's Perch (ID) 131-2
Ellsworth Mts. (Antarctica) 236
Enzo Pk. (Himalchal Pradesh, India) **325**
Erdmann, Ben 154-5, 228
Ermishina, Anastasia 259

Esperanza, Cerro (Chile) *art.* 70-7, **74**
Evans, Mt. (CO) 142-**3**

F

Fairweather Range (AK) 164-5
Falsa Aguja "Great Needle Pk." (South Shetland
    Islands, Antarctica) 239
Fastness P. (Southern Alps, New Zealand) 362
Fava, Gabriel 216, 28
Favresse, Nico *art.* 46-56; 180-2
Favresse, Olivier *art.* 46-56; 180-2
Fersmana Valley (Tien Shan, Kyrgyzstan) 265
Fiksman, Alex 246-7
Fiorenza, Luciano 218
Firey, Joe *obit.* 375
Fisher, Max 166-7
Fisher, Ryan 162-4
Fitz Roy, Cerro (Patagonia) 228
Flatiron Butte (Sierra Nevada, CA) **124**-5
Formin, Mikhail 292-3
Four Pigs Peak (Sichuan, China) **351**-2
Fox Jaw Cirque (Greenland) 188
Frances, Mt. (Alaska Rg, AK) 158
Fremont Pk. (Wind River Rg., WY) 136-8, **137**
Fry, Nathan 147
Funky Tower (Greenland) 180-**2**

G

Gamgadhi (Nepal) 284-5
Gangotri (Western Garhwal, India) 327-31
García Ayala, Luis Carlos 190
Garcia, João 299
Gasherbrum group (Pakistan) *art.* 33-7, **36**
Gasherbrum V (Karakoram, Pakistan) *art.* 33-7,
    33, 36
General (Chukotka, Russia) 254-6, **255**
General Carrera, Cerro (Central Andes) 221
Gentet, Frédérick 258-9
Ghujerab Mts. (Karakoram, Pakistan) 275
Gibbs Fjord (Baffin, CAN) *art.* 46-56; *map* 50-1
Gildea, Damien 236, 239
Giraldo, John 160-2
Glowacz, Stefan 245
Golden Fleece Pk. (Antarctic Peninsula) 236-7
Golden Sentinel (Zanskar, India) 314
Golovchenko, Dmitry 338
Gómez, Lucas 218-9
Gongkala Shan (Shaluli Shan, China) 346
Goodhart, Jamie 267-8
Goodman, Pat 350-1
Gorakh Himal (Nepal) 284-5
Goulotte West (Chile) 220-1
Gran Torre del Cortaderal (Chile) 219-21, **220**
Grand Cappuccino Tower (Waddington Rg.,

CAN) 168
Grandes Jorasses (France) 242
Great Needle Pk. (Antarctica) *See* Falsa Aguja
Green, Eitan *obit.* 376
Green, Stewart M. 376-7
Greenland 180-9
Gregory, Steffan 133
Gregson, Jim 183-4
Grigoriev Valley (Tien Shan, Kyrgyzstan) 266-7
Grobel, Paulo 284-6, 290, 357
Gu Qizhi 352-3
Guerra, Carloncho 218
Güicán P. (Colombia) 193
Guillaumet, Aguja (Patagonia) 228
Gukov, Alexander 301-3
Gunung Mulu National Park (Borneo) 360
Guras Himal (Nepal) 286
Gyao Kang (Tibet) **357**

H

Haas, Jason 145
Haathi (Himalchal Pradesh, India) 326
Haden, Jimmy *art.* 86-90
Hagshu (Kishtwar, India) 319-23, **322**
Haizi Shan (Daxue Shan, China) 346
Haley, Colin 171-2, 224-31
Hall Pk. (Purcell Mts., CAN) 173-**4**
Hana's Men (Kishtwar, India) 319-20
Haptal Valley (Kishtwar, India) 323-**4**
Harrington, Brette 168, 229
Hayes Range (AK) 160-2
Hayes, Mt. (Hayes Rg, AK) 160-2, **161**
He Chuan 356
Heald, Nathan 201-5
Helander, Clint 152-4, 158
Helen, Mt. (Wind River Rg., WY) 137-8
Herberger, Karl 313-4
Heritage Rg. (Ellsworth Rg., Antarctica) 236
Hermano, El (Patagonia) **222**-3
Herrington, Blake 112-3
Herron, Punta (Patagonia) **227**
Hesse, Mark *obit.* 376-7
Himalchal Pradesh (India) 325-7
Himlung Himal (Nepal) 290
Hindu Kush (Pakistan) 272-4
Hispar Muztagh (Pakistan) 275-6
Hkakabo Razi (Myanmar) **358**-9
Hoelzler, Walter 327-9
Hong Sung-taek 301
Honnold, Alex 227
Hooker, Mt. (Wyoming) *art.* 62-9; 138-9; **64**
Hornby, Geoff 244-5
Horobin, Chris 312-3
House, Steve *art.* 78-85

Hu Jiaping 353-4
Hua Shan (Shaanxi, China) **356**
Huang Guan Feng (Sichuan, China) 349
Huantsán Chico (Peru) *See* Quillujirca
Huaraca (C. Huayhuash, Peru) 198-201, **200**
Huayna Potosi (C. Real, Peru) 208-**11**
Hulya I, Mt. (Greenland) 183
Humantay (C. Vilcabamba, Peru) 205
Huntington, Mt. (Alaska Rg, AK) 156-7
Hydra P. (Revelation Mts, AK) 148-51

I

Idaho 131-2
Idiot P. (Alaska Rg, AK) 155-6
Igdlukasip Tunua Fjord (Greenland) 188-9
Igls P. (Karakoram, Pakistan) **275**
Ikatsky Ridge (Russia) 252-**4**
Ikerasak Island (Greenland) 180-2
Ikerasak Peak (Greenland) 180-2, **181**
Ilgner, Arno *art.* 97-107
Il-jin, Lim 289
Illimani (C. Real, Peru) 210, **214**-5
India 310-37
Iñurrategi, Alberto 276-7
Italia, Pico (C. Real, Peru) 208-9
Ives, Katie 368

J

Jabal Asala (Oman) 245
Jabal Misht (Oman) 244-5
Jabo (Shaluli Shan, China) **345**
Jackson, Brian 288-9
Jackson, Dennis 376-7
Jacquot, Raymond *art.* 97-107
Jammo (Shaluli Shan, China) **345**
Janahut (Western Garhwal, India) 329-**30**
Jarjinjabo (Shaluli Shan, China) 345-6
Jatunjasa, C. (C. Vilcabamba, Peru) 205
Jeffcoach, Daniel 127-8
Jenkins, Mark *art.* 97-107, 140
Jennings, Ryan *art.* 22-32
Jensen, Bob 115
Jin-seok Kim 290-1
Johnson, Mt. (Ruth Gorge, AK) *art.* 22-32
Jordan 244-5
Jorgeson, Kevin *art.* 12-21
Jornet Burgada, Kilian *art.* 91-5
Juárez Zapiola, Facundo 216
Jugal Himal (Nepal) 292-3
Juggernaut (Sierra Nevada, CA) **120**-1
Junaidi, Imran 280
Jurau (C. Huayhuash, Peru) 196-8, **200**
Jurau B (C. Huayhuash, Peru) **196**
Jurauraju (C. Huayhuash, Peru) 196-8

K

K7 (Masherbrum Rg., Pakistan) 280-**1**
Kadatz, Michelle 173-4
Kalous, Chris 141-2
Kanchenjunga Himal (Sikkim, India) 334-7
Kang Yatze (Zanskar, India) 314-**6**
Kangchenjunga (Nepal) 309
Kangchenjunga Himal (Nepal) 306-9
Kangcho Nup (Mahalangur Himal, Nepal) 298-**9**
Kangcho Shar (Mahalangur Himal, Nepal) **299**
Kange Ri (Zanskar, India) 314-6, **315**
Kange Valley (Zanskar, India) 314-6
Kangerdiuluk Dru (Greenland) 184-8, **185**
Kangtega (Mahalangur Himal, Nepal) **304**
Kanjiroba Himal (Nepal) 284-6
Kanjiroba Northwest (Nepal) **284**
Kanti Himal (Nepal) 284-5
Karakoram (China/Pakistan) *art.* 33-7; 274-80,
    342-5
Karakoram (India) 310-12
Karavshin (Pamir Alai, Kyrgyzstan) 257-9
Karcha Valley (Himalchal Pradesh, India) 326
Kashkaratash Valley (Kyrgyzstan) 263-4
Kasi Dalpha (Nepal) **284**
Kastelic, Domen 295
Kawarani I (Shaluli Shan, China) 346
Kelley, Maura Reynolds 382-3
Kellogg, Chad Lewis *obit.* 377-8
Kennedy, Cole *obit.* 378-9
Kenya 246-7
Kern, Cameron 353
Khafraz P. (Tajikistan) 271
Kharagosa (Kishtwar, India) 323-**4**
Khumbu (Mahalangur Himal, Nepal) 298-305
Kiager Ri "P. 6,100m" (Ladakh, India) 313
Kichatna Mts (AK) 154-5
Kichi Alai (Pamir Alai, Kyrgyzstan) 259
Kichkesuu Valley (Trans Alai, Kyrgyzstan) 260
Kilichenko, Yuri 300-1
Kings Canyon Nat'l Park (CA) 128
Kirken (Greenland) 184-**5**
Kishtwar Himalaya (India) 318-24
Kishtwar Shivling (Kishtwar, India) 323-**4**
Klepikov, Alexander 252-4
Kleslo, Michal 259
Klestinec, Martin 298
Knight, Lyle 170
Knott, Paul 164-5
Koh-e-Langar (Hindu Kush, Pakistan) **272**-4
Kokodak Dome (Kun Lun, China) 341
Kokshaal-too, Western (Tien Shan, Kyrgyzstan)
    265-7
Komandnaya Pk. (Russia) 254-6, **255**
Kooshdakhaa Spire (Coast Mts., AK) **166**-7

Korona Fifth Tower (Kyrgz Ala-too, Kyrgyzstan) 261-2
Koschitzki, Robert 232-3
Kosh Moynok Valley (Pamir Alai, Kyrgyzstan) 259
Kosmos, Pik (Tien Shan, Kyrgyzstan) 265-6
Kotur Glacier (Tien Shan, Kyrgyzstan) 265
Krajnc, Luka 242
Krakus, Cerro (Argentina) 218
Kreutner, Edith 264
Kristoffy, Jozef 244
Kruk, Jason 168-9
Kula North (India) See Chalung North
Kuldefjeld (Greenland) 183
Kumaun Himalaya (India) 331-3
Kun Lun, China 341
Kwon-sik, Sim 275-6
Kyrgyzstan 257-68
Kyrgz Ala-too (Kyrgyzstan) 261-2
Kyzyl Asker (West Kokshaal-Too, China) 338-40, **339**

L

L14 (Lenak, Zanskar, India) **317**
L15 (Lenak, Zanskar, India) **317**
Ladakh (India) 312-3
Lagan (Kishtwar, India) 319-20
Lahille Island (Antarctic Peninsula) 236-7
Lahual (Himalchal Pradesh, India) 326
Lama Anden (Kanchenjunga Himal, India) 337
Langshisa Ri (Jugal Himal, Nepal) 292-**3**
Langtang Himal (Nepal) 290-1
Langtang Yubra (Langtang Himal, Nepal) **290**-1
Langua-tai Barfi (Pakistan) See Languta-E-Barfi
Languta-E-Barfi (Hindu Kush, Pakistan) 272-4, **273**
Las Guacamayas (Mexico) 190
Las Leñas Valley (Central Andes) 221
Laurel Mt. (Sierra Nevada, CA) 119-20
Lavigne, Joshua art. 57-61
Lawrence Grassi, Mt. (Rocky Mts., CAN) 177-8
Leaning Tower Group (Purcell Mts., CAN) 173-4
Leary, Sean art. 86-90
Leclerc, Marc-André 168, 227-31
Lempe, Cheyne 118-9
Lenak (Zanskar, India) 317
Lhotse (Mahalangur Himal, Nepal) 301
Libecki, Mike 179, 364-5
Lierenfeng (Sichuan, China) 349-50
Limi (Nepal) 285-6
Lincoln Pk. (Cascades, WA) 111-**2**
Lindic, Luka 228, 319-20
Lingti Valley (Himalchal Pradesh, India) 327
Little Poobah (Tien Shan, Kyrgyzstan) 265
Little Sandy Valley (Wind River Rg., WY) **139**

Little Trango (Baltoro, Pakistan) 280
Littlejohn, Pat 263-4
Liu Zhixiong 348-9
Liushen Tag (Kun Lun, China) 341
Liverpool Land (Greenland) 183-4
Livingston Island (South Shetland Islands, Antarctica) 239
Lobuche East (Mahalangur Himal, Nepal) **300**-1
Lofoten (Norway) 243
Longs Pk. (Rocky Mtn. Nat'l Park, CO) 145
Lotos (India) See Lotus Pk.
Lotus Pk. "Lotos" (Himalchal Pradesh, India) **325**
Luba Sumba Himal (Nepal) 305
Lugula (Damodar Himal, Nepal) 289
Lumba Sumba Peak (Nepal) 305
Lungmochey Kangri (Ladakh, India) 312
Lurking Tower (Baffin Island, CAN) **179**

M

MacDonald, Dougald 10; art. 97-107; 140, 144
Machu Kangri (Zanskar, India) 314
Magro, Whit 135, 138-9
Mahalangur Himal (Nepal) 298-305
Mahle, Melissa Boyle 373
Majilis Al Jinn (Oman) 245
Mange, Gabriel 116-7
Mansail (Nepal) **287**
Manuel Rodríguez, Cerro (Central Andes) 221
Marian P. (Southern Alps, New Zealand) 362
Marinero, Aguja el (Central Andes) 218
Mariushri (Karakoram, India) 311-2
Marmolejo, Cerro (Central Andes) 219-20
Marquesas Islands 364-5
Martinez, Natalia art. 70-7
Masherbrum Range (Pakistan) 280-1
Massif des Écrins (France) 242
Matterhorn (Alps) 242
Mauthner, Kirk 173
Mayo, Will 142-3, 156-7
Mayta, David 208-9
McKinley, Mt. (AK) See Denali
McKinnon, Guy 361
Meder, Steve 201
Meije (France) 242
Melcyr Shan (Daxue Shan, China) 346-7
Melinau Gorge (Borneo) 360
Meling, Thomas 242-3
Mena, Esteban 340
Menitove, Ari 131-2
Merlon (Bighorn Mts., WY) art. 97-**107**
Messini, Vittorio 346-7
Mexico 190-2
Mighty-Seven Dwarfs, Mt. (Greenland) 183-4
Miles, Evan 291-2

Milk Tooth (Greenland) 188
Miller, Aaron 145-7
Miller, John 337
Millerious, Hélias *art.* 39-45
Mills, Jay 175-6
Milluni, Pico (C. Real, Peru) 208-9, 212-**3**
Minya Konka Range (Daxue Shan, China) 348
Miyar Valley (Himalchal Pradesh, India) 325
Mojón Rojo (Patagonia) 228
Monasterio, Erik 206-7, 215
Mont Blanc Massif (France) 242
Montana 134-5
Morales, Roberto 278
Moran, Martin 331-2
Morrell, Bradley 286
Morriss, Matthew 174
Moser, Phillip 202
Motutakae (Marquesas) 365
Mozambique 248-9
Mucci, Josh 118
Muchu Chhish (Karakoram, Pakistan) 274
Mugu (Nepal) 284-5
Muir, Mt. (Chugach, AK) 162-4
Mukherjee, Anindya 335-7
Mukot Himal (Nepal) 283
Mulkey, Aaron 135
Muni, Divyesh 310-1
Muñoz Jaramillo, Juan Sebastian 235
Musiyenko, Vitaliy 124-7
Mustang Himal (Nepal) 287-8
Muzkol Range (Tajikistan) 270-1
Myanmar 358-9

N
Nakamura, Diego 218
Nak-john, Seong *art.* 33-7
Nalakankar (Nepal) 285-6
Namuli, Mt. (Mozambique) 248-**9**
Nangamari I (Nepal) 305
Nar Phu (Damodar Himal, Nepal) 288-9
Naya Kanga (Langtang Himal, Nepal) 290-1
Negro Pabellón, Cerro (C. Frontal, Argentina-
      Chile) 218-9
Nepal 282-309
Ness, Amy Jo 123-4, 234-5
Nestler, Stefan 341
Nettekoven, Christof 344-5
Nevada 130
Nevado del Huila (Colombia) 193
Nevado del Tolima (Colombia) 193
Neverseen Tower (Himalchal Pradesh, India) **325**
New Mexico 145-7
New Zealand 361-3
Nico Made (Andes, Argentina) **216**

Nor-Este Torreón (Chile) 220-1
Normand, Bruce 342-4, 346, 348
North Dolpo (Nepal) 283
North Howser Tower (British Columbia, CAN)
      172
Norway 242-3
Nupchu (Nepal) 306
Nya Kangri (Karakoram, India) **310**

O
Octante, Cerro (Chile) *art.* 70-7
Ohkawa, Shingo 137-8
Ohmi Kangri Himal (Nepal) 305-6
Oibala Mts. (Alai, Kyrgyzstan) 261
Ololokwe (Kenya) **246**-7
Olson, Jennifer 172-3
Oman 244-5
O'Neill, Hilaree 358-9
Oregon 113-5
Organ Mts. (NM) 147
Ostrog (Russia) 252-**4**

P
P. 11,300' (Ruth Gorge, AK) 158-60, **159**
P. 12,878' (Rocky Mts., CO) 144-5
P. 4,360' (Chugach, AK) 162
P. 4,645m (Tien Shan, Kyrgyzstan) 265
P. 4,789m (Tien Shan, Kyrgyzstan) 265
P. 4,849m (Tien Shan, Kyrgyzstan) 265
P. 5,184m (Shuangqiao Valley, China) 350-1
P. 5,384m (Tajikistan) **271**
P. 5,395m (Trans Alai, Kyrgyzstan) **260**
P. 5,467m (Shuangqiao Valley, China) 350-1
P. 5,600m (C. Real, Peru) **206**-7
P. 5,680m (Kishtwar, India) 319-20, **322**
P. 5,905m (Nepal) **284**
P. 6,100m (Ladakh, India) *See* "Kiager Ri"
P. 6,123m (Tajikistan) ski descents **270**-1
P. 6,192m (Langtang Himal, Nepal) 290-2, **291**
P. 6,222m (Karakoram, India) **310**
P. 6,295m (Ladakh, India) 313
P. 6,313m (Nepal) **284**
P. 6,460m (Daxue Shan, China) 348
P. 6,490m (Karakoram, China) **343**
P. 6,622m (Karakoram, China) **344**
P. 6,745m (Gyao Kang, Tibet) **357**
P. 6,781m (Langtang Himal, Nepal) 290-1
P. 6,860m (Gyao Kang, Tibet) **357**
P. 8,290' (Fairweather Rg., AK) **164**-5
Pabuk Kang (Nepal) 305-6
Paiju P. (Baltoro, Pakistan) **276**-7
Paine, Central Tower (Patagonia) 234-5
Paine, Torres del (Patagonia) 234-5
Paint Rock Buttress (Bighorn Mts., WY) 140

Pakistan *art.* 33-7; 272-81
Pamir (Tajikistan) 269-71
Pamir Alai (Kyrgyzstan) 257-9
Pancas (Brazil) 194
Pantanos, Cerro de los (Central Andes) 221
Parchamo (Rowaling Himal, Nepal) 297-8
Park Myung-won 261-2
Parque Nacional Cascada de Basaseachic (Mexico) 191-2
Parque Nacional Cumbres de Monterrey (Mexico) 190
Patagonia 222-35
Patrasi (Kanjiroba Himal, Nepal) 286
Pedra Cara (Brazil) 194
Penitent, Pt. (Tien Shan, Kyrgyzstan) 263-4
Penitentes, Nevado (Chile) 220-1
Pennine Alps (Switzerland/Italy) 242
Peri Himal (Nepal) 290
Perito Moreno Nat'l. Park (Patagonia) 224-6
Perot Pillar (Kyrgz Ala-too, Kyrgyzstan) **262**
Peru *art.* 39-45; 195-205
Peruffo, Alberto 334-5
Petrocelli, Adrián 217
Pickles, Matt 360
Piedra Bolada (Mexico) 191-2
Pilar Meridional (Chile) 220-1
Pilar Occidental (Chile) 220-1
Pinney, Pk. (Tien Shan, Kyrgyzstan) 267-**8**
Pinto, Beto 196, 201
Piramidal del Potrero Escondido, Cerro (Central Andes) **217**
Piramidalny, Pik (Pamir Alai, Kyrgyzstan) 258-9
Pirámide "Cerro Colorado" (Patagonia) 224
Pirámide Alejandro Lewis (Northern Andes) 216
Piri Ri (Zanskar, India) 314-6, **315**
Pizem, Rob 132, 142
Poincenot, Aguja (Patagonia) 229
Point 5,182m (Sichuan, China) 353
Polar Sun Spire (Baffin, CAN) *art.* **57**-61
Pomerape (C. Occidental, Peru) 215
Pomiu (Sichuan, China) 354
Pope's Nose (Southern Alps, New Zealand) **361**
Porter, Charlie *obit.* 379-80
Portzline, Dustin 121-3
Potrero Escondido Los Clonquis Cordón del (Central Andes) 217
Poumaka (Marquesas) **364**-5
Pregar (Karakoram, Pakistan) 274
Pugliese, Mark 157
Punta Arisca (Patagonia) 223
Purcell Mts. (British Columbia, CAN) 172-4
Putha Himal (Nepal) 283
Putnam, William Lowell III *obit.* 381-2
Pyramid P. (Revelation Mts, AK) 148-52, **150**

Q
Qaquglugssuit (Greenland) 180-**2**
Qiezi Feng (Shaanxi, China) 354-**6**
Qin Mountains (Shaanxi, China) 354-6
Qionglai Shan (Sichuan, China) 348-54
Quebec 178-9
Quesillo (C. Huayhuash, Peru) 198-201, **200**
Quillujirca, Nevado (C. Blanca, Peru) **195**

R
Radio Control Tower (Alaska Rg, AK) 157
Raganowicz, Marek 243
Ramírez Carrascal, Sergio 195, 202
Ramsden, Paul 320-3
Raru Valley (Zanskar, India) 316-7
Rassa Kangri (Karakoram, India) 310-1
Ratel, Sébastien 351-2
Rauch, Robert 208-9
Red Rock Canyons (NV) 130
Reids Pk. (Uintah Mts., UT) 133
Renland (Greenland) 184-8
Renz, Peter 375
Rethel Mt. (Waddington Rg., CAN) **168**-9
Revelation Mts. (AK) 148-54
Reynolds, Gibson *obit.* 382-3
Rieger, Erik 144-5
Riga P. (Tajikistan) 271
Rikame, Rajan 326
Rinpoche's Temple Pk. (Kanchenjunga Himal, India) **334**-5
Riso Patrón, Cerro (Patagonia) 232-**3**
Riso Patrón, Cordón (Patagonia) 232-3
Roberts, David 366-7, 383-4
Rocky Mts. (CAN) 175-8
Rocky Mts. (CO) 142-5
Rongdo Valley (Karakoram, India) 311-2
Roskelley, Jess 165
Rousseau, Alan 297-8
Rousseau, Louis 178-9
Rowaling Himal (Nepal) 294-8
Roxo, Paulo 329
Rubens, Des 333
Rupshu (Ladakh, India) 313
Russia 250-6
Ruth Gorge (Alaska Rg., AK) *art.* 22-32; 158-60

S
Sahuasiray, Nevado (C. Urubamba, Peru) 202-4, **203**
Saint-Exupery, Aguja (Patagonia) 229
Sakaton (Mahalangur Himal, Nepal) 303-5, **304**
Sam Ford Fjord (Baffin, CAN) *art.* 46-56; *map* 50-1
San Juan Mts. (CO) 140-1

San Lorenzo, Cerro (Patagonia) 224-6
Sanders, Olly 188-9
Sanjines, Denys 215
Saraghrar (Hindu Kush, Pakistan) **272**-4
Sarawak (Borneo) 360
Sassara, Charlie 367
Sauter, Libby 222-3
Sawtooth Mts. (ID) 131-2
Schaffter, Stéphane 316-7
Schiera, Luca 257-8
Schurr, Mickey 375
Schweizerland (Greenland) 188
Seagram, Joie 311-2
Sedona (AZ) 131
Sella Col Pk. (Kanchenjunga Himal, India) 334-5
Selters, Andy 312
Sentinel Rg. (Ellsworth Rg., Antarctica) 236
Serra 2 (Waddington Rg., CAN) 168
Serra 5 (Waddington Rg., CAN) 168
Shaanxi Province (China) 354-6
Shakhawr (Hindu Kush, Pakistan) 272-**4**
Shaluli Shan (China) 345-6
Shaqsha (Peru) *See* Quillujirca
Shark's Fin (Sichuan, China) 352-**3**
Shark's Tooth (Greenland) 184-8, **186**
Sharkshead Tower (Purcell Mts., CAN) 173
Sharma, Chris 245
Shepton, Bob *art.* 46-56; 180-2
Shetland Islands (Antarctica) 239
Shierpra (Kishtwar, India) 323-4
Shipton Spire (Baltoro, Pakistan) **277**-8
Shivling (Western Garhwal, India) 327-9, **328**
Shoshoni Pk. (Rocky Mts., CO) 144
Shuangqiao Valley (Sichuan, China) 349-51
Shymko, Mykola 250
Siadak, Austin 224
Sichuan (China) 348-54
Sickle Spire (Western Garhwal, India) 330-1
Siegrist, Stephan 323-4
Sierra Nevada (CA) 119-29
Sierra Nevada del Cocuy (Colombia) 193
Siew, Edwin 326
Siguniang (Sichuan, China) 353-4
Siguniang National Park (China) 348-54
Sikkim (India) 334-7
Silin, Oleg 271
Sillem Island (Baffin, CAN) *art.* 46-56
Silver Wall (Pamir Alai, Kyrgyzstan) 259
Simutis, Gediminas 325
Simvu Glacier, South (Kanchenjunga Himal, India) 335-6
Simvu Twins (Kanchenjunga Himal, India) **335**-6
Siniolchu (Kanchenjunga Himal, India) **336**-7
Siniolchu Rock Needles (Kanchenjunga Himal,

India) **336**-7
Sir Donald, Mt. (British Columbia, CAN) **171**-2
Sirijuani (C. Urubamba, Peru) **203**-4
Siula Chico (Peru) *art.* 39-45, **43**
Siula Granda (C. Huayhuash, Peru) 198
Slesova, Pk. (Pamir Alai, Kyrgyzstan) 257-**8**
Smith, Nathan 133
Son Kul (Tien Shan, Kyrgyzstan) 263-4
Sonam Ri (Zanskar, India) 316-7
Sosneado Group (Central Andes) 221
South Georgia (Antarctica) ski descent 240-1
South Howser Tower (British Columbia, CAN) **172**-3
Southern Alps (New Zealand) 361-3
Spangnak Ri (Ladakh, India) 313
Spegazzina, Cerro (Chile) *art.* 70-7
Sphinx (Sierra Nevada, CA) 127
Spiti (Himalchal Pradesh, India) 327
Spohn, Matt 136-7
Squamish (British Columbia, CAN) 169
Stawamus Chief (British Columbia, CAN) 169
Stephen, Mt. (Rocky Mts., CAN) 176-7
Steurer, Lisi 245
Stevenson, David 371
Storm Creek Headwall (Rocky Mts., CAN) 175
Storm Pt. (Teton Rg., WY) 136
Straathof, Dennis 261
Straka, Jan 242
Sudt, Mt. (Himalchal Pradesh, India) 326
Sullivan, Jerome 151-2
Supercave Wall (Cascades, WA) 112-3
Suter, Mt. (Southern Alps, New Zealand) 362-**3**
Svarog (Pamir Alai, Kyrgyzstan) **257**

T
Tae-Hoon, Kim 292
Tahu Rutum (Hispar Muztagh, Pakistan) 275-6
Tajikistan 269-71
Tangra Rg. (South Shetland Islands, Antarctica) 239
Taniguchi, Kei 158-60, 287-8
Tanoguch, Pt. (Tien Shan, Kyrgyzstan) 263-4
Tara (Karakoram, India) 311-2
Tatajayco, Nevado (C. Central, Peru) 201
Tawoche Northwest (Mahalangur Himal, Nepal) 299
Tees, Alan 336-7
Telthop (Ladakh, India) 312-**3**
Temple, Pk. (Tien Shan, Kyrgyzstan) 267-**8**
Tengi Ragi Tau (Rowaling Himal, Nepal) 297-8
Teton Rg. (WY) 136
Thamserku (Mahalangur Himal, Nepal) 301-3, **302, 304**
Thielsen, Mt. (Cascades, OR) 113-5

Thistle, Mt. (Greenland) 183
Tibet 357
Tien Shan (Kyrgyzstan) 263-4
Tikona (Himalchal Pradesh, India) 326
Timpano, Seth 318-9
Tipton, Jake 131
Tischler, Stephan 275
Titanic, Mt. (Revelation Mts, AK) 152-4, **153**
Todd, Wayne 162
Tokopah Valley (Sequoia Nat'l Park, CA) 128
Tomczik, Doug 123
Tongshyong (Kanchenjunga Himal, India) 334-5
Tooth (Patagonia) 223-4
Torretta, Anna 219-20
Town, John 341
Trans Alai (Kyrgyzstan) 260
Triangular, Pico (C. Real, Peru) 210-2, **211**
Trident Glacier (Kichatna Mts, AK) 154-5
Trident Pks. (South Georgia, Antarctica) **240**-1
Trividic, Pascal 277-8
Troll Wall (Norway) 243
Tromso (Norway) 242-3
Tsacra Grande (C. Huayhuash, Peru) 198-201, **200**
Tsagan-Shibetu Rg. (Russia) 251-2
Tso Kang South (Kangchenjunga Himal, Nepal) **308**
Tunduk Gildys, Pk. (Tien Shan, Kyrgyzstan) 263-4
Tunsho Sur (C. Central, Peru) 201
Turret (Baffin, CAN) art. 57-**61**
Tushum Kangri (Karakoram, India) 310-1
Tusuhm Kangri (Karakoram, India) 310-1
Tuva 251-2
Tyrol Shan (Daxue Shan, China) 346-7

U

Ua Pou (Marquesas) 364-5
Uintah Mts. (UT) 133
Uli Biaho Gallery (Baltoro, Pakistan) **278**
Urubko, Denis 309
Utah 132-3
Uummannaq (Greenland) 180-2

V

Valle Correntoso (Patagonia) 222-3
Varmtind (Greenland) 183
Venables, Stephen 240-1, 379-80
Veronica, Nevado (C. Urubamba, Peru) 202-4, **203**
Villiger, Ralph 184
Vostochny Pk. (Tuva, Russia) 251-**2**

W

Waddington Range (CAN) 168-9
Wadi Rum (Jordan) 244

Walker Citadel (Baffin, CAN) art. 46-56, **52**
Walker, Susanna 269-70
Walsh, Jon 173, 175
Warawarani I (C. Real, Peru) 207-**8**
Ward, Emily 265
Warner, Chris 254-6
Washburn, Barbara obit. 383-4
Washington 110-3
Watkins, Mt. (Yosemite, CA) art. 86-90
Watters, Ron 136
Wehrly, Eric 110-1
Weidner, Chris 130
Wellner, Jon 375
Welsted, Ian 148-51
West Kokshaal-Too (China) 338-40
Western Garhwal (India) 327-31
Western Hajar (Oman) 244-5
Wharton, Josh 138-9, 142
Whitecrown (Chugach, AK) 162
Wickens, Phil 238-9
Wide Awake Tower (British Columbia, CAN) 173
Wiencke Island (Antarctic Peninsula) 237-9
Williamson, Jed 370
Wind River Rg. (WY) art. 62-9; 136-9
Witches Tit, West (Coast Mts., AK) 165
Wright Ice Piedmont (Antarctic Peninsula) 239
Wu Peng 354
Wyoming art. 62-9; 136-40

X

Xiao Gongga (Daxue Shan, China) 346-**7**
Xiao Kangri (Karakoram, China) 344-5

Y

Yak Pk. (British Columbia, CAN) 170
Yearsley, Simon 329-30
Yokoyama, Katsutaka 280-1
Yosemite Nat'l Park (CA) art. 12-21, 86-90; 115-9
Yubra (Langtang Himal, Nepal) **290**-1

Z

Zaalaisky Ridge (Trans Alai, Kyrgyzstan) 260
Zanskar (India) 314-7
Zhigalov, Alexander 251-2
Zhioltaya Stena (Pamir Alai, Kyrgyzstan) 258-9
Zhongming, Xia 349
Zimmerman, T. Price 381-2
Zion Nat'l Park (UT) 132-3
Zumthul Phuk Glacier (Kanchenjunga Himal, India) 336-7

the AMERICAN ALPINE club

THE AMERICAN ALPINE JOURNAL 2015

AAJ

INTERNATIONAL GRADE COMPARISON CHART

SERIOUSNESS RATING:

These often modify technical grades when protection is difficult

R: Poor protection with potential for a long fall and some injury

X: A fall would likely result in serious injury or death

YDS=Yosemite Decimal System
UIAA=Union Internationale des Associations D'Alpinisme
FR=France/Sport
AUS=Australia
Sax=Saxony
CIS=Commonwealth of Independent States/Russia
SCA=Scandinavia
BRA=Brazil
UK=United Kingdom

Note: All conversions are approximate. Search "International Grade Comparison Chart" at the AAJ website for further explanation of commitment grades and waterfall Ice/ mixed grades.

YDS	UIAA	FR	AUS	SAX	CIS	SCA	BRA	UK (tech)	UK (adj)
5.2	II	1	10	II	III	3			D
5.3	III	2	11	III	III+	3+			
5.4	IV- / IV	3	12		IV-	4			VD
5.5	IV+		13		IV	4+			S
5.6	V-	4	14		IV+	5-		4a	HS
5.7	V / V+		15	VIIa		5		4b	VS
5.8		5a	16	VIIb	V-	5+	4 / 4+	4c	HVS
5.9	VI-	5b	17	VIIc		6-	5 / 5+	5a	E1
5.10a	VI	5c	18	VIIIa	V	6	6a		
5.10b	VI+	6a						5b	E2
5.10c	VII-	6a+	19	VIIIb		6+	6b		
5.10d	VII	6b	20	VIIIc	V+	7-	6c		E3
5.11a	VII+	6b+		IXa			7a	5c	
5.11b		6c	21	IXb		7	7b		
5.11c	VIII-	6c+	22		VI-	7+			E4
5.11d	VIII	7a	23	IXc			7c	6a	
5.12a	VIII+	7a+	24			8-	8a		E5
5.12b		7b	25	Xa	VI	8	8b		
5.12c	IX-	7b+	26	Xb		8+	8c		
5.12d	IX	7c	27				9a	6b	E6
5.13a		7c+	28	Xc		9-	9b		
5.13b	IX+	8a	29				9c		
5.13c	X-	8a+	30			9	10a	6c	E7
5.13d	X	8b	31	XIa	VI+		10b		
5.14a	X+	8b+	32	XIb			10c	7a	E8
5.14b		8c	33			9+	11a		
5.14c	XI-	8c+	34	XIc			11b	7b	E9
5.14d	XI	9a	35				11c		E10
5.15a	XI+	9a+	36	XIIa		10	12a		
5.15b	XII-	9b	37		VII		12b		E11
5.15c	XII	9b+	38	XIIb			12c		